The Fashioned Body

This new edition is dedicated to my father, Dr Paul Entwistle

The Fashioned Body

Fashion, Dress and Modern Social Theory

Third Edition

Joanne Entwistle

polity

First edition first published in 2000 by Polity Press
Second edition first published in 2015 by Polity Press
This third edition first published in 2023 by Polity Press

Polity Press
65 Bridge Street
Cambridge CB2 1UR, UK

Polity Press
111 River Street
Hoboken, NJ 07030, USA

ISBN-13: 978-1-5095-4788-3 (hardback)
ISBN-13: 978-1-5095-4789-0 (paperback)

A catalogue record for this book is available from the British Library.

Library of Congress Control Number: 2022949336

Typeset in 10.5 on 13pt Swift Neue
by Fakenham Prepress Solutions, Fakenham, Norfolk NR21 8NL
Printed and bound in Great Britain by TJ Books Ltd, Padstow, Cornwall

For further information on Polity, visit our website:
politybooks.com

Contents

Acknowledgements

Many thanks to my husband for his patience, which I frequently test! I'm grateful for his support in preparing the manuscript for submission during a family summer holiday. I'd also like to thank my girls for their patience and love during the writing of this book. In terms of the intellectual development, this book has been shaped by conversations with colleagues whose support I want to acknowledge here. Elizabeth Wissinger helped me to rethink the debates about diversity and race with regard to fashion and I also thank my colleagues and co-founders of the Critical Fashion Studies Seminar (CFSS), Angela McRobbie, Agnes Rocamora and Jane Tynan, for helping shape some of my thinking in this book. I would also like to thank Kate Fletcher for her very insightful thoughts, via email, on sustainability. Finally, I would like to acknowledge the three anonymous reviewers who helped me to decide the final form of this book by their comments on an earlier draft. Though the book remains all my own work (for better or worse), it has not been produced in a vacuum but through the support of my family and colleagues.

Preface to the Third Edition

The third edition is more substantially revised and updated than the 2015 edition, which had been refreshed with a long(ish) Preface detailing developments since 2000 but had left untouched the original chapters. Only one chapter, Chapter 7, had new material added to it. When starting this third edition I knew that a more radically revised book was required. Since many points made in the 2015 Preface have now been expanded in the relevant chapters, I have removed that Preface and absorbed some of the points made there into a single Preface to this edition.

Two reasons necessitated a substantially revised third edition. First, the continued growth of fashion studies since 2015 meant that significantly more material needed inclusion. Second, this new material required more than a citational nod, either because new conceptual terms have shifted the field of fashion, or because new ideas, theories or data have subsequently challenged the older terms and ideas first aired in 2000. I am very grateful to my editor, Mary Savigar at Polity, who agreed an extended word limit; but to make space for new material I have also trimmed some of the original chapters. I am also very grateful to the three anonymous reviewers, whose comments were not only very supportive but very instructive of some changes that need to be made: their suggestions shaped the final form of this book, directing me to reflect upon my theoretical framing and incorporate some explicit reworking of the chapters. I have done my best to take on board their constructive comments. A few things noted in the 2015 Preface that did not get rehoused in one of the chapters are worth mentioning here as they are still relevant, as I write this in 2022.

First, the landscape of fashion scholarship (or 'fashion studies'), is vastly more expanded now than when this book was conceived at the end of the 1990s. Back then, a few classic texts such as Wilson's *Adorned in Dreams* (2007, first published in 1985) joined a very meagre number of early sociological work (Simmel 1904, 1971 [1904]; Veblen 1953 [1899]; and Blumer 1969), some psychology of clothes (Flügel 1930), and some early anthropological analysis (Barnes and Eicher 1992). Since 2000 and accelerating since 2015, a veritable explosion of interest in fashion, dress and the body far exceeded any predictions or expectations I had when the book came out. This has some large part to do with the explosion of interest in consumption, material culture, and continued cultural studies on subcultures. Over the last few years many sub-fields have opened up: e.g. analyses on the fashion industry, especially sustainability, histories and ethnographies of fashion modelling. Bloomsbury expanded an already extensive fashion scholarship catalogue, building on the success of *Fashion Theory: The Journal of Dress, Body and Culture* (first issue 1997). Their *Dress Cultures* series has an extensive back catalogue. Other publishing houses, notably Intellect and Routledge, have followed suit, with series on fashion and dress or journals: for example, *Critical Studies in Fashion and Beauty* (first issue 2010) and *Critical Studies in Men's Fashion* (first published in 2014), with two major interventions in the US – *Fashion Studies* published by Parsons School of Design, and the Ryerson University student-run *Bias: Fashion Studies* following the lead set. The establishment of *International Fashion Studies* (first published in 2014) is notable for its 'principal aim [...] to be a platform for fashion studies developed by non-English speakers' thus recognising the need to give voice to the growing non-Anglophone scholarship, particularly in Latin America and Asia.

Other developments in the field, noted in 2015, include the emergence of fashion theory courses at universities, such as City University of New York (CUNY), which runs an MA in Liberal Studies with a Fashion Studies Concentration, and London College of Fashion (University of the Arts, London), which offers dedicated fashion theory programmes. There have also been some fashion research centres, notably in the Nordic countries, for example, the Centre for Fashion, Stockholm University (established in 2006) and a whole host of events such as the early 'Creative Encounters' at the Copenhagen Business School (see McNeil and Wallenberg 2012 for more details on 'Nordic' fashion studies). The Critical Fashion Studies Seminar (CFSS) established in 2019 is a more recent development, discussed below.

Another point I made in the 2015 Preface remains true. I argued then that the once low status accorded to fashion within sociology, which I experienced as a PhD student studying sociology at Goldsmiths College, has since changed. While Aspers and Godart (2013), citing Kawamura (2004a), argue that fashion is still devalued within academia, I suggest that, at least in the UK, fashion is now more generally taken seriously. Much of this has to do with developments around the 'creative industries': fashion, once seen as marginal, now sits at the core of economic discourse focused on ideas about 'cultural' and 'creative' work as a major driver of developed economies. No longer seen as a frivolous bit of 'fluff', fashion features in the policy plans of many national and local governments in the UK and around the world (Pratt 2008, 2009; Jeong et al. 2021). Although fashion remains a 'cultural' entity, alignment with 'economic' forces has enhanced its status and legitimacy in academia and in policy circles, e.g. the 2020 All Party Parliamentary Group (APPG) on Creative Diversity (to which I contributed) included discussion of the fashion industry. Although an informal cross-party group within the

UK Parliament, the APPG testifies to a growing interest in examining the importance of creative industries such as fashion to social, cultural and economic life.

The fashion industry has also come to the fore in recent years because of its many negative impacts, particularly its poor environmental practices and social inequalities. Growing concerns about the environmental cost of fast fashion have been highlighted by climate-change scholars and activists, such as Extinction Rebellion, while scandals over poor labour conditions in factories in the global South, as in the collapse of the Rana Plaza garment factory in Bangladesh in 2013, highlight the urgent need for a critical, empirical study of fashion.

Throughout this rapid expansion of fashion studies in the early noughties, *The Fashioned Body* remained as core reading. However, while a refresh in 2015 breathed some new life into the material, there was no doubt that more recently the book was becoming outdated in the face of the scholarly developments detailed below. A substantial re-write has been necessary to ensure that *The Fashioned Body* is relevant to the twenty-first century as a reference point for scholars of fashion and dress and as a core text on fashion modules.

This edition, therefore, incorporates many new texts that have sprung up under the generic banner of fashion studies. Fashion studies designates a thematic area of interest rather than a discipline and captures the inter- and multi-disciplinary range of work in this area. In their excellent review essay of current sociological research on fashion, Aspers and Godart (2013) acknowledge the various disciplines close to sociology that have attempted to analyse aspects of clothing and dress, including history, philosophy, economics, geography, and cultural studies. This complex mix of fashion scholarship is evidenced in the establishment of an informal international network of Critical Fashion Studies Seminar (CFSS). This network, established in 2019 with colleagues, Angela McRobbie (Loughborough University), Agnes Rocamora (University of the Arts, London), Jane Tynan (Vrije Universiteit Amsterdam), and myself, aims to support a critical scholarship within fashion studies. The events held so far (curtailed by Covid-19 and occurring mostly online) have given a platform to new scholars within fashion studies – PhD students and early career scholars – from around the world. Indeed, while all the organisers are European, our speakers and attendees come from many parts of the world (e.g. India and Ghana), and much of the interest is in decolonising fashion scholarship and the curriculum and the climate emergency.

This vibrant scholarly community is actively growing a critical, post-colonial fashion scholarship that far exceeds anything I could have imagined in 2000 or 2015. Fashion scholarship continues to go from strength to strength and it is my hope that twenty-three years since the first publication of *The Fashioned Body* this third edition does some justice to this increasingly exciting and expanding field. I have done my best to acknowledge new debates and authors in this edition, although space prevents me from including all the excellent work I have read while preparing this manuscript. That said, I hope I have included enough new material within the significantly expanded Reference section to acknowledge recent developments and debates and capture the interest and imagination of readers and scholars who can continue to grow the field of fashion studies.

Introduction

Fashion is about bodies: it is produced, promoted and worn by bodies. It is the body that fashion speaks to and it is the body that must be dressed in almost all social encounters. Within the West, and increasingly beyond as well, fashion structures much of our experience of dress, although, as I argue in this book, it is not the only factor influencing dress in everyday life since other factors, such as sex, class, income and tradition, play their part. Fashionable dress is dress that embodies the latest aesthetic; it is dress defined at a given moment as desirable, beautiful, popular. In articulating the latest aesthetic, and in making available certain kinds of clothes, *fashion* provides the 'raw material' of daily *dress*, produced by a multitude of bodies operating across a variety of sites. In other words, we can define fashion and dress as follows (and this definition will be expanded upon in Chapter 2): fashion refers to the systems for the production and circulation of prevailing aesthetics in clothing, while dress refers to the daily, embodied practices of *getting dressed* – usefully it is both a noun and a verb. To understand fashion we need to acknowledge it is both material and discursive, concerning material things, such as clothing (and their creation/workers), as well as discourses about these things, which gives (fashion) value to them. To understand dress we need to see how individuals, located within social groups, translate the fashionable dress made available to them by the fashion system – selecting particular material things and making sense of the prevailing discursive/aesthetic ideals. In this way, fashion, to be fashion, finds its ultimate expression on bodies. We can note also how dress is part and parcel of habitual practices of embodiment. As Eckersley and Duff (2020: 36) argue, we need to examine 'the links between habit, fashion, clothing and subjectification to extend analysis of the clothed body beyond the semiotic frames that have tended to dominate discussions of fashion across the social sciences and humanities'.

Understanding fashion requires understanding the relationship between these different bodies operating within the fashion system: fashion colleges and students, designers and design houses, tailors and seamstresses, models and photographers, as well as fashion editors, distributors, retailers, fashion buyers, shops and consumers. In other words, studying fashion involves moving from production to distribution and consumption: without the countless seamstresses and tailors there would be no clothes to consume; without the promotion of fashion by cultural intermediaries, such as fashion journalists, 'fashion' as the latest style would not be transmitted very far; and without the acceptance of consumers, fashionable dress would lie unworn in factories, shops, wardrobes. Thus, when we speak of fashion we speak simultaneously of many overlapping and interconnecting bodies involved in the production and promotion of dress as well as the actions of individuals acting on their bodies when 'getting dressed'. In their account of fashion, Fine and Leopold (1993; also Leopold 1992) argue that fashion is a 'hybrid subject': the study of fashion requires understanding the 'interrelationship between highly fragmented forms of production and equally diverse and often volatile patterns of demand (Fine and Leopold 1993: 93). Thus, the study of fashion covers the 'dual concept' of fashion as a 'cultural phenomenon and as an aspect of manufacturing with the accent on production technology' (Leopold 1992: 101). However, this hybridity is not generally acknowledged by the literature, which tends towards one or other aspect of fashion without acknowledging the relationships between the different elements of production and consumption. According to Leopold (1992: 101), this duality has resulted in a separation 'in which the histories of consumption and production plough largely separate and parallel furrows'. The histories of consumption trace the rise and fall of demand of a product and link this to social developments. It tends to focus attention on individual psychology and/or the fashionable object itself, exploring it as 'the embodiment of cultural and social values prevailing at a specified time and place' (Fine and Leopold 1993: 93). Within this literature, production becomes passive, explained not only as a reflection of consumer or individual demands, but more often than not, as reflecting the fluctuating (and irrational) desires of women. The second study of fashion on the production side grapples with industrial history and deals also with the history of supply. This literature charts the innovations in technology, as well as the growth and organisation of labour within the fashion industry. It makes general assumptions about the reasons for growth in demand but does not look at the specifics of it, nor the specific characteristics of demand in particular clothing markets. Thus, as Leopold argues (1992: 101), the history of clothing production has made little contribution to an understanding of the 'fashion system'. Moreover, these different bodies of literature do not connect with each other to provide an integrated approach.

Both Fine and Leopold put forward a case for a materialist analysis of fashion. They point to the need for historical specificity in the analysis of the fashion system, arguing that within the fashion system itself there are differences in the provision of clothes. There is no one 'fashion system' but a number of systems producing clothes for different markets. Alongside mass production, small systems of 'made to measure' clothing persist in *haute couture* and bespoke tailoring, which operate with rather different modes of production, marketing, distribution and consumption than does factory production for the high street. A full account of fashion needs to acknowledge the different practices within the fashion industry and bring together the crucially linked and overlapping practices of production and consumption. However, so far little attempt has been made by social theory to bridge the gulf between production and consumption. Sociology, cultural studies and psychology have tended to focus on the consumption side, while economic theory, marketing and industrial history have tended to examine the development of production. This book provides a summary of this literature and, in doing so, explores both the literature on consumption and production, although it considers the former in rather more detail. The reason for this lies in the contemporary significance of this work, which has grown exponentially since the 1980s in comparison to literature on production. This means that this book replicates to some extent the division between literature on consumption and production: only Chapter 7 deals specifically with the literature on production, while the other chapters focus more on the consumption and meanings of fashion. However, I agree with Fine and Leopold that this division is an artificial one and that new studies on fashion and dress need to address the interconnections between production and consumption. I therefore argue in this book that a sociological account of fashion and dress must acknowledge the connections between production and consumption, considering the relationship between different agencies, institutions, individuals and practices. Such accounts of fashion, can therefore connect it to everyday dress, while everyday dress, especially in the age of social media, feeds back to fashion: the two are also crucially interconnected.

I argue in this book that a historical division existed within the early literature, between studies of fashion (as a system, idea or aesthetic) and studies of dress (as in the meanings given to particular practices of clothing and adornment). Some of the classic studies of fashion within sociology, cultural studies, costume history and psychology tended to be theoretical in scope, seen as an abstract system with theoretical explanations that are sought to explain its apparently mysterious movements. Studies of dress, on the other hand, historically the domain of anthropology, tended to be empirical, examining dress in everyday life within communities and by particular individuals, with an original focus on non-Western and traditional communities, though this has changed in recent years, with anthropologists studying Western communities. Accounts of dress by psychologists was (and still is) limited as they tend to be individualistic rather than social in their analysis of dress practices. I give an overview in this book as to this disciplinary division between fashion and dress studies, which I argued in early editions was as problematic as the division between production and consumption. More recent studies of fashion/dress within sociology and other disciplines (e.g. geography, cultural studies) now bridges the gap between these various bodies of literature and looks at the way in which fashion determines dress and dress interprets fashion.

The Fashioned Body 3.0

I want briefly to highlight the changes made in this third edition. While the whole book has had a light facelift, there are many substantially new segments worthy of commentary here. Chapter 1 on the body is unchanged in its core substantive discussion, a decision backed up by the three anonymous reviewers, whose comments did not suggest that a substantial revision was required. Indeed, one reviewer noted that 'Entwistle should not change the basic theoretical underpinning of the book. To do so would deprive audiences of a theoretical framework for thinking about fashion that has come to be an extremely important building block in fashion studies over the last two decades.' However, quite rightly, it was noted that the overly white, male, European bias in the theoretical framework required some reflexive commentary and this has been incorporated into a new conclusion to the chapter.

In proposing a study of fashion/dress as *situated bodily practice*, the original edition set out a theoretical framework for future sociological analysis that has, over time, evolved as a key approach. Thus, as before, Chapter 1 introduces and develops the concept of situated bodily practice as a framework for bridging the gap between fashion and dress. This framework offers a way of analysing fashion as a structuring determinant on dress and opens up ways to examine how fashion is translated into everyday dress. It directs attention onto the body as the link between the two: fashion articulates the body, producing discourses on the body that are translated into dress through the bodily practices of dressing on the part of individuals. This positioning of the body at the centre of the analysis of fashion/dress allows us to examine practices and strategies from the micro-level of the individual experience of dress, through to the macro-level of the fashion industry, corporate strategies and marketing, which must keep the body in mind when designing, promoting and selling fashion. A new reflexive note has now been added to this chapter to acknowledge the fact that the theorists I refer to are predominantly white European men (notably Merleau-Ponty, Foucault and Bourdieu). While their concepts still stand (hence I have retained them), they were blind to notions of gender and race. I invite future scholars to find ways to incorporate, extend and challenge theories of embodiment through critical examination of these classic sociological theorists and concepts.

Chapter 2 details the ways in which fashion has been thought of and written about. It focuses on intellectual responses to fashion, examining how early social theorists tended to ignore the body (and by implication fashion) and when they have looked at fashion/dress, tended to disembody it. Early intellectuals writing on fashion thus concentrated on other aspects, such as fashion writing (Barthes 1985), fashion photographs (Ewen 1976; Evans and Thornton 1989; Lewis and Rolley 1997) or general theory, for instance, 'emulation' and status competition (Simmel 1971; Veblen 1953) or the 'shifting erogenous zone' (Laver 1950, 1995). There were some early exceptions to this and more recent work examines how bodies and embodiment are caught up within fashion (Granata 2017; Geczy 2016; Tseëlon 1997; Twig 2013; Wilson 2007 [1985]); Wright (1992), for example, explores the way in which fashion operates on the body.

Chapter 2 also originally set out the historically accepted definitions of fashion and dress and reviewed the literature on theories for the emergence of the fashion system in European/Western societies but, more recently, these definitions have come under criticism. Likewise, in Chapter 3, criticism as to the dominant historical narrative that fashion developed out European/ Western societal conditions is now reviewed. Both these chapters now acknowledge the growing body of scholarship that has challenged the conventional fashion histories and accounts of fashion's European origins. With new material emerging from historians, archaeologists and anthropologists providing evidence of earlier, non-Western societies expressing a fashion sensibility, it was necessary to consider these debates. For example, extending traditional research on Western fashion, dress and consumption are studies of fashion and dress in communist eastern European countries pre-1989 (Bartlett 2010; Pellandini-Simanyi 2016). Thus, while the focus of this book is still European societies and the history of fashion as it emerged in European courts, these revisions see that narrative is now contextualised and historicised to make clear that this is one history of fashion. Readers are now invited to consider this new scholarly work which was not included in previous editions.

The remaining chapters consider various substantive themes within the literature, with new works within fashion studies discussed. The re-titled Chapters 4, 5 and 6, have been substantially revised and renamed to better reflect the expansion in new studies of fashion with respect to debates about identity, class, race, gender and sexuality. To signal the obvious point that all three chapters are dealing with identity, the old Chapter 4 ('Fashion and Identity'), newly named 'Fashion and Identity: From Modernity to Intersectionality', signals recent refocusing of debates from earlier fashion scholarship, which had been primarily concerned with class. It now includes a fuller discussion of religion, modesty and dress as this has been one major area of new research in recent years. Chapters 5 and 6 have also grown with the addition of new material. Debates around transgender that challenge conventional understandings of the male/female dichotomy are reviewed in Chapter 5, while the expanding literature on gay and lesbian fashion features in the discussion on sexuality.

The most significant changes in terms of new material are in Chapter 7, in recognition of many developments in scholarship critically examining the fashion industry. There is now new material on the industry that has emerged of late, specifically, discussion of digital fashion, fashion blogging and Instagram, reflecting the significant growth in scholarly work in this area. There is also a whole new section on fashion sustainability and ethics to take on board the growing literature that critiques contemporary fast fashion in terms of its poor environmental and labour relations. This discussion of ethics is extended also to include debates about fashion industry's historic (lack of) diversity and inclusion.

Conclusion

The re-evaluation of theories and literature from earlier editions and the expansion of the book in terms of new material is meant to capture the most significant developments within the field. It is not meant to be exhaustive, however. Were I to be writing a new book there would no doubt be much more scope to develop my theoretical framework, examine in more detail new research and find and include new and emerging arguments. However, within the scope of this book – a third edition of an older book/s – these additions and amendments are meant to refresh and reframe the original arguments in *The Fashioned Body* written over twenty-three years ago. This edition presents an overview of the literature, within the context of my original framing of fashion and dress as situated bodily practice. It is offered as a text to assist students (undergraduate, postgraduate alike) by providing a map of early, classic works on fashion and dress, as well as indicating current thematic issues in the literature today. It definitely sparks the end of fashion studies as the preserve of white, European scholars. Fashion scholarship today, as I hope this edition highlights, is a transnational endeavour within an expanding post-colonial curriculum; and this book is offered up to future scholars in places far from London, located in many countries such as India, China and Latin America. My hope is that fashion studies will continue to extend far beyond the Anglophone world (see for example, Bartlett 2022; Stevenson 2022).

1

Addressing the Body

'There is an obvious and prominent fact about human beings', notes Turner (1985: 1) at the start of *The Body and Society*, 'they have bodies and they are bodies'. In other words, the body constitutes the environment of the self, to be inseparable from the self. However, what Turner omits in his analysis is another obvious and prominent fact: that human bodies are dressed bodies. The social world is a world of dressed bodies. Nakedness is wholly inappropriate in almost all social situations and, even in situations where much naked flesh is exposed (on the beach, at the swimming-pool, even in the bedroom), the bodies that meet there are likely to be adorned, if only by jewellery, or indeed, even perfume: when asked what she wore to bed, Marilyn Monroe claimed that she wore only Chanel No. 5, illustrating how the body, even without garments, can still be adorned or embellished in some way.

Dress is a basic fact of social life and this, according to anthropologists, is true of all known human cultures: all people 'dress' the body in some way, be it through clothing, tattooing, cosmetics or other forms of body painting. To put it another way, no culture leaves the body unadorned but adds to, embellishes, enhances or decorates the body. In almost all social situations we are required to appear dressed, although what constitutes 'dress' varies from culture to culture and also within a culture, since what is considered appropriate dress will depend on the situation or occasion. A bathing-suit, for example, would be inappropriate and shocking if worn to do the shopping, while swimming in one's coat and shoes would be absurd for the purpose of swimming, but perhaps apt as a fund-raising stunt. The cultural significance of dress extends to all situations, even those in which we can go naked: there are strict rules and codes governing when and with whom we can appear undressed. While bodies may go undressed in certain spaces, particularly in the private sphere of the home, the public arena almost always requires that a body be dressed appropriately, to the extent that the flaunting of flesh, or the inadvertent exposure of it in public, is disturbing, disruptive and potentially subversive.

Bodies that do not conform, bodies that flout the conventions of their culture and go without the appropriate clothes are subversive of the most basic social codes and risk exclusion, scorn or ridicule. The 'streaker' who strips off and runs across a cricket pitch or soccer stadium draws attention to these conventions in the act of breaking them: indeed, female streaking is defined as a 'public order offence' while the 'flasher', by comparison, can be punished for 'indecent exposure' (Young 1995: 7).

The ubiquitous nature of dress would seem to point to the fact that dress or adornment is one of how bodies are made social and given meaning and identity. The individual and very personal act of getting dressed is an act of preparing the body for the social world, making it appropriate, acceptable, indeed respectable, and possibly desirable also. Getting dressed is an ongoing practice, requiring knowledge, techniques and skills, from learning how to tie our shoelaces and do up our buttons as children, to understanding about colours, textures and fabrics and how to weave them together to suit our bodies and our lives. Dress is the way in which individuals learn to live in their bodies and feel at home in them. Wearing the right clothes and looking our best, we feel at ease with our bodies, and the opposite is equally true: turning up for a situation inappropriately dressed, we feel awkward, out of place and vulnerable. In this respect, dress is both an intimate experience of the body and a public presentation of it. Operating on the boundary between self and other is the interface between the individual and the social world, the meeting place of the private and the public. This meeting between the intimate experience of the body and the public realm, through the experience of fashion and dress, is the subject of this chapter.

So potent is the naked body that when it is allowed to be seen, as in the case of art, it is governed by social conventions. Berger (1972) argues that within art and media representations there is a distinction between naked and nude, the latter referring to the way in which bodies, even without garments, are 'dressed' by social conventions and systems of representation. Perniola (1990) has also considered the way in which different cultures, in particular the classical Greek and Judaic, articulate and represent nakedness. According to Ann Hollander (1993) dress is crucial to our understanding of the body to the extent that our ways of seeing and representing the naked body are dominated by conventions of dress. As she argues, 'art proves that nakedness is not universally experienced and perceived any more than clothes are. At any time, the unadorned self has more kinship with its own usual dressed aspect than it has with any undressed human selves in other times and other places' (1993: xiii). Hollander points to the ways in which depictions of the nude in art and sculpture correspond to the dominant fashions of the day. Thus the nude is never naked but 'clothed' by contemporary conventions of dress.

Naked or semi-naked bodies that break with cultural conventions, especially conventions of gender, are potentially subversive and treated with horror or derision. Competitive female body builders, such as those documented in the semi-documentary film *Pumping Iron II: The Women* (1984), are frequently seen as 'monstrous', as their muscles challenge deeply held cultural assumptions and beg the questions: 'What is a woman' s body? Is there a point at which a woman's body becomes something else? What is the relationship between a certain type of body and "femininity"?' (Kuhn 1988: 16; see also Schulze 1990; St Martin and Gavey 1996). In body building, muscles are like clothes but, unlike clothes, they are supposedly 'natural'. However, according to Annette Kuhn, muscles are rather like drag, for female body builders especially: 'while muscles can be assumed, like clothing, women's assumption of muscles implies a transgression of the proper boundaries of sexual difference' (1988: 17).

It is apparent from these illustrations that bodies are potentially disruptive. Conventions of dress attempt to transform flesh into something recognisable and meaningful to a culture; a body that does not conform, that transgresses such cultural codes, is likely to cause offence and outrage and be met with scorn or incredulity. This is one of the reasons why dress is a matter of morality: dressed inappropriately we are uncomfortable; we feel ourselves open to social condemnation. According to Bell (1976), wearing the right clothes is so very important that even people not interested in their appearance will dress well enough to avoid social censure. In this sense, he argues, we enter into the realm of feelings 'prudential, ethical and aesthetic, and the workings of what one might call sartorial conscience' (1976: 18–19). He gives the example of a five-day-old beard, which could not be worn to the theatre without censure and disapproval 'exactly comparable to that occasioned by dishonourable conduct'. Of course, such norms are subject to change (historically and across cultures): in 2022 the so-called 'hipster' beard of the early noughties is still a mainline trend and does not look 'dishonourable' to the contemporary eye. But the point remains that appearances matter. Clothes are often spoken of in moral terms, using words like 'faultless', 'good', 'correct' (1976: 19). Few are immune to this social pressure and most people are embarrassed by certain mistakes of dress, such as finding one's flies undone or discovering a stain on a jacket. Thus, as Quentin Bell puts it, 'our clothes are too much a part of us for most of us to be entirely indifferent to their condition: it is as though the fabric were indeed a natural extension of the body, or even of the soul' (1976: 19).

This basic fact of the body – that it must, in general, appear appropriately dressed – points to an important aspect of dress, namely its relation to social order, albeit micro-social order. This centrality of dress to social order would seem to make it a prime topic of sociological investigation. However, the classical tradition within sociology failed to acknowledge the significance of dress, largely because it neglected the body and the things that bodies do. More recently, sociology has begun to acknowledge dress, but this literature is still on the margins and is relatively small compared with other sociological areas. A sociology of the body has now emerged that would seem germane to a literature on dress and fashion (see Shilling 2007). However, this literature, as with mainstream sociology, has also tended not to examine dress. While sociology has failed to acknowledge the significance of dress, the literature from history, cultural studies, psychology and so on, where it is often examined, does so almost entirely without acknowledging the significance of the body. Studies of fashion and dress tend to separate dress from the body: art history celebrates the garment as an object, analysing the development of clothing over history and considering the construction and detail of dress (Gorsline 1991; Laver 1969); cultural studies tend to understand dress semiotically, as a 'sign system' (Hebdige 1979; Wright 1992); or to analyse texts and not bodies (Barthes 1985; Brooks 1992; Nixon 1992; Triggs 1992); social psychology looks at the meanings and intentions of dress in social interaction (Cash 1985; Ericksen and Joseph 1985; Tseëlon 1992a, 1992b, 1997). All these studies tend to neglect the body and the meanings the body brings to dress. And yet, dress in everyday life cannot be separated from the living, breathing, moving body it adorns. The importance of the body to dress is such that encounters with dress divorced from the body are strangely alienating. Elizabeth Wilson (1985) grasps the importance of the body in terms of understanding dress and describes the unease one feels in the presence of mannequins in the costume museum. The eeriness of the encounter comes from the 'dusty silence' and stillness of the costumes and from a sense that the museum is 'haunted' by the spirits of the living, breathing humans whose bodies these gowns once adorned:

> The living observer moves with a sense of mounting panic, through a world of the dead ... We experience a sense of the uncanny when we gaze at garments that had an intimate relationship with human beings long since gone to their graves. For clothes are so much part of our living, moving selves that, frozen on display in the mausoleums of culture, they hint at something only half understood, sinister, threatening, the atrophy of the body, and the evanescence of life. (Wilson 1985: 1)

Just as the discarded shell of any creature appears dead and empty, the gown or suit once cast off seems lifeless, inanimate and alienated from the wearer. The sense of alienation from the body is even more profound when the garment or the shoes still bear the marks of the body, when the shape of the arms or the form of the feet are clearly visible. However, dress in everyday life is always more than a shell, it is an intimate aspect of the experience and presentation of the self and is so closely linked to the identity that these three – dress, the body, and the self – are not perceived separately but simultaneously, as a totality. When dress is pulled apart from the body/self, as it is in the costume museum, we grasp only a fragment, a partial snapshot of dress, and our understanding of it is thus limited. The costume museum makes the garment into a fetish, it tells of how the garment was made, the techniques of stitching, embroidery and decoration used as well as the historical era in which it was once worn. What it cannot tell us is how the garment was worn, how the garment moved when on a body, what it sounded like when it moved and how it felt to the wearer. Without a body, dress lacks fullness and movement; it is incomplete (Entwistle and Wilson 1998).

A sociological perspective on dress requires moving away from the consideration of dress as object to looking instead at the way in which dress is an embodied activity and one that is embedded within social relations. When this book was first written there were few accounts of how dress operates on a phenomenal, moving body and how it is a practice that involves individual actions of attending to the body with the body. This chapter considers the theoretical resources for a sociology of dress that acknowledges the significance of the body. I propose the idea of dress as situated bodily practice as a theoretical and methodological framework for understanding the complex dynamic relationship between the body, dress and culture. Such a framework recognises that bodies are socially constituted, always situated in culture and the outcome of individual practices directed towards the body: in other words, 'dress' is the result of 'dressing' or 'getting dressed'. Examining the structuring influences on the dressed body requires taking account of the historical and social constraints on the body, constraints that impact upon the act of 'dressing' at a given time. In addition, it requires that the physical body is constrained by the social situation and is thus the product of the social context as Douglas (1973, 1984) has argued.

Becoming a competent member involves acquiring knowledge of the cultural norms and expectations demanded of the body, something Mauss (1973) has examined in terms of 'techniques of the body'. Goffman (1971) has described forcefully the ways in which cultural norms and expectations impose upon the 'presentation of self in everyday life' to the extent that individuals perform 'face work' and seek to be defined by others as 'normal'. Dressing requires one to attend unconsciously or consciously to these norms and expectations when preparing the body for presentation in any particular social setting. The phrase 'getting dressed' captures this idea of dress as an activity. Dress is therefore the outcome of practices that are socially constituted but put into effect by the individual: individuals must attend to their bodies when they 'get dressed' and it is an experience that is as intimate as it is social. When we get dressed, we do so within the bounds of a culture and its particular norms, expectations about the body and about what constitutes a 'dressed' body.

Most of the theorists I discuss do not specifically relate their account of the body to dress, but I have aimed to draw out the implications of each theoretical perspective for the study of the dressed body. The main discussion focuses on the uses and limitations both of structuralist and post-structuralist approaches, since these have been influential in the sociological study of the body: in particular, the work of Mauss (1973), Douglas (1973, 1984) and the post-structuralist approach of Foucault (1977, 1980) are pertinent to any discussion of the body in culture. However, another tradition, that of phenomenology, particularly that of Merleau-Ponty (1976, 1981) has also become increasingly influential in terms of producing an account of embodiment. These two theoretical traditions have, according to Crossley (1996), been considered by some to be incommensurable but, as he argues, they can offer different and complementary insights into the body in society. Following both Csordas (1993, 1996) and Crossley (1995a, 1995b, 1996), I argue that an account of dress as situated practice can draw on the insights of these two different traditions, structuralism and phenomenology. Structuralism offers the potential to understand the body as a socially constituted and situated object, while phenomenology offers the potential to understand dress as an embodied experience. In terms of providing an account of the dressed body as a practical accomplishment, two further theorists are of particular importance, Bourdieu (1984, 1994) and Goffman (1971, 1979). Their insights are discussed at the end of this chapter to illustrate the ways in which a sociology of the dressed body might bridge the gap between the traditions of structuralism, post-structuralism and phenomenology.

Theoretical Resources

The body as cultural object

All the theorists discussed in this chapter can broadly be described as 'social constructivists', in that they take the body to be a thing of culture and not merely a biological entity. This contrasts with approaches that assume what Chris Shilling (2012, see also Shilling 2007) refers to as the 'naturalistic body'. These approaches, for example, socio-biology, consider the body 'as a pre-social, biological basis on which the superstructures of the self and society are founded' (2012: 41). Since the body has an 'obvious' presence as a 'natural' phenomenon, such a 'naturalistic' approach is appealing and indeed it may seem odd to suggest that the body is a 'socially constructed' object. However, while it is the case that the body has a material presence, it is also true that the material of the body is always and everywhere culturally interpreted: biology does not stand outside culture but is located within it. That said, the 'taken-for-granted' assumption that biology stands outside culture was, for a long time, one of the reasons why the body was neglected as an object of study by social theorists. While this is now an object of investigation within anthropology, cultural studies, literary studies, film theory and feminist theory, it is worthwhile pointing out the ways in which classical social theory previously ignored or repressed the body, since this may account, at least in part, for why it has largely neglected dress.

In his early intervention into the sociology of the body, Turner (1985) gives two reasons for this academic neglect of the body. First, social theory, particularly sociology, inherited the Cartesian dualism that prioritised mind and its properties of consciousness and reason over the body and its properties of emotion and passion. Further, as part of its critiques of both behaviourism and essentialism, the classical sociological tradition tended to avoid explanations of the social world that considered the human body, focusing instead on the human actor as a sign-maker and a maker of meaning. Similarly, sociology's concern with historicity and with social order in modern societies, as opposed to ontological questions, did not appear to involve the body. As Turner argues, instead of nature/culture, sociology has concerned itself with self/society or agency/structure. A further reason for the neglect of the body is that it treated the body as a natural and not a social phenomenon, and therefore not a legitimate object for sociological investigation.

However, there has been growing recognition that the body has a history and this has been influential in establishing the body as a prime object of social theory (Aldersey-Williams 2013; Bakhtin 1984; Elias 1978; Feher et al. 1989; Kalof and Bynum 2010; Laquer and Gallagher 1987; Laquer and Bourgois 1992; Sennett 1994; Sims 2003). Norbert Elias (1978) points to the ways in which our modern understandings and experiences of the body are historically specific, arising out of processes, both social and psychological, that date back to the sixteenth century. He examines how historical developments such as the increasing centralisation of power to fewer households with the emergence of aristocratic and royal courts served to reduce violence between individuals and groups and induce greater social control over the emotions. The medieval courts demanded increasingly elaborate codes of behaviour and instilled in individuals the need to monitor their bodies to produce themselves as 'well mannered' and 'civil'. As relatively social mobile arenas, the medieval courts promoted the idea that one's success or failure depended upon the demonstration of good manners, civility and wit and, in this respect, the body was the bearer of social status, a theme later explored in the culture of the day by Bourdieu (1984, 1994) in his account of 'cultural capital' and the 'habitus'. The impact of these developments was the promotion of new psychological structures, which served to induce greater consciousness of oneself as an 'individual' in a self-contained body.

Along with histories of the body, anthropology has been particularly influential in terms of establishing the legitimacy of the body as an object of social study (Benthall 1976; Berthelot 1991; Featherstone 1991a; Featherstone and Turner 1995; Frank 1990; Mascia-Lees 2011; Polhemus 1988; Polhemus and Proctor 1978; Shilling 2012; Synnott 1993; Turner 1985, 1991). Turner (1991) gives four reasons for this. First, anthropology was initially concerned with questions of ontology and the nature/culture dichotomy; this led it to consider how the body, as an object of nature, is mediated by culture. A second feature of anthropology was its preoccupation with needs and how needs are met by culture, an interest which focuses in part on the body. Two further sets of concerns focus on the body as a symbolic entity: for example, the body in the work of Mary Douglas (1973, 1979b, 1984) is considered as a primary classification system for cultures, the means by which notions of order and disorder are represented and managed; in the work of people like Blacking (1977) and Bourdieu (1984) the body is taken to be an important bearer of social status.

For the anthropologist Marcel Mauss the body is shaped by culture, and he describes in detail what he calls the 'techniques of the body', which are 'the ways in which from society to society men [sic] know how to use their bodies' (1973: 70). These techniques of the body are an important means for the socialisation of individuals into culture: indeed, the body is how an individual comes to know and live in a culture. According to Mauss, the ways in which men and women come to use their bodies differ since techniques of the body are gendered. Men and women learn to walk, talk, run, fight differently. Furthermore, although he says little about dress, he does comment on the fact that women learn to walk in high heels, a feat which requires training to do successfully and which, as a consequence of socialisation, is not acquired by the majority of men. (See Okley 2007 for an application of Mauss 'techniques of the body'.)

Douglas (1973, 1979b, 1984) has also acknowledged the body as a natural object shaped by social forces. She therefore suggests that there are 'two bodies': the physical body and the social body. She summarises the relationship between them in *Natural Symbols*:

> the social body constrains the way the physical body is perceived. The physical experience of the body, always modified by the social categories through which it is known, sustains a particular view of society. There is a continual exchange of meanings between the two kinds of bodily experience so that each reinforces the categories of the other. (1973: 93)

According to Douglas, the physiological properties of the body are thus the starting-point for culture, which mediates and translates them into meaningful symbols. Indeed, she argues that there is a natural tendency for all societies to symbolise the body, for the body and its physiological properties, such as its waste products, furnish culture with a rich resource for symbolic work: 'the body is capable of furnishing a natural system of symbols' (1973: 12). This means that the body is a highly restricted medium of expression, since it is heavily mediated by culture and expresses the social pressure brought to bear on it. The social situation thus imposes itself upon the body and constrains it to act in particular ways. Indeed, the body becomes a symbol of the situation. Douglas (1979b) gives the example of laughing to illustrate this. Laughter is a physiological function: it starts in the face but can infuse the entire body. She asks, 'what is being communicated? The answer is: information from the social system' (1979b: 87). The social situation determines the degree to which the body can laugh: the looser the constraints, the more free the body is to laugh out loud. In this way, the body and its functions and boundaries symbolically articulate the concerns of the particular group in which it is found and indeed become a symbol of the situation. Groups that are worried about threats to their cultural or national boundaries might articulate this fear through rituals around the body, particularly pollution rituals and ideas about purity (1984). Douglas's analysis (1973) of shaggy and smooth hair also illustrates this relationship between the body and the situation. Shaggy hair, once a symbol of rebellion, can be found among those professionals who are in a position to critique society, in particular, academics and artists. Smooth hair, however, is likely to be found among those who conform, such as lawyers and bankers. This focus on the body as a symbol has led Turner (1985) and Shilling (2012) to agree that Douglas's work is less an anthropology of the body and more 'an anthropology of the symbolism of risk and, we might add, of social location and stratification' (Shilling 2012: 73).

This analysis can of course be extended to dress and adornment. Dress in everyday life is the outcome of social pressures and the image the dressed body makes can be symbolic of the situation in which it is found. Formal situations such as weddings and funerals have more elaborate rules of dress than informal situations and tend to involve more 'rules', such as the black tie and evening dress stipulation. This dress in turn conveys information about that situation. In such formal situations one also finds conventional codes of gender more rigidly enforced than in informal settings. Formal situations, such as job interviews, business meetings and formal evening events tend to demand clear gender boundaries in dress. A situation demanding 'evening dress' will not only tend to be formal but the interpretation of evening dress will be gendered: generally, this will be read as a gown for a woman and black tie and dinner jacket for a man. Men and women choosing to reverse this code and cross-dress risk being excluded from the situation. Other specific situations that demand clear codes of dress for men and women can be found within the professions, particularly the older professions such as law, insurance and City finance. Here again, the gender boundary is normally clearly marked by the enforcement, sometimes explicit, sometimes implicit, of a skirt for women. Colour is also gendered more clearly at work: the suit worn by men in the City is still likely to be black, blue or grey but women in the traditional professions are allowed to wear bright reds, oranges, turquoises and so on. Men's ties add a decorative element to the suits and can be bright, even garish, but this is generally offset by a dark and formal backdrop. The professional workplace, with its norms and expectations, reproduces conventional ideas of 'feminine' and 'masculine' through the imposition of codes of dress. In this way, codes of dress form part of the management of bodies in space, operating to discipline bodies to perform in particular ways. To follow Douglas's idea of the body as a symbol of the situation, the image of the body conveys information about that situation. Even within the professions there is some degree of variation as to the formality of bodily presentation: the more traditional the workplace, the more formal it will be and the greater the pressures on the body to dress according to codes that are rigidly gendered. I return to this theme in more detail below, when I examine the applications of Foucault's work to the analysis of power-dressing, which is a gendered discourse on dress operating in the professional workplace.

While anthropology has been influential in suggesting how the body has been shaped by culture, Turner (1985) suggests that it is the work of the historian and philosopher Michel Foucault that has effectively demonstrated the importance of the body to social theory, helping to inaugurate a sociology of the body. In contrast to classic social theorists who ignore or repress the body, Foucault's history of modernity (1976, 1977, 1979, 1980) puts the human body centre stage, considering the way in which the emergent disciplines of modernity were centrally concerned with the management of individual bodies and populations of bodies. His account of the body as an object shaped by culture has never been applied specifically to dress but is of considerable relevance for understanding fashion and dress as important sites for discourses on the body.

The influence of Foucault

Foucault's account of modernity focuses on the way in which power/knowledge are interdependent: there is no power without knowledge and no knowledge that is not implicated in the exercise of power. According to Foucault, the body is the object that modern knowledge/power seizes upon and invests with power since 'nothing is more material, physical, corporeal than the exercise of power' (1980: 57–8). Foucault's ideas about the relations between power/knowledge are embedded in his notion of a discourse. Discourses for Foucault are regimes of knowledge that lay down the conditions of possibility for thinking and speaking at any particular time, only some statements come to be recognised as 'true'. These discourses have implications for the way in which people operate, since discourses are not merely textual but put into practice at the micro-level of the body. Power invests in bodies, and in the eighteenth and nineteenth centuries this investment replaces rituals around the body of the monarch: 'in place of the rituals that served to restore the corporal integrity of the monarch, remedies and therapeutic devices are employed, such as the segregation of the sick, the monitoring of contagions, the exclusion of delinquents' (Foucault 1980: 55).

Turner (1985) suggests that Foucault's work enables us to see both how individual bodies are managed by the development of specific regimes, for example in diet and exercise, which call upon the individual to take responsibility for their own health and fitness (the discipline of the body), and how the bodies of populations are managed and co-ordinated (bio-politics). These two are intimately related, particularly with respect to the way in which control is achieved, namely through a system of surveillance or panopticism. This is forcefully illustrated in *Discipline and Punish*, in which Foucault describes how new discourses on criminality from the late eighteenth century onwards resulted in new ways of managing the 'criminal', namely the prison system. From the early nineteenth century new ways of thinking about criminality emerged: 'criminals' were said to be capable of 'reform' (rather than being inherently 'evil' or possessed by the devil) and new systems for stimulating this reform were imposed. In particular, the mechanism of surveillance encourages individual prisoners to relate to themselves and to their bodies and conduct in particular ways. This is reinforced by the organisation of space in modern buildings around the principle of an 'all-seeing eye': an invisible but omnipresent observer such as that described in the 1780s by Jeremy Bentham (1843) in his design for the perfect prison, the 'Panopticon'. This structure allowed for maximum observation: cells bathed in light are arranged around a central watch tower, which always remains dark, making the prisoners unaware of when they were watched and by whom. This structure is used by Foucault as a metaphor for modern society, which he saw as 'carceral' since it was a society built upon institutional observation, in schools, hospitals, army barracks, etc., with the ultimate aim of 'normalising' bodies and behaviour. Discipline, rather than being imposed on the 'fleshy' body through torture and physical punishment, operates through the establishment of the 'mindful' body, which calls upon individuals to monitor their own behaviour. However, while from the eighteenth to the early twentieth century 'it was believed that the investment in the body by power had to be heavy, ponderous, meticulous and constant', Foucault suggests that by the mid-twentieth century this had given way to a 'looser' form of power over the body and new investments in sexuality (1980: 58). Power for Foucault is 'force relations'; it is not the property of anyone or any group of individuals but is invested everywhere and in everyone. Those whose bodies are invested in by power can therefore subvert that same power by resisting or subverting it. He therefore argues that where there is power there is resistance to power. Once power has invested in bodies, there 'inevitably emerge the responding claims and affirmations, those of one's own body against power, of health against the economic system, of pleasure against the moral norms of sexuality, marriage, decency ... power, after investing itself in the body, finds itself exposed to a counterattack in the same' (1980: 56). This idea of 'reverse discourse' is a powerful one and can help to explain why discourses on sexuality from the nineteenth century onwards, used at first to label and pathologise bodies and desires, subsequently produced sexual types such as the 'homosexual'; such labels were adopted to name individual desires and produce an alternative identity.

Foucault's account of power and how it ceases on the body/bodies/populations, is different to other, classical sociological accounts, such as that of Marx, which emphasise how power is a fixed resource held (by the bourgeoisie) over others (the proletariat). For Foucault, power is diffused through society, a force that can be harnessed by anyone – even if the only power is resistance. It provides an interesting way of analysing power at the level of dressed bodies – how bodies may resist power even in subtle ways, as when taking on forms of dress. It points to the context within which dress and bodies acquire meaning that becomes politically salient. For example, the wearing of the hijab by women might be seen as an act of oppressive power, if it is imposed by the State, as when the Taliban won the recent war in Afghanistan and sought to repress female participation in public life; but it is an expression of self-identity when adopted voluntarily by some devout women in Western societies to articulate religiosity. The issue is not so much the dress *per se*, but the meanings it acquires for the bodies who wear it and how those bodies experience the hijab. The fact that the hijab (and headscarf) has become a battleground in France – which sought to ban it for under eighteens in the so-called 'anti-separatism bill' (in 2021) and which became a battleground political issue in the 2022 presidential battle between Marine Le Pen and Emmanuel Macron – highlights the ways dress becomes entangled within discourse and power within the State. Likewise, at the time of writing (autumn 2022), Iranian women are fighting for the freedom to remove their headscarves in protest at the brutality of the regime's strict laws sparked by the killing of Mahsa Amini by the so-called 'modesty' police.

Foucault's insights can be applied to contemporary society, which encourages individuals to take responsibility for themselves. As Shilling (2012) notes, potential dangers to health have reached global proportions, yet individuals in the West are told by governments that as good citizens they have a responsibility to take care of their own bodies. Contemporary discourses on health, appearance and the like tie the body and identity together and serve to promote practices of body care that are peculiar to modern society. The body in contemporary Western societies is subject to social forces of a rather different nature to the ways in which the body is experienced in more traditional communities. Unlike in traditional communities, the body is less bound up with inherited models of socially acceptable bodies that were central to the ritual life, the communal ceremonies of a traditional community, and tied more to modern notions of the 'individual' and personal identity. It has become, according to Shilling (2012) and others (Giddens 1991; Featherstone 1991b) 'a more reflexive process'. Our bodies are experienced as the 'envelope' of the self, conceived of as singular and unique.

Mike Featherstone (1991a; see also Shilling 2007) investigates the way in which the body is experienced in 'consumer culture'. He argues that since the early twentieth century there has been a dramatic increase in self-care regimes of the body. The body has become the focus for increasing 'work' (exercise, diet, make-up, cosmetic surgery, etc.) and there is a general tendency to see the body as part of one's self that is open to revision, change, transformation. The growth of healthy lifestyle regimes is testament to this idea that our bodies are unfinished, open to change. Exercise manuals and videos promise transformation of our stomachs, our hips and thighs and so on. We are no longer content to see the body as finished, but actively intervene to change its shape, alter its weight and contours. The body has become part of a project to be worked at, a project increasingly linked to a person's identity of self. The care of the body is not simply about health, but about feeling good: increasingly, our happiness and personal fulfilment is pinned on the degree to which our bodies conform to contemporary standards of health and beauty. Health books and fitness videos compete with one another, offering a chance to feel better, happier as well as healthier. Giddens (1991) notes how self-help manuals have become something of a growth industry in late modernity, encouraging us to think about and act upon our selves and our bodies in particular ways. Dress fits into this overall 'reflexive project' as something we are increasingly called upon to think about: manuals on how to 'dress for success' (such as Molloy's classic *Women: Dress for Success*, 1980) image consultancy services (the US-based 'Color Me Beautiful' being the obvious example) and television programmes (such as the Clothes Show and Style Challenge in the UK) are increasingly popular, all encouraging the view that one can be 'transformed' through dress.

Featherstone (1991a) argues that the rise in products associated with dieting, health and fitness points not only to the increasing significance of our appearance but to the importance attached to bodily preservation within late capitalist society. Although dieting, exercising and other forms of body discipline are not entirely new to consumer culture, they operate to discipline the body in new ways. Throughout the centuries and in all traditions, different forms of bodily discipline have been recommended: Christianity, for example, has long advocated the disciplining of the body through diet, fasting, penance and so on. However, whereas discipline was employed to mortify the flesh, as a defence against pleasure, which was considered sinful by Christianity, in contemporary culture such techniques as dieting are employed in order to increase pleasure. Asceticism has been replaced by hedonism, pleasure-seeking and gratification of the body's needs and desires. The discipline of the body and the pleasure of the flesh are no longer in opposition to one another: instead, discipline of the body through dieting and exercise has become one of the keys to achieving a sexy, desirable body, which in turn will bring you pleasure.

Discourses of dress Since Foucault said nothing about fashion or dress, his ideas about power/knowledge initially seem to have little application to the study of the dressed body. However, his approach to thinking about power and its grip on the body can be utilised to discuss the way in which discourses and practices of dress operate to discipline the body. As I argued at the beginning of this chapter, the dressed body is a product of culture, the outcome of social forces pressing upon the body. Foucault's account therefore offers one way of thinking about the structuring influence of social forces on the body as well as offering a way of questioning common-sense understandings about modern dress. It is common to think about dress in the twentieth century as more 'liberated' than in previous centuries, particularly the nineteenth. The style of clothes worn in the nineteenth century now seem rigid and constraining of the body. The corset seems a perfect example of nineteenth-century discipline of the body: it was obligatory for women, and an uncorseted woman was considered to be morally deplorable (or 'loose', which metaphorically refers to lax stays). As such it can be seen as something more than a garment of clothing, something linked to morality and the social oppression of women. In contrast, styles of dress today are said to be more relaxed, less rigid and physically constraining. Casual clothes are commonly worn and gender codes seem less rigidly imposed. However, this conventional story of increasing bodily 'liberation' can be told differently if we apply a Foucauldian approach to fashion history: such a simple contrast between nineteenth and twentieth century styles is shown to be problematic. As Wilson argues (1992), in place of the whalebone corset of the nineteenth century we have the modern corset of muscle required by contemporary standards of beauty. Beauty now requires a new form of discipline rather than no discipline at all: to achieve the firm tummy required today, one must exercise and watch what one eats. While the stomach of the nineteenth-century corseted woman was disciplined from the outside, the twentieth century exercising and dieting woman has a stomach disciplined by exercise and diet imposed by self-discipline (a transformation of discipline regimes is something like Foucault's move from the 'fleshy' to the 'mindful' body). What has taken place has been a qualitative shift in the discipline rather than a quantitative one, although one could argue that the self-discipline required by the modern body is more powerful and more demanding than before, requiring great effort and commitment on the part of the individual, which was not required by the corset wearer.

Foucault's notion of power can be applied to the study of dress in order to consider the ways in which the body acquires meaning and is acted upon by social and discursive forces and how these forces are implicated in the operation of power. Feminists such as McNay (1992) and Diamond and Quinby (1988) argue that Foucault ignores the issue of gender, a crucial feature of the social construction of the body. However, while he may have been 'gender blind', his theoretical concepts and his insights into the way the body is acted on by power can be applied to take account of gender. In this respect, one can use his ideas about power and discourse to examine how dress plays a crucial part in marking out the gender boundary that the fashion system constantly redefines each season. Gaines (1990: 1) argues that dress delivers 'gender as self-evident or natural' when in fact gender is a cultural construction that dress helps to reproduce. Dress codes reproduce gender: the association of women with long evening dresses or, in the case of the professional workplace, skirts, and men with dinner jackets and trousers is an arbitrary one but nonetheless comes to be regarded as 'natural' so that femininity is connoted in the gown, masculinity in the black tie and dinner jacket. Butler's work on performativity (1990, 1993), influenced by Foucault, looks at the way in which gender is the product of styles and techniques such as dress, rather than any essential qualities of the body. She argues that the arbitrary nature of gender is most obviously revealed by drag when the techniques of one gender are exaggerated and made unnatural. Similarly Haug (1987), drawing heavily on Foucault, denaturalises the common techniques and strategies employed to make oneself 'feminine': the 'feminine' body is an effect of styles of body posture, demeanour and dress. Despite the fact that Foucault ignores gender in his account of the body, his ideas about the way in which the body is constructed by discursive practices provides a theoretical framework within which to examine the reproduction of gender through particular technologies of the body (see also Chase 2010).

A further illustration of how dress is closely linked to gender and indeed power is the way in which discourses on dress construct it as a 'feminine' thing. Tseëlon (1997) gives a number of examples of how women have historically been associated with the 'trivialities' of dress in contrast to men, who have been seen to rise above such mundane concerns, having renounced decorative dress (Flügel 1930). As Tseëlon (1997) suggests, women have historically been defined as trivial, superficial, vain, even evil because of their association with the vanities of dress by discourses ranging from theology to fashion. Furthermore, discourses on or about fashion have therefore constructed women as the object of fashion, even its victim (Veblen 1953; Roberts 1977). Dress was not considered a matter of equal male and female concern and, moreover, a woman's supposed 'natural' disposition to decorate and adorn herself served to construct her as 'weak' or 'silly' and open her to moral condemnation. A Foucauldian analysis could provide insight into the ways in which women are constructed as closer to fashion and 'vain', perhaps by examining, as Efrat Tseëlon (1997) does, particular treatises on women and dress such as those found in the Bible or the letters of St Paul.

These associations of women with dress and appearance continue even today and are demonstrated by the fact that what a woman wears is still a matter of greater moral concern than what a man wears. Evidence of this can be found in cases of sexual harassment at work as well as sexual assault and rape cases. Discourses on female sexuality and feminine appearance within institutions such as the law associate women more closely with the body and dress than men. Wolf (1991) notes that lawyers in rape cases in all American states except Florida can legally cite what a woman wore at the time of attack and whether or not the clothing was 'sexually provocative'. This is true in other countries as well. Lees (1999) demonstrates how judges in the UK often base their judgments in rape cases on what a woman was wearing at the time of her attack. A woman can be cross-examined and her dress shown in court as evidence of her culpability in the attack or as evidence of her consent to sex. In one case a woman's shoes (not leather but 'from the cheaper end of the market') were used to imply that she too was 'cheap' (1999: 6). In this way, dress is used discursively to construct the woman as 'asking for it'. Although neither Wolf nor Lees draws on Foucault, it is possible to imagine a discourse analysis of legal cases such as these, which construct a notion of a culpable female 'victim' through a discourse on sexuality, morality and dress. In addition, greater demands are made upon a woman's appearance than a man's and the emphasis on women's appearance serves to add what Wolf (1991) calls a 'third shift' to the work and housework women do. Hence, the female body is a potential liability for women in the workplace. Women are more closely identified with the body, as Ortner (1974) and others have suggested; anthropological evidence would seem to confirm this (Moore 1994). Cultural association with the body results in women having to monitor their bodies and appearance more closely than men. Finally, codes of dress in particular situations impose more strenuous regimes upon the bodies of women than they do upon men. In these ways, discourses and regimes of dress are linked to power in various and complex ways and subject the bodies of the women to greater scrutiny than men.

Returning to the issue of dress at work, we can apply Foucault's insights to show how institutional and discursive practices of dress act upon the body and are employed in the workplace as part of institutional and corporate strategies of management. Carla Freeman (1993) draws on Foucault's notion of power, particularly his idea about the Panopticon, to consider how dress is used in one data processing corporation, Data Air, as a strategy of corporate discipline and control over the female workforce. In this corporation a strict dress code insisted that the predominantly female workers dress 'smartly' in order to project a 'modern' and 'professional' image of the corporation. If their dress did not meet this standard they were subject to disciplinary techniques by their managers and could even be sent home to change their clothes. The enforcement of this dress code was facilitated by the open-plan office, which subjects the women to constant surveillance from the gaze of managers. Such practices are familiar to many offices, although the mechanisms for enforcing dress codes vary enormously. Particular discourses of dress, categorising 'smart' or 'professional' dress, for example, and particular strategies of dress, such as the imposition of uniforms and dress codes at work, are utilised by corporations to exercise control over the bodies of the workers within.

As I have demonstrated, Foucault's framework is quite useful for analysing the situated practice of dress. In particular, his notion of discourse is a good starting-point for analysing the relations between ideas on dress and gender and forms of discipline of the body. However, there are problems with Foucault's notion of discourse as well as problems stemming from his conceptualisation of the body and of power; in particular his failure to acknowledge embodiment and agency. These problems stem from Foucault's post-structuralist philosophy and these I now want to summarise in order to suggest how his theoretical perspective, while useful in many respects, is also problematic for a study of dress as situated practice.

Problems with Foucault's theory and method As a post-structuralist, Foucault does not tell us very much about how discourses are adopted by individuals and how they are translated by them. In other words, his is an account of the socially processed body and tells us how the body is talked about and acted on but it does not provide an account of practice. In terms of understanding fashion/dress, his framework cannot describe dress as it is lived and experienced by individuals. For example, the existence of the corset and its connection to moral discourses about female sexuality tell us little or nothing about how Victorian women experienced the corset, how they chose to lace it and how tightly, and what bodily sensations it produced. Ramazanoglu (1993) argues that the notion of reverse discourse is potentially very useful to feminists, but it is not developed fully in his analysis. It would seem that by investing importance in the body, dress opens up the potential for women to use it for their own purposes. So, while the corset is seen by some feminists (Roberts 1977) as a garment setting out to discipline the female body and make her 'docile' and subservient, an 'exquisite slave', Kunzle (1982) has argued in relation to female tight-lacers that these women (and some men) were not passive or masochistic victims of patriarchy, but socially and sexually assertive. Kunzle's suggestion is that women more than men have used their sexuality to climb the social ladder and, if his analysis is accepted, could perhaps be seen as one example of the 'reverse discourse'. He illustrates (unwittingly since he does not discuss Foucault) that once power is invested in the female body as a sexual body, there is a potential for women to utilise this for their own advancement.

Foucault's particular form of post-structuralism is thus not sensitive to the issue of practice. Instead, it presumes effects, at the level of individual practice, from the existence of discourse alone. He thus 'reads' texts as if they were practice rather than a possible structuring influence on practice that might or might not be implemented. In assuming that discourse automatically has social effects, Foucault's method 'reduce[s] the individual agent to a socialised parrot, which must speak/perform in a determinate manner in accordance with the rules of language' (Turner 1985: 175). In failing to produce any account of how discourses get taken up in practices, Foucault also fails to give an adequate explanation of how resistance to discourse is possible. Rather, he produces an account of bodies as the surveilled objects of power/knowledge. This, as McNay (1992) argues, results in an account of 'passive bodies': bodies are assumed to be entirely without agency or power. This conception undermines Foucault's explicit contention that power, once invested in bodies, is enabling and productive of its own resistance.

Turner (1985) commends the work of Volosinov as an alternative to this version of structuralism. In Volosinov's work, language is a system of possibilities rather than invariant rules; it does not have uniform effects but is adapted and amended in the course of action by individuals. Bourdieu (1989) also provides a critique of structuralism that claims to know in advance, from the mere existence of rules, how human action will occur. He attempts a 'theory of practice' that considers how individuals orient themselves and their actions to structures but are not entirely pre-determined by them. His notion of practice is sensitive to the tempo of action; to how, in the course of action, individuals improvise rather than simply reproduce rules. (Bourdieu's critique of structuralism is examined in more detail at the end of this chapter.)

This focus on structures (as opposed to practices) in Foucault's work is closely related to the second major problem with structuralism and post-structuralism, namely the lack of any account of agency. For Foucault, the body replaces both the liberal-humanist conception of the individual and the Marxist notion of human agency in history. However, the focus on 'passive bodies' does not explain how individuals may act in an autonomous fashion. If bodies are produced and manipulated by power, then this would seem to contradict Foucault's concern to see power as force relations that are never simply oppressive. The extreme anti-humanism of Foucault's work, most notably in *Discipline and Punish*, is questioned by Lois McNay (1992) because it does not allow for notions of subjectivity and experience. With this problem in mind, McNay is critical of the attention feminists have paid to this aspect of his work and turns instead to Foucault's later work on the 'ethics of the self'. She argues that in his later work Foucault develops an approach to questions of the self and how selves act upon themselves, thus counteracting some of the problems of his earlier work. He acknowledged the problems with his earlier work and addressed some of these criticisms by arguing that

> if one wants to analyse the genealogy of the subject in Western civili-sation, one has to take into account not only technologies of domination but also technologies of self ... When I was studying asylums, prisons and so on, I perhaps insisted too much on the technologies of domination ... it is only one aspect of the art of governing people in our societies. (Foucault in McNay 1992: 49)

Hence, Foucault's later work began to examine techniques of subjectification – how humans relate to and construct the self – and he considered how, for example, sexuality emerges in the modern period as an important arena for the constitution of the self. In the second volume of *The History of Sexuality* Foucault (1985; also 1986, 1988) goes on to consider how the self comes to act upon itself in a conscious desire for improvement. These 'technologies of the self' do go some way towards counteracting the problems of Foucault's earlier work and are potentially useful for understanding the way in which individuals 'fashion' themselves. For example, discourses on dress at work operate less by imposing dress on the bodies of workers, and more by stimulating ways of thinking and acting on the self. Power-dressing can be analysed as a 'technology' of the self: in dress manuals and magazine articles the 'rules' of power-dressing were laid out in terms of techniques and strategies for acting on the self in order to 'dress for success'. Thus the discourse on power-dressing, which emerged in the 1980s to address the issue of how professional women should present themselves at work, invoked notions of the self as 'enterprising'. As I have argued elsewhere (Entwistle 1997b, 2000) the woman who identified with power-dressing was someone who came to think of herself as an 'enterprising' subject, someone who was ambitious, self-managing, individualistic. The techniques for dressing laid out in these manuals implicated the self and stimulated one to act towards one's body in particular ways. However, the problem with Foucault's 'technologies of the self' is that they are peculiarly disembodied and this point highlights a problem endemic to Foucault's work, namely his account of the body.

The body versus embodiment

While Foucault's approach to the body is useful since it enables the analysis of the body without resorting to biological determinism, his body is peculiarly lacking in features that would seem crucial. As noted above, Foucault's account of the body and its relationship to power is problematic for feminists such as McNay (1992) and Ramazanoglu (1993) because it is not sensitive to the question of gender, which, they insist, is crucial to any account of the body and how bodies are operated on by power. As McNay (1992) argues, not only is gender the most crucial division between bodies but power does not act on male and female bodies in the same way.

Furthermore, Foucault's analysis is internally inconsistent at times and his conception of the body confused. Turner notes that Foucault vacillates between some idea of a 'real' material body and a body constructed by discourse:

> at times he treats the body as a real entity – as, for example, in the effects of population growth on scientific thought or in his analysis of the effect of penology on the body. Foucault appears to treat the body as a unified, concrete aspect of human history which is continuous across epochs. Such a position is, however, clearly at odds with his views on the discontinuities of history and with his argument that the body is constructed by discourse. (1985: 48)

Thus, on the one hand, Foucault's bio-politics would appear to construct the body as a concrete, material entity, manipulated by institutions and practices; on the other, his focus on discourse seems to produce a notion of the body that has no materiality outside the representation. Such a vacillation is problematic since the question of what constitutes a body is one that cannot be avoided – does the body have a materiality outside language and representation? The body cannot be at one and the same time both a material object outside language and a solely linguistic construction. Terrance Turner suggests that Foucault's body is contradictory and problematic in terms of his own claim to critique essences: it is 'a featureless tabula rasa awaiting the animating disciplines of discourse ... an a priori individual unity disarmingly reminiscent of its arch-rival, the transcendental subject' (1996: 37). Further, the dominance of the discursive body in Foucault's work would seem to undermine his aim to produce a 'history of bodies' and the investments and operations of power on them. What is most material and most vital about a body if not its flesh and bones? What is power doing if not operating on, controlling or dominating the material body? Turner makes this point emphatically, arguing that Foucault's notion of the body as the most material thing is 'transparently spurious. Foucault's body has no flesh; it is begotten out of discourse by power (itself an immaterial, manna-like force)' (1996: 36).

Foucault's approach denies the fact that, however difficult it might be to access the body as an independent realm, we are nonetheless embodied and contained within the parameters of a biological entity and that this experience, however culturally mediated, is fundamental to our very existence. Bodies are not simply representations; they have a concrete, material reality, a biology that is in part determined by nature. Bodies are the product of a dialectic between nature and culture. Such an acknowledgement of the body as a natural object does not automatically result in biologism and indeed, several social constructivist accounts recognise the body as a biological entity but consider how it is subject to social construction (Douglas 1973, 1979a, 1979b, 1984; Elias 1978; Mauss 1973; Shilling 2007). However, if the body has its own physical reality outside or beyond discourse, how can we theorise this experience?

With these issues in mind, Thomas Csordas (1993, 1996) details the way forward for what he calls a 'paradigm of embodiment', posed as an alternative to the 'paradigm of the body' that characterises the structuralist approach. His express aim is to counter-balance the 'strong representational bias' of the semiotic/textual paradigm found in works such as that of Douglas (1979a), Foucault (1977) and Derrida (1976). Csordas calls for a shift away from a semiotic/textualist framework to a notion of embodiment and 'being in the world' drawn from phenomenology. A similar distinction is drawn by Nick Crossley, who argues that the 'sociology of the body' is concerned with 'what is done to the body', while 'carnal sociology' examines 'what the body does' (1995b: 43; see Hawson (2005) for a feminist perspective on the sociology of embodiment). The methodological shift for which both argue 'requires that the body be understood as the existential ground of culture – not an object that is "good to think with" but as a subject that is "necessary to be"' (Csordas 1993: 135). Csordas argues for a study of embodiment that draws on the phenomenology of Maurice Merleau-Ponty (1976, 1981) as well as Bourdieu's 'theory of practice' (1989). His paradigm of embodiment thus marks a shift away from a concern with texts to a concern with bodily experience and social practice. Crossley also identifies the concern with bodily experience with both Merleau-Ponty and Erving Goffman. I now go on to detail the theoretical and methodological assumptions underlying a 'paradigm of embodiment', looking first at phenomenology and focusing on the work of Merleau-Ponty

(1976, 1981), then at Goffman (1971 1972, 1976) and finally at Bourdieu (1989), whose concepts are especially useful for developing a sociological account of embodiment.

Merleau-Ponty and embodiment

Merleau-Ponty (1976, 1981) places the body at the centre of his analysis of perception. He argues that the world comes to us via perceptive awareness, that is from the place of our body in the world. Merleau-Ponty stresses the simple fact that the mind is situated in the body and comes to know the world through what he calls 'corporeal or postural schema': in other words we grasp external space, relationships between objects and our relationship to them through our position in, and movement through, the world. Thus the aim of his work on perception, as he points out in *The Primacy of Perception*, is to 're-establish the roots of the mind in its body and in its world, going against doctrines which treat perception as a simple result of the action of external things on our body as well as against those which insist on the autonomy of consciousness' (1976: 3–4).

As a result of Merleau-Ponty's emphasis on perception and experience, subjects are reinstated as temporal and spatial beings. Rather than being 'an object in the world' the body forms our 'point of view on the world' (1976: 5). The tendency in Foucault to see the body as a passive object is thus counter-acted. According to Merleau-Ponty, we come to understand our relation in the world via the positioning of our bodies physically and historically in space. 'Far from being merely an instrument or object in the world our *bodies* are what give us our expression in the world, the visible form of our intentions' (1976: 5 [emphasis added]). In other words, our bodies are not just the places from which we come to experience the world, but it is through our bodies that we come to be seen in the world. The body forms the envelope of our being in the world; selfhood comes from this location in the body. Therefore, for Merleau-Ponty, subjectivity is not essential and transcendental: the self is located in a body, which in turn is located in time and space.

The notion of space is for Merleau-Ponty crucial to lived experience, since the movement of bodies through space is an important feature of people's perception of the world and their relationship to others and objects in the world. This concern with space is also apparent in Foucault's work, as discussed above. Foucault brings to his account of space an acknowledgement of its social and political dimensions, the way in which space is infused with power relations, something Merleau-Ponty overlooks. However, Foucault's work lacks any sense of how people experience space, how they use it and move through it; this can be found in phenomenology. For Merleau-Ponty, we are always subjects in space but our experience of it comes from our movement around the world and our grasping of objects in that space through perceptual awareness.

Dress and embodiment

It may seem difficult at first to apply these phenomenological concepts, as a philosophical method, to the analysis of the dressed body. However, in bringing embodiment to the fore and emphasising that all human experience comes out of our bodily position, Merleau-Ponty offers some useful insights for the analysis of dress as situated bodily practice. Dress in everyday life is always located spatially and temporally: when getting dressed one orientates oneself to the situation, acting in particular ways upon the body. However, one does not act upon the body as if it were an inert object but as the envelope of the self. Instead, our bodies are, in Merleau-Ponty's words quoted above, 'the visible form of our intentions', indivisible from a sense of self. What, therefore, could be more visible an aspect of the body/self than dress? In unifying body/self and in focusing on the experiential dimensions of being in a body, Merleau-Ponty's analysis demonstrates how the body is not merely a textual entity produced by discursive practices but is the active and perceptive vehicle of being. His focus on embodied being also directs attention away from the purely visual, focus on fashion – how clothes look on the body – as well as away from the linguistic or textual analysis of how clothes can be 'read', towards the felt experience of *wearing* clothes from the point of view of the wearer. In other words, how clothes *feel* on the body, which is at least as important to how they look. How many times have you changed your outfit because something didn't *feel* right even if the outfit looked good. For example, you might love a pair of trousers but not feel comfortable if the waistband is too tight (after your gaining weight or it shrinking in the wash); or you might love the style of a shirt but find the fabric too tight or scratchy. Only the other day I changed a bright green (synthetic mix) dress, which I love, and which was visually very striking, for a long, loose (cotton) black dress, solely on the basis that the former green dress would be too hot. I loved the visual *look* of the green dress, but it was the cooler *feel* of the cotton black dress that was most comfortable for a hot day around London during a heatwave in July 2022.

The visual dimensions of dress – often the focus of analysis – need to be complemented with studies of the embodied and sensual feeling of clothes. The embodied experience of clothing is captured in Sampson's (2020) material cultural analysis of shoes, which argues for a shift in analysis to pay attention to the experience of wearing clothing. Her analysis focuses on 'the sensual and embodied experience of wear' (2020: 6). It is a corrective to studies of consumption, away from 'the point of acquisition and towards the material, tactile, habitual and bodily' (2020: 9). Her argument evidences the central claims of this book, namely that clothes sit at the juxtaposition between the individual and social world, at once both private and public. Worn garments are significant social and personal records: 'our used garments hold particular place in our networks of things, at once intimate (steeped in sweat, stretched by the girth of our thighs) and public, visible and on display'

(2020: 6). Hauser's (2004) study of the FBI Laboratory's Special Photographic Unit is another example that explores clothes as embodied aspects of material culture. In 1986, the FBI identified a bank robber from the worn details of his denim trousers as caught on CCTV bank surveillance footage. As Hauser notes (2004: 298), 'the idea that worn clothing bears the individuating traces of its wearer confirms the evidence of our everyday experience'. Garments, as we know, take on the shape of our bodies. However, focusing on the materiality of jeans, she goes on to argue that '[D]enim jeans are, of course, particularly well-suited to manifesting these traces. Jeans tend to be worn in close intimacy to the body' (2004: 298). Eco's (1986: 192–4) now classic commentary on wearing jeans testifies to their ability to impinge upon the wearer's felt experience, forming an 'epidermic self-awareness' of the edges and boundaries of the body that interrupted his thinking (see Entwistle 2000 for fuller analysis).

There are, however, a number of problems with Merleau-Ponty's phenomenology. First, he neglects gender. The body moves through time and space with a sense of itself as gendered and this is the reason why the spaces of the public realm of work are experienced differently by women and men and why the presentation of the body through dress is also experientially different. Furthermore, as argued earlier, women are more likely to be identified with the body than men and this may generate differential experiences of embodiment: it could be argued that women are more likely to develop greater body consciousness and greater awareness of themselves as embodied than men, whose identity is less situated in the body. Second, Merleau-Ponty's approach remains philosophical: as a method, it cannot be easily applied to the analysis of the social world.

Despite these problems, however, both Crossley (1995a) and Csordas (1993) see much potential in Merleau-Ponty' s approach and look to the works of Goffman and Bourdieu respectively; the latter two draw some inspiration from phenomenology but develop approaches to embodiment that are sociological rather than philosophical in that they are grounded in empirical evidence of practice. The following discussion applies phenomenological concepts to the study of dress and draws not only on Merleau-Ponty but the work of these two sociologists in order to suggest some of the ways in which the study of dress might approach it as an embodied practice.

The phenomenology of Merleau-Ponty provides one way of understanding the operations of dress as it is constituted and practised in everyday life. The experience of dress is a subjective act of attending to one's body and making the body an object of consciousness and is also an act of attention with the body. Understanding dress then means understanding this constant dialectic between body and self: it requires, as Merleau-Ponty suggests, recognising that 'The body is the vehicle of being in the world, and having a body is, for a living creature to be involved in a definite environment, to identify oneself with certain projects and to be continually committed to them' (1981: 82).

By adopting Merleau-Ponty's notion of the dialectical nature of body/self, it is possible to examine the unity of the body and the self and to explore how these constitute each other. Getting dressed involves different levels of consciousness in terms of how one thinks about the body and how to present it. We are sometimes aware of our bodies as objects to be looked at, if entering particular social spaces, while at other times and in other spaces, such as at home, we do not tune into our bodies as objects to be looked at. This tuning into the body and awareness of the body as an object when in public spaces is similar to Goffman's notion of 'front stage' (1971): in public spaces we may feel ourselves to be on view, while when alone at home we are 'backstage'. In certain circumstances one might also be made self-conscious of appearance and dress if, say, dressed inappropriately. If dress is varied and always 'situated' (i.e. directed towards very different situations), then it might be that there are some moments when the act of getting dressed constitutes an unreflective act – analogous with grocery shopping or picking up children from school – and others when the act of dressing is brought to consciousness and reflected upon – such as dressing for a job interview or important meeting. The different practices of dress therefore raise phenomenological questions about the nature of consciousness of self, for example about how one makes oneself an object of attention. Tseëlon's (1997) study seems to confirm that there are different states of attending to dress and appearance. Asked to describe their dress for different occasions, the women she interviewed identified a range of situations, which varied according to the degree to which they attend to and are aware of their dress: the highest degree of self-consciousness of appearance was manifest in very formal occasions such as weddings or job interviews, while moving around the home, or doing the weekly shopping, had rather lower levels of attention. Although she does not draw on phenomenology to articulate an analysis of body consciousness, her findings can be used to demonstrate how appearance and thus dress are subject to varying degrees of consciousness according to the situation. Consciousness of bodily appearance is gendered: Berger (1972) has suggested that women more than men view their bodies as objects 'to be looked at' and this may indeed inform the choices women make when getting dressed for some situations. Tseëlon's (1997) analysis of women's relationships to their appearance would also seem to illustrate the different levels of body consciousness that inform women's dress choices. The women she interviewed indicate that they are conscious of self and appearance in complex ways: tuning in and out of consciousness, they are at times lost in the temporality of the action and at other times acutely aware of the action.

These patterns of body consciousness and dress practice are not individualistic, although they may be experienced acutely by individuals. However, as Tseëlon (1997) identifies, there are practices of dressing that operate above the level of the individual and must be seen as social and cultural. As I argued at the beginning of this chapter, dress is a technical and practical accomplishment that draws on accumulated social and cultural knowledge. In my analysis of power-dressing (Entwistle 1997b, 2000) I argue that it is a practice of dress that has to be learnt, sometimes from experiences of the workplace and sometimes explicitly through courses offered by image consultants. Many professions and careers are still male dominated and, for some women attempting to climb the ladder in particular institutions, it is important to attend to the body and dress very carefully to 'manage' or limit the potential sexuality of their bodies. Understanding dress in everyday life requires a consideration of the socially constructed categories of experience, namely time and space. Both time and space order our sense of self in the world, our relationships and encounters with others and indeed our mode of attending to our bodies and the bodies of others through dress. When getting dressed, whether unreflective or not, one constitutes self as a series of continuous 'nows'. The everyday practice of getting dressed involves conscious awareness of time because to engage with the experience of dress (in the West at least) one cannot usually avoid the temporal constraints of fashion. The experience of fashion imposes an external sense of time: fashion changes, indeed fashion is by definition temporal. Time is socially constructed by the fashion system through the circle of collections, shows and seasons that serve to halt the flow of 'now' by means of projections into the future. Fashion orders the experience of self and the body in time, and this ordering of time must be accounted for in the consideration of subjective modes of attending to one's body through clothing and style. The fashion system, particularly fashion journalism, constantly freezes the flow of everyday practices of dress and orders it into distinct entities of past, present and future ('this winter, brown is the new black', or 'forget last year's lime-green, cool beige is the colour to wear this summer'). The self, while experiencing an undifferentiated internal time, is also forever being 'caught', frozen, temporally fixed by fashion. One only has to think of the discomfort that is commonly felt when looking at old photographs of oneself in clothes that are no longer fashionable to see how fashion imposes a sense of time onto the experience of the adorned self. This moment of reflection on the presentation of self is a moment when the internal durée, the internal flow of time, is halted or disrupted and the self as experienced in the 'now' must reflect upon the 'old' presented self. In this way, then, a sociology of dress and the practices of the fashion industry could use these phenomenological terms to look at how the experience of attending to and expressing the body is socially and temporally constituted.

Dressed bodies in space

Space is the other crucial dimension of our experience of our bodies and identity. While Foucault's analysis looks at space in relation to social order and, ultimately, power, a phenomenological analysis of space such as that offered by Merleau-Ponty considers how we grasp external space via our bodily situation or 'corporeal or postural schema'; thus, 'our body is not in space like things; it inhabits or haunts space' (1976: 5). The concern with space in the work of both Foucault and Merleau-Ponty, albeit different in methodological viewpoint, is one of the points of contact that Crossley (1996) identifies between the two theorists. One could argue that in terms of dress both conceptions of space – how it is ordered and how it is experienced – need to be acknowledged and here Goffman's work is particularly useful. Space is both external to individuals, in that it imposes particular rules and norms upon them, and internal to individuals, in that it is experienced and indeed transformed by them. There is a moral order to the social world that imposes itself upon individuals who generally come to recognise that there are 'right' and 'wrong' ways of being in a space, 'correct' and 'incorrect' ways of appearing (and dressing). In this respect, Goffman's work owes much to the ideas of Emile Durkheim, who argued that social life is not only functionally ordered but morally regulated too. To be a 'good' person requires conformity to this moral order: when dressing, we have to orientate ourselves to different spaces that impose particular sorts of rules on how to present ourselves. When we fail to conform we risk censure or disapproval: the female guest at a wedding so daring as to wear white is often met with the disapproving eye of relatives who regard this as rude or blatantly disregarding to the bride.

In his acknowledgement of the moral and experiential dimensions of space, Crossley (1995a) argues that Goffman takes the analysis of bodily demeanour in social situations further than do either Mauss or Merleau-Ponty. He notes that Goffman develops Mauss's idea of techniques of the body, not only recognising that such things as walking are socially structured, but considering the situation in which an activity such as walking takes place and how walking is not only a part of the interaction order, but serves also to reproduce it. Thus, for Goffman, the spaces of the street, the office, the shopping mall, operate with different rules and determine how we present ourselves and how we interact with others. Space is also experientially different according to the time of day: at night the street is threatening and our perceptual awareness is sharper than in the daytime and the zone around our bodies is widened and monitored more closely. Goffman reminds us of the territorial nature of space and describes how we have to negotiate crowds, dark quiet spaces and so on. Another important point to bear in mind is that action transforms space: encountering objects and others is about the negotiation of space. Because his sense of space is both social and perceptual, Goffman (1972) provides a link between the structuralist/post-structuralist analysis of space delineated by Douglas (1979a) and Foucault (1977) in terms of social order and regulation and the phenomenological analysis of space as experiential. Crossley (1995b) suggests that while Merleau-Ponty is good at articulating spatiality and the perception of it, Goffman provides concrete accounts of how this occurs in the social world.

This account of space as structuring movement and presentation of self and as something that individuals must grasp and interpret is valuable to an account of dress as a situated bodily practice. Dress forms part of the micro-social order of most social spaces and when we dress we have to orientate ourselves to the implicit norms of these spaces: is there a code of dress we have to abide by? who are we likely to meet? what activities are we likely to perform? how visible do we want to be? (do we want to stand out in the crowd or blend in?) and so on. We may not always be consciously aware of all these issues; indeed only some circumstances, such as formal situations, demand a high degree of body/dress consciousness. However, even when not attending to these issues consciously, we internalise particular rules or norms of dress, which we routinely employ subconsciously. Spaces are also gendered: women may have to think more carefully about how they appear in public than men, at least in some situations; and how women experience public spaces such as offices, boardrooms, quiet streets at night, is likely to be different to how men experience them. I have argued elsewhere (Entwistle 1997a) that the profes-sional woman is more likely to be conscious of her body and dress in public spaces of work than at home or even in her private office. Space is experienced territorially by professional women, who routinely talk of putting on their jacket to go to meetings and when walking around their workplace (the reason being to cover the breasts so as to avoid sexual glances from men), but taking it off when in the privacy of their office. As this example illustrates, spaces at work carry different meanings for women and they have developed particular strategies of dress for managing the gaze of others, especially men, in public spaces at work. In a similar way, women dressing up for a night out might wear a coat to cover up an outfit that might otherwise make them feel vulnerable on the street. In a night-club, short skirts and skimpy tops might be perfectly appropriate (depending on the wearer's confidence and/or intentions), but on a quiet street late at night, the same clothing might be experienced differently and make one feel vulnerable. The space imposes its own structures onto the individual who, in her turn, may come up with strategies of dress aimed at managing this space.

Sociological accounts of the body and embodiment

Crossley (1995a) suggests that there are many other fruitful connections to be made between Goffman and Merleau-Ponty. He suggests that both depart from the Cartesian dualism that is central to much classical sociological thought. Goffman's analysis (1971) examines the crucial role the body plays in social interaction. His work (1971, 1972, 1979) highlights how 'presentation of self in everyday life' is embodied. The body as the vehicle of the self has to be 'managed' in daily interaction and failure to manage one's body appropri-ately can result in embarrassment, ridicule and/or stigma. This performative aspect of self is particularly useful for understanding and interpreting dress practice. Davis argues that dress frames the embodied self, serving as 'a kind of visual metaphor for identity and, as pertains in particular to the open society of the West, for registering the culturally anchored ambivalence that resonates within and among identities' (1992: 25). In other words, not only is our dress the visible form of our intentions but, in everyday life, dress is the insignia by which we are read and come to read others. Dress is part of the presentation of self; ideas of embarrassment and stigma play an important part in the experience of dress in everyday life and can be applied to discuss the ways in which dress has to 'manage' these as well as the way dress may sometimes be the source of our shame. However, the ridicule is not simply that of personal *faux pas*, but the shame of failing to meet the standards required of one by the moral order of the social space. A commonly cited dream for many people is the experience of suddenly finding oneself naked in a public place: dress, or the lack of it in this case, serves as a metaphor for feelings of shame, embarrassment and vulnerability in our culture as well as indicating the way in which the moral order demands that the body be covered in some way. Dressed inappropriately, we feel vulnerable and embarrassed, as is the case when our dress 'fails' us on finding that in a public place we've lost a button, stained our clothes or that our flies are undone. These examples illustrate the way in which dress is part of the micro-order of social interaction and intimately connected to a (rather fragile) sense of self. Dress is therefore a crucial dimension in the articulation of personal identity (a theme explored in more detail in Chapter 4). Understanding dress in everyday life requires, therefore, looking not only at how individuals turn to their bodies but how dress operates between individuals as an intersubjective experience as well as a subjective one. This returns me to the theme with which I opened this chapter, namely that dress is both a social and an intimate activity.

Dress, embodiment and habitus Bourdieu's work (1984, 1989, 1994) offers another potentially useful sociological analysis of embodiment, which not only builds a bridge between approaches that prioritise either objective structures or subjective meanings but provides a way of thinking through dress as a situated practice. Bourdieu is critical of approaches that do not acknowledge the dialectic relationship between social structures on the one hand and agency on the other. Objectivists, he argues, impose upon the world reified structures and rules that are seen to be independent from agency and practice but breaking from these structures should not result in subjectivism 'which is quite incapable of giving an account of the necessity of the social world' (1994: 96). His 'theory of practice' is an attempt to develop a dialectic between these two.

His notion of the *habitus* marks an attempt to overcome the either/or of objectivism and subjectivism. The *habitus* is 'a system of durable, transposable dispositions' that are produced by the conditions of a class grouping (1994:

95). These dispositions are embodied: they relate to the way in which bodies operate in the social world. All class groupings have their own *habitus*, their own dispositions, which are acquired through education, both formal and informal (through family, schooling and the like). The *habitus* is therefore a concept that links the individual to social structures: the way we come to live in our bodies is structured by our social position in the world, in particular for Bourdieu, our class position. Taste is one obvious manifestation of the *habitus* and, as the word taste itself would seem to indicate, it is a highly embodied experience. Taste forms part of the bodily dispositions of a class grouping: tastes for particular foods, for example caviar, are said to be 'acquired' (i.e. they are learnt, developed or nurtured) and are indicative of class position. In this way, the *habitus* is the objective outcome of particular social conditions, 'structured structures', but these structures cannot be known in advance of their lived practice. Thus, the notion of lived practice is not individualistic, it is more than 'simply the aggregate of individual behaviour' (Jenkins 1992). According to McNay (1999), in foregrounding embodiment in his notion of the *habitus* and in arguing that power is actively reproduced through it, Bourdieu provides for a more complex and nuanced analysis of the body than Foucault, whose 'passive body' is inscribed with power and an effect of it. The potential of the *habitus* as a concept for thinking through embodiment is that it provides a link between the individual and the social: the way we come to live in our bodies is structured by our social position in the world but these structures are reproduced only through the embodied actions of individuals. Once acquired, the *habitus* enables the generation of practices that are constantly adaptable to the conditions it meets.

Bourdieu's theoretical and methodological perspective is useful for overcoming the bias towards texts but not practices; this perspective, as I argue in Chapter 2, runs through much of the literature on fashion. His work also sets out concepts useful for a study of dress as situated bodily practice: dress in everyday life cannot be known in advance of practice by examination of the fashion industry or fashion texts alone. Choices over dress are always defined within a particular context: the fashion system provides the 'raw material' of our choices but these are adapted within the context of the lived experience of the woman, her class, race, age, occupation and so on. Dress in everyday life is a practical negotiation between the fashion system as a structured system, the social conditions of everyday life such as class, gender and the like as well as the 'rules' or norms governing particular social situations. The outcome of this complex interaction cannot be known in advance, precisely because the *habitus* will improvise and adapt to these conditions. The notion of the *habitus* as a durable and transposable set of dispositions allows some sense of agency: it enables us to talk about dress as a personal attempt to orientate ourselves to particular circumstances and thus recognises the structuring influences of the social world, on the one hand, and the agency of individuals who make choices as to what to wear, on the other.

The *habitus* is useful for understanding how dress styles are gendered and how gender is actively reproduced through dress. However much gendered identity has been problematised and however much gender roles may have changed, gender remains entrenched within the body styles of men and women or, as McNay puts it, 'embedded in inculcated, bodily dispositions' that are 'relatively involuntary, pre-reflexive' (1999: 98). To return to the issue of dress at work, it is apparent that there are gendered styles of dress within the workplace, especially the white-collar and professional workplace. Here we find that the suit is the standard 'masculine' dress and, while women have adopted suits in recent years, theirs differ in many respects from men's. Women have more choices of dress in that they can, in most workplaces, wear various skirts or trousers with their jackets; there is also a wider range of colour than the usual black, grey, navy of most male suits for the conventional office and a wider range still of jewellery and other decorative accessories (Molloy 1980; Entwistle 1997a, 1997b, 2000).

Significantly, women's adoption of tailored clothes has to do with the orientation of women's bodies to the context of the male workplace and its *habitus*, which designates the suit as the standard 'uniform'. In this environment, the suit works to obscure the male body, hiding its sexed features, as Collier (1998) has argued. Women's movement into this sphere, as secretaries and later as professionals, required them to adopt a similar need for a uniform to designate them as workers and thus as public as opposed to private figures. However, as discussed in Chapter 6, the feminine body is always, potentially at least, a sexual body and women have not been able to escape this association entirely, despite their challenge to tradition and the acquisition, in part, of sexual equality. In other words, women are still seen as located in the body, whereas men are seen as transcending it. Thus, while a woman can wear a tailored suit much the same as a man's, her identity will always be that of a 'female professional', her body, her gender being outside the norm 'masculine' (Sheppard 1989, 1993; Entwistle 2000). This is not to say that women are embodied and men are not, but that cultural associations do not see men embodied in the way that women are. Therefore, understanding women's dress for the professional workplace, how they come to wear the clothes they do, requires situating their bodies within a very particular social space and acknowledging the workings of a particular *habitus*.

As a theoretical and methodological perspective Bourdieu's *habitus* is useful for understanding the dressed body as the outcome of situated bodily practices. The strength of Bourdieu's account is that it does not see dress as the outcome of either oppressive social forces on the one hand, or agency on the other: instead it drives a steady course between determinism and voluntarism: as McNay argues, 'it yields a more dynamic theory of embodiment than Foucault's work, which fails to think through the materiality of the body and thus vacillates between determinism and voluntarism' (1999: 95). Bourdieu provides an account of subjectivity that is both embodied, unlike

Foucault's passive body and his 'technologies of the self', and which is active in its adaptation to the *habitus*. As such, it enables an account of dress that does not fall into voluntarism and assume that one is free to fashion oneself autonomously. Polhemus's analysis of 'streetstyle' (1994) is illustrative of such an approach to fashion and dress, which has tended to define recent work in this area. In his idea of the 'supermarket of style', Polhemus argues that the mixing of youth culture 'tribes' in recent years has meant less clearly differentiated boundaries between groups, while his image of the supermarket suggests that young people are now free to choose from a range of styles as if they were displayed on supermarket shelves. However, such emphasis on free and creative expression glosses over the structural constraints of class, gender, location and income that set material boundaries around young people, as well as the constraints at work in a variety of situations that serve to set parameters around dress choice.

This chapter has set out the theoretical framework for a sociology of dress as situated bodily practice. Such an approach requires acknowledging the body as a social entity and dress as the outcome of both social factors and individual actions. Foucault's work may contribute to a sociology of the body but is limited by its inattention to the lived body and its practices, and to the body as the site of the 'self'. Understanding dress in everyday life requires understanding not just how the body is represented within the fashion system and its discourses on dress, but also how the body is experienced and lived and the role dress plays in the presentation of the body/self. Abandoning Foucault's discursive model of the body does not, however, mean abandoning his entire thesis. This framework, as shown above, is useful for understanding the structuring influences on the body and the way in which bodies acquire meaning in social contexts

Dress involves practical actions directed by the body upon the body, resulting in ways of being and ways of dressing; for example, ways of walking to accommodate high heels, ways of breathing to accommodate a corset, ways of bending in a short skirt and so on. In this way, the analysis of dress as embodied and situated practice enables us to see the operations of power in social spaces (and, in particular, how this power is gendered) and how power impacts upon the lived body and results in particular strategies on the part of individuals. I have attempted to provide such an account in my own research (Entwistle 1997a, 1997b, 2000), which examines the way in which power-dressing operates as a discourse on how the career woman should dress for the professional workplace and how such a discourse, with its array of 'rules', becomes translated into actual dress practice in the everyday life of a number of career women. In sum, the study of dress as situated practice requires moving between, on the one hand, the discursive and representational aspects of dress and the way the body/dress is caught up in relations of power and, on the other, the embodied experience of dress and the use of dress as a means by which individuals orientate themselves to the social world.

Addressing the body in the twenty-first century

The original premise outlined here is still as relevant today as it was in 2000 but is no longer as original as it was back then. Many of these connections I suggest in this book have been traced extensively since the publication of the first edition of the book over twenty-three years ago, and I would need to write a new book to do full justice to the mass of literature that has arisen since 2000. My theoretical provocation – that dress is a 'situated bodily practice' – has now been widely cited. I noted in the Preface in 2015 that Edwards (2009: 35), in his review of the first edition, argued that it was 'more critique and prescript for future research than an explication of how such connections work either theoretically or empirically' and that my attempt to delineate a range of theoretical perspectives – those of Foucault, Bourdieu, Merleau-Ponty – to analyse dressed bodies was 'underdeveloped'. Although I have yet to produce the long-awaited 'sequel' Edwards requests, my later work on fashion models and buyers examines the embodied labour and practices of fashion within the industry and, perhaps, goes some way towards answering Edwards' request for some empirically evidenced analysis of fashioned bodies. In addition, since the original book was published there have been many empirical studies of dressed bodies (Black et al. 2013; Entwistle and Wilson 2001; Mitchell and Weber 2004; Paulicelli and Clark 2009; Riello and McNeil, 2010). Woodward's monograph (2005, 2007) and the 'wardrobe studies' that have followed are also good examples of ordinary dress practices as women grapple with what to wear for different contexts. She notes how women wonder what 'goes' with what and consider 'comfort' as part of their calculations (comfort meaning the fit of clothing and comfort in fitting the social context), which are orientated towards the situation they are dressing for and whether something is 'really me' (2007: 22). In recent years, many anthropological books examine dress practices globally (Akou 2001; Allman 2004; Goff and Loughran 2010; Ivaska 2011; Küchler and Miller 2005; Miller and Woodward 2011; Norris 2010). Küchler and Miller (2005) develop a 'material culture' approach to clothing that refutes long-held distinctions between the form and texture of fabric and cloth, which has been the basis of parallel material cultural analysis that is located within museums and dress conservation, with the more anthological study of dress as meaning of identity that tends to be divorced from materiality. Such a focus on materiality, of lived expressions of dress, is not a million miles away from my own theoretical approach.

Conclusion

This chapter has set out the theoretical resources for analysis of the inter-relationship between fashion and dress as a situated bodily practice, explaining how we can link fashion and dress to examine how one thing (fashion) becomes the other (dress/dressed bodies); how a system for organising the materials to clothe bodies arrives at the ultimate embodied expression in someone (mine/ your) daily dress. These links are geographical, in that they designate the movement of things (cotton, for example); they are economic, as objects of trade, retail and consumption; and they are also deeply intimate and personal, since these objects reside at the boundaries of our bodies, intimately touching our skin and seen and read by others as indicators of something intrinsic to us (our 'character' or 'personality').

With this theoretical framework described by one anonymous reviewer as 'one of the strongest contributions to fashion studies, explaining its staying power, and the reason it has remained a core text requiring a third edition', I felt justified in retaining the original chapter largely untouched, except for some recent citations. However, all three anonymous readers of the first draft of this book called on me to acknowledge some key omissions, notably failure to discuss race and the body. The obvious point is that the theorists discussed here are all white, European men and this raises questions as to their knowledge and truth claims. Theoretisations of the 'body' or 'embodiment' by Merleau-Ponty, Foucault and Bourdieu assume a universal subject, which is in fact an illusion. As early feminist scholarship (Harding 2004; Smith 2004) argues, all knowledge is produced from the knower's standpoint or position in the world, reflecting their subjectivity and values. However, while I noted in earlier editions the gender-blindness of classic social, I failed to note the importance of race and ethnicity, which needs to be acknowledged now.

Early black theorists, such as Du Bois (2004 [1094]) and Fanon (1986 [1952]) evidence the significance of race through their experience as black men within racist societies (USA under slavery) and France (under colonialism). Their complex relationship to the body and consciousness highlights how black is 'Other': for Du Bois, this experience produces a 'double consciousness' of being simultaneously black and American, while for Fanon (1986 [1952]: 111), racist experiences split his experience of the body 'schema': '[I]n the white world the man of color encounters difficulties in the development of his bodily schema. Consciousness of the body is solely a negating activity. It is a third-person consciousness.' Fanon's descriptions of racism and experience of his body in time and space read very much like Merleau-Ponty's phenomenology when he describes himself 'in the middle of a spatial and temporal world' (Fanon 1986 [1952]: 111), his body is marked as black and inferior. Race continues to be marked today, for example, when police in the UK and USA use controversial 'profiling' to target black men disproportionately for stop and search, with devastating effects, as in the case of the murder of George Floyd in 2019, which sparked the global Black Lives Matter (BLM) movement. That race is absent in the work of the key theorists discussed here is problematic, but it does not mean we cannot extend analysis of classic theories or analyse the ways racial identities are articulated through dress (for more see the discussion of race and identity in Chapter 4).

Building on earlier civil rights campaigns, the black civil rights movement in the US in the 1960s challenged racism. The rise of cultural studies (Hall 2017) and, more recently, 'critical race studies' (CRS), has meant that race and ethnicity are increasingly on the syllabus. Much as feminists of the second wave in the late 1960s and early 1970s challenged the gender-blindness of sociology, studies of 'race' have now drawn attention to the problems of classic sociology. However, these liberation movements were themselves not without problems: the critical interventions of black feminists drew attention to the ways black women were marginalised within both black liberation movements on account of their gender, and challenged second-wave feminist movements, whose notion of a 'universal sisterhood' (Breines 2006: 4), excluded women of colour. For example, black feminist scholars, such as Hill Collins (2020) and hooks (1981, 2000a, 2000b) point to the inherent racism (and classism) of earlier white feminist scholarship, such as that of Friedan (1963), which assumed all women share the same conditions of oppression. The notion of intersectionality (discussed in more detail in Chapter 4 on identity) emerged out of the experiences of black women, to note how multiple forms of oppression intersect. Thus, race is not experienced in isolation from gender (and sexuality, able-bodiness, age, etc.). These political challenges to knowledge production take many theoretical forms in scholarly debate, notably, the rise of post-structuralism and postmodernism, post-colonialism over the 1980s and 1990s, and the 'third-wave' feminist movement, coming to deconstruct the very idea of 'woman' as a social and political subject.

While the absence of race in the theoretical works cited in the early editions to this book is problematic, it does not undermine the overall theoretical approach as a way of studying fashion and dressed bodies in social space. The phenomenology of Merleau-Ponty does not preclude the study of racialised bodies (Diprose and Reynolds 2014), while Foucauldian analysis can consider power as exercised on and through racialised bodies, as Elden and Crampton (2007) do in their application of Foucault's 'state racism'. While Bourdieu concentrates attention on class, his notions of cultural capital and *habitus* can be extended to consider race (Wallace 2017). In conclusion, readers are invited and encouraged to develop the work of situated bodily practice through extension of the theoretical resources discussed here.

2
Theorising Fashion and Dress

The previous chapter argues for a study of fashion/dress that acknowledges the way in which it operates on the body, producing discourses *about* the body as well as practices of dress, which work *on* the living, phenomenal body. However, for analysis to proceed, it's necessary to define these two terms precisely and examine how they are interrelated. The idea of fashion/dress as situated bodily practice acknowledges a very basic sociological tension between structure and agency whereby structures, such as a fashion system, impose parameters around dress within which individuals creatively translate into their own practices of dress.

Various terms are employed in the literature: 'fashion' and 'dress', 'clothing', 'costume', 'adornment' and 'decoration', 'style' are among the most obvious; establishing the distinctions between them is an essential starting-point for this chapter. Different disciplines tend towards one or other term and therefore one way to make sense of the terminology is to locate these words within disciplinary traditions. For example, the terms 'dress' and 'adornment' are associated with anthropological literature, a major strand of which involves the search for universals and therefore an all-inclusive term that denotes all the things people do to their bodies in order to modify them. These words can be said to describe a more general kind of activity than either 'fashion' or 'costume'. The term 'fashion' has been used to refer to a historical and geographically located Western system of dress said to have emerged from the mid fourteenth century and accelerating under conditions of capitalist modernity. This term is the preferred one for sociological or cultural studies approaches, as well as by social or cultural historians of fashion, while the term 'costume' tends to be found in historical texts. However, in recent years this characterisation has been challenged and a broader definition of fashion proposed that is not prejudiced towards the West or modernity. For example, Welters and Lillethun (2018) explore the meanings of fashion in their discussion of terminology and propose that its meanings do allow us to define fashion as a broader practice than the earlier fashion scholarship has suggested.

Thus, while it is possible to discern a body of early anthropological literature on 'dress' distinct from a sociological, historical and cultural body of literature on 'fashion', in practice the picture is more complex than this and scholars are not in agreement as to whether fashion as a form of dress is unique to the north/west. Far from clearly employing one or other term and defining it precisely, there is a considerable degree of confusion in the various bodies of literature, with many authors employing a number of different terms ('style', 'taste', 'mode'), often using them interchangeably. A review of the literature illustrates the fact that there is no consensus on the definition and use of these words and no agreement on precisely what phenomena they describe.

Defining the Terms

Anthropology and the disciplines of modernity (sociology, cultural studies, psychology) adopt different approaches to the body and matters of its adornment. Turner (1985) gives a clear summary of the important distinctions between anthropology and sociology, at least as they were formed at the end of the nineteenth century and early twentieth century. He notes that, at its inception in the nineteenth century, anthropology focused attention on ontological questions about the nature of humanity, in particular through the distinction between nature and culture. The result of this interest was the emergence of a major strand concerned with the search for universals, the things that pertain to all peoples and cultures. He goes on to note that classical sociology, on the other hand, is not concerned with ontological distinctions and universals but with historicity and the forms of social life that emerge with modernity.

This distinction between anthropology and sociology is a historical one – a remnant of late nineteenth and early twentieth-century concerns to establish disciplinary boundaries. However, anthropology now studies modern Western societies, not just traditional communities, while, as argued in Chapter 1, since the 1970s or so a sociology of the body has emerged to address questions of the body. The historical difference between the two disciplines, however, has made for discernibly different traditions of writing: an anthropological body of literature was originally concerned with accounts of 'dress' or 'adornment', evident in the early work of Barnes and Eicher (1992), Cordwell and Schwarz (1979) and Polhemus and Proctor (1978); and another body of literature on 'fashion' in modern societies, produced by theorists from sociology, cultural studies and psychology (Ash and Wilson 1992; Bell 1976; Flügel 1930; Lurie 1981; Simmel 1971; Veblen 1953; Wilson 2007). However, in recent years, this distinction has eroded quite considerably. Contemporary anthropological literature tends to focus on the meanings and practices of adornment or dress in non-Western cultures or, in the case of some anthropological collections such as Barnes and Eicher (1992), Cordwell and Schwarz (1979) and Polhemus and Proctor (1978), there is an interest in cross-cultural variations, which might involve considering dress in the Western fashion system as well. One feature of this anthropology is an ethnographic concern with practices surrounding dress, clothing and fabric, and the rise of 'material culture' studies has seen this emphasis on everyday practice extend to looking inside the wardrobes of men and women (Miller and Woodward 2011; Woodward, 2007). In contrast, early sociological and cultural studies literature was often quite theoretical in terms of the claims made about 'fashion', seeking to explain it and account for its prevalence in modern societies but generally not empirically grounded (Lipovetsky 1994; Davis 1992; Wilson 1985). However, a growing fashion studies over the last twenty or so years has produced many PhDs, monographs and Readers covering various aspects of fashionable dress. The earlier disciplinary distinction between dress as the more anthropological term and the more universal one, versus fashion as a sociological term to describe a dress system in the modern West has entirely broken down. Indeed, today many anthropologists and sociologists lay claim to fashion as the more universal and inclusive term (Eicher et al. 2008; Craik 2009; Welters and Lillethun 2018) and critique the Eurocentrism of dominant fashion scholarship that has defined it as a specifically Western phenomenon. The definitional argument about these terms is discussed here, while debates on fashion history and its development in the West/Europe are taken up in Chapter 3.

Defining dress

The early anthropological concern with universals led anthropologists such as Benthall (1976) and Polhemus and Proctor (1978) to argue that there was a universal human propensity to adorn. This argument is now widely accepted by writers on dress and fashion, and anthropological evidence that all cultures 'dress' the body and that no culture leaves the body 'unadorned' is cited by most of the key texts in the area. Indeed, it is taken for granted in contemporary anthropological texts on dress. The nineteenth-century concern to demonstrate the universality of adornment has therefore been displaced by concern with the actual practices and meanings of human adornment and the meanings and practices of particular garments (Barnes and Eicher 1992).

However, there still remains a concern within recent anthropological works to define an appropriately universal and all-inclusive term to describe 'all the things people do to or put on to their bodies in order to make the human form, in their eyes, more attractive' (Polhemus and Proctor 1978: 9), although the notion of being 'attractive' is only one explanation for the many body modifications performed by various cultures, as I discuss below. Early anthropological works such as Roach and Eicher (1965), Polhemus and Proctor (1978) and Barnes and Eicher (1992) often open their introductions by asserting the need for, as they put it 'the most descriptive and inclusive' phrase to describe the human act of adorning. Similarly, more recently, Welters and Lillethun (2018) argue the importance of defining terms precisely. In order to make their case that it is not unique to the modern West but existed in pre-modern societies and outside of Europe/West, it is essential to delineate its characteristics.

The terms 'adornment' and 'dress' are terms favoured by early anthropologists of dress, such as Roach and Eicher. 'Dress', they suggest, signals 'an act' that emphasises 'the process of covering', while 'adornment stresses the aesthetic aspects of altering the body' (1965: 1). Given that the form of activity that constitutes most adornment in the West involves covering the body with garments, as opposed to scarification or tattooing, 'dress' is perhaps the most suitable term to use for this process in this book, since it captures the idea of the act (or series of acts) involved. Indeed, this activity is neatly summed up in the everyday words we use to describe our practices of preparing the body, since dress is both a noun and an adjective, as in 'getting dressed' or 'dressing up'. However, 'dress' does not exclude the possibility of encompassing the aesthetic concept of 'adornment': the choices made in getting dressed can be aesthetic as much as 'functional'. Moreover, dress as a noun and an adjective always takes place within the context of a fashion system. In the West, the practice of 'getting dressed' is framed by a fashion system that is increasingly speeded up as the term 'fast' fashion denotes. Fast fashion frames aesthetic choices, providing newer ones at fast turnover. This points to the issue that fashion is about more than material objects; it refers to something valued in these objects – an aesthetic value that makes these things desirable. Thus, before further discussion of fashion can take place, a more precise definition is needed.

Defining fashion

Defining fashion used to be much easier (as is obvious in earlier editions of this book). However, there is now a heated debate as to what counts as fashion, where it can be found, and whether fashion is as universal as dress. The central feature of fashion would appear to be something to do with a desire for *novelty and change*: '[F]ashion, as applied to dress, is commonly described as changing forms of dress that are adopted by a people at a certain time and place' (Welters and Lillethun 2018). In earlier fashion scholarship this 'certain time and place' was thought to be somewhere in the fourteenth century in the courts of Europe; more of this in Chapter 3. Important also to the definition of fashion is to note that it is about much more than material object (garment, form of dress) but refers to a specific value or symbolic meaning generated around it that gives it its aesthetic value *as* the current or latest 'look', taste or style (Entwistle 2009). For Kawamura (2005: 44), 'clothing is tangible while fashion is intangible … A fashion system operates to convert clothing into fashion that has a symbolic value and is manifested through clothing.' However, 'fashion' is not unique to clothing: it is found in many areas of social life, in architecture, design, even academia whenever there is aesthetic change. As discussed here and in Chapter 3, most early historians have argued that a 'fashion system' pertaining to dress refers to a particular industry, a special and unique system for the production and consumption of dress, which was born out of historical and technological developments in Europe. These two points – fashion as novelty/change and fashion referring to something given symbolic value by particular people at a particular time – provide a good definition of fashion to explore the debates about fashion's location in time and space. As a definition, it allows us to examine the lexicon of early and later fashion scholarship, from early research that locates it as a very specific historical and geographically located dress system belonging to particular (modern) societies to consideration of how this dominant definition of fashion is challenged in recent years.

Early debates among fashion scholars marked out a clear division between those seeing fashion as a prevalent even universal feature of all cultures and those arguing for a restricted definition, located to dress in Europe at a particular time. For example, Barnes and Eicher (1992) and Polhemus and Proctor (1978) disagree on the meaning of the term 'fashion'. Polhemus and Proctor argue that 'fashion' refers to a special system of dress, one that is historically and geographically specific to Western modernity. In contrast, Barnes and Eicher do not recognise fashion as a special instance of dress and indeed make no reference to it, except to argue that it is a mistake for researchers to consider fashion as 'a characteristic only of societies with complex technology' (1992: 23). Some of this clash is disciplinary. Barnes and Eicher are anthropologists and the tendency in this discipline is to search for the universal things that link all societies and culture, while Polhemus and Proctor follow in a longer tradition within sociology that tends to focus on particularities of modern societies in contrast to traditional ones. Their definition of fashion follows earlier, classic studies that also sought to define fashion as a particular system of dress originating in Europe. For example, in his classic work, J.C. Flügel (1930) made the distinction between 'fixed' and 'modish' dress: the latter type predominates in the West, 'a fact that must be regarded as one of the most characteristic features of modern European civilisation' (Flügel, quoted in Rouse 1989: 73). In contrast to 'modish' dress, 'fixed' dress is another term for traditional dress, such as the kimono or sari, which is characterised by its continuity with the past rather than change. Rouse (1989) notes that this kind of dress can also be found in traditional communities within the West such as the Hasidic Jewish community in Britain. Similarly, Polhemus and Proctor (1978) point out that the official dress of Queen Elizabeth II was likewise largely immune to fashion, her coronation clothing in 1953, for example, implying continuity rather than change. Fashion is thus claimed in this early fashion scholarship to exist only under specific social arrangements that characterise European societies from around the fourteenth century, but with later colonial expansion and trade gradually extended west, to North America and to Asia and beyond.

There has been, therefore, an orthodoxy within fashion studies, until relatively recently, that limits the definition of fashion to particular social and historical conditions. It is defined as a system of dress characterised by an *internal logic of regular and systematic change*: as Wilson puts it, 'fashion is dress in which the key feature is *rapid and continual* changing of styles: fashion in a sense is change' (2007: 3 [emphasis added]). Similarly, Davis argues that 'clearly any definition of fashion seeking to grasp what distinguishes it from style, custom, conventional or acceptable dress, or prevalent modes must place its emphasis on the element of *change* we often associate with the term' (1992: 14). This point has been made also by Breward (1994) and Lipovetsky (1994), who identify the idea of change as characteristic of modern societies as opposed to feudal societies or so-called 'traditional' societies. This history of modern dress, discussed in Chapter 3, links fashion to societies within the European/ Western context characterised by increasingly rapid social change.

Thus, fashion has typically been understood as a historically and geographi- cally specific system for the production and organisation of dress, emerging over the course of the fourteenth century in the European courts, particularly the French court of Louis XIV, and developing with the rise of mercantile capitalism (Bell 1976; Breward 1994; Finkelstein 1991; Flügel 1930; Laver 1969, 1995; McDowell 1992; Polhemus and Proctor 1978; Rouse 1989; Veblen 1953; Wilson 2007). Wilson's account, for example, situates fashion as a feature in the emergence and development of Western modernity. These authors all agree that fashion emerges within a particular kind of society, one where social mobility is possible.

One recurring theme, proposed by Bell (1976), Simmel (1971), Veblen (1953), McDowell (1992) and Tseëlon (1992a), is that during the movement towards a capitalist society and the emergence of a bourgeois class, fashion developed as a tool in the battle for social status. Fashion, they argue, was one of the means adopted by the new capitalist class to challenge aristocratic power and status, first by openly flouting the sumptuary laws imposed by royalty and aristocracy, and second, by adopting and aggressively keeping pace with fashion in an attempt to maintain status and distinction (Simmel 1971; Veblen 1953). These authors support the idea that 'emulation' is a motivating factor in fashion (this theory is discussed more fully both below and in Chapter 3) as fashion is an elite practice, which others, lower down the social hierarchy seek to copy. Thus, as Bell (1976) and Braudel (1981) argue, fashion is not found in feudal Europe, which provided little opportunity for social movement. Braudel, among others, argues that fashion is not found in non-Western cultures where social hierarchies are rigid, although it has increasingly spread to other parts of the world given global capitalism. Different temporalities can be discerned; for example, Tseëlon (1992a) argues that this history of [Western] fashion can be divided into three major stages: classical, modernist and postmodernist. The classical period of fashion, from the fourteenth to the eighteenth century, saw the feudal status order challenged by the expansion of trade and the rise of 'urban patricians'. However, dress still marked 'the courtly from common' more clearly than during the modern and postmodern period, in which the relationship between clothes and social hierarchy has been progressively challenged.

As discussed in Chapter 3, dominant histories of fashion have depended upon privileging of European ideas of social and aesthetic change within European modernity as a special and unique context for the emergence of fashion. However, more recently, there has been a reassessment of this dominant history of fashion as the story of European/Western social change and status competition exhibited in regular, systematic aesthetic change. Emerging evidence of changing aesthetics in body modification, hairstyles, textiles in much earlier periods in history (pre-fourteenth century) and in non-European/non-Western cultures challenges this restricted definition of fashion. Welters and Lillethun (2018: 4 [emphasis added]) give a comprehensive account of evidence 'that fashion existed in Europe *before* the mid-fourteenth century and in cultures *outside the West* prior to modern times'. They summarise evidence from Japan (Slade 2016), China (Tsui 2016), the Americas (and beyond). They also point to the fact that aesthetic change is seen in some areas of clothing that typify European/Western dress, such as tailoring, and not in other aspects, such as hairstyles.

This recent scholarship (Niessen 2003; Jansen and Craik 2016; Welters and Lillethun 2018) proposes that there is a propensity for all humans to enjoy aesthetic variation. However, rather than seeing all traditional dress as 'fixed' (Flügel 1930), which suggests no change takes place, we might prefer to use the alternative terminology of Polhemus and Proctor (1978) to more usefully distinguish 'fashion' and 'anti-fashion' instead of 'modish' and 'fixed' dress. They argue that 'anti-fashion' (for example folk dress) is not fixed and unchanging. However, most scholars would not claim that there is no aesthetic change in traditional dress, just that it does not change at quite the speed and with the regularity of fashion in modern societies. Rather, folk dress changes slowly, often so slowly that the changes are imperceptible to the people themselves, although this too has been progressively challenged by new evidence (Welters and Lillethun 2018). Bell (1976) similarly contrasts modern and traditional dress when he compares European dress since the fourteenth century with traditional dress in China. He argues that there must have been variations in dress from dynasty to dynasty but these would be not of the dramatic kind found in Europe, where fashionable dress is characterised by the logic of 'change for change's sake'. Here, debates about fashion change dovetail with ideas about societies characterised by change taken up in Chapter 3 and discussed in relation to the critique that what has counted as fashion has depended upon ethno and specifically Eurocentric ways of seeing and interpreting evidence.

There is, indeed, merit in seeing traditional societies and earlier civilisations as exhibiting some fashion impulse, as this growing scholarship evidences. However, I would argue that there is still a value in retaining some specificity when analysing fashion as a system/s for the provisioning of clothes. To universalise fashion, as these studies do, and to see it always occurring all over the world, is itself problematic. Rather than universalising one system of dress, it is preferable to consider specific conditions for clothing provision emerging in different places. Such a universalising gaze also undermines the call for a precise, sociological analysis of the systems of provision proposed in the Introduction by Fine and Leopold (1993). For this reason, the well-documented history of fashion within European courts and later into newly expanding cities, is detailed in Chapter 3. As Riello and McNeil (2010: 4) note, 'one cannot simply ignore all scholarship that has gone before in order to miraculously concoct a politically correct new history of fashion'.

There clearly has, however, been a European/Western bias to look at clothing systems in European and Western societies and the value of these critiques of Eurocentrism has been to focus attention elsewhere. I therefore welcome this post-colonial and transnational lens, which is shifting attention away from the North/West to other places, and which also examines the complex intersections and inter-connections between European/Western dress and East/South. As Bartlett (2022: 457) puts it: 'Cultures have always been hybridities, the products of migration, exchange and cross-fertilisation, and dress plays an important role in those processes.' Indeed, as discussed in Chapter 7, Western fashion has for centuries been dependent upon criss-crossing colonial trade routes, such as the 'Silk Road (or Silk Routes)' (Bartlett 2022: 458), while today's fast fashion depends upon long sub-contracting chains that stretch out across the globe, as discussed in Chapter 7.

Thus, we can and should extend scholarship beyond the Western fashion system and find alternative arrangements for organising dress that may share similar impulses, or which stand in stark contrast. Indeed, much of the most exciting recent scholarship on fashion has been focused outside the West and points to different systems previously ignored. For example, there is a growing scholarship examining the different understandings of fashion in the Eastern bloc of Soviet countries pre-1989 under communism, which developed an alternative economic and cultural system outside that of Western capitalism (Bartlett 2010, 2015; Pellandini-Simanyi 2016.) Similarly, Zhang's (2021) analysis of fashion during the Cultural Revolution in China argues for the importance of understanding how the different political ideology of China influenced attitudes and caused a different relationship with fashion to emerge. Zhang thus challenges many of the assumptions built into Western scholarship, specifically challenging 'the dominant model of sovereign consumers, which emphasises people's agency' (p. 961) and the Western theories of conspicuous consumption: 'unlike conspicuous consumption theory, instead of showing off their wealth, consumers displayed their poverty during this era' (p. 950). In sum, Zhang notes (p. 950), 'how status-seeking models and trickle-down theory play out differently against this unique political background' of the Cultural Revolution.

The term fashion system/s refers to conditions for the production, distribution and consumption of dress. It refers to the complex interactions between design, manufacturing, marketing and distribution of clothing into retail outlets, as well as their consumption and ultimate disposal. The complexity of fashion means that, as Leopold (1992) argues, it is 'a hybrid subject' requiring the study of the interconnectedness between production and consumption. Fine and Leopold's materialist analysis (1993) points to the need for historical specificity in the analysis of the fashion system and argues that the fashion system under capitalism comprises very particular relations of production and distribution. Indeed, as discussed in Chapter 7, there are different modes within the fashion system, as women's fashion is organised rather differently from men's and children's. Leopold (1992) states that fashion should be considered a complex system, so that it can be understood not just as a cultural phenomenon but as an aspect of manufacturing and technology as well as marketing and retail. The same acknowledgement of fashion as 'hybrid' comes from Ash and Wright (1988) and also from Willis and Midgley (1973), who suggest that the study of fashion requires an integrated approach combining the study of technology, politics, economics, social context, communities and individuals. However, as Leopold (1992) suggests, such an approach has yet to emerge, with most fashion literature focusing attention either on supply or consumption.

One central theme not examined fully in the original text is the importance of *belief* and *symbolic meanings* that make up the fashion system. In other words, it is not enough to consider the physical production of garments; we must also take account of the desire be 'in fashion' and the symbolic value created around things that promote fashion consumption. This is discussed eloquently by Bourdieu (1993c) in his analysis of field relations and the quality of 'magic' and in the work of 'cultural intermediaries' who move between production and consumption adding value and meaning to things to produce them *as fashion*. Precisely how belief in fashion is generated, and how aesthetic styles come to be popularly desired and worn, means focusing attention on key meaning-makers within fashion, who help to generate belief or symbolic meanings. This is a key theme in my own work, which examines how aesthetic value accrues within and across these markets (Entwistle 2002, 2009) and is discussed in Chapter 7. For now, it is enough to state that fashion and dress refer to a social arrangement regarding anything (object or idea) that has currency and is popular – in this case aesthetic appeal – that will be worn widely. This fashion quality is held in place by the multitude of choices and decisions that momentarily secure the appeal and celebrate it as the new.

In sum, fashion is characterised by the idea of change and novelty but what counts as change – whether or not this is fast or slow change – is disputed among scholars and, so too, the link between aesthetic change and social change characteristic of modern societies. The issue of whether evidence of aesthetic change in pre-modern cultures and societies beyond the West exhibits a 'fashion impulse' (Craik 2009) is a contentious one: is fashion a feature of *all* societies or specific to a particular historical and geographical location originating only in Europe? This question is returned to in Chapter 3. In terms of defining our terms it is important to note how the distinction between 'dress' (as a practice – to dress) and 'fashion' (as an aesthetic system) can be drawn.

Everyday dress and fashion

Having outlined the main terms to be used – 'dress' as an activity of clothing the body with an aesthetic element (as in 'adornment') and 'fashion' as concerned with novelty or change that is socially valorised within a specific system of dress – it is now important to discuss the relationship between these two. How does fashion relate to dress? Several authors, such as Wilson (2007), have argued that the fashion system provides the raw material for most everyday dress, not only producing the garments themselves, but also discourses and aesthetic ideas around the garments. These discourses of fashion serve to present clothes as meaningful, indeed beautiful and desirable for, as Rouse (1989) puts it, fashion is more than a commodity, it is 'an attribute with which some styles are endowed. For a particular style of clothing to become fashion it actually has to be worn by some people and recognised and acknowledged to be fashion' (1989: 69).

It is worth exploring the relationship between physical production of fashion (materials) with the symbolic production of fashion (values, aesthetics, taste). Fashion relates to the production of some styles as new, 'hot' or popular, but also to the production of aesthetic ideas that serve to structure the reception and consumption of styles. One of the earliest sociological attempts to understand the fashion system, Leopold (1992), argues that it comprises not only manufacturing and the provision of certain styles of clothing, but also marketing, retail and cultural processes; all of these serve to produce 'fashion' and in doing so structure almost all experiences of everyday dress, though there may be some pockets among religious communities that are outside or on the margins of this. This structuring influence is so strong that, as Wilson (2007) argues, even dress that is labelled 'old-fashioned' and dress that is consciously oppositional to fashion is meaningful only because of its relationship to the dominant aesthetic propagated by fashion. Alternative dress is 'alternative' in relation to prevailing styles and, in some cases, in relation to lifestyle. Indeed, devising an alternative 'uniform' was an important feature in many nineteenth-century Utopian movements, which aimed, according to Luck (1992: 202), to give members a 'family likeness' that 'marked their difference from outsiders, thus acting as a powerful indicator of shared values and community boundaries'.

The various dress reform movements of the nineteenth century adopted styles of dress that were oppositional to the prevailing fashionable aesthetic: campaigns against the corset posed an alternative, 'natural' waist for women, while bifurcated dress was proposed by some Utopian thinkers and feminists of the nineteenth century as an alternative to the crinoline skirts of their time (Luck 1992; Newton 1974; Ribeiro 1992; Steele 1985).

However, fashion is not the only determinant of everyday dress. While fashion is important for defining styles at a given moment, these styles are always mediated by other social factors, such as class, gender, ethnicity, age, occupation, income and body shape, to name but a few. Not all fashions are adopted by all individuals: at any one time some aspects of fashion may be taken on board, while others are rejected. Other important social factors that influence clothing decisions include historical bonds to national costume: indeed, forms of 'national' costume are often taken up as reaction to foreign/colonial power as part of a broader struggle for independence. This was the case for Moroccan dress in the years after independence (1956). In strong reaction to the promotion of European fashion by King Mohammed V as a sign of modernity, there was a move away from it by some of the Moroccan elite, who favoured traditional dress at least some of the time (Jansen 2016: 146).

The social context one is to enter is also important in defining everyday dress. Different situations impose different ways of dressing, sometimes in the form of rules (school uniforms), or codes of dress (business attire), or sometimes simply through conventions that most people adhere to most of the time. Weddings, funerals, job interviews, shopping, hiking, sports, clubbing and so on all impose ways of dressing and serve to constrain dress choices. Even when individuals choose to ignore such codes of dress, they are likely at least to be aware of the pressure to conform and that their decision not to do so might be read as rebellious. The factors listed here are not meant to be exhaustive but are intended to suggest some of the kinds of social factors influencing everyday dress within the fashion system. I now discuss these factors in more detail in order to demonstrate how fashion is only one determining factor on dress.

Polhemus and Proctor (1978) have considered the social influences impinging on dress, suggesting, for instance, that class is effectively marked out by dress and that these class associations do not necessarily come from fashion. Writing in the 1970s, they noted how members of the upper class in the UK use clothes to mark out their identity, adopting their 'own traditional anti-fashion costume' the symbolism of which is 'lasting quality' and aggressive 'anti-fashion' (1978: 68). They give the example of opera dress at Glyndebourne, which cannot always be accurately dated. The symbolism of 'quality' and 'classic' style adopted by the upper class contradicts the view that 'fashion is the prerogative of the upper class' (1978: 68) and they cite the Burberry, a light raincoat (worn by the Queen and aristocracy), which has changed little over the years. Even the middle classes, who once used fashion as a weapon for social climbing, now have their own styles of dress, which are resistant to fashion: for example, the style of the businessman, which they argue has remained quite consistent. However, their definition of anti-fashion is perhaps dated today. Given the arbitrary swings of fashion, the trench coat is no longer anti-fashion: Burberry has since become a high-fashion brand after its re-invention by Christopher Bailey. Yet associations with class have prevailed. The fluctuating fortunes of Burberry after it became associated with 'chavs' (a code word for working class) in the late 1990s highlight what Appleford (2013) argues are class values and judgements relating to dress.

For one thing, class has a material bearing on clothing choice, as it is a factor in choices of purchase (see Crane 2000 for a full discussion). Only a tiny minority can purchase *haute couture* (Colderidge 1989) and even 'off-the-peg' designer clothes, offered by many couture houses, remain beyond the reach of most people. Class also structures dress decisions through taste, as Appleford argues. A taste for high-quality clothing will have a bearing on how much money is spent: the upper-class notion of 'quality and not quantity' will be reflected not only in decisions about the amount spent on individual items, but on the fabrics chosen (for example, silk, linen and cashmere as opposed to their synthetic substitutes). The predisposition to certain kinds of fabric and the notion of 'quality' may be explained in the notion of 'cultural capital' (Bourdieu 1984). Indeed, in an age when jeans and casual clothes are worn by all, making class less obviously discernible in dress, it could be argued that finer gradations of difference require an ever-greater degree of cultural capital. Those 'in the know' are likely to spot the distinction between a Savile Row suit and a high-street one, a designer dress and its cheap high-street imitations. Taste is closely linked to the body, indeed it is a bodily experience, since to talk of having a taste for a particular food or item of clothing is to refer to the sensual qualities of the thing itself. The taste orientations of classes are therefore, in part, bodily orientations or *habitus* (Bourdieu 1984). This concept, discussed in more detail in Chapters 1 and 4, is used by Bourdieu to convey the idea that class position is reproduced through bodily dispositions.

Along with class, peer groups, in particular subcultures, also play a part in predisposing their members to particular styles of dress and involve the deployment of 'subcultural capital' in the interpretation and understanding of style (Thornton 1995). As Brake (1985) (Brill 2008; Geczy and Karaminas 2013; Kawamura 2012; Spooner 2004; Winge 2012) notes, style is important in marking out the subcultural group identity not only to those within the subculture, but to those outside. In his now classic study of youth subcultures, Hebdige (1979) considers the important role played by style in the subculture. He notes that the subculture plunders consumer culture, adopting certain commodities as its own, often to the extent that the commodity becomes shorthand for the group itself: the moped for the mods, the safety pin or ripped clothes for punks. This plundering or 'appropriation' sees the subculture 'inflect' these commodities with its own meanings, often subverting the original meaning of the commodity in mainstream culture. The teddy boys' adoption of the Savile Row gentleman's suit is one example of a style of dress 'inflected' with a rather different meaning from its original association as upper-class dress. On the body of the teddy boy, the 'zoot suit' became inflected with a menacing, working-class aggression (Cosgrove 1989).

A further aspect framing the clothing choices of individuals comes from occupation. Many occupations within the working or lower middle classes prescribe a uniform or lay down clear rules of dress, restricting the types of garments and colours suitable for work. The professions, on the other hand, generally operate with looser codes of dress that are left up to the individual to interpret. As shown in my analysis of the dress choices of female professionals (Entwistle 2000), different occupational settings exhibit different codes of dress: law and banking will tend to be less fashion conscious than the media and creative professions. Within these constraints, individual professional women interpret what is and what is not appropriate to wear to work.

Finally, while the social factors thus far discussed mediate everyday dress, they do not in themselves produce a singular and uniform method of dressing for a particular class or peer or occupational group. Most individuals do not wear the same clothes to all occasions, but rather adapt their dress for the particular social context they are to enter. This is true in the case of some youth subcultures, such as the mods, who, as Hebdige (1979) suggests, adapted their dress to the demands of work (usually clerical work) and the demands of the 'weekend' when they could devote greater attention to subcultural activities such as dress. The social situation therefore plays an important part in structuring dress choices.

Of all the structuring constraints, gender is perhaps the single most important factor in practices of dress in almost all social situations where dressed bodies meet. Fashion is 'obsessed with gender ... constantly working and reworking the gender boundary' (Wilson 2007: 117) and thus any consideration of dress cannot leave out recognition of gender. This is discussed in more detail in Chapter 5, but it is important to note here that it is difficult to consider gender as a category separate from class, peer group and occupation, since the concept of gender is constituted differently by each and is constituted differently according to the social context. Codes of gender vary enormously, depending on all sorts of factors operating in a given context. The skirt, for example, is the most heavily gender-coded garment, worn almost exclusively by women in the West, often explicitly enforced in certain dress codes, for example those of exclusive restaurants and nightclubs where women are supposed to look 'feminine', or more subtly enforced by social convention as in the case of certain professional occupations such as business, politics or law, where a skirt is 'preferred'. However, it is also possible for some women never to wear a skirt if their occupation and lifestyle do not demand it, while in several different contexts skirts are worn by men (at an official ceremony in Scotland, at a 'drag night' in a club, at an avant-garde fashion event and so on). Indeed, this gendering of the skirt is quite unique to the West, since in many other societies men wear skirted garments (kaftans in Arab countries, for example). If fashion is 'obsessed with gender' as Wilson argues (discussed in Chapter 5) and constantly plays with the gender boundary, precisely how it does so and precisely how gender gets codified in dress is highly variable and dependent upon factors operating within the social context. Gender is refracted through these many factors and is produced differently within different situations.

The discussion above points to the complexity of fashion and the necessity of employing an analysis of it which examines the interactions between fashion and a host of other social factors. To understand dress in everyday life requires acknowledging a wide range of social factors that frame individual clothing decisions, of which fashion is important, but by no means the only factor.

Approaches to Fashion and Dress

Sociology and fashion

As a discipline of modernity, arising out of European industrialisation, sociology has not always treated fashion with the seriousness of other aspects of social life, reflecting, perhaps, early predispositions, judgements of value and prejudices. The reasons why much of sociology has not tackled fashion, until relatively recently, are not clear. Edwards (1997) suggests that this neglect of fashion could be explained in terms of its historical location in the arts. This neglect by much twentieth-century sociology is surprising when one considers that fashion has been important to the development and character of Western modernity and remains an industry of considerable economic and cultural significance today.

One possible explanation, however, is that from its inception in the nineteenth century sociology tended to focus on action and rationality, a fact that meant the subsequent repression of the body as an object of sociological investigation and thus the neglect of practices, such as dress, which surround it (Benthall 1976; Berthelot 1991; Turner 1985). Furthermore, as Polhemus (1988) suggests, Western society has largely dismissed body decoration and adornment as unimportant, ephemeral nonsense, unworthy of serious analysis. Fashion has also been subject to prejudices that prevent it from being taken seriously; it has been viewed as trivial, frivolous, irrational, wasteful and ugly. Bell argues that 'the seeming triviality of such questions, the virtual impossibility of linking our sartorial decisions with the grand spiritual passions of mankind, make clothes not less but more important to those who seek to understand their fellow men' (1976: 16–17).

Even several of the few classic studies that have attempted to treat fashion in a serious manner have fallen prey to some of these prejudices (Baudrillard

1981; Flügel 1930; Veblen 1953; see also Wilson 2007 for an account of these). An additional ingredient that makes fashion even more prone to condemnation is its connection to 'vanity'. This is one example of how fashion is often the subject of moral discussion and censure. However, as Bell (1976) and McDowell (1992) point out, this moral component is itself testimony to the power and significance of dress in the social world: 'that dress is burdened with so many moral provisos is a proof of its power and significance within society'. And yet 'in clear contradiction of the fact, many writers have persisted in denigrating an interest in fashion as proof of vanity, or worse, and are critical of those who take more than a fleeting interest in appearance' (McDowell 1992: 15). Despite the influence of postmodernism, which has served to re-evaluate old hierarchies of cultural value, these prejudices still linger and fashion is still the subject of moral and aesthetic condemnation (Baudrillard 1981; Veblen 1953).

A further explanation for the low status of fashion *vis-à-vis* sociological analysis, according to Polhemus (1988) and Tseëlon (1997), is its association with the 'feminine'. The subject (or object?) of fashion is commonly thought to be the woman who falls prey to the 'dreadful' delights of fashion. Moreover, Polhemus (1988) argues that pursuits labelled 'frivolous' and 'foolish' tend to be those associated with women. Until around the 1980s consumption practices associated with women were neglected or treated with derision. A number of feminists, in particular those associated with cultural studies, have pointed out that, within the Academy, feminine consumer behaviour such as the reading of romance novels or the enjoyment of soap operas has traditionally been downgraded as silly and trivial (e.g. Ang 1985; Radway 1987). By implication, condemning fashion as trivial, silly and vain has meant an implicit condemnation of women and women's culture (Tseëlon 1997). Some of this condemnation of fashion has come from feminists who have not meant to criticise the women who wear fashion but characterise women's relationship to fashion as one of exploitation. This kind of critique has been directed at certain garments, such as the corset, which some feminists regard as oppressive (Roberts 1977). In addition to medical and aesthetic criticisms of the corset enunciated by the Dress Reform Movement, feminist voices have been raised against it (see Kunzle 1982; Newton 1974; Steele 1985 for a summary of these arguments). Feminist theory has become rather more confused on the matter of women's relationship to fashion but has at least begun to recognise the pleasure it affords women (Evans and Thornton 1989; Wilson 2007).

However, the few early scholars, such as Simmel, did give it consideration and demonstrate the social importance of fashion enacted at the individual level: for him, it is a perfect example of structure and action. Likewise, fashion, as Edwards (1997) argues, is about the individual and the social, a creative force on the one hand, and a structured (and structuring) phenomenon on the other, and he is right to point out that these facts alone make it an obvious candidate for sociology. This is particularly true when one considers how important fashion is in framing our everyday choices about dress (discussed above), how it reflects and performs existing socialising structures (class, gender, etc.) and how it is a major structuring influence in the social presentation of the body in everyday life; it seems quite remarkable that sociology should have largely ignored it for so long. However, these sociological questions were not the prime focus of early studies of fashion in disciplines such as art history, psychoanalysis, social psychology and cultural studies, all of which attended to other issues. Among these were a few recurring questions: how and why does fashion change as it does? (a common concern of costume history); or what does fashion *mean* and what form of communication is it? (a frequent concern of social psychology and cultural studies). There is, therefore, it seems, a tendency in the literature on fashion to seek to identify a general theory or overarching explanation for its presence in Western society. This all too often leads to explanations that are reductive and deny the complexity of fashion. However, a proper sociological study of fashion needs to analyse the way in which social forces framing dress – such as the fashion system, social location, class, income, gender, ethnicity, region and occupation – structure dress in everyday life. In other words, I advocate a study of fashion and dress that would analyse how they relate to each other: how fashion structures dress and how dress always involves the creative interpretation of fashion by individuals. Such a study takes for granted Edwards' contention that fashion is a phenomenon involving both agency and structure and would counteract the tendency towards generalisation and simplification characteristic of the current literature.

Addressing the literature on fashion

As the discussion above indicates, addressing the literature on fashion and dress requires crossing many disciplinary boundaries. The diversity of disciplines and approaches within the literature is further testimony to Leopold's claim that fashion is a 'hybrid subject' (1992: 101). Fashion is treated as an aspect of industry, manufacturing, marketing, design and aesthetics, consumption and lifestyle. It has attracted the attention of theorists working in different fields and operating from very different viewpoints. As argued above, anthropology has treated dress with some seriousness as a universal feature of human culture. Some of the earliest studies of Western dress costume history developed out of art history as a means of dating paintings. This body of literature emphasises the development of styles and techniques of dress, usually *haute couture* and elite fashions, and is largely descriptive (e.g. Gorsline 1991; Kohler 1963; Ribeiro 1983; Tarrant 1994). However, out of this literature has sprung cultural and social histories (Breward 1994; de la Haye 1988; and Hollander 1993, 1994), which analyse the historical and cultural context of fashion. Some have challenged the focus on elite dress, such as Taylor and Wilson (1989), who examine styles of dress from the Victorian era to the present day, focusing on what 'ordinary' people have worn. A further branch of fashion literature includes histories and contemporary accounts of the economic and technological aspects of the fashion system (e.g. Leopold 1992; Fine and Leopold 1993) and those accounts that examine the exploitation of sweated workers within the fashion system (e.g. Chapkis and Enloe 1984; Coyle 1982; Elson 1984; Phizacklea 1990; Ross 1997). Joining this classic body of literature, the recent explosion of fashion studies over the last twenty-five years has focused on multi-dimensional aspects of this complex industry: from analysis of fashion representations (Brooks 1989; Evans and Thornton 1989; Jobling 1999; Lewis 1996; Nixon 1996; Lynge-Jorlén, 2017), fashion industry work and workers (Armstrong and McDowell 2018; Lynge-Jorlén 2022; Mears 2008, 2011, 2012a, 2012b; Wissinger 2015) identity and difference (MacKinney-Valentin, 2017). This work has been framed by several theoretical perspectives: Marxist materialist analysis (Leopold 1992), structuralism (Barthes 1985), semiotics (Hebdige 1979), psychoanalysis (Flügel 1930, 1996; Silverman 1986), social psychology (Soloman 1985; Tseëlon 1997) and post-structuralism (Entwistle 1997a, 1997b; Nixon 1996; Wilson 1992).

Some common themes and approaches can be discerned across the literature, defined not by discipline but by the kinds of question they ask and the theoretical and methodological approach taken. The first starts out by asking such questions as, why wear clothes? These are questions that tend to lead to simplistic answers. A second approach within the literature attempts a more sophisticated analysis, exploring the relationship of fashion to 'modernity'. While broad in scope, these theoretical approaches do not provide an account of how fashion is experienced and practised in everyday dress. They provide a theoretical account of fashion, which results in the neglect of dress as practice. They also often fail to address the way in which fashion is intimately connected to the body, treating fashion as a social and communicative phenomenon but not a phenomenon of the body. The third approach is less concerned with theoretical explanations than with examining specific dress practices in a culture. This concern with practice can be found in some recent anthropological literature (Barnes and Eicher 1992, Freeman 1993, Hoodfar 1991, Weiner and Schnieder 1991), which examines the cultural significance, meanings and practices around adornment, as well as in social psychology (Cash 1985, Ericksen and Joseph 1985, Tseëlon 1992a, 1997), which looks at what people do and mean by their dress in daily life. However, they are of limited value to an account of fashion in the West.

Theoretical approaches I: 'why' questions

Early explanations of dress and fashion, and indeed many contemporary accounts, have tended to start from 'why' questions: why do we wear clothes? They may also ask questions about the nature of fashion: why a fashion system based on continual change?; why do fashions change as they do?; why the difference between men's and women's fashions? An examination of these 'why' questions is quite revealing of the ways in which fashion has been theorised and can also demonstrate how thinking on fashion has tended to be reductive, producing a theory of dress or fashion that is simplistic in its attempt to be all-inclusive. The net result of such 'why' questions is the reduction of fashion to simple causes and effects and to overly deterministic and reductive accounts.

In answer to the question why do we adorn? anthropology has come up with a number of different explanations: protection, modesty, display and communication, each one being progressively more inclusive than the former. Barnard (1996), Polhemus and Proctor (1978) and also Rouse (1989) give good summaries of these different approaches and begin by noting the early influence of the late nineteenth-century anthropologist Malinowski, who posed the narrower question, why do we wear clothes? One answer is that human beings have basic needs, one of the most fundamental of which is to protect the body from the elements. However, this theory is problematic: in some cultures people do not wear clothes and indeed, as Rouse (1989) notes, many are able to survive in extreme temperatures without much protection from clothes. This is true of clothes in the West as well as in non-Western cultures: skimpy clothes, for example, are worn for the sake of fashion, often regardless of freezing temperatures. Polhemus and Proctor (1978) and Rouse (1989) therefore note that this explanation ignores the fact that many styles of dress both in the West and in traditional and non-Western cultures are not practical and often cause bodily discomfort.

The second explanation that has been put forward is that of modesty: clothes are worn in order to cover the sexual organs. However, anthropo-logical evidence suggests that there is no universal notion of modesty but a high degree of cultural variability, making modesty problematic as a founding principle. As Rouse (1989) notes, modesty and shame are relative to social context. Psychological literature has also asked why we wear clothes and has sought to explain the fact in terms of psychological processes. Flügel's work (1930) in this area constitutes the classic text. He does not reject the two theories of protection and modesty but proposes that a third might be of more significance, that is the purpose of decoration and display. Clothes are worn not to reduce sexual messages but to make us more sexually attractive. Adapting Freud's psychoanalytic approach, he goes on to suggest that clothes express two contradictory tendencies, that of modesty and exhibition, and also argues that clothes themselves (such as the male necktie) may symbolise the sex organs. In this way, clothes express an ambivalence, and this leads him to suggest that 'the use of clothes seems, in its psychological aspects, to resemble the process whereby a neurotic symptom is developed' (Flügel 1930: 20). Clothes, for Flügel, constitute 'a perpetual blush upon the surface of humanity' (1930: 21). A fourth explanation for adornment, that it stems from a universal human propensity to communicate with symbols, has become a dominant theoretical framework, accepted by anthropologists on dress as well as by theorists concerned specifically with fashion. Given its dominance, this explanation of fashion/dress as communication is discussed in more detail below, but first I examine some of the theories put forward to explain fashion.

Theoretical explanations: why fashion?

There are numerous fashion histories that attempt to find a theoretical explanation of fashion. This literature seeks to explain fashion as a unique system of dress and to understand why such a system exists at all, perhaps also addressing the question of why fashions change the way they do. This propensity to ask 'why' questions of fashion is evident in the now classic *Theory of the Leisure Class*, by the late nineteenth-century sociologist Thorstein Veblen, first published in 1899 and reissued 1953. Implicit in his theory of fashion are two 'why' questions, the first of which is: why a fashion system at all? His answer is one that needs to be historicised, since it could be argued that it tells us more about fashion at the end of the nineteenth century than about the meanings of fashion today. Veblen explains fashion in terms of the characteristics he argues are particular to the leisure class, the new bourgeois class who, he argues, adopt fashion as a tool in the battle for social status. The newly emerging bourgeoisie expresses its wealth through conspicuous consumption, conspicuous waste and conspicuous leisure. Since fashion has no utility, members of this class adopt it as a means of showing their distance from function: only the rich and leisured can afford to discard clothes before they are worn out. Dress is a supreme example of the expression of pecuniary culture, since 'our apparel is always in evidence and affords an indication of our pecuniary standing to all observers at the first glance' (Veblen 1953: 119). The second question asked by Veblen is: why do fashions relentlessly change? He suggests that the need for conspicuous consumption and waste may explain the need for fashion to keep changing. However, this alone is not enough, since it leaves unexplained not only the motive for making and accepting changes in style, but why conformity to fashion is necessary. Instead, he goes on to argue that wastefulness is innately offensive, and this makes the futility and expense of fashion abhorrent and ugly. He therefore suggests that the movement of fashion and its being followed by people can be explained as our attempt to escape the futility and ugliness of fashion, with each new style welcomed as relief from the previous aberration until that, too, in all its futility and wastefulness, is also rejected.

According to Veblen, women's dress displays these dynamics more than men's since the only role of the bourgeois lady of the house is to demonstrate her master's ability to pay, his pecuniary strength to remove her entirely from the sphere of work. Veblen's account of the leisure class constructs the bourgeois woman as servile (he compares her role with that of domestic servants); they are passive beings or 'men's chattel' and the clothes they wear are indicative of this. Women's dress was closely linked to fashion and

therefore was an important means by which the bourgeois class could conspicuously consume and be fashionably wasteful. The Victorian woman's dress
was also an important indicator of vicarious leisure. The bourgeois lady wore
clothes that made her obviously incapable of work – elaborate bonnets, heavy
skirts, delicate shoes and constraining corsets – testimony to her distance
from productive work and of her consumption of leisure. Veblen condemns
these traits of fashionable dress and calls for dress that is based on rational,
utilitarian principals reminiscent of the principals of many dress reformers
(see Newton 1974 for a summary).

There are several problems with Veblen's theory. His account of fashion
and fashion change relies on the idea of emulation (the limitations of which
are examined in more detail below and in Chapter 3). His analysis of the
bourgeois woman lacks any sense of agency: fashion is conceived of as an
over-determining and negative force in the life of the Victorian woman. Both
Kunzle (1982) and Steele (1985) offer a rather different view of the Victorian
woman's relationship to fashion and revise the standard fashion story of the
corset as oppressive to women (Veblen 1953; Roberts 1977). Steele's account
sets out to consider the role of erotic display in fashion, arguing that the traditional image of the Victorian woman as sexually and socially repressed 'needs
to be radically revised' (1985: 3). Instead, she posits the view that 'Victorian
fashions revolved around an ideal of feminine beauty in which eroticism
played an important part' (1985: 3) and in this way there is more continuity
between the nineteenth and twentieth centuries than previously thought.
Kunzle (1982) goes further than this, arguing that the wearing of the corset by
the Victorian woman was not a sign of her servile status, but that instead the
female tight-lacer was a sexually and socially assertive woman. Both Kunzle
and Steele see the Victorian woman as an active subject and support their
argument by historical evidence of what Victorian women did in their daily
practice (although Steele takes issue with Kunzle's evidence of tight-lacers,
taken from the correspondence of corset fetishists, which, she suggests may
have been exaggerated for the sake of erotic effect).

It is also worth noting at this point that Veblen's account of women's
relationship to dress, if ever appropriate, is now significantly out of date. As
I have argued elsewhere (Entwistle 1997a, 1997b) the entry of women into
the professions has brought with it a shift in the public/private, production/
consumption dichotomy, which had women confined to the home and the
realm of consumption. It also brought with it a shift in the terms operating
around female dress. As a player within the productive world of work, and a
wage earner in her own right, the career woman is no longer 'man's chattel'
and her dress no longer about vicarious display of leisure. The entry of women
into the professional job market resulted in the emergence of dress that was
not incapacitating but indeed almost 'rational', at least in its principal aim of
enabling women to get on in the world and not be encumbered by fussy and
feminine dress.

Despite the problems with Veblen's account it provides a good example of an early sociological study and one that is still influential today. Many of his ideas can be traced through the work of other theorists of fashion and indeed, as Wilson (2007) notes, in general Veblen's ideas have gone largely unchallenged by fashion writers. This may have something to do with the fact that he is one of the few social theorists to have treated fashion with any seriousness. One sympathetic reading of Veblen comes from the work of Bell (1976), although his analysis produces a far less negative picture of fashion and does not condemn fashion as ugly or irrational. A similar line of argument can be traced through the work of Baudrillard (1981), who argues that fashion continually fabricates the 'beautiful' on the basis of a radical denial of beauty, by reducing beauty to the logical equivalent of ugliness. It can impose the most eccentric, dysfunctional, ridiculous traits as eminently distinctive. This is where it triumphs – imposing and legitimating the irrational according to a logic deeper than that of rationality (1981: 79). Wilson takes issue with Veblen's and Baudrillard's account of fashion as wasteful and futile. In condemning fashion, Veblen assumes that the world should be organised around utilitarian values; this is a world where 'there is no place for the irrational or the non-utilitarian; it was a wholly rational realm' (Wilson 2007: 52). A further problem with Veblen, according to Wilson, is his causal account of fashion change. His theory that fashion is constantly changing in an attempt to get away from ugliness and find beauty is reductive and over deterministic. In his assertion of utility in dress, Veblen attempts to 'explain away' fashion as essentially useless, unnecessary, and irrational, thus failing to acknowledge its ambivalent and contradictory nature as well as the pleasures it affords. The same is true of Baudrillard, whose account, according to Wilson, is 'over simplified and over-deterministic' in that, he, like Veblen, 'grants no role to contradiction, nor for that matter to pleasure' (2007: 53). Moreover, Baudrillard's attack on consumption *per se* is ultimately nihilistic, producing an account of individuals as caught up in a 'seamless web of oppression' (2007: 53).

The problem of causality is one that dogs several other classic accounts of fashion and dress. A number of theorists begin by asking why questions: why does such a seemingly 'irrational' system of dress exist and why do fashions change in the way they do? Many theories have developed to explain fashion's dynamics in terms of a logic inherent to the fashion system. Three theories in particular have become quite influential as explanatory frameworks: the theory of emulation or 'trickle-down'; the theory of Zeitgeist; and the theory of 'the shifting erogenous zone'. All three attempt to explain fashion by reference to a singular force and are highly problematic, in that in seeking to find the 'causes' of fashion, they tend to be reductive and mechanistic.

Veblen (1953) and Simmel (1971) are the most famous proponents of the theory of fashion as emulation, according to which styles start at the top of the social hierarchy with an elite class opting for a distinctive style of dress; the classes below, seeking to emulate the status of this class, gradually adopt the style and fashion thus 'trickles down'. By the time a particular style has been adopted by the working class, the elite, in order to maintain their distinction and status, have moved on to another style, thus fashions continually shift. Georg Simmel (1971) argues that fashion expresses a tension between uniformity and differentiation: it expresses the contradictory desire to fit in and connect with a group, and simultaneously to stand out and assert an individual identity. According to Simmel, adopting extreme and new styles of dress is one means by which the elite differentiate themselves from the rest but, given their high social status, the things they choose to wear become desirable and are copied by the social class below them in an attempt to emulate their status. Once the style has 'trickled down' to the lower classes, it can no longer serve to differentiate the 'leading edge' elite who have to move on to adopt another, often more extreme style to maintain their status position. This oscillating rhythm produces fashion with its logic of constant innovation.

Emulation has come under attack by several theorists (Campbell 1989; Partington 1992; Polhemus 1994; Wilson 2007). Rouse (1989) outlines three main criticisms of this approach: first, change does not occur because the lower classes begin to wear the clothes of the rich; second, there have been occasions when fashions from working-class and other low-status groups such as black youth have become influential; and third, that the 'trickle-down' theory is dependent upon a time lag between styles worn by the rich being adopted by the lower classes, which, given today's production turnover, is no longer the case. Partington (1992) attacks emulation more radically in her account of working-class women and Dior's 'New Look'. She suggests that working-class women did not emulate this look but adapted it in their own way, which was not a 'watered down' or less creative version of the 'real' thing. McCracken (1985) has attempted to re-evaluate the emulation model, updating it by examining power relations between the genders. His account looks at the professional and business woman's emulation of the male business suit at work. He argues that this new breed of professional woman wanted the same status as men at work and, in order to achieve it, emulated the suited look long established as the uniform of men in business. However, in order to develop this argument, he has to 'prove' that the dominant group (i.e. men) is now altering its style as more women start to wear the suit. This seems patently not the case: McCracken provides little evidence to substantiate this point. The main issue, however, is that emulation as a model for explaining dress is too mechanistic and too simplistic. (Further discussions of emulation and its problems are offered in Chapters 3 and 7.)

The question of why fashion changes as it does is answered by some authors with reference to Zeitgeist (e.g. Ditcher 1985). This approach argues that fashion responds to social and political changes. It is an explanation of style that has become part of everyday 'folklore', evident in the commonly cited idea that hemlines drop during economic depressions, as was the case in the 1930s, and rise in times of economic boom, as in the 1960s. Wars are given great importance in this approach. During the First World War, for example, women went out to work in greater numbers than before, and it is assumed that this resulted in the abandoning of the corset and the long hobble skirts of the preceding period; and it is in terms of this explanatory framework that commentators interpret Dior's 'New Look' as part of the 1950s move to make women more feminine and decorative after the masculinising influence of the Second World War. However, there are numerous problems with this approach, one being that it tends to over-simplify fashion: as Wilson notes, 'such statements are too obvious to be entirely true, and the history they misrepresent is more complex' (2007: 46). The 'New Look' can in fact be traced back to before the outbreak of the Second World War: Bell (1976), for example, argues that Vivien Leigh's dresses in the film of Gone with the Wind (1939) anticipated Dior's post-war look. The quantitative study of women's fashions from the 1600s to the 1930s conducted by Richardson and Kroeber (1973) is perhaps the most exhaustive attempt to correlate fashion change with social change. In examining fashion plates of over three centuries, they could not find any conclusive evidence to suggest that social changes influenced any particular dimension of the female silhouette. Instead, as Bell suggests, dress often fails to mirror social climate: while some connections might be established for some of the time, the connection is 'not one of mechanical causality' (1976: 102). If we try to pin changes down to political and social movements, we will always find exceptions to the rule because fashion cuts both ways. Bell also goes on to say that if we allow Zeitgeist theory a free hand it becomes almost a supernatural hypothesis, one of metaphysical rather than social proportions.

A third strand in answering the question of why fashions change as they do focuses on attempts to explain why women's fashions change so rapidly. Laver (1969, 1995) argues that there is a single rule governing women's fashions, namely the 'seduction principle': women's dress is primarily about the enhancement of their sexual attractiveness to men. On the other hand, men's dress does not change as rapidly as women's and is governed instead by the 'hierarchical principle': it is about the enhancement of their social status. The rapidity of change in women's fashions is explained by Laver through the theory of the 'shifting erogenous zone'. At different times, women's clothes display a particular part of the female body but, in order to keep men's desire, the emphasis must continually shift. Thus, for example, he argues that men became tired of the emphasis on female legs in the 1920s so shifted attention to the female back in the 1930s, hence causing a shift in women's fashions. As several authors testify (Bell 1976; Hollander 1994; Polhemus and Proctor 1978; Rouse 1989; Steele 1985, 1996; Wilson 2007), there is a definite link between dress and eroticism. Wilson, for example, argues that 'it seems so obvious that dress must bear some relationship to sexuality that the assumption goes virtually unquestioned' (2007: 91). Even in societies where few clothes are worn, it is common to dress up for ceremonies in ways that serve to enhance sexual appeal. Fetishistic dress, as I demonstrate in

Chapter 6, is also testimony to the power of clothes to incite sexual desire and indeed in the West many items of clothing, for example corsets, and such fabrics as leather and rubber have become closely associated with sex (Kunzle 1982; Wilson 2007; Polhemus 1994; Steele 1985, 1996). However, while there is an undoubted link between dress and sexuality, Laver's account (1969), which places eroticism as the prime mover of women's fashions, is inadequate. As Wilson argues, it is very difficult to determine what erogenous zone clothes display: 'trousers might reveal the leg or the bottom', for example? (2007: 92). She also suggests that there are a number of instances of women's dress, such as their dress for work, which seeks to 'muffle' sexuality, not enhance it, demonstrating that eroticism and display do not explain all fashion. Polhemus and Proctor (1978) also suggest that the theory of erotic attraction cannot take account of many styles of dress that are not erotic. For example, it fails to explain the fashion for combat trousers for women in the late 1990s; these garments seem to be neither obviously erotic nor particularly revealing of the body.

Among the problems with historical accounts and theories that take 'why' questions as their starting point is the fact that the literature is over-simplistic and methodologically naive. It tells stories of fashion as a self-evident, unfolding narrative of change explained by a single motivating force: status competition (Veblen 1953); 'the shifting erogenous zone' (Laver 1969); the 'neurotic impulse' or 'perpetual blush on the face of humanity' (Flügel 1930). This kind of theory results in the organisation of fashion history in terms of narratives that are unilinear and reductive. A further problem is that, more often than not, fashion is depicted as 'ugly' and 'irrational' or indeed trivial and vain, thus producing theories that are heavily moralistic. Since fashion literature traditionally tends to focus on women, these macro-theories have therefore often produced simplistic, moralising and patronising accounts of women's involvement in dress: for example, Laver's account (1969) produces women as passive victims of the 'male gaze' (Mulvey 1975); Veblen's account of women's relationship to fashion constructs them as 'exquisite slaves' and victims to the irrationality of fashion.

However, perhaps a more general and fundamental problem with all these 'why' questions is that they result in macro-theory, which attempts to explain the fashion system in an all-inclusive way. As demonstrated above, each theory has its limitations primarily because each attempts to find an all-inclusive explanation of adornment or fashion. This kind of approach to dress and the fashion system reduces to singular cause and effect what is actually a complex phenomenon. The literature fails to recognise fashion as a socially constituted practice that cannot be understood in isolation but as part of a wide range of other social forces, in particular class, race and gender. Moreover, the 'why' approaches, with their propensity to over-generalise, fail to give an account of agency on the part of women and men. There is no account of dress practice: the theorist sits at a distance, interpreting fashion without seeking to grasp the meanings given to it in daily life or indeed the ways in which it is transformed and resisted by people in practice.

In contrast to these theories, the argument put forward here is that dress needs to be understood as a situated practice that is the result of complex social forces and individual negotiations in daily life. An approach to dress that adopts the framework of situated practice opposes crude reductionism and rejects any attempt to isolate fashion as an all-powerful and determining force. Instead, the fashion system sets parameters around dress but within these parameters are many practices of dressing that are dependent upon a variety of other social structures. A consideration of dress from this perspective involves investigating experiences and practical understandings of fashion as well as the factors that mediate it. It would counteract the tendency to generalise about all dress which 'grand theory' tends to.

Dress and fashion as communication This discussion has so far examined the problems associated with many of the universal explanations of adornment from anthropology, as well as the limitations of numerous classic accounts, attempting to explain the specific dynamics of the fashion system. However, as indicated above, one explanation of all forms of adornment, traditional and modern, is that they stem from the human propensity to communicate through symbols. The idea that humans share a fundamental need to communicate has now become widely accepted as the dominant explanatory framework among anthropologists of dress and theorists of fashion. Anthropology has provided evidence to indicate that all human societies modify the body through some form of adornment and that this, along with language, is posited as a universal propensity. The idea that dress is communicative is adopted by theorists such as Barnard (1996), Calafato (2004, 2010), Davis (1992), Lurie (1981), Polhemus and Proctor (1978), Rouse (1989) and Wilson (2007), and used to explain the purpose of fashion in modern societies. This explanation is more fruitful than other theories for dress, adornment and fashion: clothes and other adornments may be worn for instrumental purposes or for protection, but they are also part of the expressive culture of a community. It follows that if clothes are expressive or communicative aspects of human culture, then they must be meaningful in some way. One clearly discernible approach to the issue of meaning in fashion/dress has emerged from structuralism and semiotics, as has a more nebulous body of work that explores the communicative aspects of fashion and consumption within modernity and postmodernity. The latter ranges from historical works that examine the emergence of fashion and the role played by fashion in modernity to accounts of the significance of fashion in late modern life, an approach that focuses particular attention on the role of fashion in the construction of identity.

One example of the approach to fashion as communication draws analogies between fashion and language, considering the way in which fashion operates 'like a language'. The language-like nature of fashion and dress is considered by such theorists as Davis (1992), Polhemus and Proctor (1978) and Rouse (1989) but is carried to extremes in the work of Lurie (1981). She suggests that fashion has a 'grammar' and a 'vocabulary' like spoken languages, with dress being theoretically larger than verbal language, extending to hairstyle, the way the body is held, how it walks and so on. There are sartorial equivalents of 'anarchic words', taboos (e.g. dresses for men) and 'slang words' (e.g. jeans), while accessories like earrings and hats can be compared to adjectives. There are a number of problems with this direct application of language models to fashion. Davis (1992) suggests that clothing can be thought of like a language but suggests that the more ambiguous language of music is better suited to capturing the equally ambiguous nature of clothes. He therefore argues that the idea of language should be applied to fashion metaphorically and not literally and goes on to suggest that the idea of a code is particularly useful: a code is 'the binding ligament in the shared understandings that comprise a sphere of discourse and, hence, its associated social arrangements' (1992: 5). There are social codes of dress but these are very context bound, and there is no equivalent to a sentence in dress and no way that dress can give as precise a message as a spoken sentence. Clothes, then, for Davis are meaningful but their meanings are ambiguous and imprecise. Their real power comes from their ability to suggest, evoke and resist a fixed meaning. Tseëlon (1997) also demonstrates the ambiguity of clothes. Having asked a group of women to come to a focus group dressed in a way that 'expresses who they are', she compared the intentions of the women with the interpretation made of them by others: the result was considerable misunderstanding and misinterpretation. It would seem, therefore, that if the meanings of dress are not as clear or precise as verbal language, Lurie's analogy becomes untenable. This inability of clothes to be 'read' effectively is noted by Campbell (1997), who criticises the very premise that fashionable dress is communicative. He suggests that the considerable misunderstanding involved in reading the dress of others reflects the difficulty of fixing any meaning to clothes.

While the direct application of language models to fashion is problematic, however, the structuralist model and its method, borrowed from the structural linguistics of Ferdinand de Saussure, has become a dominant framework for considering fashion, particularly within cultural studies. Structuralism is interested in meaning and how meaning in communication systems is possible. Saussure proposed that signs gain their meaning not from anything intrinsic to them, but from their ability to stand in for things. The sign comprises two elements, the signifier (i.e. the sound or image of the sign) and the signified (i.e. the concept associated with it). Signs gain their identity from one another through their difference to other signs, and meaning (in language or any other sign system) comes from the way in which signs combine with other signs. While Saussure developed his theory in relation to language, he saw the potential of his approach for the study of all signs systems and prophesied that a 'science of signs', which he called semiology, would develop. Such a 'science' would provide a method for understanding meaning in all communicative practices, including dress. Semiotics draws upon Saussure's system of language but moves from looking at written communication to non-verbal phenomena. The focus of semiotic accounts has been to explain fashion as a system rather than everyday dress, and to address fashion texts rather than practices (Jobling 1999, 2005). The reasons for this focus of attention are purely methodological. Roland Barthes, who played an influential role in establishing semiology (or semiotics), provides a classic structuralist account of fashion in *The Fashion System* (1985) and demonstrates very clearly the structuralist's methodological concerns. Barthes recounts his decision to focus on the written fashion text, as opposed to its visual representation or the real garments worn, in his search 'to reconstitute step by step a system of meaning, in a more or less immediate manner' (1985: x). He says it is the 'structural purity' of the fashion text that governed his choice: real clothing and its representation are burdened with practical problems but the magazine's text offers the best possibility of studying a slice of fashion at a given moment: only written clothing has no practical or aesthetic function: it is entirely constituted with a view to a signification: if the magazine describes a certain article of clothing verbally, it does so solely to convey a message whose content is: 'Fashion; ... written clothing is unencumbered by any parasitic function and entails no vague temporality' (1985: 8). Barthes therefore recognises the limitations of this choice in terms of a sociology of fashion, suggesting that an analysis that looks only at the written system may disappoint sociologists because it does not deal with fashion as an institution and may indeed tell us only about semiology. The structuralist approach as Barthes develops it effectively 'brackets off' other equally important aspects of the fashion system, such as its industrial and commercial aspects, as well as how it is incorporated into everyday practices of dress. The structuralist approach, governed by methodological concerns, is thus propelled towards texts rather than practices. The 'structural purity' of the text comes from its being a 'frozen' or 'static' moment, whereas social action is complex and dynamic and difficult to capture. As Barthes' account testifies, it is much easier to study a slice of text than it is to study the complex mechanisms of an industry such as the fashion industry, or the complex and nebulous negotiations that make up everyday dress practices. The relative ease of the structuralist method, which can indeed be done from the armchair, makes it a popular choice with theorists. Fashion literature of this ilk has focused on 'reading' photographs, magazines and advertisements as texts. Evans and Thornton (1989), for example, attempt to re-evaluate theories of female narcissism and theories of masquerade through women's magazines and fashion photographs. In one chapter they analyse six fashion photographs and proceed to analyse semiotically the internal arrangement of the elements in the photograph. In a similar vein, Brooks (1989) analyses the way in which Helmut Newton orchestrates 'the look' within his fashion photographs. Moving beyond semiotics, Nixon (1996) draws on psychoanalysis and Foucauldian post-structural analysis (as well as empirical work on marketing and advertising practices) to examine the organisation of the look in style magazines for men, focusing in particular on fashion photography and the various representations of the 'new man' popularised in the 1980s.

In his analysis of youth subcultures, Hebdige (1979) draws directly upon the Saussurian tradition in order to talk about the 'signs' adopted by the subculture to create meaning within, and give identity to, the group. His semiotic analysis moves from written texts as in Barthes' analysis to the uses of objects by youth subcultures. Hebdige uses this concept to suggest that subcultures 'steal' or 'appropriate' objects from mainstream culture but in doing so 'inflect' them with their own meaning. A humble object such as a safety pin with its associated domestic meanings is inflected with subversive and aggressive meanings when worn through the nose of a punk. In this way, Hebdige gives an account of the meaningful role played by 'style' within youth subculture. Although Hebdige's account focuses not on fashion texts but 'real' garments and their uses within social groups, this account of style remains a structuralist one by virtue of its methodological approach. Hebdige textualises subcultural dress practice: he reads the body/style of the subculture as if it were a text. Such textualism makes no distinction between reading a fashion magazine and reading the body of a punk or a mod. This ability to textualise everything serves to 'bracket off' real live bodies as they are lived and experienced. The structuralist method, in seeking to find the relations between elements in a structure, puts a distance between the theorist and the subjects under investigation, since semiotic analysis can be done in the armchair or office and does not require entering the field of action itself (Bourdieu 1989).

This 'bracketing off' of the world beyond the text is a deliberate epistemological and methodological stance taken by structuralists, who claim that we cannot know the world beyond its representations. This stance effectively displaces the idea of embodiment and the individual and can give us no account of experience or agency. It can therefore tell us nothing about what sense people make of fashion, what pleasures it affords, or how fashion structures the experience of dress and the clothing decisions made in everyday life. There is a further problem with this method as with other studies of fashion which focus on texts, and that has to do with the position of the theorist who, in 'reading' representations remains at a distance from actual practices. In his critique of structuralism, Bourdieu (1989, 1994) argues that structuralism maintains a position of distance from the world but assumes a position of superiority; the implicit claim of the structuralist is that he or she knows more, has greater understanding and insight, than those they observe. Thus, Hebdige's work on subcultures does not give us an account of what people do and mean by their dress: his analysis does not consider what subcultural participants say about their dress. Instead, we are offered Hebdige's interpretation of their dress and what it means. The structuralist reading assumes that there is an objective meaning that can be discerned from the surface and which the method of structural analysis can unlock.

Structuralism, however, is not entirely responsible for this focus on texts. Contributions to the study of fashion within art history and film theory have been equally concerned with texts rather than practices. Gaines and Herzog (1990) explore the meaning of the dressed body in texts, mainly film texts, while Hollander (1993) explores 'how clothes in works of art have been connected with clothes in real life' (1993: xi). Hollander suggests that the formal qualities of art are important in illuminating the way in which clothes should be worn and how the body should look in them: so much so that 'the way clothes strike the eye comes to be mediated by current visual assumptions made from pictures of dressed people' (1993: xi). However, while Hollander's focus on art to illuminate dress, although not unusual (it is the standard approach within art/costume history) is problematic because she extends her analysis of the representations to suggest how these representations may have influenced the way clothes and nakedness are perceived in general. Bell (1976), for example, advises caution in relying on paintings and fashion plates, since the painter might have exaggerated the dress, and the person depicted might have chosen to wear particularly elaborate dress for the purpose of the painting. Paintings therefore do not necessarily tell us what dress would have been worn in everyday life. It is also problematic because the clothes depicted in art tend to be the clothes of the elite, not those of 'ordinary people'. For this reason, de la Haye (1988) and Taylor and Wilson (1989) focus not on paintings but on other sorts of representation in order to examine fashions through the ages. A further problem with focusing on art images, or indeed any image, is noted by both McDowell (1992) and Bell (1976), who argue that visual information is just one part of clothing: what we lack in these historical records is the sensual sound and feel of clothes. Hollander's claim that 'the clothed figure looks more persuasive and comprehensible in art than it does in reality' (1993: xi) points to a methodologically driven quest not unlike Barthes' desire to investigate the workings of the fashion system by looking at fashion journalism. The body in art might present a static, tidy, more 'comprehensive' image than in reality and might therefore be easier to study. However, clothes in everyday life are not like art, nor do they pretend to be: clothes in everyday life take on the form of the body and in doing so get crumpled, creased, ripped and so on. Textual approaches therefore do not tell us of the many other aspects of fashion and dress.

I do not wish to suggest that these textual approaches are in themselves invalid, since they serve the purpose of illuminating the way in which clothes are represented, albeit in idealised form. However, what is problematic is the dominance of approaches that focus on texts to the exclusion of other issues concerning fashion and dress, as well as the tendency to extend the analysis of texts beyond the text itself, as Hollander (1993) does. By textualising fashion and dress these approaches can sometimes be reductive; if practices are reduced to texts, the complexity of fashion and dress and the way in which it is embodied is largely neglected. Studies of fashion and dress in terms of how they are lived and experienced are equally valid but have found little place within historical or contemporary literature. The study of fashion/ dress as situated bodily practice moves away from looking solely at texts, although such structuring influences as paintings and fashion magazines are not to be ignored. It looks at how people take account of their involvement with fashion and the way they dress in particular social situations. A concern with subjective accounts necessitates a move into the 'field' of action itself rather than maintaining a position of distance occupied by structuralism. The notion of situated bodily practice also recognises dress as an experience of embodiment and the outcome of practical actions taken by individuals on their bodies.

Theoretical approaches II: fashion and the condition of modern life

Another body of literature on fashion has emerged, which examines its communicative abilities and its role in modern and late or postmodern life. The works of Breward and Evans (2005), Evans (2003, 2005), Finkelstein (1991), Giddens (1991), Sennett (1977) Simmel (1971) and Wilson (1985, 1992, 2007) have all attempted to understand fashion as an integral aspect of modernity and/ or postmodernity. While these approaches are discussed in detail in Chapters 3 and 4 – and have been challenged of late, as discussed above – it is worth noting some important points about this influential literature here. There are several themes which unite these accounts: they focus on the nature of identity under conditions of rapid change, exploring the resources for the self that modernity opens up in order to cope with these changes and examining the role played by dress in the presentation of the self on the modern social stage. These accounts deal with sociological concerns in that they examine the fashion system not from the point of view of human psychology, or from the idea of disembodied sign systems, but examine the social forces at work within a system of dress and situate fashion within the context of the development of modernity.

Wilson makes a strong case for considering fashion in terms of modernity in *Adorned in Dreams* (2007). She is critical of the various theories put forward to explain fashion (emulation, Zeitgeist, fashion as language, psychoanalysis and so on) as generally reductive, missing 'fashion's purposive and creative aspects', its 'tantalising and slippery essence' (2007: 58). She proposes instead that the concepts of 'modernism' and 'modernity' capture this essence. Fashion, she suggests, has an affinity with modern art and a number of fashion designers have purposively borrowed from modern art. This argument is pursued in detail in Wallenberg and Kollnitz's (2018) more recent anthology. The concept of modernity is mobilised because it 'seems useful as a way of indicating the restless desire for change characteristic of cultural life in industrial capitalism, the desire for the new that fashion expresses so well' (2007: 63). Fashion is also part of the modern experience because it is central to the experience of the modern city; dress is one 'technique of survival' in a metropolis that brings one into contact with strangers.

The theme of display and self-presentation in the city is also central to Richard Sennett's classic analysis *The Fall of Public Man* (1977). In his account, the development of the bourgeoisie and the increasing separation of public and private that ensued during the late eighteenth and nineteenth century have eroded the public life of the individual. Over the course of the eighteenth century and with the rise of Romanticism, the public sphere was eroded by the intrusion of the private sphere and this was coupled with the injunction to be 'authentic' in public. This can be traced through the kinds of dress worn at the time. Up until around the mid-eighteenth century, appearance was not seen to express the self, but instead to be a performance 'at a distance from the self'. The eighteenth-century aristocratic figure, both male and female, would have worn highly elaborate dress, heavy make-up and flamboyant wigs; but this striking impression did not attempt to present the individuality of the person. The elaborate dress would set the body (and thus the identity) of the wearer at a distance as 'costume' does in the theatre: the body was a 'mannequin'. Appearance was all about play and performance and this enabled individuals to live fully in the public world. However, as Romanticism took hold, challenging artifice and celebrating 'natural' and 'authentic' man, the sense that dress and appearance should be related to one's identity emerged.

The modern individual, then, is one who is aware of being read by his or her appearance (as discussed in Chapter 4). This theme is also pursued by Joanne Finkelstein (1991). Like Sennett, she is interested in the development of 'authenticating narratives' that link one's appearance with identity. While the physiognomic theories popular in the nineteenth century might now seem quaint, Finkelstein argues that they have not disappeared: the common form they take is reading people by reference to their body, dress and overall appearance. Given that people are aware of the significance given to their appearance, more and more are choosing to manipulate it through cosmetic surgery or dress; it is also true that we are increasingly aware that appearance can be 'inauthentic' or artificial. The modern world, says Finkelstein, is thus a strangely contradictory one.

As I argue in Chapters 3 and 4, increasing importance has been attached to the body and this can be traced back much earlier than the eighteenth century and could be deemed part of a longer 'civilising process'. Elias (1978) points to the way in which the body became a site for marking out status and distinction in European court societies. In the court, social roles and status were indicated by the degree of bodily control, good manners and gentility exhibited, and knights could rise or fall on the degree to which they managed their bodies and maintained a 'civilised' appearance. Elias maintains that this civilising process is never ending. It could be argued that the processes identified by him are the pre-history to Sennett's and Finkelstein's analysis of the different emphases placed upon bodily appearance in the seventeenth, eighteenth and nineteenth centuries. In contemporary society, not only are bodies bearers of status and distinction, as Bourdieu (1984) points out, but the body has increasingly come to be seen as the container of the self, signifying 'individuality' and 'authenticity'. Featherstone (1991b) catalogues the social and cultural changes that have brought about the 'performing self', which he argues emerged in the early twentieth century. He examines the extension of new forms of representation into everyday life, in particular photography and Hollywood films, arguing that these have, along with the cosmetics industry, placed increasing attention on bodily appearance and health, youth and beauty. According to Featherstone, this has brought about a modern self that is acutely interested in how it appears to others; appearance has become important in the pursuit of happiness and fulfilment. Shilling (2012) pursues a similar theme when he talks about the emergence of a number of 'body projects' in the late twentieth century, such as dieting and body building, which attempt to gain control over the appearance of the body and which are thought to enhance one's ability to achieve greater personal satisfaction out of life. The advent of social media in the twenty-first century has only served to exacerbate this emphasis on bodily appearance, as discussed in Chapter 7 in this third edition.

Another attempt to understand the nature of modernity and its impact upon the self centres on one important aspect of modernity noted by Bauman (1991), Davis (1992), Finkelstein (1991) and Giddens (1991), namely, ambivalence. The modern or postmodern world is a social maelstrom characterised by a loss of certainty, a world where 'all that is solid melts into air' (Berman 1983). For the modern self, this fragmentation results in anxiety and a crisis in identity, although not all individuals experience the modern as threatening or alienating. It is in such a world that fashion opens up possibilities for framing the self, at least momentarily, since fashion is always moving, never stable. As Davis (1992) argues, fashion provides symbols, however ephemeral, for fixing identity while simultaneously playing with the instability of identity. Baudelaire's *flâneur* (Baudelaire 1986; see also Benjamin 1989) and the dandy are examples of the modern self (discussed in Chapter 4), who exploits the freedoms of the city and traverses its avenues and boulevards to see and be seen. However, clothing in the modern world is deployed to deal with the ambivalence although, as Davis (1992) argues, fashion does not produce permanent symbolic solutions, only temporary ones. The way in which identity is the site for work is a theme explored in the work of Giddens (1991) and Beck (1992). Although they do not deal specifically with dress, both posit the idea that modern identity has become a 'reflexive project'. The modern self is increasingly aware of itself, including its appearance, and able to intervene and act upon it.

These theories of modernity are insightful, offering accounts of how identity in contemporary society is constructed. They are particularly useful for understanding how fashion develops as a technique of dressing, employed self-consciously to construct an identity suitable for the modern stage. This literature on fashion and modernity is of considerable value in terms of understanding and historicising practices of dress today. However, one problem is its failure to ground these ideas in empirical work on practices of the self. Tseëlon (1997) is one notable exception to the theoreticist tendency. She attempts not only to interpret the ways in which femininity has been constructed in Christian and other texts, for example, but has also explored the way in which these ideas have framed women's understandings of their appearance and impacted upon their strategies of dress. She has therefore stepped into the field itself, interviewing women about their self-presentation and clothing choices, and therefore comes closest to understanding dress as 'situated practice'.

Conclusion

To conclude this chapter, I want to argue that the two broad theoretical approaches examined above tend to theorise but not to investigate dress in everyday life empirically. This is a major failing as it does not attend to bodies as they are dressed *in real life*. My approach is, therefore, concerned to argue the need for empirical studies of dress; that is to say, studies of dress that look at how it is practiced in the world not how theorists imagine or theorise about it.

The two bodies of literature that have conducted empirical work on practices surrounding dress are anthropology (see, for example, Shukla 2005) and social psychology (Tiggemann and Lacey 2009). The ethnographic approach adopted by anthropology has resulted in detailed and grounded accounts of the meanings and practices of dress within particular cultural contexts. For example, work has been conducted on the construction of gender among the British community in colonial India (Callaway 1992), the meanings surrounding maternity wear (Bailey 1992), the meanings given to cloth in different cultures (Weiner and Schnieder 1991), and the practices of veiling in Egypt by women white-collar workers (Hoodfar 1991; Lewis 2013; Tarlo 2010; Tarlo and Moors 2013). These studies all pay close attention to the culturally specific meanings and practices of dress within a particular context. Hoodfar, for example, shows how veiling practice in Iran is very different from that of women in Egypt, demonstrating the complexity of this practice.

While it would be inappropriate to generalise across all these studies, since their value comes precisely from the fact that they deal with the specificities of dress in different contexts, one thing they do share is an interest in the local practices surrounding dress. These accounts are quite different from structuralist accounts of fashion in that they are concerned with the meanings of dress as they are understood and lived by a group. Unlike the semiotician, the ethnographic researcher does not stand outside or at a distance, but builds up a picture of dress practice from observation and engagement. Since they are accounts of dress practices in non-Western cultures, however, they are not intended to contribute to the understanding of dress in the West. For this, one has to look to social psychology, where some detailed studies have been carried out. Social psychology is interested in dress in terms of how it is utilised by the individual and what role it plays in interpersonal communication. Tseëlon (1997, 2012a), for example, is concerned with how individual women dress and explores the constraints on their choices. There is also a small body of literature on the issues at stake in female professional dress. Two studies on female professional dress are brought together in a collection edited by Soloman (1985), Cash (1985) and Ericksen and Joseph (1985). These studies adopt a (rather crude) methodological framework of hypothesis testing, starting with a particular 'problem' or question. For Cash the problem is 'the impact of grooming style on the evaluation of women in management'; for Ericksen and Joseph it is 'achievement motivation and clothing preferences of white-collar working women'. Ericksen and Joseph propose that 'achievement-motivated white-collar working women wear business-like costumes more than their non-achievement motivated counterparts' (1985: 357) and this hypothesis is then tested by large-scale questionnaire-based surveys and the testing of images of women in different kinds of outfit. Such psychological studies are, however, highly problematic. The framework of hypothesis testing is flawed: the methods are naive and there is no critical reflection upon the methodology, which is taken to gain access unproblematically to the 'truth' of female white-collar dress. Such accounts are also flawed in that they do not give any account of the subjective meanings of dress. These approaches are therefore of little sociological relevance to a study of fashion and dress. This chapter has set out to examine the literature on fashion, dress and adornment and has sought to point out the strengths and weaknesses of various approaches. It has also explored the complex relationship of fashion and dress and examined how the various bodies of literature distinguish between both. I have argued that, in general, early theories of fashion and fashion change tended to be reductive and mechanistic while the literature on modernity has avoided such over-simplistic accounts, framing the role played by fashion in contemporary culture by giving a more complex account of modern society. However, these accounts tend to be theoreticist and do not address the way in which dress is lived and experienced. A further problem with much of this literature is the tendency to neglect the essentially embodied nature of dress. Wilson (2007) has acknowledged the body to some extent in her account of fashion, recognising that dress is 'incomplete' without the body. However, in general, the tendency to theorise has resulted in a neglect or 'bracketing off' of the body and embodiment. As argued in Chapter 1, the body and embodiment are crucial to the understanding of fashion and dress. Fashion is an important contemporary site for discourses on the body and plays an important role in framing particular practices of dress, along with a host of other social factors. I also argue that dress is a necessary aspect of socialisation and, from babyhood, individuals are called upon to turn to and act upon their bodies in particular ways. Discourses on fashion and practices of dress therefore form an important component of culture, crucial to the micro-order of daily life (imagine what would happen if you walked into your local supermarket stark naked) and crucial to one's relationship with self and others. A sociology of dress as situated bodily practice aims to give an account of dress within everyday life that is not reductive or theoretically abstract, but theoretically complex and empirically grounded.

3
Fashion, Dress and Social Change

Introduction: Theorising Fashion and Dress: Twenty-First-Century Debates

In their detailed analytic overview of literature on fashion within sociology, Aspers and Godart (2013) argue that research on fashion has been hampered by a lack of clarity as to what it is and how to distinguish it from related concepts, like fads or trends or style. Other questions still persist: does fashion only refer to dress found in developed industrial and capitalist modernity? Aspers and Godart (2013: 174) argue that fashion *might* be found anywhere, 'its extent and feature depend on several factors related to the type of social order at play' and their definition of fashion as 'an unplanned process of recurrent change against a backdrop of order in the public realm' (p. 174) might be open enough to include non-Western development. However, the most dominant fashion system, historically, has arisen in Europe and 'several factors' can be identified to explain and describe it, as many historians have done (Breward 1994; Wilson 2001) These factors may not explain all fashion systems in other places but do form the basis of Western fashion. This chapter therefore is largely about this specific fashion system although this edition has been updated to acknowledge newer literature that challenges this Eurocentric narrative.

The history of Western fashion locates fashion within Europe as a feature of Court societies, characterised by status competition, as opposed to societies where people's social position is relatively fixed and stable. These battles are played out through dress in the Court and then later, with industrialisation and urbanisation, became a feature of modern urban life in the emerging modern cities. This narrative is premised upon the idea of fashion as connected to – in some way, responding, reflecting, reproducing – social change. This history of fashion therefore restricts it to particular social, economic, and cultural conditions within the European/West – a narrative that has been challenged recently as Eurocentric. While Chapter 2 dealt with definitional issues, the issue of fashion and change (changing aesthetics and societies characterised by high degrees of social change) is taken up in more details.

Western Fashion History

Numerous historians of fashion have typically focused attention on the sorts of social conditions thought to account for its emergence and significance within early, mid, and now late (post)modern culture (for example, Breward 1994; Wilson 2003; Lipovetsky 1994; Davis 1992). Fashion has been embedded within the culture of Europe for many centuries, a feature of European modernity, which, while seemingly trivial, 'touches on every issue – raw materials, production processes, manufacturing costs, cultural stability ... and social hierarchy' (Braudel 1981: 311). As well as analysing the particular social conditions for its emergence, the chapter also considers how fashion has been thought and written about by intellectuals, moralists, clergymen and historians who have discussed, criticised and often condemned fashion, hinting at its place within the unfolding modern society. Fashion has been accorded significance in the development of class: as Fernand Braudel argues, 'subject to incessant change, costume everywhere is a persistent reminder of social position' (1981: 311). It has been seen to play a part in the challenge to old hierarchies and power structures made by a newly emerging capitalist class. Sumptuary laws and discourses on luxury and taste illustrate the threat that fashion posed to the old aristocratic order, which saw its own power and influence diminished by the *nouveau riche*. Fashion has also been seen to articulate gender and sexual difference, gradually becoming associated with femininity and frivolity; a fact which may go some way to explaining why it has been attacked and condemned as well as marginalised within much social theory.

This chapter gives a historical account of fashion but not in terms of a straightforward chronology of fashionable dress, as there are plenty of histories that give a detailed account of fashion changes over time. Instead, the chapter focuses on the recurring themes in the literature on fashion, exploring the relationship between fashion and social change, as well as suggesting how the body and its relationship to dress has been understood at different times. In order to do this some chronology is needed to explore the social, industrial and technical conditions required for the development of fashion at particular times. It is also necessary in order to situate debates about fashion, dress and the body within their historical context, to examine what historical circumstances frame these discourses.

Fashion and Social Change

Before embarking on this historical excursion, it is necessary first to consider what constitutes good fashion history and, indeed, to reflect on the relationship between fashion and society. Common sense dictates a link between the two but precisely how is it formed? What sort of society produces a fashion system or systems? What historical, social, technological and cultural conditions are necessary for the continual development of fashion? And what of fashion's relationship to the surrounding culture – does it, as some would argue, move with and reflect the Zeitgeist?

To a social theorist interested in the uses, meanings and practices of fashion and the relationship of fashion to everyday dress, fashion history is a source of some disappointment. Traditional accounts of fashion have tended towards description as opposed to analysis or explanation. These histories focus on the details of dress, the development of the buttonhole, the changing shape of the corset, the dropping and raising of hemlines, to provide a chronology of fashion and fashion change. Breward (1994), who is critical of such histories, argues that they neglect the context and meanings of dress. However, he does suggest that criticisms levelled at such histories are sometimes unwarranted and perhaps unfair. Fashion history arose out of art history as one means of authenticating paintings and this explains the emphasis on chronology and the attention to detail. He also notes that such rich and painstaking detail often provides invaluable documentary evidence. However, he argues that fashion needs to be placed in the context of historical, technological, and cultural change and this requires going beyond the terms of aesthetic details.

Breward (1994) is also aware of the problems of historical evidence used by historians of fashion, namely, visual and literary representations. The privileging of such representations has also led to the exclusion of other documentary evidence that might point to the existence of fashion elsewhere, in oral societies, or indeed earlier points in history in the West (see Welters and Lillethun 2018 for a fuller critique). While sculpture, paintings, engravings and literary texts are important sources of information, one needs to be careful when connecting the dress to the prevailing culture. The interpretation of historical evidence requires sensitivity to the fact that representations of fashion and dress are not neutral descriptions. For example, paintings of royalty and gentry in their finery present idealised versions of dress, flatter the sitter and generally provide a representation of him or her congruous with their status and power. Representations of peasants might idealise peasant life, as in Romantic literature and painting, or might portray them as idle or debauched, as in the paintings of Brueghel.

A further problem that needs to be addressed when considering the relationship of fashion to society is that of causation. As argued in Chapter 2, when fashion histories do try to explain and analyse fashion change there is a tendency for the historian to ask 'why' questions and seek out the causes of fashion by reference to some all-inclusive force: the Zeitgeist, the 'shifting erogenous zone', emulation. Of these, theories of emulation have been the most influential and have become very much embedded within accounts of fashion (McKendrick et al. 1983; Veblen 1953; Simmel 1971). For this reason, such theories will be given greater attention in the following chapter (and in Chapter 7).

The question of why fashion changes as it does is answered by some authors with reference to Zeitgeist (e.g. Ditcher 1985). This approach argues that fashion responds to social and political changes, reflecting and reproducing these changes. However, there are numerous problems with this approach. One problem is that such accounts tend to over-simplify fashion, which focuses on those styles that seem to correspond with social change, while neglecting styles which do not. However, dress often fails to mirror social climate, as Bell (1976), Wilson (2007) and Steele (1985) argue. Valerie Steele suggests that fashion 'has an internal dynamic of its own that is only very gradually and tangentially affected by social change within the wider culture'; she goes on to say, 'fashion is not a power unto itself, but the principal dynamic of fashion is an internal one ... Roots of change in fashion precede the great event – be it the French Revolution or the First World War' (1985: 5).

Events such as wars might contribute to an understanding of how and why certain styles get adopted on a wide scale, but they do not explain how such styles originated. Fashion does not directly or simplistically reflect the times; the fact remains that it is always and everywhere situated within a society and culture. How then can one analyse the relationship between fashion and social and cultural life in a way that avoids the problems discussed above? There are several significant questions to consider: what stimulated the development of fashion in Europe and what conditions have served to promote its spread to more and more of the population? To put it another way, what, if anything, can fashion tell us about the society in which it emerges? Can it shed any light on the forms of social order in modern society, for example, formations of class and gender or other forms of identity in modern society? Given that clothing is intimately linked to the body, what is the relationship of fashion styles and fashion change to changing notions of embodiment and changing discourses on the body, appearance and identity?

There are no simple answers to these questions precisely because fashion is embedded within culture and cannot be isolated as an independent variable. Indeed, one further problem with fashion histories is that they are often prone to isolate fashion change from the rest of the society in which it is found. A sociological approach to the study of fashion is one that situates it within context and looks at the social, political, technological discourses and practices surrounding it, as well as at the prevailing aesthetic discourses framing it. Breward (1994, 1999, 2003; Breward and Evans, 2004, 2005) provides an excellent account of fashion, which situates it firmly within a range of social and cultural developments, as does Steele (1999 [1988], 2001, 2013; see also English 2007). The following summary and analysis of fashion owes much to their insights. In addition, numerous histories of consumption have brought together economics, politics and culture to suggest some of the ways in which the idea of fashion and the extension of fashionable commodities became an important feature in the development of modern European consumer culture. This literature focuses primarily on the eighteenth century, when a 'consumer revolution' is said to have occurred. However, the idea of fashion goes back much further and we will begin by discussing its emergence in medieval society.

The Beginnings of European Fashion

The origins of European fashion have long been said to have emerged out of very particular social and historical conditions linked to the emergence of European court, mercantile and capitalist society. Fashion histories have documented this fashion history: from the development of medieval and Renaissance court society, the expansion in trade across the globe, the emergence of new social classes, and the growth of city life, and 'consumer society', processes of industrialisation and modernity are all said to play a part in the development of a system of dress based upon continual and quite rapid stylistic change. Pinpointing exact dates for the emergence of fashion in Europe has always been difficult, if not impossible, and the dates for its origins disputed. However, there are a number of general periods and features seen as significant in the development of fashion, identified in classic fashion histories. For example, Braudel pinpoints the mid-fourteenth century although 'one cannot really talk of fashion becoming all-powerful before about 1700' (1981: 316) and it is not until even later that fashion could be said to be widely available to all, working classes included. However, the idea of fashion may have been around longer: the medieval historian Orderic Vitalis (1075–1142) condemned what he saw as the foolishness of fashion, arguing that 'the old way of dressing has been almost completely thrown over by the new inventions' (Braudel 1981: 317). Braudel argues, however, that Vitalis was probably exaggerating, since the shape of clothes 'did not fundamentally alter' during this period and it was some centuries later before fashion as we would recognise it developed.

One important contrast between the dress that emerged in medieval Europe and that worn by the 'ancients' is between 'fitted' and 'draped' clothes. Modern clothing falls into the first category and requires stitching, while dress in ancient civilisations, was generally made from lengths of fabric tied in elaborate ways. The draped cloth would have hung from the shoulder or the waist and was considered a mark of civilisation: indeed, tailored clothing was considered 'barbaric' in Roman times (Laver 1995). However, this emphasis in classic fashion history on tailored as opposed to draped clothing is one critique of the Eurocentrism of Western fashion scholarship in recent years. In defining fashion only or mainly through changing tailored dress, classic histories of fashion overlooked or failed to see aesthetic change in other dress forms, notably excluding changes in fabric, hair styles and jewellery that characterised dress in earlier Western societies and non-Western cultures (see Welters and Lillethun 2018 for full discussion).

The key to the emergence and development of fashion for Braudel (and other fashion historians such as Breward 1994 and Wilson 2003) seems to be societies characterised by social change and movement, including movement within the class system. The orthodoxy within early cultural histories of fashion seems to be the idea that fashion emerges in societies that have some social mobility rather than a fixed and stable class structure. For Braudel, as for other historians and writers on fashion (Bell 1976; Breward 1994; Wilson 2003; Lipovestsky 1994), a society that remains stable is less likely to exhibit changes in dress than one which sees social mobility. As noted by Braudel (1981: 312), 'if a society remained more or less stable, fashion was less likely to change – and this could be true at all levels, even the highest in established hierarchies'. It is for this reason that feudal society in Europe was dismissed by early fashion histories as not exhibiting fashion as we know it today. This view of European societies and changing is also contrasted in Braudel's work, with 'other' societies, such as ancient China, where he claims the dress of the mandarin remained constant from Peking to Szechuan for many generations (Braudel 1981), while the kimono was thought not to have changed for centuries in traditional Japanese society. In contrast to European societies, Braudel describes these traditional societies as 'conservative'. Steele does not entirely agree with this argument: 'far from having "ancient" and "unchanging" costumes, many Eastern cultures were characterised by intense (if restricted) fashion competition' (1999 [1988]: 19). However, she concedes that in both East and West during the thirteenth and early fourteenth centuries, the choice of clothing was restricted according to rank and that the movement of fashion was kept in check because of a resistance to movement in hierarchical societies. It would therefore seem that limited stylistic change might occur in ancient societies but fashion, as defined by Western scholarship on European dress, revolved around constant stylistic change coinciding with more fluidity in the class hierarchy. Thus, as Steele argues, 'from the fourteenth century onwards, in both the courts and cities of Europe, there was an inexorable movement toward fashion orientated behaviour' (1999 [1988]: 19).

There have, however, been numerous criticisms of this view of feudal society as monolithic, traditional societies as stable. More recently, the 'birth of fashion' – the search for origins – pushed the date back much further in time. Welters and Lillethun (2018: 156) cite two authors – Waugh and Heller – who have 'pushed back the date of fashion's arrival in Europe after studying contemporary written sources', which include monastic texts. As early as 1094 evidence of young men wearing tight-fitting tunics and pointed shoes appear as playful challenges to the prevailing dress of the day and exhibiting a desire for change. While there is comparatively less physical evidence, new fashion scholarship is unearthing aesthetic changes in many pre-modern settings, as early as the Bronze Age, where tastes and choices in jewellery have been documented as fashion (Philips 2012). Indeed, in their comprehensive overview of emerging historical evidence of pre-modern tastes, Welters and Lillethun (2018) persuasively argue that fashion has existed long before the oft-claimed origins of fashion in the fourteenth century across the entire globe. For example, evidence they cite from Bronze Age settlements already mentioned suggests some aesthetic change in very ancient civilisations; other evidence of status competition has been found in non-Western societies, with sumptuary laws found in places such as China and Mesoamerica indicating evidence of status competition in these apparently traditional societies. Social changes in China after the Manchu invasion overthrew the Ming dynasty and, despite 'the Manchu degrees of 1644 instituting the most regulated dress systems in sartorial history ... the Chinese followed their fashion impulses in other ways, specifically through cosmetics, hairstyles, embellishments, and trims' (Welters and Lillethun 2018: 133). Such evidence points to the existence of alternative fashion systems operating in other parts of the world during the same period as European courts.

However, returning to the dominant historical narrative in classic fashion histories (Boucher 1966; Laver 1969; Newton 1974) of Europe, the origins of European fashion are identified somewhere in the middle of the fourteenth century. The fashionable society for Braudel is the society that desires to shape and modify the world, breaking with tradition and seeking the new. Innovation, which he argues is 'the source of all progress', stems from a 'restlessness which may express itself in such trifles as dress, the shape of shoes and hairstyles' (1981: 24). However, Braudel does not see fashion as 'trivial', but notes that 'the future was to belong to the societies fickle enough to care about the changing colours, materials and shapes of costume' (1981: 323). This restlessness could be found initially in Italy, probably the birth-place of fashion 'where it is closely associated with the rise of cities – and with the rising middle class' (Steele 1999 [1988]: 17); this, according to Steele (1999 [1988]), was part of a broader cultural Renaissance, although the court in Burgundy and France acquired important positions within the world of fashion around the same time (Bradley 1955). The demise of the feudal system during the fourteenth and fifteenth centuries coincided with the emergence of new merchant classes, whose wealth stemmed not from inherited land, but from trade, often on an international scale, with a concomitant effect on the promotion of fashion. It seems that during the fourteenth century there was a sudden change in dress styles, particularly for men, and a speeding up of style changes among the nobility. Between 1300 and 1500 men's and women's dress continued to become looser and simpler, but there was also the beginnings of fitted dress, pulling in tighter to the body (Breward 1994). Around 1350 the tunic worn by upper-class men shortened dramatically and, together with tight hose on the legs, revealed more of the male form than ever before, much to the dismay of the old and the conservative, who considered it scandalously indecent (Braudel 1981). The chronicler Guillaume de Nangis notes how 'men, in particular, noblemen and their squires, and a few bourgeois and their servants, took to wearing tunics so short and tight that they revealed what modesty bid us to hide' (Braudel 1981: 317).

This style of dress seems to have originated from military dress, which had developed a short plate of armour over the chest in place of long chain mail (Steele 1999 [1988]). Women's dress also changed, fitting closer to the body, and becoming quite elaborate, while a low *décolletage* provided further cause for outrage. The fact that clothing is by its nature close to the body, the 'mere flesh' that is the seat of desires and longings both gastronomic and sexual, has not surprisingly given rise to much religious condemnation over the centuries. The body in Christian teachings is the source of distraction from Godly thoughts and is to be mortified and chastised into submission. Luxurious dress, dress that reveals parts of the body, and changing fashions that attract the eye and distract the soul, are therefore condemned, particularly, by the Puritans of the Reformation. Fashionable dress has therefore been a matter for much moral discourse and, with the development of more modern notions of sexuality, is increasingly condemned as sinful. However, although seeming to deny the body, as Breward (1994) argues, asceticism draws attention to the body (hence also bodily desires and sexuality) in a similar way to the cut of cloth, except that the emphasis is negative as opposed to positive. (For further detail on the debates about dress, sexuality and gender, see Chapters 5 and 6.)

Throughout the fifteenth century, European dress became more and more exaggerated: large hats, long sleeves and long, trailing gowns. However, while the standard narrative of the birth of fashion tends to consider the link between the end of feudalism and the emergence of a new class system, Breward (1994) cautions us about taking this for granted. This kind of descriptive history comes from representations depicted by and for the rich and places a high degree of emphasis upon status. Thus, argues Breward (1994: 23) if one can say that a moment for the birth of fashion can be found in the fourteenth century, it describes the emergence of fashion only for the very rich; 'what is missing from such a narrative is any explanation or description either of variety within such a system' when it is likely that other systems of clothing continued 'which, while not dominant in terms of wealth and status, must have presented similar shifting codes and styles'. Thus, the dominant histories of fashion have been histories of elite dress changes. For Welters and Lillethun (2018: 161) this focus on elite dress to the detriment of peasant dress, is problematic:

[E]vidence favors the wealthy who could afford to have their portrait painted … Peripheral to the fashion discourse have been the dress practices of the common people … the so-called folk of Europe, and slaves from Africa.

They note new archaeological evidence of aesthetic variation in so called 'folk' or peasant dress (Welters and Lillethun 2018) which shifts the emphasis on elite dress. That said, the 'consumer revolution' of the eighteenth century gathered pace in Europe did see '"many social milieus engaged in creative self-fashioning"' (Lemire 2011: 50 quoted in Welters and Lillethun 2018: 161).

Numerous social, cultural and technological changes encouraged the development of fashion in Europe. Breward (1994) notes how the manufacture of garments from the preparation of raw material to alterations in garment was largely in the hands of women until the late Middle Ages. This arrangement was broken down by the emergence of male-dominated guilds and systems of apprenticeship for weavers and other textile workers, which laid the foundations for the development of fashion. This proto-capitalist organisation moved the production of clothing out of the home and 'preceded speeding up of fashion change in the following century' (Breward 1994: 30–1). Thereafter, female labourers were consigned to unskilled production and would, in later centuries, find themselves in 'sweated' working conditions (see Chapter 7).

The expansion in the trade of cloth, as well as numerous technological developments, such as the spinning-wheel, also helped to stimulate fashion in Europe, increasing the choice and availability of different sorts of fabric. The Crusades of the eleventh, twelfth and thirteenth centuries brought Europe into contact with Eastern civilisations, and there was considerable excitement about the new silks and furs that began to be traded between Asia and Europe. According to Said (1985) the European encounter with the 'exotic Other' played an important part in the formation of the identities of both Occident and Orient over the next few centuries, as well as shaping the destiny of many countries whose natural resources were plundered for cheap raw materials and commodities which would become increasingly common in the households of Europe.

Over the course of the fourteenth and fifteenth centuries, the so-called 'Silk Road' trade routes criss-crossed Europe and beyond, carrying silk and cotton from Italy and wool from England to different corners of the continent. This expansion in world trade played its part in the establishment of fashion: 'the dramatic evolution of fashion from the mid-fourteenth century is certainly resonant with the heightened language of commerce and a new material worth that arguably takes clothing into the sphere of a "modern" fashion system' (Breward 1994: 22). Italy of the fourteenth century with its trade in silks and cotton could be described as 'proto-capitalist': according to Steele (1999 [1988]), the structure of Renaissance city-states in Italy enabled the development of fashion and helped to disseminate it in a way that would not be possible in a remote place. Breward further argues that the fashionable body is closely associated with the growing city 'as focus of social interaction and display and an allied sense of cosmopolitanism' (1994: 35). (The relationship between fashion and city life is examined in Chapter 4). In addition to the newly emerging city, the court also provided a platform for fashion and the court society, most notably in seventeenth and eighteenth-century France, and was to take on particular significance in the setting of fashions.

Class, status and power in late medieval and early modern European culture

During the fourteenth and fifteenth centuries, power across Europe became increasingly concentrated on the courts, which sought to tame and co-ordinate territorial domination. While court societies developed, there was a progressive reduction of violence and factional fighting as power became increasingly monopolised within the hands of noblemen and, more importantly, monarchs:

> royal courts were centres of national power, arenas where the struggles and alliances between monarchs and nobility were played out. Increasingly, as kings tried to reduce the military might of their most powerful subjects and as nobles came to accept humanist ideas that valued learning and taste as much as martial prowess, courts became centres of culture and refinement. (Brewer 1997: 4)

The courts played an important role in the 'civilising process' (Elias 1978) by engendering new codes of corporeality. The 'animalistic' functions of the body were progressively constrained: codes and rules were developed for eating and sleeping and even for defecating and reproduction, functions which had previously been openly conducted and discussed, but were now increasingly 'hidden away' as they became subject to shame and embarrassment. Life at court demanded greater emotional control than had existed in early medieval society and instituted more and more finely differentiated codes of behaviour. This development is detailed by Norbert Elias in the first volume of *The History of Manners*, entitled *The Civilizing Process* (1978). Elias's evidence is taken from the writings of various fifteenth and sixteenth-century social commentators, in particular Erasmus, whose popular treatise on manners 'On Civility in Children', published in 1530, details the sorts of body management required at court. The prohibitions he records about eating, sleeping and other such matters (don't blow your nose on the tablecloth; don't throw your bone in the communal pot after gnawing at it and so on) shed light on some of the ways in which ('uncivilised') bodies must have behaved at the time and illustrate the sorts of constraints increasingly imposed upon bodies over the course of the 'civilising process', a process which for Elias (1978) is never ending.

During the shift from medieval to Renaissance court society the body increasingly became the bearer of social value, carrying information about a person's social status. The court societies of this period enjoyed relative social mobility: a courtier or knight could catch the eye of the king and curry favour by illustrating good taste, manners and deportment. As Elias puts it:

> To keep one's place in the intense competition for importance at court, to avoid being exposed to scorn, contempt, loss of prestige, one must subordinate one's appearance and gestures, in short oneself, to the

fluctuating norms of court society that increasingly emphasise the difference, the distinction of the people belonging to it. One must wear certain materials and certain shoes. One must move in certain ways characteristic of people belonging to court society. Even smiling is shaped by court custom. (1978: 231–2)

In such a society as this, based on relative social mobility, new relationships between clothing, appearance and identity emerged and fashion played an increasingly significant role in the life of the court. According to Breward (1994: 34), the pervasiveness of fashion had direct impact on the emergence of the individual's 'sense of self-knowledge': in late medieval society 'the body was prioritised as the dwelling place of the soul'. Increasingly, in the court, and in the city, appearance was used as a 'classifying tool', a means of marking out class distinctions in which dress played a crucial part. Notions of 'good taste' and refinement were emphasised and embodied in the courtier 'in his manners and elegant comportment – the gesture of a hand, the subtlety of a bow, a witty remark – but also in the objects with which he surrounded himself' (Brewer 1997: 4).

For Breward (1994), this courtly society and the fashions emerging out of it, emphasised symbolic display that put the body at a distance from the clothing worn. Beneath acres of elaborate fabric, the body was hardly visible: clothes caught the eye because of their richness and grandeur, not because they revealed the body. 'The existence of skin and the concrete conception of the body were largely forgotten in the presence of the coverings of wool and fur … The envelope assumed the role of the body' (Vigarello in Breward 1994: 34). The relationship between body and clothing is also described by Sennett (1977), who argues that up until around the mid-eighteenth century the body of the court aristocrat was something like a mannequin (see below). Well-established conventions of dress would indicate one's position within the class structure or one's membership of a guild, rather than articulating individuality or inner feelings. Thus, elaboration, artifice or even unnaturalness came to characterise styles of dress that put the body at some distance from the clothes.

The spread of fashion during the Middle Ages was very uneven. Only the rich could afford to participate fully in fashion, and this created some uniformity in dress among the elite across Europe, although cultural variations did also emerge. Claims made by some historians that peasant dress changed little depend upon the lack of evidence, according to Welters and Lillethun (2018), but affluence among merchants and traders enabled them to participate in fashion. From Italy, fashion spread to the court of Burgundy, the most splendid in Europe, prefiguring the stature of Versailles (Steele 1999 [1988]). The Burgundian dukes under the house of Valois (1364–1477) were far wealthier than their counterparts in Versailles or Paris and this was reflected in dress. Certain colours, in particular red and purple, were restricted to the ruling class, although this was progressively challenged. Such sumptuary laws indicate the link between fashion and social class: fashion not only emerges in societies with looser class structures, but itself becomes a site of class conflict. By the fourteenth century, status had come to be based less on the traditional standard of birth than on visible and acquirable markers of social identity, such as civic offices, land holdings, houses, household furnishings, coats of arms, seals and apparel. As a result, the regulation of these material status signifiers came under increasingly greater scrutiny (Sponsler in Emberley 1998: 46). Sumptuary laws aimed at regulating consumption from food to clothing took several forms, ranging from Acts of Parliament to proclamations from monarchs and local ordinances. Beginning in the Middle Ages with Edward III (1327–77) almost all monarchs in Britain until the seventeenth century introduced some legislation on consumption (Emberley 1998). Thus, as Slater (1997: 29–30) notes: 'the *ancien régime* inherited a feudal idea, if no longer quite the actuality, of a social structure comprising fixed and stable status: a world in which social position is ascribed by birth and is fixed as part of a cosmological order'.

Increasingly during the late Middle Ages and through the Renaissance, those at the top end of the class structure sought to police and regulate fashion, while those lower down periodically challenged or simply flouted such regulation. Among the motivations behind sumptuary laws was a concern to preserve class distinctions, enabling identification of persons' status. They also served to preserve certain commodities for the wealthy, restricting symbolic displays of wealth to the property and land-owning classes. In addition, sumptuary laws attempted to restrict the import of luxury goods from abroad and so protect the interests of merchants at home. However, these laws do not describe what people actually wore and it is difficult to know to what extent such laws were enforced or followed. What they show is the competing interests at work in the area of consumption and how class and status had become matters of concern requiring political intervention. As status became more fluid and more accessible, it follows that clothing became the target of political elites attempting to regulate such status. For this reason, 'clothing laws are crucial texts in the dynamics of social change and social control in late medieval England' (Sponsler in Emberley 1998: 46). Fashion tells a tale of class struggle, albeit heavily mediated. Many condemnations of fashion can be explained as reactions by some intellectuals towards the breakdown of traditional order and the loss of their own power and status as the *nouveaux riches* became able to purchase the same signifiers of status without the inherited right to do so.

Over the course of these centuries concern about fashion was expressed not just in terms of extravagance, which had previously been seen to break down the social order of the classes, but also with the breakdown of moral order. In her analysis of sumptuary legislation on furs, Emberley (1998: 9) argues that

the hierarchy of furs and social positions created by these regulatory acts also influenced notions of sexual propriety among different classes of women and contributed to the construction of feminine and masculine genders and sexual differences between men and women.

In terms of sexual morality, the distinction between the 'respectable' and the 'fallen' woman was particularly significant. A British parliamentary ordinance of 1355 attempted to police this distinction, forbidding prostitutes to wear fur. It read: 'no known whore should weare from henceforth any hood, except reyed or striped of divers colors, nor furre, but garments reversed or turned the wrong side outward upon paine to forfeit the same' (in Emberley 1998: 54).

Fashion in the Renaissance Court

While medieval Europe became increasingly fragmented, different centres of fashion rather than a single capital came to be developed (Steele 1999 [1988]). Fashion began to take on a distinctly nationalist character, with styles of dress becoming associated with different European courts. Italy maintained its importance as the home of the Renaissance but after 1492 and Columbus's discovery of the Americas, Spain became particularly influential in political and economic terms and also, not surprisingly, in terms of fashion. England under Henry VIII had grown in importance as a trading nation and this new prosperity served to enhance her status abroad. Catherine of Aragon and her entourage are credited with introducing the Spanish farthingale skirt to the English court and it was worn by all but peasant and working-class women. However, this transmission of fashions from abroad was sometimes commented upon and sometimes seen as a problem. The English dramatist Thomas Dekker (c. 1570–1632) commented in his Seven Deadly Sins that

> the Englishman's dress is like a traitor's body that hath been hanged, drawn, and quartered, and is set up in various places; 'his cod-piece is in Denmark, the collar of his doublet and the belly in France; the wing and narrow sleeve in Italy; the short waist hangs over a Dutch butcher's stall in Utrecht; his huge slops speak Spanishly' ... And thus we that mock every nation for keeping of one fashion, yet steal patches from every one of them to piece out our pride. (Quoted in Braudel 1981: 321)

The simile of the 'traitor's body' in this quotation highlights a concern that the consumption of goods from abroad threatened the body politic of the nation; it was treachery against the trade interest of one's own country. As Slater puts it, 'the health of the body politic is represented by the healthy household of the sovereign. Consumption will tend to deplete this wealth by drawing on imports' (1997: 176). This mercantile line of thought is not surprising given the importance of trade to England at this time. London had established itself by the mid-sixteenth century as a major trading port, which developed through the seventeenth and eighteenth centuries, and therefore also as a centre for consumption and style.

As such cities as London and Paris grew wealthier – and indeed, as the population of cities increased – it became more and more difficult to know the class of people one met. By the same token sumptuary laws became ineffectual: how can one know when a person is dressing above his or her station in a city of strangers? According to Sekora (1977), sumptuary laws responded to fears about breakdown of economic order or morality if members of the lower classes consumed goods above their basic needs or station in life. Breward (1994) notes that there is some evidence to suggest that by 1560 the concerns of clergymen and moralists about the breakdown of order was having an effect on the enforcement of sumptuary laws. This contrasts with accounts of unbridled fashion consumption during the same period; but for Breward these two accounts are not in contradiction – sumptuary laws were always difficult if not impossible to enforce and suggest the prevalence of fashion rather than its suppression. If, as Breward suggests, there was some attempt to enforce such laws more vigorously in the sixteenth century, this would suggest that fashion had indeed become more widespread and therefore more threatening.

European elite dress at the end of the sixteenth century is encapsulated in the notions of elaboration, excess and artifice. Great importance was attached to appearance and its manipulation in the Renaissance and there was an emphasis on art and creativity in the construction of outward appearance. The style of dress for men and women 'polarised into aggressive masculinity, accentuated at the shoulders and throwing emphasis on to the narrow hips, muscular legs and padded codpiece, contrasted with an angular femininity, exemplified through a balanced, symmetrical pairing of bodice and skirt' (Breward 1994: 44).

Men's and women's clothing was elaborate and stiff – for both sexes the neck was encumbered with stiff white collars. Slashing and embroidery could be found on all wealthy male and female garments. This style remained the same until the early seventeenth century, though changes in cut and colour made fashions 'seem to take on their own self-contained momentum' (Breward 1994: 52). These minute details in dress seemed to preoccupy the Elizabethans. Clothing was governed by complex codes both hidden and blatant, which could be decoded only by those with genteel refinement: 'the importance of overt and indirect symbolism in dress to Elizabethans across the social scale is difficult to over-estimate' (Breward 1994: 63). Dress was not about individual choice but 'recognition and comprehension of a complex set of formal visual codes' (1994: 65). For example, there was a highly developed language of colours in heraldry and coats of arms were one means of marking out family status. For Breward, the overriding emphasis on the symbolic and the high degree of artificiality and elaboration in elite dress lend an archaic quality to current perceptions of Elizabethan dress, derived mainly from paintings.

In portraits of Queen Elizabeth I, for example, her dress is so elaborate as to obscure the body altogether:

> the exaggerated sleeves and the gigantic skirt efface between them all other indications of a human body ... the effect of the richly lined oversleeves is of a sumptuous casing which, without attributing to the Queen anything so specific as broad shoulders (she had, indeed, no bones at all), extends the dimensions of the figure to make of the arms an anatomically improbable, embracing, encompassing semicircle. (Belsey and Belsey 1990: 11)

The body is lost in the clothing which bears little relationship to it; the line and contours of the limbs almost completely obscured.

Historical evidence from portraiture and etiquette books has isolated the mid to late sixteenth century as 'a significant moment of change in relation to attitudes towards individuality and a new sense of self' (Breward 1994: 69). According to Greenblatt:

> in the sixteenth century there appears to be an increased self-consciousness about the fashioning of human identity as manipulable, artful process'; although the word 'fashion' had long been in use 'as a term for the action or process of making, for particular features or appearance, for a distinct style or patter ... it is in the sixteenth century that 'fashion' seems to come into wide currency as a way of designating the forming of a self. (1980: 2)

This fashioning 'may suggest the achievement of ... a distinctive personality, a characteristic address to the world, a consistent mode of perceiving and behaving' Greenblatt cites the poets and writers of this period, such as Spenser and Shakespeare, as embodiments of the new self-fashioned gentleman.

In manuals on etiquette and manners one finds further evidence of a new concern with the body, its decoration and deportment: the 'gentleman's body emerges as a totality to be continuously and minutely governed according to principles of grace and decorum' (Bryson 1990: 141). Such fashioning was not restricted to men: Elizabeth I was particularly artful in her construction and representation of herself as a great, almost mystical being, a virgin queen and mother to England. Indeed, as Greenblatt notes, her ability to turn her 'potentially disastrous sexual disadvantage' (1980: 167) into a cult of secular virginity is evidence of her extraordinary ability to fashion her identity. George Gower's portrait of her at the time of the Spanish Armada is among those to proclaim 'the sovereignty and the right to rule: the splendour of her appearance, her vision and her self-control are evidence of the majesty and the authority which inhere in the person of the Queen' (Belsey and Belsey 1990: 15).

Figure 1. Miniature of Queen Elizabeth I by Nicholas Hilliard (1547–1619), showing how the body was a mere mannequin to the heavy and elaborate clothes that obscure and abstract it. © Victorian and Albert Museum, London

Moralists complained that overt concern with fashionable dress indicated vanity and unfettered individualism incompatible with class and duty. This was more marked in the city than in the country, where traditions were more likely to encourage people to 'know their place' in the social hierarchy. Contemporary pamphlets and treatises focus on declining standards in metropolitan centres and illustrate the sorts of concern expressed by some in the sixteenth century about fashion and sartorial display (Breward 1994). For example, excessive interest in clothing is singled out by some writers as a moral problem that upsets the 'natural' order of things, both the 'natural' hierarchies of class and the moral propriety of a good, God-fearing society.

Judaeo-Christian attitudes towards the body have also left an indelible mark on the progress of fashion. Nonconformists from the time of Martin Luther to Oliver Cromwell reacted against what they saw as the excesses of Rome and condemned sartorial extravagance. The sombre clothing of the Reformation continued in Protestant countries, particularly in Holland, and was carried to the New World, where it was embodied in such religious communities as the Shakers. However, with the growing influence of Spain, the Spanish style, dark, formal and highly elaborate, swept through much of Protestant Northern Europe as part of the Counter Reformation. It was adopted by most European courts; the marriage of Mary Tudor to Philip II of Spain in 1554 ensured its widespread adoption in courtly circles. There were many who resisted the style as wicked and excessive, objections being at their strongest in Germany.

During the final decade of the Elizabethan period another feature developed, that of naturalism in dress. People sitting for their portraits in the 1590s 'are beginning to want to see themselves depicted less as symbols and more as vehicles of human emotions and feeling' (Strong in Breward 1994: 68). This is manifest in the sitters' untidy appearance and a preference for pastoral settings which 'signifies most of all ... the ability of clothing to reflect a new sense of "private self" as much as it symbolised public status and history' (1994: 69).

Fashion in the Seventeenth Century

The seventeenth century was one of massive political and religious upheaval. The Thirty Years War exposed the tension between Catholic and Protestant states, which struggled for dominance not just in Europe, but the colonies abroad. The reign of Charles I represented the 'English apotheosis of ... Renaissance kingship' (Brewer 1997: 5). The court was as rich and extravagant as it was large and sprawling and was the focus of rituals, displays, ceremonies and tableaux, some of which were performed by the king and queen themselves before an audience of courtiers (Brewer 1997). Male and female clothing was rich and elaborate – the padding, starch and drapes of varying textures from velvet through to lace obscured the body. The contrast between this and Oliver Cromwell's rule is sharp and the Civil War is often seen as a clash of strait-laced Puritans and Roundheads and flamboyant Cavaliers and Royalists. The Puritans under Cromwell swept away the luxurious and decadent styles of James I and Charles I and introduced sombre, undecorated dress: face patches, for example, were banned. In their ideology, moral rectitude was closely linked to plain dress and can be seen most clearly in the austere style of the Quakers. However, these are simplistic characterisations and it makes more sense to look at wider social and political changes, in particular the evolution of the private sphere and developing ideas about the individual that informed attitudes to appearance and consumption. According to Campbell (1989, 1993), the Puritans, while seemingly anti-fashion and anti-consumption, brought about a change in attitudes that helped to promote modern hedonism and consumption, thereby stimulating the consumer revolution of the eighteenth century.

The return of the monarchy with the Restoration of Charles II in 1660 did not see the restoration of calm but continuing religious and political strife. Charles II tried to emulate his father's opulent kingship and even looked to emulate the splendour of Louis XIV in France, but his court was 'a weak copy of the extravagant absolutist regime across the Channel' (Brewer 1997: 8). Dress remained opulent but elements of informality crept into both male and female dress. Gender divisions were lessened by the similarity of some aspects of dress: deep lace collars, long hair dramatically curled and high heels were worn by both sexes. The most distinctive development in male dress was the integration of doublet, jerkin and breeches into a unified whole, the tunic or coat; and a similar integration of female dress took place in the final decades of the century in the form of the mantua – based on night-dress – which linked the top or bodice to the skirt to make an entire gown (Breward 1994). These developments served to make the line of clothing more fluid and the body's contours more apparent.

As the balance of power shifted towards Holland and France, dual fashion paths developed in the French court and the Dutch bourgeoisie. The Dutch carried the stark black and white Catholic style of the Spanish into the next century – transforming it into a Protestant, bourgeois and urban style, suited to Calvinist religious ideology (Steele 1999 [1988]). This style extended to the nineteenth century, becoming the 'uniform' of the bourgeoisie all over Europe, part of an attempt to redress the excesses of the aristocracy. Although the stark dress of the Dutch continued to dominate some parts of Europe, during the mid-seventeenth century the French court emerged as a powerful force in fashion. The court of Louis XIV established France as the supreme trend-setter among the elite in Europe, a position retained by that country until the mid-twentieth century. Although only five when he ascended the throne in 1643, 'when Louis came of age he ushered in an era of unprecedented extravagance and splendour, and Paris very shortly became the fashion capital of the world' (Bradley 1955: 193). Luxury, excess, and elaboration, along with splendorous texture and colour, were to become the style of Versailles, not only in terms of dress, but in the architecture and interiors of the grand palace itself. Louis XIV, known as the 'Sun King' for his emblem of the sun and snake, was aware of the symbolic nature of clothing. As early as 1665 he recognised the potential importance of fashion to French industry: various attempts were made to protect French textiles from the rival luxury fashion industries in Italy and Holland, in particular, the promotion of silk weaving in France to challenge that of the Italians (Steele 1999 [1988]); the heavy duties on foreign fabrics and precious metals along with incentives to help French manufacturers also served to stimulate the French fashion industry (Yarwood 1992). However, as Steele puts it, 'economics alone does not explain the shift from international Spanish black to modish French fashion' (1999 [1988]: 23); more important than state support, argues Steele, was the power of the French court, consolidated by the marriage of Louis XIV to the Spanish infanta, Maria Theresa, in 1660 and leading to the triumph of French Baroque splendour in the seventeenth and eighteenth centuries. While black and white remained dominant in other parts of Europe, particularly among Spanish noblemen and Dutch and English Puritans, sumptuary legislation in Louis XIV's court kept fashion in check and established complex codes of etiquette: clothing was restricted and regulated, gold and silver trimmings, for example, being reserved for the king's family and some favoured courtiers. Despite the rigid rules, which actually slowed down the pace of change in fashion, the styles of the French court were copied across Europe. In these days before the fashion magazine, fashion dolls transmitted the latest court fashions and acted as 'ambassadors'.

In contrast to the over-elaborate and formal style of court dress, often slow to change, a more genuinely modern fashion was emerging in the city of Paris (Steele 1999 [1988]). Thousands of tailors worked to produce clothes for court but towards the end of Louis' reign, younger princesses and ladies revolted against the court style in favour of the new styles originating in Paris. Steele notes how on one occasion in 1715 the Duchesse d'Orléans and the Princesse de Conti presented Louis XIV with the newest fashion from Paris, to which he gave his approval. On the King's death that year, however, fashion came to be determined between individual ladies and dressmakers and this served to accelerate the pace of fashion. Nevertheless, with such figures as Mme de Pompadour and Mme du Barry, and later Marie Antoinette, as fashion setters for courtly, aristocratic dress in other European courts, the French court retained its prestige. The dominance of French, especially Parisian, fashion remained unchallenged until the mid-twentieth century.

Dress, class and social identity in the eighteenth century

Compared with sixteenth and seventeenth-century court society, the society emerging in the eighteenth was increasingly urban in style. London came to occupy an important place within the imagination, which is not surprising given that 'one in ten English people lived there; one in six spent part of their working life in the metropolis. Ten times larger than any other English city, it dwarfed the other British capitals ... and, with nearly 750,000 inhabitants at the mid-century, was the largest city in western Europe' (Brewer 1997: 28). The eighteenth century was an era of great sociability, when cities 'developed networks of sociability independent of direct royal control, places where strangers might regularly meet' (Sennett 1977: 17). One might encounter others in the new pleasure gardens of Paris and London, or in the new streets that were developing for pedestrians, or in the numerous coffee bars and cafés where one could spend hours reading, chatting or simply observing others. Coffee-bar clubs like the influential Kit-Cat Club flourished between 1690 and 1720, encouraging regular discussions on literature, art, theatre and politics (Brewer 1997: 40). John Brewer notes how 'the Kit-Cat Club exemplifies the shift that took place in the early eighteenth century from court to city, from raffish courtier to polite man-about-town' (1997: 41). This shift can be perceived in the changing style of portraiture introduced into England at the time by

Godfrey Kneller, who painted the portraits of the Kit-Cat Club members. 'There is none of the grand self-absorption of the court portrait; these are men engaged with society' (1997: 41–2).

'Society' became an object of attention and discussion for an increasing number of urbanites as well as the gentry in small provincial towns. Members of 'society' would go visiting, promenading and shopping, in settings ranging from pleasure parks and gardens, such as the Vauxhall or Ranelagh Pleasure Gardens, to theatres, exhibitions, grand shops, masquerades and balls held at assembly rooms across the country. These settings had their 'season' – Bath and London were visited at different times in the social calendar by the gentry living in the provinces. Although these activities were primarily the focus of attention for a small privileged set, activities such as promenading, once the preserve of the elite, were taking off as popular pastimes among wage labourers in the big cities, and the theatre, once a restricted form of enter-tainment, opened up to a wider audience than ever before (Brewer 1997). As Brewer notes, one's ability to participate in such cultural activities depended not just on having the price of a ticket, but on looking 'respectable'.

Patterns of consumption began to change with the increase in wealth and many historians have argued that there was something of a consumer revolution during the eighteenth century (Brewer 1997; Brewer and Porter 1993; Campbell 1989; McKendrick et al. 1983; Slater 1997; Weatherill 1993, 1996). With incomes rising 'it is likely that many had surplus disposable income; as this translated into higher consumer demand, growth in manufacturing was stimulated' (Porter 1990: 205–6). The commodities purchased were likely to be beyond necessity: table linens, silverware, pottery, clocks and furniture, along with personal adornments such as bonnets, parasols, handkerchiefs, gloves, perfume, watches. This expansion in consumer goods, alongside an expansion in 'society', opened up more opportunities for social display. The audiences at public settings 'made publicly visible their wealth, status, social and sexual charms' (Brewer 1997: 69) and the new consumer durables became a popular means of transmitting such charms.

It is no surprise then that around this time the idea of emulation came to preoccupy social theorists and has since been put forward as an explanatory model to account for the consumer revolution in the eighteenth century (see in particular McKendrick et al. 1983). Theories of emulation propose that fashions start at the top of the social ladder and percolate down as the 'lower orders' consume elite fashions to copy or emulate their 'betters'. Emulation was seen by contemporary philosophers and moralists as a problem since it was said to disrupt the natural or cosmological order of the universe wherein status is fixed and ordained by God. As the modern society of commerce swept away the old agrarian order, it brought with it new sources of status not dependent upon land and blood but money. New social groups – merchants, industrialists, the new middle classes – could afford to purchase, 'above their station', luxury items once exclusive to kings and nobility. In the eyes of traditionalists, this was seen as 'a form of sin, rebellion and insubordination against the proper order of the world, and represents moral, spiritual and political corruption' (Slater 1997: 69; see also Sekora 1977). Discussions about luxury, the control of sumptuosity illustrate this preoccupation with maintaining the boundaries of class and status in the face of change. However, while emulation is seen by some intellectuals as a sin and therefore a problem, it comes to form the basis of modern sentiment. Emulation for Adam Smith (1986) is the source of modern virtue, since it is through the selfish pursuit of riches and status that the general wealth of a nation is increased. Moreover, for Smith, emulation encourages greater sympathy and sociability among people.

Emulation theories have since formed the backbone of many discussions of the eighteenth-century consumer revolution and they remain a dominant explanatory framework for understanding fashion ever since. For Slater, emulation is not a single theory but part of a vocabulary of modernity, 'a pre-occupation for western modernity from its start' (1997: 157). The idea of emulation, also known as the 'trickle-down' model, has been proposed by different theorists as an explanation for the extension of fashion in the eighteenth and nineteenth centuries (McKendrick et al. 1983; McCracken 1985; Veblen 1953), although Braudel (1981) also links it to the very origins of fashion in the fourteenth century. Veblen (1953) and Simmel (1971) are two of the commonly cited proponents of this framework and they both refer to fashionable dress in their accounts (see Chapter 2). In providing a neat and tidy account of fashion and fashion change, emulation has been immensely popular. However, emulation as a concept is very problematic. For one thing, this theory assumes rather too much based on little or no evidence (what is 'human nature' after all and how can we prove emulation to be 'natural'?). An example of how difficult it is to establish emulation as the basis for consumption can be illustrated by examining one 'fact' commonly noted by social commentators in the eighteenth century to support the idea, namely, that of the lady's maid who wore the grand clothes of her mistress. The maid in her finery was seen by some as a problem, an illustration of naked social ambition on the part of the maid to climb the social ladder or be mistaken for a lady. The sight of a servant girl's grand clothes may not, however, be traceable to her desire to emulate her mistress, as thought by some social commentators in the eighteenth century. First it should be noted that it was common practice for a mistress to pass 'hand-me-downs' to her female servants and these gifts would have been seen as part of her wages (Fine and Leopold 1993). Second, it is also true that maids often sold on clothes bequeathed to them in wills in the lucrative second-hand clothing market, 'the preference for cash (from selling hand-me-downs) over the pleasures to be had from keeping and wearing the master's old clothes' suggesting 'a definite limit to the allure of emulation', according to Fine and Leopold (1993: 126). Even when the clothes were kept and worn, Campbell (1993) argues that we cannot assume this as evidence of emulation; to do so is to assume intentions that are not apparent in the mere act of wearing the fancy clothes. Indeed, even if emulation is the intention, he argues, we do not know what it is exactly she is emulating and why. In other words 'to dub an activity "emulative" is in this sense merely to begin the process of understanding' (Campbell 1993: 41). There may be a whole range of reasons why a maid would wear the clothes of her mistress, as Campbell (1993: 41) notes:

> does the maid's intention to compete with her mistress in the style and opulence of her dress merely imply a desire to rival her in fashiona-bleness or does it stem from a more general ambition to be considered her social equal? Is she seeking, through this emulative conduct, to impress her fellow servants, her family and friends, her mistress, any strangers she meets on the street, or indeed herself? Does this striving to impress stem from envy of her mistress, from a need to boost her own feelings of self-esteem, or from naked social ambition?

The flaw in this theory for Campbell is that it confuses consequence with intention. It also illustrates the problem with reading dress of others from a theoretical distance. As argued in Chapter 2, theories of fashion tend to abstract it from the social context, resulting in general statements about fashion/dress without testing these against actual practices. In other words, they are reductive: too much is assumed based on too little evidence. Fashion and dress in such theorisations are divorced from the body and from the practices of dress in daily life, which are complex and over-determined. Other critiques of emulation theories point to its mechanistic view of social class and status (Slater 1997) and its assumption that only the elite innovate, when certain evidence would suggest that working-class styles can in fact 'bubble up' to become the latest style (Partington 1992; Polhemus 1994; Wilson 2007). Further problems arise from the lack of specificity in the theories: it is hard to identify who the 'elite' trendsetters might be at any one time – are fashions set by court, king and aristocracy, or by the new bourgeoisie? If the former classes for the seventeenth or eighteenth centuries, why would the new bourgeoisie take over in the nineteenth century, as is sometimes claimed? Campbell (1989) argues that the increased propensity to consume came from the bourgeoisie not because of a desire to emulate the aristocracy but because of a change in attitudes towards consumption. Indeed, he suggests that far from being emulators, the middle classes of the eighteenth and nineteenth centuries were setters of taste: empirical work on probate inventories shows a greater concern with fashion in households of urban tradesmen than landed gentry living on great country estates (Weatherill 1993, 1996).

Emulation theories fail to explain fashion and why the idea of 'fashion' and 'fashionability' extended through so much of the population in the eighteenth century to encompass all aspects of life (and lifestyle, although this concept is a twentieth-century one). Art, literature, music, interior décor, along with dress, styles of hair and make-up, were caught up in the universe of fashionable society of the eighteenth century. 'Society' was overly concerned with fashion and the urban and provincial gentry would have kept their eye on what the 'fashionable set' was doing, where they were going, how they decorated their houses, and what they were wearing. Indeed, 'provincial towns put on London airs' and developed their own equivalents to the pleasure gardens of Ranelagh or Vauxhall, or the theatres of Drury Lane (Porter 1990: 223–4). In the literature of Jane Austen and in the diaries of rich ladies, concern with fashion is overt. Anna Margaretta Larpent, wife of Chief Inspector of Plays in the Lord Chamberlain's office, represents one such cultured lady (Brewer 1997). She took her refined activities, such as reading, art, theatre and concert going, very seriously as part of an overall project of self-improvement and, although she might protest at the superficiality of some of those she encountered – 'how horrid is the life of (too many) people of fashion, one might forget they had souls' – but as Brewer notes, 'this did not prevent her from pursuing these pleasures' (1997: 70). Indeed, as he argues, 'in this culture of display, vanity, pride and greed as well as the finest clothing were on show' (1997: 73). Even those who professed not to care all that much about fashion, such as Elizabeth Shackleton (1726–81) of Alkincoats in Lancashire, were interested to know of the latest London styles in dress and interior decor (Vickery 1993). It was not just women who were caught up in the consumer revolution, although commentators at the time and historians of consumption since have tended to assume this. Affluent men of fashion would have done their share of shopping, buying their own snuffboxes, handkerchiefs and gloves as well as supervising the purchase of large consumer goods for the home such as furniture (Vickery 1993).

According to Porter (1990) and McKendrick et al. (1983), advertising helped to fan the flames of the new consumer revolution, although it alone cannot account for the spectacular explosion of demand for new commodities, which must reflect a change in attitudes towards consumption (Campbell 1989; Weatherill 1993). Campbell argues that the birth of consumer culture came with the birth of modern hedonism among the Puritan bourgeoisie. This is far removed from the ethics of envy and imitation that traditional histories and theories of emulation emphasise. As discussed in Chapter 4, modern hedonism involves the use of the imagination to control external stimuli. This produces both the longings and dissatisfactions associated with modern consumption. Modern consumerism, according to Campbell, is 'anything but materialistic'; the 'basic motivation is to experience in reality the pleasurable dramas which they have already enjoyed in imagination' (1989: 89). So as Breward (1994) suggests, the servant girl dressing like a lady encodes goods with dreamlike properties and escapism rather than envying the style. None of these new modes of sociability entirely swept away old privileges or hierarchies of class and status – indeed, the increased affluence for some served to heighten the division between 'haves' and 'have nots' (Porter 1990) – but they did see a progressive challenge to such hierarchies. Sumptuary laws provide a good example of the contrast between the old and new order: while the laws remained on the statute books, few arrests were made since 'people in very large cities had little means of telling whether the dress of a stranger on the street was an accurate reflection of his or her standing in the society' (Sennett 1977: 66). Sennett provides further evidence of the contradiction between the desire to fix class identity and the impossibility of doing so. The new social classes, not just merchants and traders, but those in offices of government and private finance, occupied an ambivalent position: their identity was not underpinned by tradition and they could not be located within the existing class hierarchy. So, while laws on dress were unenforceable, attempts were made to 'bring order to the mixture of strangers on the street' (1977: 66) with the establishment of costumes for different occupations. However, these too were unenforceable, since people had no way of distinguishing impostors, given that people would take to the streets wearing the costume of a particular profession or guild whether they belonged to it or not. It would seem that 'whether people were in fact what they wore was less important than their desire to wear something recognisable in order to be someone in the street' (1977: 67). A shipping clerk going for a walk wearing the dress of a butcher is wearing a costume and in doing so is observing a convention. 'Codes of dress as a means of regulating the street worked by clearly if arbitrarily identifying who people were' (1977: 68).

How did the clothing of this period relate to the body? For much of the eighteenth century, public dress for aristocratic men and women was highly elaborate. For women, skirts were full and long, sometimes slashed to reveal the petticoat, and richly decorated with ribbons, jewels and buttons. The dress worn in public was as elaborate for men as for women: breeches and waistcoats in luxurious fabrics such as velvet, brocade, taffeta, satin or damask would have been decorated with lace or embroidery and would have been brightly coloured in apple-green, wine-red, orange and violet. Ribbons and garters would have adorned the costumes of both men and women and make-up and patches worn to add lustre to the complexion. However, as Sennett notes, while such finery attracted attention to the wearer, it 'did so by the qualities of these adornments as objects in themselves, and not as aids to setting off the peculiarities of his face or figure' (1977: 69). The body, he suggests, was like a mannequin. Men and women wore wigs, which, along with large and ornate hats, would have totally obscured the natural shape of the head and would have been the real focus of attention, not the individual beauty of the face. The surface of the body operated in a similar way – the increased exposure of women's breasts over the course of the century was intended as a showcase for the jewels worn around the neck.

As public life expanded, with many more occasions for sociability than before, there was a significant change in the relationship of the body and dress. Whereas in the seventeenth century, dress for the elite was always

Figure 2. Les Adieux, De Launay after Moreau le Jeune, c.1777. Eighteenth-century fashionable dress was elaborate and excessive. Dressed for the opera, this fashionable woman has to pass through her opera box sideways to accommodate her large skirt. © Farewells, engraved by Robert Delaunay, 1777 (engraving), Moreau, Jean Michel the Younger (1741Ð1814) / Private Collection / Bridgeman Images

elaborate, whatever the occasion, by the mid-eighteenth century a division
had opened up between public and private dress. 'On the street ... clothes
were worn which recognisably marked one's place' while in the private realm
clothes were 'more natural [and] the body appeared more expressive in itself'
(Sennett 1977: 66). A common metaphor to describe this division between
public and private, and one that Sennett draws on, is the stage: in public one
was 'on stage', playing a role that might or might not be 'authentic'; at home,
one was 'backstage' and could relax, wearing loose dress and concentrating
on 'comfort'. For women, this might mean wearing a negligee. In public, a
different standard of bodily presentation was demanded and dress played its
part in this performance, marking out roles, conventions or status that might
or might not relate to the actual status or identity of the wearer. This performance was accepted for what it was – a more or less convincing appearance,
as that of an actor's might be. As Sennett suggests:

> at home, one's clothes suited one's body and its needs; on the street one
> stepped into clothes whose purpose was to make it possible for other
> people to act as if they knew who you were. One became a figure in a
> contrived landscape; the purpose of the clothes was not to be sure of
> whom you were dealing with, but to be able to behave as if you were
> sure. (1977: 68)

Conventions of dress, speech and interaction in the eighteenth century were
taken as straightforward social conventions, not as symbols behind which lies
some inner truth (as they are today). For Sennett, this element of playfulness
with one's public appearance and identity is a positive thing, enabling one to
be artful and expressive and enjoy open social interaction. Indeed, Sennett
argues that people are more sociable when there are tangible barriers such
as social conventions between them. However, when one treats things as
symbolic, as embodying a hidden meaning, the playfulness of conventions is
lost and so too the freedom it allows in terms of sociability. 'Human beings
need to have some distance from intimate observation by others in order to
feel sociable. Increase intimate contact and you decrease sociability' (1977: 15).
Such a concern with inner reality results in a more psychological view of the
other, a questioning of the inner reality of the other often leading to mistrust.
The result is that the public arena is 'dead public space' and leads to a search
for truth and intimacy, which ultimately results in a retreat into the private
sphere. Sociability, enjoyed in and of itself when governed by social conventions, is consequently viewed as unsatisfying and without meaning. Sennett
is therefore critical of the Romantic concern with authenticity that invaded
the public realm in the nineteenth century and in doing so, he argues, it
diminished the possibilities of an active and artful social life. (Discourses on
authenticity inspired by Romanticism and the rise of bourgeois individualism
are discussed in Chapter 4.)

As Sennett's focus is primarily on Paris, he does not draw attention to the differences in styles of dress across Europe. The *habit à l'anglaise* grew in popularity in France towards the end of the eighteenth century, possibly reflecting the current republican admiration of liberal England. Ironically, the informal English country style was in fact adopted by the English aristocracy in the eighteenth century (Steele 1999 [1988]). Tensions between the older formal French style and the English country style had repercussions both in France and abroad. In France, the 'Macaroni' style (as in the song 'Yankee doodle-dandy') became associated with the ultramodern young noblemen in France; this style spread to England, where it was adopted by some of the more conservative aristocracy. The fashion was foppish, elaborate and considered effeminate; some condemned its tight short coat as obscene. The Macaroni style was censured in France on the grounds that a country with such feeble people who sported it could not defend itself. Partly as a result of this condemnation and growing nationalism, the fashion in men's dress changed as people began to see sober dress as a reflection of patriotic values, country and city (as opposed to court) life and enterprise (as opposed to gambling and frivolity) (Steele 1999 [1988]).

During the eighteenth century the city emerged as an alternative space to the court for fashion (Brewer 1997). Rules of court gave way to urban society and city life. This expansion of industrialisation and the city coupled with the growth in the urban bourgeoisie continued into the nineteenth century, undermining the power and privilege of the aristocratic elite. Such a dramatic shift in power and such sweeping social changes brought with them changes in the relations between public and private life, the effects of which we are still feeling today. Romanticism, with its powerful critique of industrialisation and urbanisation, became an increasingly popular antidote to the new modern life. As discussed in the next chapter, this helped to upset the balance between public and private life that had been carefully maintained in the eighteenth century and to promote new relations between appearance and identity.

Fashion from the Nineteenth Century Onwards

Fashion thrives in a world of social mobility, a dynamic world characterised by class and political conflict, urbanisation and aesthetic innovation, so it is not surprising that fashion flourished in the nineteenth century, when social upheaval reached a new zenith with the French and the Industrial Revolutions. The frenetic pace of change continued into the early twentieth century, most notably in further social and political unrest, which culminated in the two world wars. As the term 'modernity' captures the idea of a society in dramatic transition, it is equally applicable to the accelerating rate of changes in fashion during this period. Thus, as Breward notes, 'if there is one major theme amongst many in which ... a discussion of Victorian clothing can be situated, it is this problem or idea of "modernity"' (1994: 146). Wilson also draws on the concept of modernity to consider fashion in the nineteenth and twentieth centuries because it 'seems useful as a way of indicating the restless desire for change characteristic of cultural life in industrial capitalism, the desire for the new that fashion expresses so well' (2007: 63). Modernity invokes a number of developments: industrialisation, the growth of capitalism, urbanisation, the rise of privatised individualism and the development of 'mass' culture, to name but a few.

Capitalism emerged out of revolutions that shook western Europe in the first few decades of the nineteenth century: in Britain it took the form of a social revolution sparked off by industrialisation and fuelled by bourgeois individualism and liberalism; in France, it took the form of a bloody political revolution, which threw off the shackles of the *ancien régime*. In both cases, a new capitalist class emerged to challenge preconceived ideas of power and wealth: their wealth was tied to factories, capital or merchandise rather than land or blood and brought them into conflict, at least in status terms, with the old aristocracy and nobility. Except in France, for the most part the challenge was fought out obliquely less with swords than through symbols, of which dress was one of the most significant. The nineteenth century was an era dominated by 'capital'; 'new money buys landed estates, it can wear the clothes of court and "society", it can indulge in the leisure pursuits of the aristocracy' (Slater 1997: 70). In the history of European fashion so far, trends had been set by the royal and aristocratic dress worn at court but by the late eighteenth century, in both Britain and France, changing fashions had come to be set by the new bourgeoisie. Steele notes how, after the Revolution of 1792, women's dress became increasingly that of 'undress', with new lines from the Directory (from 1795) to Consulate (1799–1804) and Empire (1804–15) inspired by classical design (1999 [1988]); such dresses as chemises were possibly also influenced by French colonial involvement in the Caribbean, where women wore simple straight dresses.

The common story that the Revolution brought about the fashion for the chemise is too simplistic. According to Steele, the simplicity of this dress compares with the over-elaborate Bastille style and the two do not correspond neatly: the chemise had in fact made appearances before the fall of the Bastille. One portrait shows Marie Antoinette in a simple dress, which caused an outcry at the time and was removed from public view. The portrait was painted by Elisabeth Vigée-Lebrun, whose own style of dress was simple (she hated the elaborate court dress at Versailles). After the pared-down elegance of Regency fashions, women's dress became ever more fussy – as 'Romantic' dress: a profusion of lace, frills and ribbons. By the mid-nineteenth century, skirts were wide and heavy, the crinoline cage being introduced in the 1850s. Men's dress changed comparatively little, though it lost much of its decoration and the dominant colours were sober in contrast to the commonly worn pinks, reds, mauves and yellows worn by eighteenth-century aristocratic men. Discourses on fashion draw attention to the sharp distinctions between men's and women's dress during the nineteenth century, when women became increasingly associated with 'frivolity'. The standard history has tended to

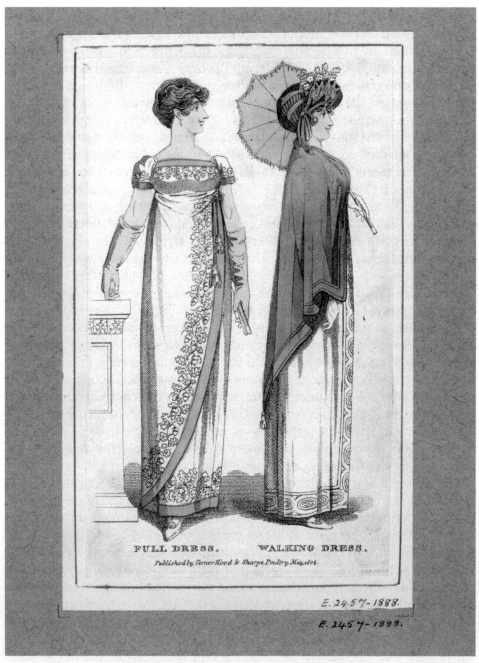

FULL DRESS.   WALKING DRESS.

Published by Verner Hood & Sharpe Poultry May 1808.

E. 2457 - 1888.

E. 2457 - 1888.

Figure 3. Hand-coloured fashion plate of two women in full (evening) dress and walking dress, showing the classical straight lines of the Regency period, c. 1805. © Victoria and Albert Museum, London

equate the restriction of women to the family with the restriction of her dress of whalebone corset and cage of crinoline, accepting without qualification the notion of a masculine renunciation of fashion. The story is, of course, more complex than that (see Chapter 5) but the striking image of the Victorian period is one of marked gender division.

Nineteenth-century industrialisation changed the nature of fashion: the development of new technologies for producing clothes, such as the sewing machine, was spurred on by new demands for cheap mass-produced clothing, particularly for men. Furthermore, wars stimulated a demand for uniforms and new industrial work (on the railroads of the United States, for example) demanded cheap, strong clothes. To this day, men's clothing remains more industrialised than women's, which has remained modelled more on *haute couture* than mass production (Fine and Leopold 1993; Leopold 1992). This shift in the production of clothing to factories altered the structure of the fashion system, which had hitherto been based on a 'putting out' method. As discussed in Chapter 7, this resulted in the emergence of the sweatshop, the harsh, inhumane and often dangerous factory.

Increasing urbanisation also helped to stimulate fashion, providing an expanded stage for the display and transmission of clothing, and providing a useful cloak of armour for city life (see Chapter 4). The increasing anonymity of the city brought with it new possibilities and new problems: new opportunities for social encounters, particularly for late nineteenth-century women, who were able to visit 'respectable' places such as department stores and cafés in the city. It also brought with it problems on both a macro and a micro-level: fears about social order grew with the expansion of the city and some intellectuals expressed fear at the emergence of a 'mass' society, an anonymous and sometimes violent 'mob' society. There is a close link between the burgeoning new capitalist class and Romanticism as an aesthetic and intellectual movement, which both prioritise the individual and celebrate individual isolation, as well as seeking refuge in the imagination as a place apart from the horrors of modern life. Romanticism privileged a peculiarly privatised individual whose retreat and isolation enabled him to find 'himself' in among the debris of modern life. These developments placed a new emphasis upon the self and stimulated the rise of privatised individualism.

How do all these developments relate to fashion and dress? In such a world as this, fashion takes on new significance; it is how people negotiate their identity, move through the city unnoticed (or noticed, depending on the style) and comes to serve almost as 'armour' protecting the individual. Fashion can be used to give a person impressive 'individual' identity, while simultaneously being capable of signalling commonality, since it enhances uniformity. These dualisms, between conformity and individuality, between private self and public appearance, introduce themes that have dominated debates about fashion and dress. A further dualism, between artifice and authenticity, has played a significant part in academic debates about fashion as well as informing a 'common-sense' understanding of fashion: does fashion conceal the 'authentic' self and serve as 'artifice'? This questioning stems from a Romantic concern with self and authenticity.

While fashion was a protective 'armour' for some, it was a tyrannous, irrational force for others. The growth of dress reform movements during the nineteenth century led to the fashionable dress of the day being condemned, on various grounds. These movements were often associated with political campaigns, such as socialism or feminism, which were set on eradicating social and political inequalities. Many of the reform movements advocated the devising of a 'uniform' as one way to encourage equality; as the 'tyranny of fashion' encourages competition between individuals, it should be eradicated. Fashion was criticised by some (e.g. Veblen 1953 and Flügel 1930) as frivolous, useless, unnecessary or just plain ugly. Veblen's functionalism led him to see fashion as essentially useless; it was also tyrannous to women, who were constrained by heavy and elaborate dress. As discussed in Chapter 5, other dress reformers were associated with feminism and called for women to wear trousered dress rather than heavy skirts (Newton 1974). However, it was not just female dress that was criticised: Flügel was associated with the Men's Dress Reform Movement and argued that men's dress was similarly constraining and oppressive.

The belief in a progressive style of dress is very much a product of late nineteenth-century faith in progress and Utopia and, in some cases, science (Newton 1974). Some dress reformers were concerned with health and hygiene and many were associated with 'water-cure' medicine and advocated looser dress on the grounds that it was more 'hygienic' and 'natural' (Luck 1992; Newton 1974). The Aesthetic Movement in England reacted against what its adherents considered the ugliness of fashion and advocated a more 'natural' style of dress. A certain strain of Romanticism runs through these attitudes to dress and it relates to the simplistic view of the body and 'nature'. Aesthetic dress, as worn by those associated with the pre-Raphaelites, assumed that a 'natural' form of dress could be devised, when in fact no dress is ever 'natural' since, whatever its shape or form, it is always an expression of culture and represents an attempt to modify the body in some way. One final point to note about dress reform, however, is that not all dress reformers were progressive (Kunzle 1982; Steele 1985). Some were actually conservative; for example those who opposed the corset in the nineteenth century on the grounds that it damaged women's reproductive organs and thus her child-bearing capacities.

Conclusion: Fashion, Social and Aesthetic Change

This chapter has looked at the development of the European fashion system and at how fashions have changed in response to a complex range of social forces over the course of modernity. I have chosen to summarise the dominant

Figure 4. Photograph of Jane Morris (wife of William Morris), wearing Aesthetic dress 1865. In contrast to standard Victorian female dress of the day, Morris wears her dress without a corset and a profusion of skirts and decoration. Posed by Dante Gabriel Rossetti. © Victoria and Albert Museum

narrative of fashion by most fashion historians to account for the origins and spread of the European fashion system, which is still dominant in the twenty-first century.

The simplistic assumption that fashion reflects the spirit of the times has been challenged; but this is not to say that fashion is unaffected by shifts in social life. When considering how and why fashions change, it is not enough to isolate a single spirit or feeling associated with the times and look for modifications in dress that might correspond. Dress is tied up to social life in more than one way: it is produced out of economic, political, technological conditions as well as shaped by social, cultural and aesthetic ideas. Fashionable dress does depend to some extent on particular social and economic circumstances, as discussed in this chapter. However, the forms of dress are not reducible to the social or economic.

Wilson (2007) argues once more for a pairing of fashion and modernity and keeps to a definition of fashion closely tied to very particular processes of modernisation. Her essay, situated in an edited collection on modernity (Breward and Evans 2004) locates fashion within the west/north. Likewise, Buckley and Fawcett (2002: 4–5) suggest that 'fashion was the embodiment of modernity … it was urban and it constituted the type of visual spectacle, which characterised the city'. The focus on fashion as a textile industry at the core of the social, political and economic transformations in Europe from the eighteenth century is central to Paulicelli and Clark's edited collection (2009) and central to colonialism and struggles for independence, as Ross's (2008) analysis acknowledges. In the latter analysis, Ross examines the global exporting of Western fashion to the colonies, noting the take up of Western dress globally as well as the pockets of national resistance in some African and Asian countries.

For Parkins (2012), modernity is defined as transformations from the Renaissance onwards, which wrought changes in governance and subjectivity and which, later in the nineteenth century, set the conditions for the emergence of a modern fashion system as 'a quintessentially modern form' that emphasises constant change and newness. Her specific point concerning the role of fashion in modernity is that the close association of fashion with femininity places women at the heart of modernity in challenging conservative associations of women as static and unchanging. Buckley and Fawcett concur: '[F]ashion provided a unique opportunity for women to experience modernity, which connected both the domestic and the public spheres.' It afforded women new opportunities for display in the drawing room and beyond. Further, as Parkins (2012: 3) notes, 'in place of such conservative representations of woman: Fashion's tempo intervenes … it offered a very different account of femininity. It seemed to admit women into modern time'. Indeed, the modernist writers – Baudelaire, Simmel, Benjamin – in giving space in their writings to fashion and its tempo, unwittingly place women centre stage in modernity. This narrative of Western modernity does, of course, contrast to other places where the spread of Western modernity has been uneven, or where there are alternative modernities. European fashion travelled to other parts of the globe as European colonies and new settlements in the Americas and Australia were formed and continues to tie East/West, North/South together in complex networks of production and consumption.

As discussed in Chapter 2, however, this dominant narrative of fashion has been contested by some scholars, who point to Eurocentric assumptions in this narrative. Firstly, questions have been raised as to the idea that fashion is *only* found in modernising societies where there is rapid change, social mobility and status competition, in contrast to traditional societies thought to be more stable, unchanging and lacking in social mobility. Such a dichotomy of 'West versus the Rest' (Niessen 2007; Welters and Lillethun 2018; Craik 2009) has been described by some scholars as Eurocentric in over-emphasising characteristics of European societies and constructing European/Western particularity that denies/fails to see change (social or aesthetic) in other cultures.

The focus on tailored clothing in European fashion history is also criticised as Eurocentric. The dramatic swings in the silhouette of the body make the draped dress of ancient societies (Greece, Rome) and in non-Western societies, such as the kimono in Japan or sari in India look less dramatic by comparison. Recent critiques suggest that if attention focused on other forms of aesthetic change, for example, fabric patterns or hairstyles, we might see fashion occurring. Western accounts have also been methodologically limited in their range of artefacts, reliant on documentary evidence characteristic of Europe (oil paintings, portraiture), which document the dress of the elite and forms of representation not found outside of Europe/the West. In other words, the 'fashion impulse' (Craik 2020) may have existed beyond modern Europe if other documentary evidence, artefacts and methods were employed to analyse material culture. For example, Styles (cited in Welters and Lillethun 2018: 162) charts changes in fashion beginning in 1660, which show that 'ordinary English people enjoyed access to new fabric and fashion'. This evidence of 'ordinary' fashion uses alternative documents – traveller accounts, court records and advertisements – to focus on 'ordinary' people. Another example cited in Welters and Lillethun draws evidence from London's foundling hospital records of billet books in the 1700s:

> clerks snipped small swatches from the clothing of infants dropped off at the hospital by impoverished mothers to provide identification if someone came back for the child … The textiles, which may have been recycled from adult clothing, calicos, flowered silks, embroidered flannels and silk ribbons. (Welters and Lillethun, 2018: 162).

This critique challenges the dominance of European fashion – both the timeline and content of fashion scholarship – to find fashion in many places.

In other words, ideas about *social change* said to prompt a fashion system have been based on Eurocentric modernity (described in this chapter), and ideas about *aesthetic change* have been similarly biased around European standards and methodology. These alternative fashion histories are calling for a methodological, even paradigmatic change in fashion scholarship (Welters and Lillethun 2018) This is refreshing: it is exciting to see new areas of research introducing new methods and artefacts.

While the desire to decolonise the curriculum, however, and to recognise dress practices from many places, the question as to whether fashion can be found everywhere beyond the Global North/West is contentious; likewise, whether fashion can be found in pre-modern times. The tendency to see everything as fashion risks flattening out regional variations and differences and alternative systems of dress production, distribution and consumption that have existed across history and in different places. If we approach a study of fashion as a system of provision, then clearly over time and across places there have been very different systems for provisioning dress. Searching for a universal fashion impulse risks seeing fashion as a trans-historic and trans-cultural phenomenon, rather than detailing the local and the specific.

Of course, there are more complex flows of dress styles and motifs between West and non-West today. Production of much Western fashion is now located in India and China, who are therefore participants in the fashion system and today's 'fast fashion', and increasingly a new middle class in the South and East consumes Western fashionable dress. Further, as Geczy's (2013) work demonstrates, Eastern motifs enter Western fashion all the time. But acknowledging the complex historical relationships between East and West should not result in a collapsing of all these practices into one universal fashion system.

Finally, I would argue that detailing the origins of European fashion does not diminish or undermine other, earlier systems of dress, or see other forms of dress in the Global South/East as inferior in any way. We can retain a precise, historically, and geographically located European fashion while also striving to study and understand the rich variation in dress practices within and beyond the modern fashion system.

4

Fashion and Identity: From Modernity to Intersectionality

Fashion has been said to express or articulate identity, although precisely what this means has changed over time. This chapter focuses attention on some of the early thinking around fashion and identity, which explores what identity meant within the context of early modernity through to contemporary understandings of identity as complex, multi-faceted and intersectional. As this chapter discusses, the idea of the 'individual' – as a separate and unique self, housed within the body – emerged out of historical conditions relating to the development of capitalism alongside industrialisation, urbanisation, and the rise of social class. It also ties in with developments within Western philosophical movements, such as Liberalism and Romanticism.

Under these conditions, the exterior envelope of the body became increasingly expressive of individual identity. Initially, it was class identity that was significant, progressively developing within Court societies and later cities. Early fashion scholarship was, therefore, likewise interested in social class and how battles over class identities formed through distinctions (Bourdieu 1984) in clothing. This historical focus has since shifted, with scholarly debates concerned to examine many dimensions of identity – predominantly, gender, race, sexuality (the focus of the subsequent three chapters) – as well as ethnic and religious affiliations, as these now increasingly feature as central to experiences of identity, and are part of how we understand and read dressed bodies. However, it is worth noting here that these are not separate and distinct aspects of identity, but elements that intersect as part of contemporary identities. Intersectionality captures the multifaceted experience and ways of analysing identity in the twenty-first century.

Fashion and Identity in Modernity

Fashion and dress have a complex relationship to modern identity: on the one hand the clothes we choose to wear can be expressive of identity, telling others something about our gender, class, status and so on; on the other, our clothes cannot always be 'read', since they do not straightforwardly 'speak' and can therefore be open to misinterpretation. This tension between clothes as revealing and clothes as concealing of identity runs through much of the literature on fashion and fits into broader thematic concerns with identity described by Sennett (1977), Finkelstein (1991) and others. These theorists examine the ways in which identity can be said to be 'immanent' in appearance and yet, how it can also be mistaken, hidden behind a 'disguise'. This tension is felt particularly strongly in the modern city, where, without tradition or established patterns for recognising others, we mingle with crowds of 'strangers' and have only fleeting moments to impress one another. Thus, when we encounter a stranger as initially mysterious and inaccessible, we refer to clothing styles and physical appearance, in the absence of any other means, as a reliable sign of identity. Clothing is frequently seen as symbolic of the individual's status and morality, whether actual or contrived (Finkelstein 1991: 128). Anonymity increases the emphasis placed upon appearance and indeed, with the development of large sprawling cities in Europe in the nineteenth century, two strategies for dealing with the anonymity of the city begin to pull in opposite directions: the idea that character is immanent in appearance (Finkelstein 1991), an idea that pulls one in search of the authenticity of the 'other', the 'truth' behind the appearance; and an alternative desire for artifice and play with appearance, through fashion and disguise, provoked by the anonymous nature of the city. The contradiction between these two strategies serves to heighten the drama of the city and focuses attention on the body and on dress as indicators to be read for hidden meaning. In the figures of the dandy and the Romantic one finds the contradiction between artifice and authenticity played out through styles of dress. For Campbell (1989), the figures of the dandy and the Romantic in the nineteenth century represented two divergent practices of dress and consumption, which co-existed. The dandy style was an older aristocratic style of dress that articulated a concern for individual distinction, a never-ending concern to appear 'distinguished', while the Romantic style represents a more familiar desire within contemporary culture, namely to be an expressive individual and be 'true to oneself'. Thus, the dandy style emphasised the artifice of appearance, the self as performed and perfected through self-conscious use of dress and the body, while the Romantic style was concerned with authenticity and the self as 'genuine' and 'natural'.

This tension between artifice and authenticity, between the self as constructed and self-styled and the self as natural and authentic is one that recurs in contemporary literature. As Finkelstein (1991) argues, there is a fundamental contradiction running through our readings of appearance and identity: while we look to read the other through appearance and hope we can do so accurately, at the very same time we are aware that 'appearances can be deceptive'. This awareness of the problematic nature of appearance does not stop us from attempting to control how we look and calculate our appearance in order to 'put our best face forward' or 'make a good impression', and we employ a whole host of strategies to enhance our appearance. Fashion and dress are the tools for this calculation, but various health projects, such as diet, fitness exercises and cosmetic surgery all contribute to the appearance of the body as well. Featherstone (1991a), Giddens (1991) and others (Crossley 2006) have argued that these body projects are an indication of the way in which the self in late modern culture is increasingly a 'reflexive self' who is increasingly called upon to think about and act upon the self in particular ways. This theme can also be found in Foucault's work (1988) on 'technologies of the self', in which he examines the historically specific ways we are called upon to make ourselves particular sorts of human beings. Different styles of dress can be said to form part of these 'technologies of self'. In this respect, the dandy and the Romantic could be said to be two nineteenth-century 'technologies of self' both derived from particular styles of dress as well as owing much to different social and political allegiances.

However, the options open for the performance of identity are not unconstrained. How we perform our identity has something to do with our location in the social world as members of groups, classes, cultural communities. The clothes we choose to wear represent a compromise between the demands of the social world, the milieu in which we belong, and our own individual desires. 'Fashions are bonds that link individuals in a mutual act of conformity to social conventions' (Finkelstein 1991: 122). This tension between social structure and individual agency is a familiar one to sociologists and is described succinctly by Simmel (1971 [1904]) in his account of 'individuality and social forms' As one of the few early sociologists to consider fashion, Simmel accords it some degree of importance in modern society as a phenomenon that exhibits the contradictory desires for social imitation and individual differentiation. Fashion embraces not only the desire to imitate others and to express commonality, but to express individuality. In other words, while dress signals our membership to communities and expresses shared values, ideas and lifestyle, at the same time we do not want to be 'clones' dressed in identical fashion to our friends. To understand how fashion and dress are linked to identity, Simmel's analysis, with its emphasis on these contradictory tendencies is pertinent here.

Simmel's analysis points to the essentially social nature of dress: individuals are located within communities and their style of dress expresses this belonging. Thus, a further theme when discussing identity in relation to the fashioned body is how fashion and dress articulate group identities and how distinctions between classes and groups of people are marked out in the process. This issue touches on questions of status and how status is embodied through fashion, dress and deportment and returns us to discussions of how the body has come to be the bearer of social status. This theme is discussed in Chapters 1 and 3 through the work of Elias (1978) and Bourdieu (1984, 1994). The importance of the body as the bearing of status and distinction is a theme also explored by Bourdieu (1984, 1994). In his analysis of class, status and power, he argues that the body holds a crucial place as the mediator of this information through inscriptions, tastes and practices he refers to as the 'habitus'. Bourdieu's account looks at how this battle for distinction is a battle for power – economic, social and symbolic since to acquire distinction potentially raises one's stakes: a debutante at a Swiss finishing school who cultivates certain manners and cultural knowledge, stands to increase her socio-economic position by 'marrying well'.

It is impossible to talk of status and status competition without talking of class. At one time, indeed until as recently as the early twentieth century, class was visible through uniforms or styles of dress known as livery, making butchers, bakers, milkmaids, coal miners, clearly identifiable. However, even in the nineteenth century new social classes, including the petite bourgeoisie and emerging white-collar workers, were already pushing forward and competing for status, old and fixed ideas of class were fast disappearing. In contemporary Western culture, class is no longer so readily apparent to the eye through dress alone, but this is not to say that social divisions are no longer apparent through styles of dress: it is still the case that dress can mark out divisions between different groups, and this is particularly true in the case of youth subcultures. Subcultures, such as Skaters, use dress along with other popular cultural artefacts to mark out differences of taste, lifestyle and identity.

Figure 5. Skater style. Kokulina/Shutterstock

However, if distinction is about setting oneself apart, it is also always about signalling to others that one is like them. Thus, the manners and bodily dispositions of a royal or aristocratic women signal her belonging to a particular class (for example, consider how the Duchess of Cambridge sits with legs demurely crossed at the ankles).

Other social groups, such as subcultures, also deploy cultural goods and dress in particular ways to distinguish themselves from each other and from 'mainstream' culture. Members of royalty, aristocracy, youth subculture, indeed all of us (since we all belong to social groups of one kind or another) illustrate the tension described by Simmel (1971 [1904]), between imitation and differentiation: showing membership of a particular cultural community by dressing in a similar way to their class or subcultural group, while also expressing 'individuality' and difference from others through bodily style and dress.

These tensions and contradictions were most visible in the nineteenth century, heightened by the rapid social changes in social life at this time. I therefore consider the characteristic features of the world described as 'modern', paying particular attention to the city as the stage par excellence for sartorial display. I then explore in detail the themes outlined above: imitation and differentiation; artifice and authenticity; body, dress and social status.

Modernity: Imitation and Differentiation

During the nineteenth century there was an unprecedented population explosion in the capitals of Europe; in England increasing numbers of peasants were displaced by the enclosure system and moved to London in search of work. The increasing industrialisation of work severed the urban populace from the rhythms of nature and, as more and more people went to work outside the home, to factories, to coal pits and to offices, the working day did not have to begin at dawn and end at dusk. These developments changed the geography of social life: cities became bustling and congested, dirty, noisy, often dangerous places to live and work; they also provided an 'expanded stage for the public drama of modern life' (Steele 1999 [1988]: 135) and fashion flourished on such a stage. In such an environment 'strangers' meet with no more than fleeting moments to make an impression on each other. Thus, increasing anonymity led to greater emphasis on appearance as the means by which to 'read' the other.

The intensity of this environment brought with it new pressures and new possibilities. Simmel characterises the society emerging in the nineteenth century as 'modern': it is highly abstract and complex in structure, reaching an apotheosis with monetarisation. During the nineteenth century there was a quantitative rise in material culture – the extension of the world of goods, of consumption, shopping and symbolic display – all of which offered new possibilities for individuals to recognise themselves as consumers 'who have come to determine their own development in this world of goods' (Miller 1987). Simmel sees modernity as inherently contradictory: it simultaneously opens up new opportunities for individualisation not possible in traditional, rural communities, and also closes down possibilities for social coherence. Problems arise when the world of objects outstrips individuals' attempts to come to terms with it; when subjects do not appropriate objects in ways that relate to their projections but confront the world as alien. As Simmel argues, 'our freedom is crippled if we deal with objects that our ego cannot assimilate' (1971: 462). The excessive array of objects for purchase always threatens to overwhelm us. He explores the contradictions of modernity, arguing that modern life exhibits a desire for generalisation, 'of uniformity, of inactive similarity of the forms and contents of life', and for differentiation, 'of separate elements, producing the restless changing of an individual life' (1971: 294). These two antagonistic principles are expressed through adornment, which 'creates a highly specific synthesis of the great convergent and divergent forces of the individual and society' (Simmel 1950: 344). Fashion articulates a tension between conformity and differentiation: it expresses the contradictory desires to fit in and stand out: 'fashion is the imitation of a given example and satisfies the demand for social adaptation … at the same time it satisfies in no less degree the need of differentiation, the tendency towards dissimilarity, the desire for constant change and contrast' (Simmel 1971: 296). The idea that fashion is always about the differentiation of a particular group is generally linked to the theory of 'trickle-down' and emulation which, as argued in Chapters 2 and 3 is flawed in terms of fashion. However, without accepting the proposition that fashions develop at the top or that emulation is the key motivation of fashion, one can still argue that what is 'fashionable' or in today's parlance, 'trendy' or 'hip', has always to be differentiated from the mainstream. Once a style becomes widely adopted, it is no longer 'different' and thus no longer 'hip'. At any one time, one or more group may be associated with 'hip' and be responsible for setting a trend. Today this group is often likely to come from the street, from youth subcultures rather than from an elite at the 'top' of the social strata. Fashionability thus depends. upon distinction or differentiation which, once copied universally, is negated. A trendsetting group whose identity depends upon being 'hip' will therefore move on to adopt another style. This process is a highly commercialised one today, the fashion industry being constantly geared to find 'new looks' each season (a new colour, line of skirt, shape of jacket). The speed at which this happens and the concomitant effect on the interconnections between designers, fashion buyers, journalists and 'street' cultures is examined in Chapter 7.

Pertinent here is the way in which fashion could be deployed for different groups at various times and used to differentiate that group, making it visible and its members identifiable. The same can be said for all dress, even that characterised as 'anti-fashion' or 'oppositional' to mainstream fashion. For example, the dress of various nineteenth-century Utopian movements, based often around a 'uniform', 'gave the members a "family likeness" and marked their difference from outsiders, thus acting as a powerful indicator of shared values and community boundaries' (Luck 1992: 202). In the twentieth century the dress of rebellious youth subcultures similarly served to mark out and distinguish an identity for these groups. Dress is therefore how identities are marked out and sustained. While this has always been the case, certainly in relation to class identity, it is important to note that modernity opened up new possibilities for the creation of identity: it unfixed individuals from traditional communities, placing them in the 'melting-pot' of the city, and it extended the commodities available for purchase to an ever-widening circle of people, thereby providing the necessary 'raw material' for the creation of new identities. As the nineteenth and twentieth centuries progressed, one's identity depended less on a fixed place in a stable social order: one's group affiliations could be 'elected' and one's identity 'invented' in the modern world.

Fashion as artifice

Industrial capitalism and urbanisation not only changed the contours of the landscape of the nineteenth century, it transformed social and temporal relations. Class conflict was a marked feature of the period. City life had its own rhythm and pace quite unlike that of the country: industrial life shifted the rhythm of the day and reordered the relationship between private and public life. As discussed in the previous chapter, the intimate life of the home and the public life of the street and 'society' had been held as separate and distinctly different realms in the eighteenth century. Public roles as performances put a discreet distance between self and 'other' and between public and private life, thereby enhancing the sociability of people. However, according to Sennett (1977), the nineteenth-century urban, industrial bourgeoisie altered this harmonious relationship. Partly because of the shocks administered by industrialisation and partly as a result of changes in morality, the public sphere came to be seen as 'dead space': space which was alienating and lacking in spiritual or moral virtue. It became a place to escape from rather than, as in the eighteenth century, a place of virtue and pleasure to be enjoyed and valued. The nineteenth century was the era when the privatised family became the bedrock of social life, the refuge of meaning and authenticity. In this 'intimate vision of society' people came to expect psychological benefits from their experience of the world; precisely because so much of life in the public realm doesn't reveal psychological rewards, it is experienced as impersonal, empty and alienating. This sets the scene for the emergence of the city as a place of danger, filled with 'strangers' who by virtue of their strangeness are unknowable and therefore potentially threatening.

In the large cities that sprang up during the nineteenth century, individuals were brought into contact with an ever-increasing number of 'strangers'. In such an alienating environment, surrounded by unfamiliar faces, appearances were the only means of reading the 'other'. In such a world as this, fashion becomes central to the experience of the modern city; according to Wilson (2007), dress can be a 'technique of survival' in a metropolis that brings one into contact with strangers. Thus, as she argues, 'the nineteenth-century urban bourgeoisie, anxious to preserve their distance from the omnipresent gaze in the strangely inquisitive anonymity of the crowd where "anyone" might see you, developed a discreet style of dress as protection' (2007: 137).

However, appearances can be therefore deceptive and indeed, as Wilson notes, mystery, suspense and disguise preoccupied the Victorian era, an era that gave birth to the murder mystery, the detective novel and the thriller. The most famous of nineteenth-century sleuths, Sherlock Holmes, was preoccupied with uncovering mysteries and secrets and deployed his powers of deduction to penetrate the appearance of things and people. However, as Sennett (1977) notes, the ability to read the appearance of others and to fix their identity was made more difficult by the mass production of clothing, particularly with the growth in mass-produced patterns, which blurred the lines that demarcated recognisable class identities. In the nineteenth century, one might wander around the city in the disguise of a lady, as did the mistress of diarist Arthur Munby. A servant to Munby, Hannah mostly wore the garb of the nineteenth-century female servant – simple dress, coarse apron and shawl, and plain bonnet. But later, once secretly married, she could pass for a lady, although not without gloves to hide her tell-tale rough hands. When a country rector's wife introduced herself to Hannah (who was dressed as a lady outside the church) and later left a card at their residence, Munby and Hannah were obliged to pay her a visit, which would require Hannah to masquerade as a 'lady' in company. For this tense meeting Hannah 'wore her pretty broad hat of black felt, with a violet veil wrapt around it; it made a picturesque background for her shining hair and sweet loving face; and she wore a dress of pale grey with black ornaments; and grey gloves, which she was on no account to take off' (Munby in Hudson 1974: 373). The meeting passed off well enough, except for Hannah's farewell: an accidental 'Goodbye Ma'am'. But in general, dressed appropriately, Hannah could attend lectures with Munby in her 'disguise' and no one could tell that her 'station' in life was as lowly as a maid. Other disguises were perhaps even more 'deceitful', such as the character Munby encountered on Oxford Street: 'I saw before me, striding along in company with an Italian organ grinder, a tall young man in full Highland costume; wearing a Glengarry bonnet, a scarlet jacket, a sporran and a tartan kilt and stocking, his legs bare from knee to calf. It was not a man – it was Madeleine Sinclair the street dancer' (Munby in Hudson 1974: 131).

Cross-dressing has been common throughout history and, in Chapter 5, the role played by dress in the construction of gender is examined in more detail. In this chapter it is appropriate to discuss how some instances of cross-dressing illustrate the uncertainty and instability of appearances in the modern city. Fashion serves to protect one from prying eyes and enables one to put a distance between self and other – it is the 'armour' of the modern world. It opens up possibilities for disguise, for the construction of a self that is 'artificial' in the sense of being a work of artistry.

Such a world also demands a particular attitude (Simmel calls it 'blasé'), which involves a mode of being and a style that enables one to cope with the 'heat' and frenzy of modern life in the city. Rather than registering shock, disapproval, dismay at the sights and sounds of the city, the individual strikes a pose of cool indifference and observes without seeming to observe. Dress and the 'blasé attitude' are techniques for survival in the city; both serve as shields against the eyes of strangers. The *flâneur* who idles along the streets of the city, yet always on the lookout, strikes such a pose of nonchalance. The *flâneur* was distinctly Parisian in character, who 'lived on the boulevards, and made the streets and cafés of Paris his drawing room' (Wilson 1991: 54); as Baudelaire put it, to 'be away from home, and yet to feel at home; to behold the world, to be in the midst of the world, and yet to remain hidden from the world – these are some of the minor pleasures of such independent, impassioned and impartial spirits' (1986: 33).

The ability to walk the streets freely was an option more open to men than to women and the *flâneur* was generally a dandy, a man of aristocratic disposition. However, Wilson (1991) suggests that the prostitute was a *flâneur* whose street-walking put her in an ideal position from which to observe the city. For Baudelaire, the painter Constantin Guys exemplified the *flâneur*, although he went beyond that of indifferent observation to be a 'passionate spectator' able to capture the fleeting beauty of the street (Steele 1999 [1988]). This 'painter of modern life', this *flâneur*-painter, was an acute observer who is aware of shifts in fashion: 'if a fashion or the cut of a garment has been slightly altered; if buckles or bunches of ribbons have been dethroned by rosettes ... his eagle's eye will already have perceived it' (Baudelaire 1986: 35). In this respect, 'fashion was the key to modernity' for Baudelaire (Steele 1999 [1988]: 90). It was essentially about the continual desire for the beautiful; 'an ideal towards which the restless spirit of mankind is incessantly spurred' (Baudelaire 1986: 63). The painter who depicted his subjects in older costume and not the contemporary styles of the day betrayed a certain laziness, but the true painter of modern life was one who could capture the transient ephemera of modern life in addition to the eternal and unchanging elements of beauty.

Fashion and authenticity

While some adopted disguise and artifice as methods of 'hiding', this posed problems for others: how could one be sure of the veracity of the people one encountered? As Sennett (1977) argues, until around the mid-eighteenth century the problem of the veracity of appearances produced congenial sociability and one accepted the other at face value; in the nineteenth century it produced suspicion and unease. The 'intimate society' of the nineteenth century sought to probe beneath the appearance, to find the 'inner truth' of the 'other'. This attitude encouraged the idea that if there is an inner reality, then it should relate to one's outer appearance. As Sennett notes, 'when street clothes and stage costume come to be seen as having something to do with the body, as they did with house clothing of the mid-eighteenth century, they will also come to appear to have something to do with the character of the person wearing them' (1977: 72).

In other words, as clothing began to connect more closely to the body and individuality of the wearer, it was read for its 'authenticity'. Arguably, the pressure of clothing to reveal the 'authentic' intentions of the wearer was greater for women in the nineteenth century who, according to Halttunen (1982), were constructed as the moral guardians of Protestant, bourgeois culture and therefore had to be 'honest' and 'true'. She argues that the connection between inner sentiment and outer appearance was most clearly articulated by advocates of 'sentimental' dress popular in the mid-nineteenth century. Sentimental dress, which threw off the excessive decoration apparent in female dress from 1815 to the 1830s, drew attention to the body and face of the wearer: bonnets, for example were plain and simple and drew close to the head, so framing the face and its features.

The idea that character is immanent in appearance became increasingly popular in the nineteenth century, although the idea stretches back much further. The desire to find inner truth behind the mask of appearance is tied to the cult of Romanticism as much as it is tied to the rise of the urban bourgeoisie. Romanticism as a philosophical and aesthetic movement stretching back to the eighteenth century prioritises the 'natural' over the social or cultural and challenges what it sees as the artifice and superficiality of appearances. In such a moral universe as this, dress and appearance are thought to reveal one's 'true' identity; gone is the eighteenth-century idea that appearances within the public realm can act as a playful façade set at a distance from one's intimate life. Romanticism encouraged a more psychological vision of self and society. It brought with it a new focus on individual uniqueness, explored in the work of philosopher Jean-Jacques Rousseau – a concern with the self which is narcissistic: 'the Romantic is one who discovers himself as centre' (Campbell 1989: 184). The Romantic strives for perfection, having found the world to be wanting, and the 'conflict between sincerity and propriety solidifies into clear-cut opposition between self and society ... as estrangement became the natural state for artists and romantically inclined intellectuals' (1989: 194). This leaves the Romantic seeking out an escape-route from what it sees as ugliness and inauthenticity.

Alongside the rise of Romanticism, the ascendancy of the bourgeoisie in the nineteenth century accentuated the cult of individualism. Their fortunes created out of their own enterprise and initiative, the bourgeoisie helped to forge the idea that one's fate depended upon one's skills and ingenuity and the nineteenth-century bourgeois male came to epitomise the 'self-made man'. The political-economic philosophy of liberalism further extended the emphasis on the individual and a laissez-faire attitude to political and economic fortune. With these philosophies of Romanticism and liberal individualism merging to form part of the 'Protestant ethic', the individual came to be seen as the source of meaning and authenticity. While seemingly 'common sense' this version of the self is a historical creation. Elias (1978) has argued that the idea of the self-contained self, hermetically sealed within an individual body, is a peculiarly modern one. As discussed in the previous chapter, the civilising process has changed the way we view our bodies and, over the course of the nineteenth and twentieth centuries, this induced a more psychological version of the self.

This process is further examined by Finkelstein (1991) who, like Sennett, focuses attention on narratives on authenticity. While stemming from Romanticism, she argues that these 'authenticating narratives' are also linked increasingly to 'scientific' discourses (this being the age of Darwin and his *Origin of the Species*). Finkelstein looks in particular at eighteenth and nineteenth-century studies of physiognomy, which produced various theories on how to read a person through the body: 'Physiognomy was a means of calculating and understanding the invisible from the visible; it assumed that the nature of human actions and intentions were recorded in the obvious signs of the face and body' (1991: 28).

Anything from the arrangement of the face, the shape of the skull, the line of the skeleton, even the shape and texture of the eyelashes was supposed to reveal the 'true nature' of the person. These theories led to crude characterisations of people into stereotypes; for example, crooked mouths were thought to indicate a corresponding skew in character and criminality, full lips, viciousness. The nineteenth-century physiognomist Samuel Wells considered that his branch of science enabled individuals to improve themselves: by learning to read character through facial features we could 'reconstruct ourselves on an improved plan, correcting unhandsome deviations, moderating excessive developments, supplying deficiencies, moulding our characters' (Wells in Finkelstein 1991: 32). This is of course an idea full of significance in today's plastic culture, which continues the idea that one's appearance is important in how one is read and is something that can be changed or modified.

If, as in the nineteenth century, appearance comes to stand as an important indicator of inner character, then the smallest of details can become important in fixing or establishing identity. Dress plays its part in this, indeed, its smallest features are often the most telling. As Sennett notes, a gentleman could be identified precisely because he did not make any great claims to be one: 'one could always recognise gentlemanly dress because the buttons on the sleeves of a gentleman's coat actually buttoned and unbuttoned, while one recognised gentlemanly behaviour in his keeping his buttons scrupulously fastened, so that the sleeves never called attention to this fact' (1977: 166). However, as

Finkelstein (1991) argues, it was not just gentlemen who used dress to fashion a particular identity. In the United States during the nineteenth century there was a movement towards individual self-promotion through dress among upwardly mobile young men. For them, 'how they looked was important not only as a means of business advance, but also as a measure of self-esteem' (Branner in Finkelstein 1991: 114).

Modernity is therefore strangely contradictory: authenticating narratives, such as physiognomy, make claims to know the self from its surface appearance, while at the same time there is a heightened awareness that appearance (such as the cool exterior of the blasé attitude) is constructed and can therefore not be trusted as 'authentic'. While such theories might now seem quaint, Finkelstein argues that they have not disappeared and that we continue to read people by reference to their body, dress and overall appearance. The suspicion as to what is a 'true' appearance is heightened by the fact that appearance is malleable and can therefore be 'inauthentic' or artificial. The significance of appearance meant that people began to be concerned with the control of appearance, and clothing and demeanour were therefore employed as techniques to control how one was perceived. Goffman (1971) recognises this when he examines people's 'impression management' in social situations. When the body diverges from the norm in any way, whether in terms of proportion, movement, or symmetry, it becomes a traitor to social rules and the moral order. 'The aberrant individual will be responded to differently and will be judged in comparison with the limits of normative order' (Finkelstein 1991: 67). In this respect, our outward physical appearance has become an important means for obtaining social status.

This theme is linked to my earlier discussion of debates about the body as the bearer of status (see Chapters 1 and 2). Featherstone (1991a) argues that the contemporary body has increasingly become the focus of attention as the prime location of identity. Whereas once the body was subject to controls such as diet and exercise aimed at subduing the flesh and enhancing the spirit, the body in consumer culture is now subject to a myriad of 'disciplining' techniques aimed at manipulating it to 'look sexy'. In addition to endless diet and exercise programmes, there are a range of other forms of body work that can be performed to enhance one's physical attractiveness. The aim of all this is the production of the 'body beautiful' and the maximisation of pleasure, since the beautiful body is a valued one. Initially promoted through Hollywood and the cosmetics industries, the modern 'care of the self' has become one of the defining features of consumer culture. Rather than imposed upon us, these practices call us to be self-conscious and self-disciplining. Control is produced less by brute force and more by surveillance and stimulation. As Foucault notes:

> mastery and awareness of one's own body can be acquired only through
> the effect of an investment of power in the body: gymnastics, exercises,

muscle-building, nudism, the glorification of the body beautiful ... we find a new mode of investment which presents itself no longer in the form of repression but that of control by stimulation. 'Get undressed – but be slim, good-looking and tanned!' (1980: 56–7)

Thus the body is the source of our identity and, if we keep 'working' on it, can potentially enhance our social status. However, any discussion of social status must accord some significance to class since, historically at least, class has determined status. The link between body, dress and class identity needs further examination also by virtue of its significance within the literature on fashion and dress and is especially pertinent for any discussion about modernity which saw progressive challenges made to old class allegiances.

Clothing, class and fashioning identity

In his analysis of fashion Simmel (1971 [1904]) argues that the elite set out to differentiate themselves from the majority by wearing extreme, modish styles. However, given the demise of the court, who were the new elite in the nineteenth century? How were battles of social class played out through status symbols such as fashionable dress? How did a recognisably modern form of consumerism emerge and what were the factors stimulating it? Finkelstein (1991: 114) suggests that during the nineteenth century there was a 'dawn of the self-styled, fashioned individual who was concerned with self-promotion, and who employed clothing and various items of fashion and conspicuous consumption to celebrate his new status'. This individual, like the figure of the Regency dandy exemplified by the socialite George Bryan Brummell, known as Beau Brummell (1778–1840), might therefore come from a humble background but climb the social ladder through elegant dressing and conscious self-fashioning. According to Finkelstein, Brummell ushered in an era when 'social ascendancy and character were no longer needed to be viewed as inherent. In the figure of Beau Brummell, there was the declaration of the self-produced modern individual, whose identity was fashioned from material possessions' (1991: 114).

However, while the dandy may have heralded an era of elaborate self-fashioning, he was not a self-made man in the bourgeois sense; indeed, in style he was aristocratic and anti-bourgeois. Nor did his style of self-fashioning resemble modern-day consumption with its hedonistic spirit and search for novelty, but was undertaken with an attitude of stoicism rather than pleasure. Moreover, the dandy was not 'fashionable' in the sense of leading or promoting new fashions. While some elements of dandy style have become established, in particular, the dandy cravat (the forerunner of the modern-day man's tie), the dandy was not an innovator as such.

In his search to find the spirit of modern consumption (and thus modern fashion) Campbell (1993) has analysed different styles or modes of consumption, focusing particular attention on the dandy and the Romantic bohemian. He argues that the dandy represents an older style of consumption, an 'aristo-cratic ethic' that is at odds with modern-day hedonistic consumption. The origin of modern-day consumption lies with the development of a 'Romantic ethic'. Whereas the dandy's dress was based upon an older, aristocratic attitude to appearance, which privileged a mannered and artificial performance of the self, the Romantic bohemian seeks to be authentic and natural. The figures of the Romantic bohemian and the dandy epitomise these two distinct styles, although in the case of the artist dandy there are important overlaps between the two styles. They also represent two strategies for dealing with the contradictory nature of modernity. The dandy is a figure who emphasises the performative nature of modernity, the possibilities it opens up for self-creation through appearance. In this respect, the dandy celebrates artifice over authen-ticity, the latter being of central concern to the Romantic bohemian. However, as we shall see, the dandy is an inherently contradictory character and thus this distinction, while useful, is a crude one.

The dandy

The man of wealth and leisure, who, even though weary of it, has no other occupation than the pursuit of pleasure; the man brought up on luxury and accustomed since his youth to the obedience of other men; the man, in short, who has no other profession but that of elegance, will always have a distinctive appearance, one that sets him utterly apart. (Baudelaire 1986: 54)

Dandyism originated in Britain towards the end of the eighteenth century, reached a peak during the Regency period and lasted through much of the nineteenth century. In France the dandy style of simple, elegant English country costume was adopted by new republicans and some artists as well as by disaffected aristocrats, 'Incroyables' (Incredibles). The style was, according to Wilson (2007), 'highly erotic', the tight breeches and finely tailored jacket calling attention to the male form, as did the lack of make-up, perfume and 'foppish' decoration. As Wilson points out, however, the term 'dandy' is sometimes confused with the 'fop', or eighteenth-century aristocrat known for his vanity, elaboration and rather effeminate appearance. However, the dandy style was quite the opposite of this and introduced a style of masculinity that is more recognisably modern. The term 'dandy' is frequently used even today to describe a man who takes great pride in his appearance, but *dandyism*, as the nineteenth-century French poet Charles Baudelaire (1986: 55 [emphasis added]) defined it, goes much beyond this:

dandyism is not ... an immodest interest in personal appearance and material elegance. For the true dandy these things are only a symbol of the aristocratic superiority of his personality. In his eyes, therefore, which seek, above all, distinction, the perfection of personal appearance consists in complete simplicity – this being, in fact, the best means of achieving distinction.

As a figure who made it his occupation to be a man of leisure, who prided himself on his aesthetic superiority, seeking distinction through the exercise of his exquisite taste, the dandy is a contradictory character, part modern hero, part aristocrat. On the one hand, the dandy was a new kind of social climber, a truly modern figure, whose status depended less on blood and inheritance than on good manners and impeccable taste; on the other he represented 'the last gleam of heroism in times of decadence' (Baudelaire 1986: 57), rejecting modernity and harking back to an older, English aristo-cratic style. Frequently without occupation, with no regular source of income and generally no wife or family, the dandy lived by his wits. In this sense, then, there is also something Romantic about the dandy whose attachment to dress and style in general draws on the idea of the individual as creative and self-creating as well as original. The figures of socialite Beau Brummell in

Figure 6. French, dandified *Incroyable* (Incredible) with a well-dressed woman, dressed in clean-cut, elegant costume popularised in Regency England by Beau Brummell. Les Français sous la Révolution; Challamel & Tenint; 1843. Drawing by H. Baron, engraving by L. Massard. Source: Wikimedia Commons

Regency Bath and Baudelaire in mid-nineteenth-century Paris represent two versions of the dandy. They also demonstrate a new shift in male dress; as Finkelstein (1991) argues, the dandy is an important figure in the development of modern fashions for men, his appearance marking a distinctive break with the masculine style of the *ancien régime*. In contrast to the elaboration of aristocratic male dress of the eighteenth century, with its colour, embroidery and decoration, the dandy fashioned an appearance of stark simplicity. Brummell, the archetypal Regency dandy, summed up the formulae for dandyism as 'no perfumes ... but very fine linen, plenty of it, and country washing. If John Bull turns round to look after you, you are not well dressed; but either too stiff, too tight, or too fashionable' (Laver 1968: 21). Although representing a different, distinctly Parisian version of the dandy, Baudelaire's dandyism similarly rejected eighteenth-century elaboration and colour in favour of a pared-down style based largely on black, offset only by a flash of brilliant white at the neck and possibly a pair of pink gloves.

The elegant simplicity of the dandy did not come without considerable effort. Brummell would spend hours each day at his toilette, shaving and scrubbing until his skin all but shone, preparing his linen and perfecting the knot in his cravat. For Baudelaire, the dandy aesthetic was almost a religion, demanding conscious effort and painstaking care akin to monastic rule. However, as Campbell notes, the dandy's style was based not only on dress which had to be 'perfect but understated', but on 'all gestures and expressions of feeling, whilst an emphasis upon refined and subtle conversation led to a premium being placed upon wit. To attain this ideal of refined behaviour was successfully to display a superiority of self' (1993: 51). The body was therefore the most important 'tool' for the dandy: the style depended not just on wearing particular clothes, but on managing bodily demeanour, gesture and mobilising wit to win status, and, in Brummell's case, approval from the Prince Regent (later George IV, at one time a companion) and 'society' as in exclusive Regency social circles.

The look represented not only a new style for men, but a new relationship between surface appearance and political and social allegiance. It was during the Regency that a 'new balance was being struck in which the external appearance, particularly for men, was becoming a significant index of political and social interests' (Finkelstein 1991: 112). According to Baudelaire, dandyism appears 'in periods of transition, when democracy is not yet all-powerful, and the aristocracy is only partially tottering or brought low' (1986: 57). The period of the dandy was indeed one of political instability: the turn of the century was characterised by revolutionary social and political turmoil and in such an environment, the old class order, particularly in France and Britain, was fast fading. In this atmosphere, 'the fate of an individual could be decided because of his or her political allegiances, the individual could increase his or her social security by demonstrating a disinterest in any political questions' (Finkelstein 1991: 112). And so it was that 'a certain number of men, detached from their own class, disappointed and disorientated, but still rich in native energy, formed a project "a new sort of aristocracy", based on superior indifference and the pursuit of perfection' (Baudelaire 1986: 57).

In his quest for the best starched linen and elegantly knotted necktie, the dandy made visible his distance from more 'substantial' issues such as politics and demonstrated a greater concern with his individual social standing, as did Brummell. Social climbing or 'distinction', as Baudelaire puts it, was the aim. Although Brummell's social background was humble and his income by no means large, he came to be known throughout Regency Britain for his exquisite taste and elegance. His social standing thus depended upon the degree to which he could mobilise his body, his appearance, manners and deportment on which his fame rested. Matters of dress were important to the dandy because they revealed one's sense of taste, and hence 'one's essential quality of self' (Campbell 1993: 52). Therefore, as Finkelstein (1991: 114) argues, Brummell's emergence on the social scene heralded an era when 'fashionability became increasingly common as a means of self-promotion'; an era when identity could be forged out of material objects. As Campbell (1989: 168) notes, it was not so much fashionability that was prided, but 'his ability to create and maintain an overall image of refinement'. Brummell's self-fashioning depended largely on his famous cravat, and Finkelstein finds it fitting that his identity was forged from a decorative piece of clothing, an item of conspicuous style through which 'Brummell could declare his primary interests were in his own elegance and sense of aesthetics' (1991: 114).

Baudelaire's political allegiances were characteristically difficult to pin down (once a revolutionary, he aspired to be aristocratic as well as Bohemian) and, as Steele (1999 [1988]: 83) notes, his clothing was 'designed to set him apart from the bourgeoisie, the bohemians and the conventionally elegant aristocrats'. In other words, in style he resisted any firm political allegiance, as did Brummell's. Baudelaire's fascination with the dandy is expressed most clearly in his homage to the painter Constantin Guys. However, his depiction is not without contradiction, since he notes how the true dandy is coolly indifferent, unlike the passionate Mr G. with his keen involvement in modern life (1986: 57). Also, the true dandy was a man without paid employment, which means that the artist-dandy, like Baudelaire himself, is a rather corrupted version. However, in the artist-dandy Baudelaire describes, one finds an essential feature of all dandyism, namely, the 'burning need to acquire originality' (1986: 56). The dandy's road to originality was a road that led away from the natural and authentic to artifice and performance. A highly mannered style, not only in dress but in deportment and rhetoric, held the key to superiority. And all manner of artifice could be employed. Although Baudelaire did not think women capable of dandyism, his depiction of female beauty is based on the same idea of artifice. Artifice is the privilege of culture which is, according to Baudelaire, of a higher order than nature and, with this in mind, he sings the praises of cosmetics, which enhance a woman's beauty; 'the lamp-black that outlines the eye', 'the rouge that emphasises the upper part of the cheek' all serve to represent a distinctly modern desire to exceed nature (1986: 64). Hence 'artifice … can but be a servant only to beauty' (1986: 64). For Baudelaire, artifice was an ennobling thing in itself since it severed one from nature; embellishing and improving on nature.

It would therefore seem that the dandy is the antithesis of Romanticism, which seeks out the authentic and celebrates the natural. However, in developing a 'cult of oneself', the artist-dandy has something akin to the Romantic about him, although there are important differences. Romanticism, in its celebration of the individual, indulges the senses and in doing so emphasises pleasure, in stark contrast to the cold 'melancholy' of dandyism. In this respect then, dandyism for Campbell represents a version of the 'aristocratic ideal', which, in harking back to a bygone era of distinction, is reactionary. In order to find the ancestor of modern-day consumption and fashion, one must look elsewhere, to the figure of the Romantic.

The Romantic bohemian

According to Campbell (1989), while seemingly out of kilter with the modern age, the Romantic is crucially linked to the modern spirit of hedonism, which, from the eighteenth century onwards, had the paradoxical effect of inducing a new attitude to consumption. The Romantic revolt stems back to the eighteenth century and is fundamentally an attack on modern ideas of empiricism, rationalism and materialism. Above these narrow ideas, Romanticism values 'change, diversity, individuality and imagination' (1989: 181). Creativity was valued and with it, the imagination, the ability to recreate oneself as well as create artworks. It was through the imagination that one glimpsed the possibilities for a perfect world, a 'bohemia', where one could escape from the imperfections of modern life. Although the Romantic ethos was linked to spirituality and not materiality, it laid the foundations for a hedonistic attitude towards the world and the objects in it, 'by providing the highest possible motives with which to justify day-dreaming, longing and the rejection of reality, together with the pursuit of originality in life and art; and by so doing, enabled pleasure to be ranked above comfort' (Campbell 1993: 54).

The desire to seek out the pleasures afforded by the senses drives the Romantic spirit in a never-ending quest for novelty and amusement, a 'longing to experience in reality those pleasures created and enjoyed in the imagination, a longing which results in the ceaseless consumption of novelty', in other words an autonomous pleasure-seeking that is characteristic of modern-day consumption and 'self-illusory hedonism' (Campbell 1989: 205). Bohemianism not only articulates Romantic ideals but is a way of life devised along the principles of Romanticism. Like the dandy, the bohemian might not work, making leisure an end in itself. Unlike the dandy, however, the bohemian seeks out pleasure while relinquishing comfort (the bohemian frequently lives in poverty), and looks for new experiences by which to indulge the senses. This mentality is not, however, limited to the Romantic bohemian, who is essentially an outsider, but spread out across the eighteenth and nineteenth centuries, stimulating a new taste among middle classes for novelty, which is the basis for modern fashion and consumption. According to Campbell (1989, 1993), there is, therefore, a close link between Romantic bohemianism and periods of expanding cultural consumption: the 1890s, the 1920s and the 1960s are the examples he cites. The link is also evident when one considers the place occupied by Paris, which was the spiritual home of bohemianism as well as the fashion capital of the world for most of the modern era. Paris was also the place where one found the most sumptuous and the most excessive department stores of the nineteenth century, temples of consumption and places for imaginary wanderings. It is the Romantic ethic that sent the consumer of the eighteenth and nineteenth centuries to department stores and markets, and a similar impulse drives shoppers to the malls of our own time. It also introduced an unquenchable thirst for novelty and fashion. The new department stores of the nineteenth century were Romantic spaces that opened one's eyes to a dreamlike world of sensory delight; a world of imaginary illusions where the shopper might indulge in the fantasy of owning the objects found there. In setting out their wares in fantastic and sumptuous displays, the department store was born out of the same spirit of self-illusionary hedonism described by Campbell (1989). The fact that more often than not consumption leads to disappointment and disillusionment – how often the object's magic wanes as soon as the parcel is unwrapped at home – is beside the point; indeed, such disappointment is a necessary element in the unquenchable appetite of the modern-day consumer. This restless Romantic spirit, this indulgence in dreams and fantasies, is what drives fashion. In order to explore this further, it is necessary to examine the role played by department stores in the propagation of fashion in the nineteenth century.

Therefore, according to Campbell (1989, 1993), to find the new 'modern' thirst for fashion one should not look to the aristocracy, whose attitude to consuming objects is derived from a stoicism quite at odds with the playfulness of modernity; one should look instead to the bourgeoisie, the middle classes. Their style, far from emulating the fashions of those higher up the social ladder, was based on a new attitude towards the self, a concern with the imagination and a desire to seek out pleasure and novelty. However, as we have seen, in the figure of the Romantic one finds the emphasis upon 'authenticity', a concern which has become an important feature in contemporary understandings of identity. Instead of the playful artifice of a public self found in the eighteenth century, when public performance was held at a distance from the 'inner' private self, we have, as Sennett (1977) argues, placed an increasing emphasis upon the 'authentic' self locked inside the body and seek to 'read' this through appearance. Psychology, particularly 'pop' psychology, has aided this process, creating the idea of an inner realm of the self whose motives can possibly be read and understood. Modern books on social behaviour, whose topics range from flirting to management and business success, offer advice on how to 'read' the appearance of 'others' through their bodily appearance as well as how to control appearance to 'win friends and influence people'. Identity is therefore thought to be immanent in our appearance even while we are aware of the potential mistakes we can make when relying on surface information such as dress, body, hair, makeup and so on. The potential is there for the conscious manipulation of such tropes.

Fashion and identity in contemporary culture

Why this long discussion of dandies and romantics in the nineteenth century? What this discussion highlights are the origins of themes of fashion and dress in the nineteenth century that have resonance even today. As well as illustrating the tension between appearance as artifice and authenticity, the two contrasting figures of the dandy and the Romantic illustrate the link, tenuous and ambiguous though it may be, between different cultural identities (in this instance, class) and dress styles. As Finkelstein (1991) argues, these themes can still be found in contemporary culture and indeed, the ancestors of these two characters, the dandy and the Romantic, can also be traced. Dandy figures litter the twentieth century: according to Hebdige (1979), the mods of the 1960s were typically lower-class dandies, exhibiting an obsessive interest in the finest details of dress. Further, the dandy celebration of artifice and performance runs through a variety of popular cultural styles from glam rock to punk rock. Similarly, Romanticism and a concern to be 'natural' runs through many understandings of identity, as exemplified in such figures as the hippies of the 1960s and 1970s.

However, the links between fashion and class identity are far less apparent in the twentieth century than they were in the nineteenth. In particular, 'high' fashion, once the preserve of a small elite, has been democratised and has extended to more people than ever before. Further, the fashion hierarchy between classes has been inverted with 'high'-status styles no longer necessarily residing at the 'top' of the social ladder but 'bubbling up' from the street, from youth subcultures (Polhemus 1994). There is much evidence to suggest that fashion today emanates from a wide range of sites within youth culture. Distinctive identities are therefore still marked by dress and style but their status challenges traditional notions of status tied to class. In order to examine distinction in dress in contemporary culture we need to bring subcultural style into the picture. In the following discussion, I begin by exploring the links between dress/body styles and class in the twentieth century and then move on to consider the relationship between dress/body in subcultural style. Analysis of the youth subculture also provides an opportunity to return to Simmel (1950, 1971) and explore the way in which style articulates a concern with imitation and differentiation.

Class, distinction and style

At the beginning of the twentieth century, one could still distinguish between working class and upper class by observing their dress: working-class men and women often wore clogs rather than shoes, while the cloth cap was often the symbol par excellence of the working-class man as opposed to the top hat of the elite. Although these are obvious clichés, they do illustrate, at least symbolically, the associations between dress and class identities that once existed but have since become obsolete. By the mid-twentieth century, developments in the mass production of fashion, along with the increasing affluence of the working class, had led to fashion being extended to a greater number than ever before, blurring the boundary between the classes in terms of style. Today, class identity is less clearly bound to particular styles of dress than ever. There are, of course, instances of class-specific dress: a member of the aristocracy used to be clearly identified by her Burberry, tweed suit and Alice band, for example. However, while *haute couture* has long been associated with a small elite group, in the 1980s designer fashion labels were marketed to an increasing number of people through the 'ready to wear' collections, extending the kudos of couture to an unprecedented number of people. For Crane (2000) this change signals the move from 'class' fashion to 'consumer' fashion'. Labels such as Christian Dior, Giorgio Armani and Calvin Klein, once exclusive, were opened to a wider clientele and could be purchased by young urban professionals (the so-called 'yuppies' of the 1980s, for example) as well as by working-class children who might not own the real thing, but a good replica bought at a market stall. Moreover, today's fashion industry is geared up to produce the latest catwalk styles almost as soon as they are displayed (see Chapter 7). The democratisation of fashion blurs yet further the distinctions between a fashionable 'elite' and most people.

However, while obvious symbols of class identity have become less distinguishable, smaller details can still mark out distinctions. 'Quality', for example, is the key distinguisher of class: such fabrics as cashmere, linen and leather are associated with 'quality', as are good seams and proper lining. In order to decode these signs one needs to be 'in the know': like all signs, dress depends upon the cultural knowledge of the reader in order for it to be meaningful. With the increased emphasis on the need for sustainable fashion, there is likely to be a class divide between those who can afford to pay more and those will still be tempted, or only able to afford 'fast' fashion (further discussion in Chapter 7).

Styles of dress and taste in clothes are only one part of the equation; how one wears these things, indeed, how one 'wears' the body, are equally important. The body is the bearer of social status not just in how it is dressed, but in how it is held, how it moves, how it walks and talks. These bodily dispositions, the *habitus* (Bourdieu 1984), refer to the seemingly natural bodily demeanour we learn as members of a particular family/class. I say 'seemingly' since there is nothing 'natural' about these body styles: they are acquired through family and other cultural institutions such as the school. These acquired bodily traits come to be experienced as natural since we learn them at a very early age and come to take them for granted. The fact that these can convey subtle information about our social class position is evidenced by the fact that at one time the elite and those aspiring to be the elite sent their young ladies of marriageable age to 'finishing school', where they were trained more thoroughly in how to walk tall and graceful, get in and out of a car, eat at a formal dinner party and so on. The supposed 'natural' grace of a lady was thus nothing more than a body style. Here the body is clearly marked out as the bearer of social status.

Subcultural style, subcultural capital

As Simmel (1971 [1904]) argues, distinction is a characteristic feature of fashion. However, in contemporary culture, distinction does not run along class lines alone but across a wide plane of social identities. In particular, youth subcultures with their distinctive style have become a source of fashion to the extent that, according to Polhemus (1994), such styles now 'bubble up' from street to designers rather than the reverse. Furthermore, subcultures employ dress to mark out distinctive identities both between themselves and mainstream culture, as well as between themselves and other youth subcultures. Thus, as Clarke et al. have argued:

> the peculiar dress, style and focal concerns, milieu, etc. of the Teddy Boy, the Mod, the Rocker or the Skinhead set them off, as distinctive groupings, both from the broad patterns of working class culture as a whole, and also from the more diffused patterns exhibited by 'ordinary' working class boys (and, to a more limited extent, girls). (1992: 56)

Thus, the subculture is a subset of a class culture but is 'smaller, more localised and differentiated' (Clarke et al. 1992: 55; see also Hall and Jefferson 1977). They share some of the same material conditions as their 'parent culture' or class culture but express their own particular concerns through a distinctive use of style. Because of their distinctiveness, they have attracted a lot of attention. After the Second World War, in Britain in particular, there was a wave of passing subcultures, many of them attracting the attention of the media until they faded away to be replaced by another. 'Spectacular' is the word often used to describe these groups since their use of style and their distinctive patterns of life marked them out as different, exotic, even dangerous. Youth subcultures have been associated with a number of 'moral panics' since the 1950s: teddy boys were associated with excess and with violence; later it was the turn of the mods, rockers and skinheads to be the focus of obsessive media attention as 'deviant', 'violent' or 'hooligan'. The most discussed subcultures have been predominantly working class, male and generally oppositional to mainstream, white, middle-class culture. Indeed, McRobbie (1981, 1991, 1994a) finds this aspect of the research to be problematic since it neglects the experience of girls, who have played only a marginal role in post-war youth subcultures, primarily because they tend to be excluded from a culture that involves 'hanging around' the street late at night.

However, while distinction is one aspect of subcultural style, as Simmel (1971) has cogently pointed out, fashion relies on the contradictory tendency towards similarity; this too is clearly visible in the youth subcultures, which use style to articulate a clear identity to members within the groups as well as to those outside. Brake (1981, 1985) argues that style expresses the degree of commitment to the group, indicating to those outside it the group's opposition to the dominant values. He goes on to note three aspects of subcultural style: image, such as costume; such accessories and artefacts as scooters or motorbikes; gait or postural expression, 'cool' for mods and 'angry' for punks; and lastly, argot, the special vocabulary of the group, and how it is delivered.

The style of the subculture articulates the particular issues or problems that the youth attend to and attempt to resolve. As mentioned above, the style of the mod was, according to Hebdige (1979), that of a lower-class dandy, the painstaking attention to the smallest detail of dress not unlike Brummell's obsession with tying his cravat. According to Hebdige, this style articulated a desire for upward mobility, a longing to 'escape' the monotony of working-class life. Not only did the dress manifest this concern, but so too the 'cool' body style of the mods, which put a 'blasé' distance between them and their immediate environment (high-rise flats in the East End of London, low-status jobs, for example). The term used by Paul Willis (1975, 1978) to describe this 'fit' between the focal concerns of the youth subculture and their overall dress, style, bodily demeanour and leisure activities is 'homology'. The motorbike rockers he examines demonstrate this fit very well: their focal concerns to express a 'hard' masculinity are articulated through dress that is 'hard' or 'tough' (leather being the preferred fabric), while their body posture is one of 'toughness' as opposed to mod 'cool'.

These distinctive styles and patterns of behaviour illustrate the way in which the dressed body can articulate identities, making them recognisable to those both inside and outside the community itself. Style then, that combination of dress and the way in which it is worn, is expressive not only of class identity but of subcultural identities. In this respect, style is the 'connective tissue' to which Wilson (2007) refers: it heightens our sense of connectedness to particular groups, making visible our commitment to that community. It is linked to class groupings and can articulate class allegiances (upper-class elites) or can be the substance that brings together a group that is a subdivision of a particular class as in a youth subculture. In all cases, the boundary between the inside and the outside of the group is policed in some way: style is one way in which one can tell if the other is a member of the same group.

Figure 7. Cyber fashion: an example of youth subcultural style. Source: Wikimedia Commons/ Danny Sotzny

Subcultures depend upon forms of knowledge and behaviour and require particular ways of being. This is closely linked to what Bourdieu (1994) termed the *habitus*: subcultures produce their own practices, which are in part bodily orientations or ways of moving, walking and talking, which are worn like a 'second skin' on the body of the skinhead, punk, raver. In her account of club cultures, Thornton (1995) argues that these represent 'taste cultures' who share similar tastes in music, media and values. These club cultures are 'fluid', allowing entry to others for the duration of a single summer or event and operate with 'hierarchies of what is authentic and legitimate in popular culture – embodied understanding of which can make one "hip"' (1995: 3). She conceives of 'hipness' as a form of 'subcultural capital'; this might not have the legitimacy of middle-class culture but nonetheless operates with its own hierarchies of legitimacy, depending on differentiation from the 'mainstream'. In focusing attention on the forms of knowledge and the hierarchies employed by club cultures, Thornton's account focuses much less attention on style than earlier studies of subculture.

Contemporary debates on fashion and identity: 'race', ethnicity and religious identities

Recent scholarship within fashion studies continues to examine the relationship between identity and fashion but attention has moved away from class to other aspects of identity considered more significant in contemporary societies, in particular, gender, sexuality, race, ethnicity, and religious affiliation. On the one hand, there has been a concern to examine the ways fashion, dress (as well as hair and beauty) are used by marginalised or oppressed groups to articulate their identities, sometimes in resistance to oppression or dominant power structures. Indeed, very often their identity is already marked as 'Other' or different with respect to white/European standards: as Reed and Medvedev (2019: 23) argue, '[A] black woman is considered the "Other" in the realm of beauty in the United States.' Adopting a particular style of dress affords the opportunity to construct a visible identity that opens a space, if only symbolically, for a group often denied expression politically. For example, the flamboyant and visually striking zoot suit has been widely studied. As Peiss (2011: 3) notes, 'African-American historians place zoot-suiters within a long-standing tradition of black style and performance, and consider them in relation to the resurgent civil rights activism of the war years.' As an exuberant and extravagant style of dress (almost a 'caricature' of the male suit) she notes: African-American scholarship attributes to style 'significant political behaviour by those who had little formal power or ability to represent themselves through speech or texts' (Peiss 2011: 3–4). (See also Cosgrove, 1989 and also Ramírez, 2009 for history of women zoot suiters.) What this style – and other forms of dress – offer is the possibility for African Americans in America to gain some control or agency over their lives – it is a symbolic battleground that articulates marginalised identities and challenges dominant norms of dress. For Tulloch (2019), addressing the 'style narratives of black people'(p. 86) in the US and UK, 'the styled body is a sincere identifier of the individual within an activist movement'(p. 85). Some forms of dress are less spectacular and overtly political, but no less symbolic. Williams (2019: 3) notes how he has adopted the Kangol hat and '[B]y sharing my individual style narrative of Kangol hats I'm able to tap into the rich collective narrative of black men who have used headdresses to challenge stereotypical notions of black masculinity.'

Another area of concern regarding identity through fashion and dress is religion and how this intersects with other identity markers. For millennia, religions in all forms have regulated bodies through moral discourses (such as shame within Judaeo-Christian traditions) and overt bodily practices (chastising the flesh by wearing sack cloth, or asterism, for example) and dress codes (the saffron robes of Buddhist monks, habits of Christian nuns, or the covering of the female head inside mosques, etc.). Dress, in all its aspects, including religious symbols (crucifix, Star of David), is often the most visible aspect of religious identity. The wearing of the hijab, for example, has been taken on board voluntarily by many women in the West to articulate their devotion (Lewis 2013) in what is often, post-9/11, a hostile environment for Muslims. Indeed, post 9/11, the figure of the Muslim woman has taken on political significance, sparking many debates and even new government policies, as happened in France, where a law banning the wearing of hijab in state schools was introduced in 2004; more recently, in 2021 the French Senate has debated outlawing all minors from wearing it in public ('Law against Islam': French vote in favour of hijab ban condemned | Religion News | Al Jazeera). Such an example points to the complex intersection of religion with gender and race: the Muslim woman's body is both racialised and gendered in such debates, marked out as racially 'Other' and also seemingly 'passive', 'oppressed' and in need of 'saving' to Western eyes. Thus, much public debate has centred on the relationship between dominant Christian norms in the West and the rights and claims made by other minority religions in the West. Interestingly, Karademir-Hazir (2020) questions the emphasis placed on religion, arguing that the dichotomy between religious and secular dress is perhaps 'over-emphasised' and 'politicised' and this matter is discussed in more detail below.

It is not surprising, given recent political events and growing 'culture wars' between Christianity and other religions, especially Muslim, that one expanding area of concern within fashion studies in recent years has been the attention given to forms of 'modest' dress, exemplified by, though not unique to, Muslim women's dress and the hijab. One line of enquiry has focused on what 'modesty' means and its relationship to fashion. As Lewis notes, '"modest" and "fashion" are mostly regarded as antipathetic' (2013: 1) even if modest fashion comes into fashion periodically. Indeed, I am writing this in early 2022 and there is currently an abundance of long, maxi dresses with large lace collars not dissimilar to something the formal, modest dresses Mormon women might wear. Modesty is, of course, contextual and mutable. What counts as modest will invariably change according to religion and situation. Indeed, even *within* the three main religions – Christianity, Judaism and Islam – there are significant differences (secular Jews versus Hasidic Jews, for example, or differences within Christian sects). While seemingly at odds with one another, modest fashion has emerged in recent years as a segment of the mainstream fashion industry, to cater for different religious and secular consumer demands. The internet has helped to foster many ways for these consumers to acquire dress that might not be readily available on the high street (Moors 2013; Tarlo 2013). Of interest is not just the fashion or representation of women who wear modest fashion, but also the ways in which this style of dress circulates and mediates identity, and the ways in which women themselves operate within the fashion industry as producers, mediators, and consumers (Lewis 2013b)

Intersectionality

Identity has remained a key concern within fashion literature but is now analysed along multiple axes. One of the legacies of decades of feminist scholarship, much of it critical of the 'second-wave' feminist movement of the late 1960s and 1970s, has been a questioning of identity and a questioning of structures of inequality and power. Responding to the whiteness of second-wave feminism 'Women's Liberation' activism and the gender-blindness of black liberation activism in the US in the 1960s, black feminist scholarship challenges *both systems* of power (patriarchy and racism) to argue for an intersectional analysis of how gender and race work together to oppress women of colour. This posed a challenge to both academia and activism and has been profoundly influential to emerging debates about identity within academic thought, especially post-structuralist, postmodernist debates on identity emerging over the 1970s and 1980s. Collins and Bilge (2016: 11) define intersectionality as follows: '[W]hen it comes to social inequality, people's lives and the organisation of power in a given society are better understood as being shaped not by a single axis of social division, be it race or gender or class, but by many axes coming together and influencing one another.' Crucial to understanding this is Critical Race Theory (CRT). Thus, as one of the key authors, Crenshaw (1989) argues, understanding the marginalisation of black women requires both feminist and anti-racist critique. Acknowledging both forms of discrimination and violence against black women is important for understanding the very particular vulnerabilities of women of colour. According to Collins and Bilge (2020) organisations, companies and people use intersectionality as an 'analytic tool' to help them deal with social problems and issues they face: rather than see only single issues (gender equality at work, for example), it is more productive to consider the intersecting nature of racial or age discrimination, since these multiple markers of identity work in combination not isolation.

Intersectionality is a powerful concept that is pertinent to analysis of fashion. For example, critiquing poor industry practices, an intersectional analysis points to how this industry is particularly impactful and exploitative on black and minority working-class women in the Global South and vulnerable immigrant women who sew cheap clothes in the West. In fashion scholarship, intersectionality means not only is it important to recognise that distinctions in dress can be classed (as earlier studies have shown), but to consider multiple and intersecting aspects of identity, such as gender, race, ethnicity, religion, etc. In recent years, intersectionality has had broad appeal and application beyond CRT for understanding multiplicity of identity articulated in/through fashion and the characteristics through which identities are read and understood. Indeed, even though she does not use the term explicitly, Appleford's (2013) analysis of women's dress in the UK points to the intersecting nature of class and gender. With a sample of predominantly white women, her analysis reveals how 'notions of femininity are created and performed within a classed context' so that ingrained assumptions about working-class women's femininity, sexuality and colour intersect with ideas about middle-class taste and respectability. Class is also the focus of critical re-examination in Karademir-Hazir's (2020) analysis of Turkish women. She argues that class remains a salient feature among Turkish women, something that recent scholarship on modest dress (discussed above) has overlooked because this literature has 'quite over-empathised and politicised dichotomy between pious and secular embodiment styles, ignoring the sociologically meaningful heterogeneity that exists within each'. Rather than diminishing class as a relevant marker of identity, these two studies suggest that it is still important and in complex interaction with other categories, such as gender, religion and modesty.

This discussion demonstrates the complexity of discussions around identity as it has been thought about in relation to fashion and dress. My original analysis in 2000 and 2015 over-played the argument that the issue of identity and dress is a peculiarly Western phenomenon. For example, in Tarlo's work (1996) 'the problem of what to wear' and the issue of class identity is examined in India. Tarlo (1996: 1) challenges head-on our assumptions about clothing and identity and questions 'the conventional academic view that Indian identity was, until recently, neatly prescribed by caste or religious tradition, and that people dressed in the clothes dictated to them over generations'. This is tied to complex issues of identity similar to that of the experience of Western women's dress. By examining specific examples of moments when clothing in India changes, or when new combinations emerge, she attends to 'the active role that clothing has played in the identity construction of individuals, families, castes, religions and nations' (1996: 1). Part of the problem, she argues, lies in classification – 'modern' versus 'traditional' being a key one, of course – which has been flagged as a critical distinction subject to ongoing contestation, as detailed in this chapter and in Chapter 2.

This simplistic distinction tends to be replicated in those museums that curate 'traditional' dress: they may favour one classification over another and select things that conform to 'authentic' 'traditional' dress so that identity is seen as singular rather than 'multiple and conflicting' (ibid.: 15). Tarlo's analysis points to the many competing identities that co-exist in India and may conflict with one another in what is a highly stratified society '(social, sexual, religious, political, economic, cultural, regional)' where 'the likelihood of wishing to identify with more than one group simultaneously is considerable' (ibid.: 45). Thus, the 'problem of what to wear' in India is not unlike the problems of dressing in the West, even while the 'system of provision' may differ, possibly radically, if the dress is in a rural Indian community as opposed to more urban locations, such as Delhi. As discussed in this chapter, the rise of academic interest in 'alternative', faith-based fashionable dress complicates discussions of modern and traditional communities/societies and requires an intersectional approach. The hijab-wearing woman has become the focus of attention, post-9/11, politicised within Western societies. An intersectional approach to the study of religion and modest dress attends to the complex practices and understandings of fashion and identity.

Conclusion

The body, and our ways of presenting it in public, is a focal point and major site of identity. Within Western modernity, there has been specific emphasis upon our bodies as separate from others – the location of our unique *individuality* and the vehicle to express ourselves *as* individuals. It is also the location of our expressions of group membership and marker of social differences and inequalities. Thus, dress articulates our 'uniqueness' and difference from others, although as members of classes and cultures, we are equally likely to use dress to connect us to others as well. This play of difference and similarity is a constant theme in fashion literature, as argued above. In modernity, this tension seems exaggerated, since we live in a post-traditional world where identities are no longer as stable as they once were. The anonymity of the city opens new possibilities for creating oneself, giving one the freedom to experiment with appearance in a way that would have been unthinkable in a traditional rural community, where everybody knows everything about everybody else. The modern or postmodern world where 'all that is solid melts into air' offers up new dangers and new pleasures and this is nowhere more apparent than in the city.

The essentially ambivalent nature of the modern city, described by Bauman (1991), Davis (1992), Finkelstein (1991) and Giddens (1991), is experienced as threatening to some, such as the Romantic who feels alienated from modern life, and exhilarating to others such as the *flâneur* or the dandy who enjoy the freedom of the city and feel at home in its bustling streets. Fashion, dress, and consumption provide ways of dealing with the problems of the mode world, characterised by increasing fragmentation and a sense of chaos. Fashion opens possibilities for framing the self, however temporarily: as Davis (1992) suggests, fashion expresses two contradictory tendencies, taking inspiration from ambivalence and yet also trying to fix identity in the form of an image or style. In other words, as Wilson (2007: 63) puts it, fashion 'opens up, yet simultaneously undercuts the possibility of individual self development, and of social co-operation'. However, as Davis (1992) argues, fashion does not produce permanent symbolic solutions: its symbols are too ephemeral, and its ambivalence too deeply rooted. But clothing comes to play a part in how we deal with ambivalence. As Davis suggests, because dress frames our embodied self, it seems 'to serve as a kind of visual metaphor for identity' (1992: 25). Thus, the modern self is increasingly aware of itself, including its appearance, and able to intervene and act upon it (see for example, Gonzalez and Bovone 2012; Holland 2004; Paulicelli and Clark 2009). Classes and subcultures employ style, dress, body, posture and so on to create identity self-consciously, both to affirm group affiliation and difference to those on the outside and within. Thus, when talking about individuality and identity and the role played by fashion and dress it is important to recognise that identities are socially meaningful. The individual may want to 'stand out' but she or he also wants to 'fit in' with a group.

Identity remains of central concern in contemporary fashion literature, alongside the focus on 'meaning', though perhaps the two are one and the same, since the accounts often given of fashion's 'meaning' boil down to questions of identity: what do clothes say about the wearer? While, as I have argued elsewhere (Entwistle 2013), we might say this pairing of 'fashion' with 'identity' is something of a cliché – 'we are what we wear' – there remains a lot to say, especially considering the more recent scholarship in this area, which is much more nuanced and detailed than earlier work. Partly we need to see what, indeed, is the connection between fashion and identity: do our clothes say more about us than, say, our furniture or interiors? Moreover, what are the limits of this expressiveness in dress? Tseëlon (2012b: 109) challenges the prevailing 'homogeneity of dressing meaning' in academic scholarship with 'the diversity of looks and meanings in ordinary people's wardrobes' by testing the 'accuracy and reliability of clothing communication' in actual interactions and interpretations. Whether I would go along with this methodology is beside the point: we need to continue to question the close associations of fashion/dress with identities.

5

Identity: Gender and Fashion

Introduction

According to Wilson, 'fashion is obsessed with gender, defines and redefines the gender boundary' (2007: 117). While it would seem that today's fashions are more androgynous, even 'unisex', clothes display an overriding obsession with gender. Indeed, fashions in androgyny are further evidence of the degree to which fashion likes to play around at the boundaries of gender difference. More recently, the rising awareness of trans, non-binary or gender-neutral identities by trans and queer activism has challenged the binary male/female and the very idea of two-sexed bodies, preferring to emphasise the multifarious ways of expressing (or challenging) gender. This has put definitions of sex and gender under scrutiny like never before. However, despite such challenges, in terms of dress, gender has been, and remains a salient feature of fashion and daily dress with some distinction between male/female part of most social settings. Once we begin to examine fashion in daily dress, it is apparent that gender remains a salient feature, with distinctions between male/female in place in most social settings for most people.

The obsession Wilson notes translates into dominant styles of dress for men and women in everyday life, which also shows a concern to mark gender difference. In many contemporary situations, particular clothing is demanded of men and women. Take, for example, commonly seen dress codes outside night clubs (I'm writing this in July 2022 in London), which specify 'heels only' or with 'laid on' special club nights, which apply solely to women, whose appearance has to be overtly decorative and feminine. Clothes don't merely reflect natural difference, they construct and stabilise gender, drawing attention to of the body so that one can tell, usually at first glance, whether they are a man or a woman. These features of dress impact the body of the wearer in significant ways: high heels enforce a particular gait and movement of the body for women, which reinforces their difference from men. Thus, what Woodhouse (1989: ix) noted, some time ago, is still true today: 'we expect men to dress to "look like" men and women to "look like" women'. This process starts early: babies, whose sex cannot usually be established at first glance are very often dressed in colours, fabrics and styles of clothing that differentiate them and announce their sex to the world. With the popularity of the 'gender reveal' on social media and parties, even foetuses are gendered with blue or pink balloons and clothes purchased in advance of the birth. Such practices are culturally and historically specific: the common association, pink for a girl, blue for a boy is a recent historical invention. According to Garber (1992: 1), 'in the early years of the twentieth century, before World War I, boys wore pink ("a stronger, more decided color" according to the promotional literature of the time) while girls wore blue (understood to be "delicate" and "dainty")'. That the reverse is true today only shows that taken-for-granted gendered norms marking difference are arbitrary. For the most part, when we meet someone for the first time 'we think we see their sex, but in fact we do not. What we see is their gender appearance and we assume that this is an accurate indication of their sex' (Woodhouse 1989: 1). Gender neutral or trans identities may be changing our views of gender but male/female gendered norms are still prevalent.

As noted above, dress practice often draws attention to, and helps construct, gendered bodies. The gendered body is so frequently invoked through clothing that we take for granted the effects of dress, that the jacket worn by a man exaggerates his broad shoulders and *décolletage* emphasises a woman's throat and breasts. But clothing does more than emphasise bodily signs of difference. It imbues the body with significance, adding layers of cultural meanings, so naturalised they are mistaken as natural. Thus, the male suit does not just accentuate male bodily features, it adds 'masculinity' to the body; indeed, until about the 1950s the transition from boyhood to manhood was marked by casting off short trousers and wearing long ones. So significant are clothes to our readings of the body they can stand for sexual difference in the absence of a body where a skirt can signify 'woman' (or offensively be used to refer to a woman), while trousers signify 'man', as these icons often do on public lavatories. In the West, bifurcated garments have always signalled female, and trousers, male, because historically women were prohibited from wearing such garments. So strong are the connotations that items of clothing can even transcend the actual biological body: the commonly used expression 'she wears the trousers' is used to describe a dominant woman in a relationship who has acquired characteristics normally associated with men. Here 'trousers' signify 'male' and 'masculine'.

It is obvious from these examples that we are far removed from the realm of 'brute' biological facts and firmly located within the realm of culture. Clothing is one of the most immediate and effective examples of the way in which bodies are gendered, made 'feminine' or 'masculine'. Our ideas about masculine and feminine are tied not just to sex difference but to *sexuality* since there is a close relationship between the gendered codes of dress and dominant ideas about sexuality. In this chapter, I consider the ways in which clothing articulates ideas about gender and explore the role it plays in constructing 'masculinity' and 'femininity'. The connections between gender and sexuality (in particular, the way in which femininity is conflated with sexuality) are addressed here because there is a historical association of 'woman' with the body evident in Western, especially Christian teachings. However, other aspects of fashion's relationship to sexuality are explored further in Chapter 6. First, it is necessary to define the terms, sex and gender and their relationship to sexuality.

Sex, Gender and Sexuality

Sex, gender, and sexuality are often conflated so that there would appear to be a 'natural' and inevitable link between them. As Judith Butler (1990) argues, in Western discourse our notions of what makes a man and a woman, i.e. our ideas about sex and gender, arise out of common-sense understandings of sexuality, generally applied to refer to hetero-sexuality. Before we can untangle this complicated knot, it is important to begin by establishing a distinction between all three terms, if only to see how they are inextricably linked.

The distinction between sex and gender has been crucial to feminist thinking of the 'second wave' (corresponding to the second half of the twentieth century) and is associated in particular with social constructivist feminists, of which Ann Oakley's (1976) *Sex, Gender and Society* is a classic example. The aim of her book is to 'disentangle "sex" from "gender" in the many fields where the existence of natural differences between male and female has been proposed' (1976: 17). She defines sex and gender as follows: '"sex" is a word that refers to the biological differences between male and female: the visible difference in genitalia, the related difference in procreative function. "Gender" however is a matter of culture: it refers to the social classifications into "masculine" and "feminine"' (1976: 16).

Thus, biological material determines sex, making us male and female, but does not determine the traits of 'masculinity' and 'femininity' which are the products of culture. This distinction is important since it enables one to see how bodies acquire meanings which are not the result of nature but the imprint of culture. So, while all cultures mark out a difference between two sexes, not all cultures draw the line in the same place or agree on the characteristics of men and women. The fact that sexual difference is in part a culturally ordained difference has been demonstrated repeatedly by anthropological accounts that show how other cultures interpret sex and 'make-up' gender, of which Margaret Mead's (1935) *Sex and Temperament in Three Primitive Societies* is the classic study.

The lack of any universal correspondence between sex and gender means that there is no 'natural' link between the biological categories of 'male' and 'female' and the cultural characteristics of 'masculine' and 'feminine'. Ortner (1996: 18) thus describes gender as a game, or more correctly, a multiplicity of games, which take on different 'forms of bodily activity' as well as 'complex rules' according to time and place. Further evidence that sex does not determine gender in a 'natural' way can be found in studies of hermaphrodites (individuals with characteristics of both sexes), who can go on to assume 'normal' gendered characteristics (masculine or feminine) despite the ambiguity of their biological sex. Studies of intersex (e.g. Stoller 1968) suggest that the acquisition of 'masculinity' and 'femininity' is not 'natural' or purely 'biological' but is the result of socialisation – parental and cultural expectation. Similarly, the existence of transsexuals gives further evidence of the discontinuity between sex and gender. Transsexuals might be born with the biological characteristics of one sex but identify with the gender character-istics of the opposite sex. As Oakley notes, 'to be a man or a woman, a boy or a girl, is as much a function of dress, gesture, occupation, social network and personality, as it is of possessing a particular set of genitals' (1976: 158).

Clothing, as an aspect of culture, is a crucial feature in the production of masculinity and femininity: it turns nature into culture, layering cultural meanings on the body. There is no natural link between an item of clothing and 'femininity' and 'masculinity'; instead there is an arbitrary set of associa-tions that are culturally specific. Thus the way clothing connotes femininity and masculinity varies from culture to culture; while trousers are commonly associated with men and considered 'indecent' for women to wear in the West (until the twentieth century that is) they have been worn for centuries by women in the Middle East and elsewhere. Furthermore, the skirt which still potently communicates 'femininity' in the West has no such associations in cultures where men and women wear sarongs. In the West, the skirt helps to maintain an arbitrary but crucial gender distinction. However, while distinc-tions of gender drawn by clothes are arbitrary, they often become fundamental to our 'common-sense' readings of bodies. In this respect, fashion also turns culture into nature, it naturalises the cultural order. As Woodhouse (1989: xiii) notes:

> clothing forms part of a system of social signalling; it is used to indicate belonging ... above all, it is used to demarcate gender, so that although the symbols change with fashion the gender/sex message remains the same, namely that feminine appearance indicates female sex and masculine appearance male sex.

In this way, says Woodhouse, we 'announce' our sex when we dress according to conventions of gender. This supposedly 'natural' link can be found in fashion magazines, which frequently proclaim 'vive la différence!', as if there was a natural, unproblematic difference between men and women that clothing simply reflects. However, the transvestite who masquerades in the clothing of the opposite sex challenges these cultural assumptions. When the masquerade is so convincing that they can 'pass off' their appearance as 'reality', it testifies not just to the importance of clothing in marking out gender, but to the way in which sex can be radically discontinuous with gender. The two are not fixed and stable as commonly thought but linked by cultural threads that can be willingly broken.

While a distinction between sex and gender is useful in that it denaturalises common associations between the characteristics of the body and the characteristics of 'femininity' and 'masculinity', many feminists are sceptical about the possibility of drawing a clear line between sex and gender (for a summary of this debate, see Entwistle 1998). Such a dichotomy assumes that sex is an unadorned 'fact' of nature, a pre-social state onto which a social meaning is pinned. However, as argued by Butler (1990), biology and nature do not stand outside culture as 'raw facts', which then acquire a social meaning: biology and nature are themselves socially constituted.

The dichotomy of sex and gender is made more complicated by the close association of both with sexuality. Sexuality is extremely difficult to define, as discussed in Chapter 6. It is often assumed to be natural, an innate 'force' within us but, like sex and gender, it is a cultural phenomenon. The sexual experiences, appetites and practices of men and women are often said to be derived from their biology, corresponding with the 'common-sense' gender characteristics assigned to them. These associations, while relying on nature, are in fact based in culture. However, rather than seeing ideas about sex and gender as the basis for cultural assumptions about sexuality, Butler (1990) argues the reverse: it is Western ideas about heterosexuality that inform common understandings regarding sex (biology) and gender (cultural characteristics); sex is therefore not an unadorned 'fact' of nature but culturally prescribed, 'compulsory heterosexuality' shapes dominant Western understandings of sexed bodies as binary.

The social and political implications of this dominant male/female binary are far-reaching. Modern social theory (here 'modern' encompasses the ideas and writings of the Enlightenment thinkers) has constructed the world with respect to dominant ideas about men and women, shaping their social and political roles. Women have typically been constructed as closer to the 'animal' or natural world because of women's role in reproduction (see Entwistle 1998; Sydie 1987 for summaries of this) with women's bodies seen by some philosophers to be the source of characteristics associated with women: wombs, for example, were also thought to make women's brains smaller, more delicate and less reasonable than men's (Sydie 1987). Thus, for Rousseau, women lacked the capacity of reason necessary to function in the public realm and must therefore remain confined in the private sphere of the home, the sphere of intimacy and emotions suited to their natures as carers of children (and men). When it comes to clothing, these connections between woman, the body and sexuality remain strong even today. Cases of rape or sexual harassment at work sometimes come with claims that 'she was asking for it' by her behaviour or style of dress and provide instances of this pairing of woman with the body

(Lees 1999; Wolf 1991; see also Beiner 2007). This leaves many women anxious about what clothing is appropriate to wear to work, as discussed below.

Looking Back: Dress and Gender in History

Sexual difference has been marked out progressively through different styles of dress; it has also been marked out through discourses on fashion and finery, which have linked them to the 'natural' vanity and weakness of the feminine soul. For centuries woman has been associated with 'fickle' fashion, vain display and indulgent narcissism. Indeed, this association may explain in part the marginalisation of fashion within social theory, why it has been seen as 'frivolous', ephemeral nonsense, unworthy of serious academic attention. Typically, as feminists have pointed out (e.g. Ortner 1974), the things associated with women tend to have lower social status than the things associated with men, and women's pastimes and preoccupations have been trivialised and mocked (Ang 1985; Modleski 1982; Radway 1987). The characterisation of women with the 'triviality' of fashion and men with more 'serious' business was challenged with the rise of the 'new man', whose narcissistic preoccupation with his appearance became the stuff of advertisements and men's magazines from the 1980s and whose relationship to clothing and adornment presented a sharp contrast to the no-nonsense 'wash and go' masculinity, which had dominated much of the nineteenth and twentieth centuries. Therefore, when considering fashion and gender it is worth asking the question: why are women associated with fashion more than men are?

Femininity and fashion

There is a strong relationship between women and fashion that is both literal and metaphorical. Women have long been associated with the making of clothes and women's prowess with textiles was one means of enhancing their reputation as ladies and suitable wives at a time when they had little economic independence from men. From the preparation of raw material (spinning, for example) to the sewing and altering of garments in the home, the manufacture of garments was for centuries in the hands of women. By the seventeenth century, needlework was thought to be 'feminine' work, unfit for men to do. Indeed, as Jones (1996) points out, stitching was thought to be morally good for women, thought to promote devotion and discipline and instilled in convent schools during the seventeenth century. She notes that women also enjoyed some control over fashion as *marchandes de modes* in the *ancien régime* of pre-Revolutionary Paris. One such *marchande de modes* was Rose Bertin, dressmaker to Marie Antoinette, whose power and influence over her famous client 'provoked considerable censure' and exorcised those who were critical of the queen's sartorial excesses (Jones 1996: 25). The blame for this extravagance was laid at the door of Bertin for provoking, tempting and exploiting Marie Antoinette's love of finery. According to Jones, it was not just the *marchandes de modes* who were thought to have considerable influence over the spread of 'frivolous' and excessive fashions, but the shop girls or grisettes who sold directly to aristocratic ladies and whose sexual jealousy of these rich women was said to 'make their rivals "pay dearly" for their pretty clothes' (1996: 44). Jones argues that by the nineteenth century these concerns about women's involvement in commercial culture helped to produce new ideologies of womanhood, which swept female merchants 'to the back room, where they could stitch and sew but never command and control' (1996: 48). Women's control over the fashion system as *marchandes de modes* was also gradually broken down by the emergence of the modern male couturier in the person of Charles Worth, who became famous in the 1850s as dressmaker to the Empress Eugénie. Therefore, female labour was progressively confined to unskilled production and later to 'sweating' and poor conditions of work and pay.

However, at least in medieval times 'woman became entwined with concepts of weaving, textile work and fashion as "feminine" pursuits' (Breward 1994: 33). These associations were 'simultaneously constricting and empowering': restricting in that they confined women to particular sorts of activity but empowering in that they gave the medieval lady power over purse strings (1994: 33). In medieval times, says Breward 'the management of the wardrobe took on a special significance ... viewed as a feminine prerogative, specifically concerned with the display of power through a wealth of textiles and the cultivation of physical beauty' (1994: 33). This power, associated with personal and social display and with the management of household expenditure, persisted for centuries as women became progressively responsible for making a home. Women's prowess in this field was seen to enhance the overall status of the household, a theme pursued by historians of the eighteenth century, who have examined women's central role in the consumer revolution. As de Grazia has suggested, women's efforts to make a home 'served to define their family's history, to signal their social position to other bourgeois, to differentiate their class from that of aristocrats and workers' (de Grazia and Furlough 1996: 19). Thus, according to Breward, women (especially bourgeois women), 'became well versed in rhetoric of clothing, its growing importance as a communicator of status, taste and gender roles' (1994: 34). This is illustrated in Vickery's study (1993) of the consumption practices of one eighteenth-century lady, Elizabeth Shackleton of Alkincoats (1726–81), who spent much time and took great pride in the artefacts she bought, recording them in her journals and letters. As far as Mrs Shackleton was concerned, shopping was a form of employment most effectively carried out by women; but it was an occupation considered 'unskilled' even though it required time, effort and a good degree of knowledge about commodities and taste. Given that women stood to inherit personal products and not real estate it is not surprising to find them investing in moveable goods, and with no paid occupation and no 'skill', Vickery suggests that it is 'small wonder if, in consequence, she turned to personal and household artefacts to create a world of meanings and ultimately transmit her history' (1993: 294).

Alongside women being associated with the making of clothes, textiles and with consumption, there has existed also a metaphorical association of femininity and the very idea of fashion. According to Jones, 'women had for centuries been associated with inconstancy and change' (1996: 35), characteristics that also describe fashion. It is also the case that, as Breward (1994) and Tseëlon (1997) note, up until the eighteenth century, fashion had been considered a sign of the weakness and moral laxity of 'wicked' women, the daughters of Eve. After this, in the more 'enlightened' eighteenth century, women's association with fashion was explained more in terms of her distinctly 'feminine' psychology (Jones 1996).

In her analysis of the relationship of femininity to fashion, Tseëlon (1997) examines how ancient myths about femininity have informed Western attitudes towards women. In particular, she examines the myths of Eve, Pandora, Lilith and the Virgin Mary. She notes that between them, these archetypal figures inform Western moral attitudes towards woman and through these 'she is portrayed as disguising behind false decoration, using her beauty and finery as a vehicle to dazzle men to their destruction' (1997: 12). This attitude has taken on a very particular complexion within Judaeo-Christian teachings; from the tales of the First Testament, through the apostolic letters of St Paul, woman has been associated with temptations of the flesh and decoration, just one of the ways in which she can ensnare men. This history of Christian Europe 'bears witness to the fact that even though finery in general was considered a vice, it became conflated with the very conception of the essence of woman' (1997: 12). At the heart of this attitude towards woman was a fear of the body which, in Christian teachings, is the location of desires and 'wicked' temptations which had to be disavowed for the sake of the soul. As a descendant of Eve, woman was perceived to be more susceptible to temptations of the flesh and could also use her body to tempt men from the path of God.

Thus the decorated (female) body is inherently problematic to Judaeo-Christian morality, but so too is the naked, or unadorned body. As Tseëlon notes, in Judaeo-Christian teachings, nakedness became a shameful thing after the Fall and, since the Fall is blamed on woman, then 'the links between sin, the body, woman and clothes are easily forged' (1997: 14). Given its associations with sexuality and sin, it is not surprising that (female) clothing is the subject of such heated debate among moralists and clergy in the medieval period. According to Tseëlon, Christianity countered its fears about woman by attempting to control her sexuality, producing a discourse of modesty and chastity in dress which became encoded into female sexuality. Christian doctrine taught that redemption lay in the renunciation of decoration and modesty in dress, a moral duty born of Eve's guilt. This was carried over to female adornment in general but with the added frisson that no amount of modesty can entirely undo the potential sexuality of the female body once encoded as such. Clothes, 'through their proximity to the body encode the game of modesty and sexual explicitness, denial and celebration of pleasure' (1997: 14). So, while they veil the body and hide its nakedness, clothes can also enhance the body and draw attention to flesh tantalisingly out of sight. This play of modesty and exhibitionism is a common one in Western culture. According to Flügel (1930), who draws on psychoanalysis to analyse clothes, humans have innate but contradictory desires for modesty and exhibitionism, which explains the purpose of clothes in the first place. Clothes represent an (inadequate) attempt to resolve this psychic contradiction and as such are a 'neurotic symptom'. Since they cannot effectively do so, they are a continual reminder of our highly developed sense of shame, becoming the 'perpetual blush on the face of mankind' (1930: 21).

If, as Tseëlon (1997) argues, women are more closely associated than men with the body, sexuality, sin and clothing, then it is understandable that they are more likely to be condemned for their dress on the grounds that it is immodest or sexually alluring. One can find particularly misogynistic diatribes on femininity and dress in the medieval writings of clergymen, as well as in the writings of later moralists of the seventeenth and eighteenth centuries. For example, she quotes Edward Cooke, who in 1678 wrote: 'a double crime for a woman to be fashion'd after the mode of this world, and so to bring her innocence into disrepute through her immodest nakedness; because she her self not only sins against shame, but causes others to sin against purity, and at the same time, renders her self suspect' (1997: 16).

From 1100 to the beginning of the seventeenth century, men's fashions were often highly erotic but it was women's immodest display that was the focus of religious and moral condemnation. Only a woman could be accused of seduction in dress. However, by condemning all forms of display, the Church 'has been instrumental in instilling into the female collective consciousness a permanent awareness of the way she appears, and the impact of her appearance on others' (Tseëlon 1997: 13). Little wonder, then, if women have developed a finely tuned self-consciousness about appearance that has nothing to do with their innate 'nature' but is a result of cultural attitudes and pressures. What is striking about this attitude to female display as seduction is that it not only holds woman responsible for her own sexual behaviour, but for man's sexual behaviour too: if a man succumbs to sexual temptation in thought or deed, it is considered *her* fault for dressing provocatively. This also explains the victim blaming that occurs when women are sexually assaulted or raped when wearing a short skirt or revealing dress (Lees 1999; Wolf 1991).

As this discussion suggests, women's fashion and dress has historically been regulated along the lines of gender and sexuality as well as the lines of social, i.e. class, distinction. However, these two often converge: as discussed in the previous chapter, sumptuary laws attempted to regulate status but, in the case of women, they also differentiate between the good, gentle wealthy woman and her 'fallen' sister, the prostitute. As Emberley (1998: 9) notes, the hierarchy of furs and social positions created by these regulatory acts also influenced notions of sexual propriety among different classes of women. At certain times prostitutes were forbidden to wear fur as a means of differentiating them from 'respectable women'. However, it is not just sexual morality that is at stake in discourses on women and fashion: women's supposed love of fashion and all that glitters and shines is equally problematic in terms of the general social and moral order. In the seventeenth century and the early eighteenth fears about the spread of luxury sometimes focused on women's supposed insatiable desire and the threat it posed to the family. A tract of 1740, for example, includes the following: 'although her children may be dying of hunger, she will take food from their bellies to feed her own insatiable desire for luxury. She will have her silk fashions at any cost' (Jones 1996: 37). Thus moral discourse gave way to other kinds of rhetoric: 'sartorial offence moved from being defined as a moral transgression to being defined as a social transgression' (Tseëlon 1997: 16). While the former was considered indicative of character flaw, the latter indicates a lack of gentility, education and civility. Moral transgression was also of great concern for both sexes but a woman might transgress moral codes in more ways than a man. By being too highly decorated she might be seen to have fallen prey to the sin of vanity. However, by the eighteenth century, women's excessive interest in fashion was thought legitimate if its aim was to please a husband or attract a suitor (Jones 1996). Indeed, for some philosophers of this period, women's interest in fashion was an inevitable result of their 'feminine' psychology. Women, it was claimed, were peculiarly susceptible to finery 'because of their heightened sense of sight and lively imaginations' (1996: 36).

While men of aristocratic birth were decorated to much the same extent as women, for much of the early modern period this simple fact did not dilute the association of fashion with femininity. Indeed, when male peacocks were criticised it was often on the grounds of 'effeminacy' for showing too great an interest in fashion. Sometimes this criticism was levelled on the grounds that male interest in fashion transgressed the rightful division of the genders. At other times, effeminacy was seen as problematic to the image of a nation. The equation of effeminacy in male attire with the diminution of national interests can be seen in Elizabethan England: in the sermon 'Homily against Excess', which Elizabeth I ordered to be read out in churches such associations are described as follows:

> yea, many men are become so effeminate, that they care not what they spend in disguising themselves, ever desiring new toys, and inventing new fashions ... Thus with our fantastical devices we make ourselves laughingstocks to other nations; while one spendeth his patrimony upon pounces and cuts, another bestoweth more on a dancing shirt, than

might suffice to buy him honest and comely aparel for his whole body
... And every man, nothing considering his estate and condition, seeketh
to excel in costly attire. (Garber 1992: 27)

As Garber notes, effeminacy here does not mean homosexuality (as it
often does today) but 'self-indulgent' or 'voluptuous' and therefore close to
'womanly' things. Criticism is levelled at the money, time and energy devoted
by the effeminate man to the feminine and trivial frivolities of fashion.
Similar criticism was directed at the 'Macaroni' style (described in Chapter 3),
which was popular among young aristocratic men of the eighteenth century.
The term 'Macaroni' appeared in an English lexicon of 1764 to describe the
style assumed by ultra-fashionable young men of noble birth. It was a rather
'foppish' style, Italianate and Frenchified, and was criticised on the grounds
that this type of gentleman had 'become so effeminate and weak, he became
unable to resist foreign threats and might even admire European tyranny'
(Steele 1999 [1988]: 31). Men have therefore not been immune to sartorial
criticism. The criticism levelled at them at various times has often been on
the grounds that they should be 'above' fashion. However, historical evidence
illustrates that men have in their own way been under the sway of fashion.

Dress and gender differentiation

If one compares clothing today with the clothing of classical antiquity or
medieval and early modern civilisations, it is possible to conclude that gender is
probably more important today and more clearly differentiated. Indeed, 'until
the seventeenth or even the eighteenth century, sexual difference in dress was
not strongly marked' (Wilson 2007: 117). Laver (1995) suggests that the more
significant division in terms of clothing has not been between genders but
between 'draped' and 'fitted' clothes. Draped clothing is the simplest method
of using cloth and involves tying a rectangle of material around the waist in
the form of a sarong, as in Ancient Egypt, or from the shoulder as in Ancient
Greece and Rome. It would seem that in these civilisations, clothing marked
out class more prominently than gender; for example, in Egypt slaves were left
almost naked as a mark of their low social status.

In medieval Europe, sexual difference was marked out more clearly through
dress, although class remained a pre-eminent feature. A prohibition on seeing
the female leg meant women's costume took the form of a long skirt or robe in
contrast to male dress, which took the form of tights or breeches emphasising
the leg. This established separate patterns of costume for men and women:
male dress in the form of bifurcated garments, tights, breeches and later
trousers; and female dress in the form of skirts or such full-length garments
as the cotte, mantle or gown. In other respects, however, male and female
dress was remarkably similar. Until around the eighteenth century, as Wilson
notes, 'for riding and sport women dressed almost exactly like men, carried

purses and daggers suspended from their belts' (2007: 118). Moreover, in terms of decoration there was nothing between the dress of men and women, with the nobility of both sexes wearing ornate clothing in rich colours and fabrics, as well as make-up, wigs and perfume. The differences in dress were therefore less significant than one might have thought and 'by the close of the fifteenth century, fashionable dress had become so fantastical and absurd that it was difficult to tell men and women at a distance' (2007: 118). Moreover, tall hats and high heels worn by both sexes would have evened out differences in height between men and women. Later, the differences became more marked, as Breward (1994) suggests, with an aggressive masculinity asserting itself in the sixteenth century in the form of excessive padding around the shoulders, legs and, indeed, the genitals of men as codpieces became ever more exaggerated and elaborate. For all the obvious differences, it is also true that for much of the sixteenth century (and indeed even the seventeenth) male and female fashionable dress often converged with elaborate ruffs and large puffed sleeves for both men and women. Jewels, ribbons, lace and embroidery also decorated the clothing of both men and women in the seventeenth and eighteenth century.

Over the course of the eighteenth century, partly because of the growing power of the bourgeoisie, excessive ornamentation, elaboration and artifice in dress was renounced in favour of a more 'natural' appearance. After the French Revolution male and female dress took on new, more relaxed contours, influenced in part by the classical republics of Ancient Greece and Rome. Wigs went out of vogue for both sexes at the turn of the century (although this was, in part, a reaction to taxes on hair powder) and hair for men became self-consciously unkempt and untidy, snatched back into a ponytail, or left loose and wild. This more 'relaxed' style began to influence aristocrats and bourgeois men alike (Steele 1999 [1988]). A relaxed country costume was adopted by some, but not all, aristocrats – breeches, riding jacket, suitable for outdoor pursuits such as hunting and fishing. It was a style of dress that was to influence the dandies of the Regency and Victorian periods of the nineteenth century. Among some aristocrats however, a rather 'foppish' style, elaborate and perfumed, still prevailed.

However, as discussed in Chapter 4, the undecorated style for men of the late eighteenth century and the early nineteenth is commonly seen to be more closely aligned to the rise of the bourgeoisie. By the end of the nineteenth century, this style had solidified into a stiff and sombre appearance for men, based largely around elements that would make up the modern three-piece suit – slim trousers, fitted jacket and waistcoat. This paring down of male dress is referred to as 'the great masculine renunciation' by Flügel (1930), who draws on psychoanalytic theories to analyse fashion and dress. According to him, at the end of the eighteenth century 'man abandoned his claim to be considered beautiful. He henceforth aimed at being only useful' (1930: 111). He suggests that the only importance clothes had for men from this point onwards was the claim to be not elegantly or elaborately attired, but 'correctly' so. The causes of this were primarily of a political and social nature: 'it is not surprising, therefore, that the magnificence and elaboration of costume, which so well expressed the ideal of the *ancien régime* should have been distasteful to the new social trend and aspirations that found expression in the Revolution' (Flügel 1930: 111–12).

According to Flügel, the fraternal, democratic spirit that swept through Europe and North America caused male dress, which had previously emphasised social differences, to emphasise solidarity and uniformity; and instead of excessive elaboration, previously separating rich from poor, there took place an increasing simplification in male dress. The cries of democracy came from a bourgeoisie who had to work for a living, whose wealth was not the product of inheritance but their own labour. Thus, whereas the aristocracy had shunned all associations with economic activity considered degrading to the dignity of gentleman (the only significant activities being leisured ones, for example riding, and hunting, possibly extending to battle), the bourgeois made work an honourable thing in itself. A renunciation of 'decadent' plumage on the part of the bourgeois male signalled one's commitment to a life of industry, sobriety and work as opposed to a life of aristocratic idleness, sloth and leisure. Kuchta (1996) agrees with Flügel that the 'great masculine renunciation' emerged out of the struggle for political power between middle-class and aristocratic men, but puts it back much further in history, arguing that it had its roots 'in an aristocratic response to the increasing diffusion of fashion in the eighteenth century and to the political culture that emerged after 1688' (1996: 56). In other words, Kuchta suggests it goes back as far as the 'Glorious' Revolution in England and not the French Revolution of 1789–92 or the Industrial Revolution of the nineteenth century.

The social, political and religious upheavals, Republican sympathies and classicism were woven into female dress of the late eighteenth century and the early nineteenth, which took on classical contours similar to that of the ancient civilisations of Greece or Rome. According to Laver (1995) and Steele (1999 [1988]), women's dress during this period was also influenced by the development of colonies that brought the European powers into contact with the simple dress of so-called 'primitive' civilisations (Steele 1999 [1988]). In particular, Napoleon's expedition to Egypt 'induced in his compatriots a new wave of Orientalism, which made turbans fashionable' (Laver 1995: 156). The dress of the period was indeed simple, a chemise or tunic, which, from 1795 until about 1815, developed successively from the Directory, through to the Consulate and Empire lines. The look was studied 'naturalness', the long line of the body and absence of a corset allowing for greater mobility. Indeed, historians often comment on the visibility of the female body at this time, arguing that 'perhaps at no period between primitive times and the 1920s had women worn so little as they wore in the early years of the nineteenth century' (Laver 1995). This simplicity of line did not last long: early in the nineteenth century corsets began to make a return in the form of long and short stays aimed at keeping a smooth, flat stomach. The classical long chemise was also soon replaced with the re-emergence of bell-shaped skirts. Over the course of the nineteenth century, changing fashions in corsetry and skirts altered the outline of the female body: crinolines, bustles, padding and a succession of different shaped corsets served to raise or lower the waist, flatten the stomach or the hips, raise or lower the bottom, pad out or flatten the bust. The crinoline made its appearance in the 1850s and was welcomed by many women for the freedom of movement it gave after the heaviness of layers of petticoats worn earlier. Among its disadvantages was that it could be a fire hazard, since the skirt could swing quite freely, and that it was also difficult to control in high wind, which created some embarrassing moments for some women. By the end of the 1860s, it was considered ugly and replaced by the long 'Princess' line of the 1870s.

During the Industrial Revolution gender differentiation in the public and private spheres became increasingly exaggerated: work was separated from the home and, although many working-class women went out to work, 'respectable' bourgeois ladies were confined to the home in the role of wife and mother (Davidoff and Hall 1987). The exaggerated emphasis on gender differentiation has been seen to translate into the dress styles of men and women, with many traditional costume histories emphasising these differences and

Figure 8. Cutaway view of crinoline costume, *Punch*, August 1856.
Source: Wikimedia Commons

neglecting some of the ways in which they converged during the late eighteenth and the nineteenth century. For example, dress of the Victorian period has been described as follows:

> men were serious (they wore dark clothes and little ornamentation), women were frivolous (they wore light pastel colors, ribbons, lace and bows); men were active (their clothing allowed them movement), women were inactive (their clothes inhibited movement); men were strong (their clothes emphasised their broad chest and shoulders), women were delicate (their clothing accentuated tiny waists, sloping shoulders, and a softly rounded silhouette); men were aggressive (their clothing had sharp definite lines and a clearly defined silhouette), women were submissive (their silhouette was indefinite, their clothing constricting). (Roberts 1977: 555)

Hence, the renunciation of decoration on the part of men is contrasted with the increasing fussiness of women's dress, particularly over the Victorian period, when decoration with lace and ribbons seemed to reach a new zenith. The silhouettes of both sexes as well as differences are also noted in terms of colour contrast (the invention of new aniline dyes in the mid-nineteenth century meant that women's dress was seen to be bright, even garish, while men in an age of dandies and industrialisation are typically depicted predominantly in black). Finally, commentators tend to associate Victorian women with the relentless movements of fashion, each new season bringing a new line that changes the contours of the female form, in contrast to men whose dress seems frozen, their clothes unyielding to the fickleness of fashion.

The question of how these differences can be explained is implicitly asked by some theorists, and the tendency is to interpret these rather simplistically. For Laver (1995), the differences can be located primarily in the 'nature' of the sexes; for Roberts (1977) and Veblen (1953), differences of dress reflect the socio-economic positions of the sexes in the nineteenth century; while for Flügel (1930), whose ideas I discuss first, the differences are the result of both the natural psychic predispositions of men and women and social and economic conditions specific to the nineteenth century. These accounts tend to gloss over many other aspects of male and female dress at the time, downplaying the many similarities and exaggerating the differences between male and female dress. Thus the fact that women's dress took on many male items of clothing during the nineteenth century is neglected, as is the fact that men's dress did not solidify into the stoical uniform of the bourgeois gent until very late in the century, succumbing to the movement of fashion, as well as giving in to some quite vivid splashes of colour for much of the century. Moreover, the discomfort of the tight, fitted male clothes is also generally overlooked. Such explanations, relying on common gendered assumptions, have been quite influential and are therefore worth considering in detail.

Figure 9. Photograph by Roger Fenton of Queen Victoria and Prince Albert, 1889 copy after an original of 30 June 1854, showing how gender was increasingly differentiated in nineteenth-century dress. Royal Collection Trust © His Majesty King Charles III 2022

Explaining the differences – a 'natural' difference

The idea of a natural difference has been used to explain differences in the dress of men and women in the nineteenth century and the early twentieth, as has the supposed difference in male and female interest in dress. As a psychologist, Flügel (1930) explains male and female dress in terms of psychic drives. He asks why men renounced their fine feathers for the sombre clothes of the nineteenth century and also ponders how men can stand the sacrifice of relinquishing decoration; given their desire for exhibitionism (which Flügel sees as a basic human drive), he wonders where it may have gone. His response draws on the idea that men and women are 'naturally' different. Women, he says, are more narcissistic than men and have a keener sense of sexual rivalry, which makes them more inclined to compete with one another for sexual attention. Therefore, 'as long as individualism is permitted, women struggle with one another for wearing the "latest" or most costly frocks' (1930: 114). Men, on the other hand, must operate in the social and political world and are therefore more likely to be affected by it. The drabness of their costume has the desired social and political effect of producing 'greater sympathy between one individual and another, and between one class and another' (1930: 114). However, since exhibitionism is a fundamental 'natural' psychic drive, the male will seek some form of compensation for its repression and will do so by displacing this desire to 'show off' onto other things. In this respect, work can act as a form of 'showing off', as can military uniform, which remained highly elaborate and decorative. He suggests that a modification in direction of this desire may occur, shifting men away from passive exhibition to active scopophilia: 'the desire to be seen being transformed into the desire to see' (1930: 118). Thus he suggests that men enjoy a 'vicarious display', in which they can enjoy and feel proud of the splendour of their woman. This displacement involves 'clearly some element of identification with the woman' (1930: 118–19) and may provide complete satisfaction in itself. However, where the projection of exhibitionism fails to satisfy male exhibitionism, 'the man may consciously seek to identify himself with a woman by wearing feminine attire', in other words, he may resort to transvestism (1930: 119).

In his discussion of male and female dress, Laver (1995) comes to similar conclusions to those of Flügel. He also suggests that women are more 'naturally' narcissistic than men and their dress exhibits what he calls the 'Seduction Principle', the aim being to enhance sexual attractiveness. He notes that, 'in general, the purpose of clothes for women has been to make them more sexually attractive and the purpose of men's clothes has been to enhance their social status' (1969: 14). So although men and women wore ruffs around the neck in the sixteenth century and although this was a status symbol for both sexes, Laver argues that for women it was also 'an attempt to exploit the wearer's charms' by drawing attention to her *décolletage*. Thus clothes play a part in attraction to the opposite sex, with men in particular looking for attractiveness in a woman.

These explanations provide examples of how the fundamental sexual differences between men and women, i.e. 'nature', are drawn upon to explain differences in behaviour, practices, roles, which feminists would argue are based in the social world. Rather than describe 'facts', explanations such as these, which suggest women are 'naturally' more narcissistic than men, reproduce social attitudes about men and women. However, these ideas are

not so much about biology or sex but gender. In particular, these explanations reproduce commonly held myths about women as seducers of men that
have their origins in Judaeo-Christian attitudes (as described by Tseëlon 1997).
There is, in fact, no evidence to suggest that women are in any way 'naturally'
more narcissistic than men and plenty of evidence to the contrary. Indeed, one
only has to look back through costume history to find that men took just as
much interest in their appearance as women and spent at least as much time
and effort. Furthermore, male dress may very well have been closely linked
to exhibitionism and erotic display: codpieces worn by men for considerable
periods in history are one item of clothing that was all about such display,
while the focus on the male leg for many centuries, with tights and breeches,
was similarly erotic, drawing attention to the male form. It could also be
argued, as Sennet (1977) has, that the *décolletage* fashionable from time to time
for women, was not about display of her 'charms' (as Laver 1995 would have
it), but before the eighteenth century provided a 'canvas' for the display of fine
jewels. By the nineteenth century, when women wore highly elaborate and
ornate clothes, it was not because of any 'natural' inclinations but more likely
the result of her limited social role. 'One only has to think of what it meant
to a Victorian girl to attract a good husband to understand the reasons for her
narcissistic proclivities. What else could she do, other than concentrate on her
appearance?' (Roberts 1977: 566).

There are also specific empirical problems with the idea of a 'great masculine
renunciation' at the end of the eighteenth century. For one thing, men did not
renounce all colour and finery at this time. Indeed, as Edwards notes, 'the
development of the dark modern suit for commerce did not start until well
into the Victorian era. Indeed, it was not until the 1880s and 1890s that the
stoic uniform of commerce really took off and, even then, the smartness of
evening dress in top hat and spats also reached its peak of popularity' (1997:
19). Moreover, once the dark suit became popular, it would have been worn
in addition to other garments. As Edwards notes, Victorian bourgeois men
would have also worn tweed walking suits, hunting jackets, seaside jackets
with bright stripes, as well as dinner jackets and velvet smoking-jackets in
rich, jewel colours, such as emerald and purple. Even the dandy would not
have been predominantly dressed in black until much later in the nineteenth
century. The Regency dandy exemplified by Beau Brummell would have worn
breeches in a buff, fawn or nut colour, a duck-egg blue or dark blue cutaway
coat, a crisp, white shirt and, on occasion, a canary-yellow waistcoat, pink
gloves or a yellow cravat (Laver 1995). It was not until the 1860s that the
dandy style, epitomised by the melancholic Baudelaire, became exclusively
black. Moreover, ornate male dress persisted in military dress, which to this
day remains brightly coloured and highly decorated (a fact that Flügel himself
recognised). However, what these examples show, and what Edwards argues, is
that the history of male dress, interpreted as the unfolding and uniform development of the dark three-piece suit, is misleading, as is the history of male

GENDER AND FASHION   159

dress that sees it as resistant to fashion. If one considers the male silhouette throughout the nineteenth century, it is possible to see a number of modifications: the introduction of breeches to replace tights in the early part of the nineteenth century and the later evolution of breeches into trousers towards the end of the century. So 'whilst it is true that fashion cycles and changes in overall form were, and to a certain extent still are, faster for women than for men, the more muted changes in decoration, detail and nuance are far more similar for each of the sexes' (Edwards 1997: 15). In fact, as Edwards notes, the overall shape of dress changed little for either sex, at least in the Victorian era, when sexual difference was marked by the wearing of either trousers or skirts. Further, while this difference was still quite marked, there was some degree of convergence between men's and women's clothing, with female dress taking on such aspects of male dress as tailored jackets from the 1860s onwards. Indeed, except for the skirt, women's walking outfits from the late nineteenth century through the Edwardian period were remarkably similar to men's.

Explaining the differences – 'social' divisions

While differences between male and female garments can sometimes be exaggerated, it is the case that the early and mid-Victorian fashions were notable for their constant gender coding. A persuasive argument for marked gender difference in the dress of the nineteenth century is put forward by Veblen (1953) and Roberts (1977). They both argue that dress conveys information about the social and economic status of the wearer and suggest that the dress of the Victorian upper class and bourgeois lady symbolised her subordinate position, symbolic of her role as 'man's chattel'. Veblen's account of fashion is based on his overall analysis of the so-called 'leisure class', the newly affluent class that emerged in the United States during the nineteenth century and attempts to re-create an 'aristocratic' way of life in the mercantile 'New World' Republic. This emerging class expressed its wealth through conspicuous consumption, conspicuous waste and conspicuous leisure; in other words, it demonstrated its 'pecuniary' strength by purchasing goods and discarding them when they were deemed out of fashion (rather than worn out) and living a leisured life (much as the life of an old-style aristocrat). Dress is a supreme example of the expression of 'pecuniary' culture, since 'our apparel is always in evidence and affords an indication of our pecuniary standing to all observers at the first glance' (Veblen 1953: 119). He suggests that the need for conspicuous consumption and waste may also explain the relentless movement of fashion. Wastefulness, he argues, is innately offensive and makes the futility and expense of fashion abhorrent and ugly. New fashions are taken up by people in an attempt to escape the futility and ugliness of fashion, with each new style welcomed as relief from the previous aberration, until that, too, in all its futility is also rejected.

According to Veblen (1953), women's dress of this milieu displays these dynamics more than men's, since the only role of the lady of the house is to demonstrate her master's ability to pay, his pecuniary strength to remove her entirely from the sphere of work. Veblen's account of the leisure class therefore constructs this upper class but *nouveau riche* woman as servile and he compares her role with that of domestic servants. These women are passive beings, 'men's chattel', and the elaborate, heavy, impractical as well as restricting clothes they wear indicate this. Their dress is also closely linked to fashion, signifying the ability to consume conspicuously and be fashionably wasteful. Moreover, the Victorian woman's dress was an important indicator of vicarious leisure: the clothes made her obviously incapable of work and were testimony to her distance from productive work as well as her consumption of leisure. Veblen describes the dress of these women as follows: 'the high heel, the skirt, the impracticable bonnet, the corset, and the general disregard of the wearer's comfort which is an obvious feature of all civilised women's apparel' (Wilson 2007: 52).

Although Veblen's account refers to the United States at the end of the nineteenth century, his analysis has been applied more extensively. Indeed, as Wilson argues, it 'continued to dominate discussions of dress by a variety of writers in the fashion history field' (2007: 53). Roberts's analysis of the Victorian lady's dress (1977) is an example of Veblenesque theorising. She argues that the heavy and restrictive dress conditioned women into a submissive-masochistic role, making her into an 'exquisite slave' who languished in her subordinate position. Her analysis focuses attention on the symbolism of the corset as the prime indicator of this submissive-masochistic position and she concentrates on the problem of the tight-lacing of corsets.

There are a number of problems with Veblen's account and these problems apply to Roberts's analysis also. Veblen is a functionalist: he begins by asking questions about why fashion emerges and what function it serves to the leisured class, concluding that it is ultimately dysfunctional, i.e. irrational. In doing so, he thereby reduces the role of fashion, failing to understand its more complex cultural and aesthetic role. However, there are further problems with their accounts of women's relationship to fashion that are worth noting here. In Veblen's and Roberts's analysis, women of a certain class are denied any sense of agency: fashion is conceived of as an over-determining and negative force in the life of the upper and middle-class Victorian woman. Both Kunzle (1982) and Steele (1985) offer a rather different view of the Victorian woman's relationship to fashion and revise the standard fashion story of the corset as oppressive to women told by Veblen (1953) and also Roberts (1977). Steele's account sets out to consider the role of erotic display in fashion, arguing that the traditional image of the Victorian woman as sexually and socially repressed 'needs to be radically revised' (1985: 3). She points to the problem of envisaging nineteenth-century fashions as literally 'enslaving' of women and twentieth-century fashions as 'liberating' when, in fact, the story is far more complex and the continuities greater than one might assume from this crude characterisation. Kunzle (1982) goes further than this, arguing that the wearing of the corset by the Victorian woman was not a sign of her servile status, but that instead, the female tight-lacer was a sexually and socially assertive woman, a social climber who used her appearance and sexuality to rise up the social ladder. Both Kunzle and Steele see the Victorian woman as an active subject and their argument is supported by historical evidence of what Victorian women did in their daily practice. (Steele, however, takes issue with Kunzle's evidence of tight-lacers; see Chapter 6.)

Victorian dress reform

Women's dress was singled out in the nineteenth century for criticism on the grounds that it was unhealthy (it was said that corsets damaged the spleen and internal organs, particularly the reproductive organs); or unhygienic (long skirts picked up mud, debris and horse manure that were a constant feature of city streets in the nineteenth century). In addition, feminist reformers condemned the way in which narrow shoulders, tight waists, and expansive and awkward petticoats constrained the locomotion of the female body. However, it was not just women's dress that was criticised as constraining; men's dress with its tight collars, fitted waistcoats and jackets was also criticised by those, such as Flügel, associated with the Men's Dress Reform Movement. Furthermore, the dress of both men and women was seen by some to be 'irrational' in that it contorted the body into 'unnatural' shapes and was driven by the 'crazy' rhythms of fashion, which were considered not just archaic to a scientific age, but wasteful and unnecessary. These reform movements came from a wide spectrum of society and were motivated by different concerns, some more progressive than others (Newton 1974; Steele 1985).

Various attempts were made in the nineteenth century to find an alternative, less restrictive female outfit. By the early 1850s, a form of dress known as the 'Bloomer' after its most famous proponent, the young American Mrs Amelia Bloomer, was received with much mirth by commentators on both sides of the Atlantic. The 'Bloomer' costume was loosely devised around an Oriental costume – a calf-length full skirt over billowing pantaloons; it was too much at odds with contemporary dress to appeal to many women at the time. Its association with Women's Rights campaigns at the time meant also that many regarded it with suspicion. However, while the Bloomer received much attention, Luck argues that it was not the first occurrence of trousered dress for women, which dates back much further than this and was 'championed by members of a number of different, but overlapping reforming constituencies, most vigorously by socialist communalists and practitioners of water-cure medicine' (1992: 201). She further suggests that among these Utopian groups, trousered dress 'provided a focus for discourses around women's physiological development, professional capacities, the nature of her sexuality, and place in nationalist politics and, as such, had anticipated most, if not all, of the questions which were to occupy the supporters of Bloomerism' (1992: 201).

The first trousers for women were worn by those American women associated with the Utopian movement of the 1820s to the 1860s. Several such communities, such as Robert Owen's New Harmony, Indiana (1825–8), were established across the United States as an alternative to industrial capitalism and devised their own uniforms. Luck (1992) suggests some possible reasons for the adoption of trousers by the women in New Harmony, not least their practicality, especially for manual work.

AMELIA BLOOMER, ORIGINATOR OF THE NEW DRESS.—FROM DAGUERREOTYPE BY T. W. BROWN.—(SEE PRECEDING PAGE.)

Figure 10. Amelia Bloomer (1818–1894), American reformer who wore full trousers for women now known as 'bloomers'. © *Illustrated London News Ltd*/Mary Evans

However, Owen's unconventional views of marriage as an equal partnership between men and women helped to associate trousered dress with sexual impropriety. Furthermore, in the mid-nineteenth century, there persisted a taboo on women's legs and trousered dress, in drawing attention to them, was considered by most as 'indecent'. Thus, 'from the mid-1850s, critics of Women's Rights could easily cash in on the identification of trousers with communal socialism and sexual unorthodoxy' (Luck 1992: 211). Trousered dress therefore failed at this time partly because it was seen to challenge a 'natural' and God-given distinction between the genders, which deemed that men should wear the trousers. This might, in part at least, explain why the Bloomer costume was so negatively received and ridiculed as 'masculine' in the 1850s by British magazines such as *Punch*. It was also criticised by clergymen such as the Revd Mr Talmadge, who 'quoted Moses from the pulpit as the authority who had forbidden women to wear men's clothes' (Newton 1974: 3). Mrs Bloomer's response similarly alluded to Old Testament imagery; 'her comment was that the first fashion was set by Adam and Eve when they assumed fig leaves, and nowhere was it stated that while Adam's were bifurcated, Eve's were not' (Newton 1974: 3). These associations did not stop other nineteenth-century dress reformers from advocating bifurcated dress for women on the grounds of health. However, those who continued to advocate this dress had to fight not just against 'public hilarity at the sight of such an eccentric dress, as has sometimes been supposed'; the real obstacles 'were the shibboleths of unrestrained female sexuality and social liberty' (Luck 1992: 211).

Working–class dress

So far, this discussion has considered how gender has been progressively marked out by dress, concentrating on the upper and middle classes of the nineteenth century. In the case of working-class women, however, the gender boundary is to some extent different. For example, bourgeois respectability reproduced a sharp differentiation of gender in terms of dress, which was not fully replicated among the industrial working classes of the nineteenth century. Analysis of working-class dress has been neglected, mostly because of a dearth of evidence. There are relatively few surviving examples of working-class costume in pictorial representations; the political economy of paintings, its exclusivity, meant that elite fashions were predominantly recorded and working-class clothes largely neglected. By the late nineteenth century this had begun to change, albeit slowly, and with the development of photography the field of vision extended to include more representations of 'ordinary' people.

One useful resource for the analysis of the (female) working-class dress in the nineteenth century are the photographs and journals of Arthur Munby. Although not a photographer himself, Munby developed a passion (a 'benign perversity' as the editor of his journals, Hudson, calls it) for recording working-class women: 'throughout his life he entered innumerable cottages to buy photographs or persuade women to come to the local village photographer's' (Hudson 1974: 77). He would commission local photographers to take pictures of milkmaids, lady's maids, pit women, farm hands and the like, and recorded his expeditions, encounters and photo sessions with these women in his journals.

Together his collections of photographs and journals provide a valuable insight into the dress and appearance of working women in the nineteenth century. These women, with their sunburnt faces and calloused hands, were quite the antithesis of the Victorian lady (in whom Munby showed no interest whatsoever) and their work clothes quite the opposite of what a 'respectable' woman would have worn. He describes meeting a pit woman as follows:

> a woman in flannel trousers, waistcoat (with livery buttons, in this case) and pink shirt and lilac cotton bonnet ... about thirty and married: hair yellow, complexion golden brown, quite clean ... A quite respectable woman ... her dress was not noticed in the streets: in Wigan, a woman in trousers is not half so odd as a woman in a crinoline. Barbarous locality. (Hudson 1974: 76)

Figure 11. Photograph of Ellen Grounds, pit worker in Wigan, with Arthur Munby, 1873. Trousered dress was acceptable for working-class women at a time when bifurcated dress was still taboo for the respectable lady. Cambridge, Trinity College, MUNB/112/1c

Barbarous indeed! Her appearance was quite striking given the standards of dress of the day. In London and in other 'genteel' provincial towns, trousers would be unthinkable for a 'lady' to wear. Respectability was so closely tied to sexual propriety that to wear trousers delineating the outline of the legs would be considered improper, immoral and licentious. However, trousers were common enough among working-class women in the nineteenth century, especially those whose work was dirty and hard. When he visited a brewery, he saw young trainee girls dressed in

> a loose cotton shirt, a waistcoat, and flannel or fustian trousers (petticoats would be in the way, as Mr. S. [the manager] says), with skirt pinned up around the waist. Cotton bonnets are worn for the outdoor work. Such a dress is very picturesque and serviceable; and being perfectly clean – not blackened as at the pits – is extremely becoming. (Hudson 1974: 76–7)

Trousers would also have been worn by actresses on the stage, although such women occupied a marginal status in society and, like working-class women, were considered not quite 'respectable'. Munby's descriptions illustrate the fact that while dress plays a crucial part in the gendering of bodies, it does not operate in isolation from class, occupation and locality. His descriptions of these women also link the body with dress – he was particularly fascinated by the 'hardness' and of the working-class female body roughened by heavy labour as well as by the 'coarseness' of their smocks and pinafores. Thus, exactly how the difference in terms of gender is marked out is dependent upon the class position, responsibilities of work and region of birth. A division between the genders, while strongly demarcated among upper and middle-class circles by the wearing of either trousers or a skirt, did not necessarily carry over into the working classes, where this boundary was, at least for female manual workers, semi-permeable.

Today class is still a salient feature in everyday dress not only in terms of specific clothes, but in terms of how dress is evaluated and judged. Class inter-sects with gender in various ways. One example, the 'chav', a term of ridicule in the British press to describe working-class people who wear prestige labels, such as the Burberry check (Renouf 2007: 75). Chav is very much a gendered term since it is most frequently applied to working-class women, such as UK celebrity Katie Price, who is often condemned for 'chavy' behaviour. As Appleford (2013: 109) argues, chav is 'often cited by middle-class women as a point of distinction, in order to establish themselves as respectable and simul-taneously create distance from any working-class connotations of sexuality and/or deviance.' Class-based perceptions of public space mean that working-class and middle-class differ in how they view items of dress and explains differences in daily dress practices. Appleford (2015) also argues that middle-class women view any public space as public and, fearful of being judged, express concerns to be dressed up and 'respectable' in public (see Skeggs 1997,

2004) while working-class women deem their immediate neighbourhood as an extension of private space, which explains why they are not embarrassed to wear their pyjamas to the supermarket. Class is a feature of how both classes of women dress and the evaluations made of their dress.

Dress and Gender in the Twentieth Century

Continuing this short history of gender, fashion, and dress, it is worth noting that while the twentieth century began with women in corsets and long skirts it ended with them able to wear bifurcated garments in public without risk of shame or censure. The same degree of freedom has not yet been afforded to men, for the most part. This shift was the result of myriad social, economic, political, and cultural developments, as well as the inevitable outcome of fashion's relentless search for the 'new'. According to Steele (1985: 224), 'the First World War was in many respects the dividing line between the nineteenth century and the modern era'. However, while female dress of the Edwardian period seems strikingly different to the looser style of dress of the immediate post-war period, one must not assume that the War caused the change in fashion. In fact, while corsets, tight bustles and heavy skirts were replaced by more flowing garments, it is also true that the designs of Paul Poiret from 1908 and 1910 'can be seen as the precursor of the Twenties look' (1985: 213). Indeed, Poiret was himself influenced by dress reform movements before the war.

Widening job opportunities for women had given them economic freedom and independence from men and are sometimes seen to have brought about a direct change in women's dress. Steele and Kidwell (1989), for example, argue that as women sought to be accepted in the man's world of business, they often adopted elements of men's clothing, for example suits and neckties, to appropriate some of the symbols associated with masculinity. However, according to Taylor and Wilson (1989), it is too simplistic to equate women in shorter skirts with full social and political emancipation. Women did not achieve the same status as men during this period and, to some extent, 'emancipation' in fashions and social mores (such as women smoking in public, or dating without a chaperone) 'served as a substitute for possibly more solid economic freedoms' (1989: 79). Furthermore, the shift in fashions for women was 'evolutionary, not revolutionary' (Steele 1985: 226). As Steele argues, while fashions may appear to change in step with the times, they are more likely the result of cyclical change within fashion than the simple reflection of social, economic or political developments beyond it.

However, attitudes were changing regarding gender. During the Edwardian era, more and more women played tennis, badminton, netball, hockey and the like, thus promoting a more relaxed, less constrained style of dress for girls and women. The look was encapsulated by the 'Gibson Girl', whose 'distinctive S-shaped body dominated the iconography of women into the

Figure 12. Edwardian dress in the early twentieth century, showing the convergence that has taken place between male and female dress. Shutterstock/Donna Beeler

1900s' (Craik 1993: 73–4) and whose attitudes and lifestyle represented the outspoken, active woman of the era and marked the beginning of the twentieth century 'cult of youth'. The bicycle also played its part, its growing popularity in the late nineteenth century and the early twentieth, giving women more freedom of mobility and gradually breaking down the taboo on bifurcated garments. Trousers, however, remained socially unacceptable for the 'respectable' woman even in the 'emancipated' 1920s. The transformations in female dress of the early twentieth century are encapsulated in the style of Gabrielle Chanel who, by the First World War, had 'begun to design some of the first modern fashions' for women (Wilson 2007: 40). Chanel's pared down style of sweaters, simple dresses and suits captured the essence of the modern woman's wardrobe, so much so that Wilson argues that 'the Chanel style was to become the paradigm of the twentieth-century style' (2007: 40).

While some of the age-old sartorial barriers were breaking for women, in menswear the story is a little different. Despite the best efforts of the French designer Jean-Paul Gautier, the skirt remains a potent symbol of 'femininity'. The taboo on men in skirts is so profound that men who dare to go in public wearing one risk ridicule. At various times this taboo is challenged. At the time of writing, a news story picks up the story of a Spanish boy, Mikkel Gomez, expelled for wearing a skirt to school in Spain. This prompted a Scottish primary school to call on male teachers and pupils to 'Wear a Skirt to School Day' in support of Gomez, which many did (Sharman 2021). However, the fact this is considered newsworthy is testimony to the strong prohibition on men wearing skirts. It is worth noting that Scotland is one country which does, already have an acceptable skirt for men in the form of the kilt.

Challenges to gendered dress

Twentieth-century dress did see some blurring of the gender boundary, particularly with the growth of sportswear. Indeed, various styles of dress have come in and out of fashion and departed from the strict gendered codes, including androgyny, unisex. The fact that such trends are marked at all indicates the extent to which dominant fashion and everyday dress still have gender differentiation as a persistent feature. While some recent fashions might appear androgynous, such styles have not abolished gender distinctions in clothing.

Indeed, androgyny has been a persistent theme in twentieth-century fashion and took on numerous forms over the course of the century. The 1920s 'flapper' and *garçonne* look, represent the first expression of something approximating to an androgynous look. Although for the Duchess of Westminster 'bosoms and hips were definitely out. A lovely figure meant a perfectly straight figure and the slightest suggestion of a curve was scorned as fat' (Steele 1985: 237); this was, says Steele, something of an exaggeration. This more masculine look caused some controversy because it represented a loosening of sexual morality; the woman of the 1920s was worldly wise and supposedly more sexually active than women of the previous generation. The conventions of feminine beauty were also challenged as fashions became 'chic and casual, very young and "semi-masculine", and certainly not traditionally "feminine" and "beautiful"' (1985: 240). Certainly, the emphasis on reed-like slenderness was new after the Edwardian 'matronly' figure and the curves of the 'S' shape. However, while the flapper with her cropped hair and straight dress was considered 'boyish' in her day, according to Wilson (1985: 239), the style was more about youth than either boyishness or androgyny. Indeed, androgyny as a concept in fashion has had an interesting history, as discussed below.

The 1950s stands out as the period that promoted a return to old-style notions of 'masculine' and 'feminine'. After the angular contours of the 1940s, when male and female silhouettes were broad shouldered, Dior's 'New Look' of the 1950s promoted a return to a Victorian shape for women, narrow waist and full

Figure 13. A 1920s 'flapper', whose haircut and loose dress exemplify the new 'boyish', youthful look of the period. Bain Collection/Library of Congress

skirt. The post-war New Look was subject to censure by some as 'wasteful' at a time when material was still scarce; it was also said to signify an ideology of femininity that put women back in the home after their war efforts. However, while the look was overtly 'feminine', the meaning of the New Look was far more complex than this, as Partington (1992) has argued. Partington examines the way in which working-class women appropriated the New Look, adapting it to their own circumstances, and argues that in modifying it, these women inflected the dress with their own meanings.

Menswear: male peacocks and the 'new man'

Gendered assumptions about the essential nature of men tended to assume men to be as less interested in fashion, a prejudice that resulted in less scholarship on men's fashion as a result. As Edwards (1997), arguing in the late 1990s, states, modern men's fashions have been largely neglected and where it received attention it was generally limited to the question of utility, omitting the nuances of male dress. The early and influential theories of Veblen (1953),

Flügel (1930) and Laver (1995), discussed above, powerfully shaped under-standings of modern male dress in terms of the renunciation of decoration in favour of the utility of the sober and constrained suit. However, as Edwards argues, 'the main example of the utility of menswear, namely the suit, is as much a symbol of masculine sexuality in terms of broadening the shoulders and chest and connecting larynx to crotch through collar and tie, as it is a practical (if historically uncomfortable) uniform of respectability' (1997: 3). Note here in this description of the suit that this form of dress is a way of shaping and exaggerating the male body, adding masculinity to it not merely reflecting some natural form beneath.

These assumptions of men's assumed uninterest in fashion have been progressively challenged since the 1990s with a growth area in scholarship on men's fashion and dress(see for example, Barry, 2015, 2019; Breward 1999; Bowstead 2018; McNeil and Karaminas 2009; Kutulas 2012; Ugolini 2007). For example, while the sober male suit has the power to convey more than 'respectability' and the desire to be 'business-like' or 'professional', these associations by no means exhaust all the possible meanings of the suit in different contexts. In his analysis of 'men in suits' in the legal profession, Richard Collier (1998) argues for consideration of male corporeality at work, suggesting that different styles of masculinity operate in legal practice but that the 'sexed specificity of this style has, in contrast to the growing literature on the corporeality of women in the profession, remained largely unexplored' (1998: 32). In other words, men's bodies are taken for granted or rendered invisible, in contrast to the attention paid to female bodies at work and in other public arenas. However, Collier (1998: 32) argues that this 'de-sexing' of men has been dependent 'on certain deeply problematic assumptions' and asks:

> does this mean that a courtroom consisting solely of men is without, or beyond the erotic? Such an argument would presume, first, that intra-male relations are asexual ... and secondly, that as sexed beings, men's eroticism is confined to the private, affective sphere.

By examining different styles of dress and corporeality at work, Collier argues that the male body at work attempts to distance itself from connotations of the body and eroticism: the suit serves the purpose of desexualising the male body, 'not in the sense of rendering men in suits beyond erotic attachment (far from it) but rather in terms of erasing the sexed specificity of the individual male body' (1998: 34). In other words, rendering 'invisible' the male body, the suit hides sexed characteristics, but more importantly, 'this body is normative within the public sphere, it has come to represent neutrality and disembod-iment' (Thornton in Collier 1998: 34).

The suit has also taken on different and more exaggerated forms in other contexts. Polhemus (1994: 17) notes how the 'zoot suit' of the 1940s was the focus of an 'extravagant use of expensive fabric', its 'luxurious accessories' loudly proclaiming, 'I've got it made.' He goes on to note that whereas for Flügel (1930) the suit declared the renunciation of decoration, for the emerging black cultural identity in American cities of the 1940s, it became 'a showy extrovert garment' (1994: 18), while other studies of the zoot suit (discussed in Chapter 4) point to its associations with race and identity.

What this discussion of the male suit highlights is two-fold. Firstly, no garment or style of dress is ever stable but is subject to fluctuating meanings and associations, which are contextual. This points to the importance, stressed in this book, of studying dress in context and as part of the practices of a group rather than merely interpreting or 'reading' it semiotically. Second, it demonstrates how clothing shapes our ways of seeing the body and in turn genders the body. There is nothing essentially 'masculine' about the suit, only dominant associations with it that convey prevalent attitudes towards masculinity that have seen it to typify men's apparent concern with utility and function, thereby constructing men as uninterested in the frivolities of fashion and clothes beyond absolute necessity. Moreover, the associated gendering of fashion as feminine, combined with hetero-normative ideas about masculinity, meant male fashion was tainted with effeminacy, which enabled the persistence of 'gendered attitudes, gender relations and gendered stereotypes concerning men, masculinity and their place in society' (Edwards 1997: 4).

That said, changing cultural forms and representation in the post-war era have gradually undermined some of the dominant associations about men as uninterested with fashion. The period from 1960s and 1970s have been seen as a significant period of change in men's fashion (Bowstead 2018; Kutulas 2012; Paoletti 2015). Referred to as the 'peacock revolution', from the mid-1960s a succession of male fashions provided alternative looks to conventional masculinity. For example, the Mod style of suit: '[T]ypified by long hair, stylish suits, short boots, [...] and vivid colours' (Kutulas 2012: 171), was characterised by 'softer fabrics and a profusion of decorative details' (Paoletti 2015: 10). This young man's style, 'represented a very direct challenge to the conformity and drabness of menswear at mid-century' (Paoletti 2015: 10) that 'both challenged and affirmed traditional markers of masculinity.' (Kutulas 2012: 171)

The 'new man' in the 1980s was another significant moment in the history of men's fashions, representing a break in traditional notions of masculinity and producing, as Frank Mort (1988, 1996) argues, opening up new representations of the male body. This new man was an amalgam of many representations and cultural developments and discussions, with much attention focused on representations in the style press and advertising, as well as retailing during this decade. This attention on men and men's fashion showed up 'the lack of previous attention to men's fashions' as well as the inadequacies of theorising around men's fashions' (Edwards 1997: 3). Whereas traditional masculinity has tended to locate it in the realm of production (i.e. work), the new man of the

1980s was seen indulging in pleasures of consumption previously associated only with 'femininity'. Nixon (1996) singles out four key sites for the 'circulation' of the new man: television advertising, press advertising, menswear shops and magazines for men. He argues that the new man was the focus of marketing, design and retailing, all of which targeted the male consumer and constructed a range of masculinities from products made increasingly available for purchase on the high street. In the 1980s menswear increased significantly with the growth in retail of 'flexible specialisation', which allows for greater market differentiation in products. High-street stores such as Next were at the fore of these developments, bringing quality fashion garments with strong design to the high street and 'average' male consumer. The growth and importance of design was also reflected in the rise of style magazines for men such as Arena and GQ, which opened up new, differentiated forms of masculinity. A 'striking feature' of such magazines was 'the sheer volume of visual representations of men' (Nixon 1996: 167).

These representations challenged conventional representations of masculinity up to that point, with a more overt eroticisation of the male form, particularly in relation to the female gaze (as opposed to the homosexual gaze). Masculinity, once uncharted and unquestioned, has now become the subject of inquiry, not just by academics, but by the press. Since the 1980s and the supposedly 'narcissistic' but also 'caring' male, we've seen other depictions of masculinity as in the 'new lad', which emerged in the 1990s as a backlash to return to conventional masculinity orientated towards football and sex (Crewe 2003; Bowstead 2018). While it is tempting to see such representations as a 'mirror' that reflects reality, it is more useful to think of them as constructive of identity, shaping our ways of seeing and understanding gender. Mort (1996) argues, that this 'new man' was 'certainly not mere chimera'; instead, he suggests that 'the debate over men's changing roles was concretised in a wide variety of settings' with the realm of consumption playing a key role as the place where such debate about masculinity was given an 'extended hearing' (1996: 17). He goes on to examine how, in the 1980s, 'the dynamics of the marketplace occupied a privileged place in shaping young men's wants and needs' (1996: 18). Cultural studies' analysis of the 'new man' and later discussions of 'lads' marked the beginning of serious examination into men and consumption that has grown exponentially in recent years. Significantly, an entire journal, Critical Studies in Men's Fashions, launched in 2013, is now dedicated to the study of men, masculinity, fashion and dress.

Traditional notions of masculinity have also centred on changing norms of sexuality often challenged through pop music. Many of these musicians, such as Bowie or Boy George, challenged the standard conventions of masculine self-presentation and sexuality. Their exaggerated costumes, elaborate hair and dramatic make-up were the antithesis of conventional sobriety associated with masculinity, wearing make-up, nail varnish, hair ribbons and skirts, provocatively playing with conventions, not just of gender, but sexuality too.

Whereas heterosexuality has been the standard to which all masculinity has aspired, Boy George (and also David Bowie before him) brought to the fore from previously underground sexualities a style suggesting both homosexuality and transvestism. The term 'gender-bending' was used at the time to describe the ways in which such taboos concerning (largely male) self-presentation challenged the basic conventions of gender. Oddly enough, however, neither Mort, nor Nixon or Edwards gives any space to popular music in their analyses of masculinity, choosing instead to focus on the 'mainstream' development of the 'new man' in the growth of men's lifestyle magazines and retailing. This may have something to do with the fact that these styles had little impact upon mainstream male fashions and the consumption practices of the average 'man in the street'; indeed, these pop stars had more young girls than young men as their principal fans.

The growing research on men's fashions represents an unfixing of the historical connections between fashion and femininity. Ugolini's (2007) study of men and menswear consumption from 1880 to 1939, and McNeil and Karaminas's (2009) edited collection demonstrates some of the range and depth of analysis on men and fashion. Although much academic attention around men's dress remains focused on subcultures and spectacular dress, there is greater acknowledgement of the more 'ordinary' aspects of male sartorial display, as Barry's (2019) work has done.

Challenges to the gender binary: androgyny and unisex clothing

One of the significant trends in fashion, especially promoted by subcultures and pop stars has been androgyny. Androgyny overtly plays with the gender dichotomy and fashion editorial statements and representations and has come in and out of style over the twentieth and twenty-first centuries. It was in the early part of the twentieth century, that androgyny became mainstream and popular with the garconne and flapper style that saw women cut their hair and wear straighter lines that did not emphasise hips and bosom. Then, over the course of the twentieth century, various influences from pop music (from glam rock in the 1970s to New Romantics in the 1980s), to film and subcultures, especially in the gay and lesbian communities, have seen androgyny come in and out of style. The 1960s and 1970s saw successive waves of androgenous dress. For example, in Woody Allen's film *Annie Hall* (1977) the central character, Annie, played by Diane Keaton is famously dressed in men's shirts, coats and a tie, while there are many examples in 1980s pop music of male stars wearing makeup and feminine ruffs, even skirts (as Boy George did). A few female pop stars similarly popularised androgenous styles, such as Suzi Quatro and Grace Jones. Often picking up these trends, fashionable clothing and fashion editorials show female models wearing menswear or male models wearing makeup. Some fashion designers, like Jean Paul Gautier, famously put men in skirts on the runway.

However, these examples highlight the problem of androgynous style; it only works by keeping in place male and female styles of dress as the norm. Annie's choice of masculine dress does not challenge the gender binary as she is evidently still a woman wearing masculine clothing. Meanwhile, the elaborate and subversive styles worn by male pop stars is never fully embraced by men in their everyday dress but remains an extreme and newsworthy subversion of male dress. In terms of fashion editorials, androgyny is usually always playing with the gender dichotomy, in ways that maintain the gendered styles of dress that remain clearly coded as 'masculine' or 'feminine'. Therefore, while androgyny has dipped in and out of fashion, it merely played at the boundaries of gender, which have otherwise been accentuated at other times. In her book on unisex fashions, Paoletti (2015: 6) argues, '[F]or the most part, androgyny meant more masculine clothing for girls and women. Attempts to feminise men's appearance turned out to be particularly short-lived.'

Indeed, what does unisex fashion truly look like? While Paoletti, uses the term unisex as a synonym for androgynous, in fact, I would argue that unisex is, perhaps, the more radical of the two terms. If one could imagine unisex clothing – clothing that is truly marketed and worn by both men and women without distinctions between them – this could potentially do away with the idea of male and female fashions and eliminate industry practices for menswear and womenswear Collections, departments and clothing stores. However, this has not yet happened: the gender dichotomy lives on through these industry distinctions and we are no closer to having unisex clothing a quarter of the way into the twenty-first century than we were at the start of the twentieth century.

Cross-dressing, unisex, and transgender challenges

Gender norms of fashion and dress, promoted by industry categorisations, strongly regulate dress practices but there are many instances historically of challenges to these gender conventions. Some of these challenges come in the form of subcultural practices that sit at the margins of dominant culture, such as historic case studies of cross-dressing and transvestism, as well as recent trans debates, as well as cultural shifts and changes within the fashion industry with trends for androgyny and unisex fashion. Indeed, the industry has responded to cultural shifts in gender and calls by queer and trans people to be gender neutral.

Of all these developments, cross-dressing has the longer history within Western fashion, and it is an interesting phenomenon as it exposes the arbitrary nature of gender conventions. Garber (1992) has examined both the 'fact' of cross-dressing in its different contexts (from medieval saints to contemporary pop stars) as well as the recurrent fascination with it in the West (see also Suthrell 2004). Cross-dressing cuts into debates about sexuality and illustrates the difficulty of separating it from gender. For example, cross-dressing has been a recurrent theme in lesbian culture and been considered a sexual perversion or disorder. Cross-dressers are also sometimes referred to, historically, as transvestites. However, such classifications are not only problematic, but they are resisted by the very constituency they seek to classify. Given its close association with underground and marginal sexualities, Garber examines cross-dressing's historic connections, bound up with 'homosexuality and gay identity, from "drag" to "voguing" to fashion and stage design, from the boy actors of the English Renaissance stage to Gertrude Stein and Divine' (1992: 4; see also, Karaminas 2013). However, she argues that no account of cross-dressing should restrict itself to the gay and lesbian community, since it frequently crosses over into high culture and mainstream popular culture. Cross-dressing was a feature in Renaissance literature, as well as in nineteenth and early twentieth-century novels: e.g. Virginia Woolf's *Orlando* is centred on a cross-gendered character, while Honoré de Balzac's *The Girl with the Golden Eyes* and Théophile Gautier's *Mademoiselle de Maupin* both feature cross-dressing female characters, who subsequently masquerade as men to woo female lovers. Cross-dressing has been a recurring theme in popular culture also: films such as *Some like it Hot*, *Tootsie* and *Mrs Doubtfire* saw famous male actors, Jack Lemmon, Tony Curtis, Dustin Hoffman and Robin Williams in drag. For Garber (1992: 10) 'one of the most important aspects of cross-dressing is the way in which it offers a challenge to easy notions of binarity, putting into question the categories of "female" and "male", whether they are considered essential or constructed, biological or cultural.'

Gender is one of the more 'plastic' aspects of identity; it is no surprise that it is open to playful sartorial negotiation. Indeed, Suthrell's (2004: 2–3) analysis of cross-dressing makes this point:

> clothing is unusual in artefactual terms because it allows us to play – temporarily or permanently – with identity and self-image. It can fix us into the gendered space we occupy on a daily basis as we get dressed or [...] it can function as the means by which gender is slipped on and off.

She asserts that a study of cross dressing does more than examine a rather minority pursuit but 'highlights key areas of the ongoing discourses on sex, gender and sexuality [...] it illustrates how fundamental aspects of our lives – the lived realities of men and women – differ, and why it matters' (2004: 2).

According to Garber, what cross-dressing produces is a crisis in the traditional binary division of male and female, masculine and feminine. Increasingly, attention is being paid to the idea of a 'third term', a third sex whose very existence calls into question the stability of the categories of 'male' and 'female'. However, all too often, says Garber, cross-dressing, which she often refers to as transvestite, is appropriated 'as' one or other of the sexes: it is assumed to be either a male or female phenomenon but for Garber, this denies or underestimates the practice, which she argues produces a third term which 'is not a term', or even a sex but a 'space of possibility' for the diminution or disappearance of gender (1992: 11). She goes on to note that the third term is always a space of negation – it signals something that is not rather than something that is, as in the case of the 'Third World', which has no unity beyond the fact of its being not the First or the Second World. This negation of the fixed categories of male and female makes cross-dressing so potent: as she puts it, 'transvestism is a space of possibility structuring or confounding culture; it is the disruptive element that intervenes, not just a category crisis of male and female, but the crisis of category itself' (1992: 17). Gamman and Makinen (1994) are not so confident that cross-dressing is always and necessarily transgressive, since much depends on the context in which drag is worn. This is echoed by Hotchkiss (1996), who argues that transvestism can sometimes confirm traditional order and. at other times overturn it or remain an ambiguous trope. Gamman and Makinen are also critical of Garber's failure to make a distinction between cross-dressing and transvestism. The former may be undertaken by individuals for all sorts of social reasons; for example, women in medieval times right through to the early twentieth century cross-dressed to experience greater social mobility than that normally allowed for their own sex (Hotchkiss 1996; Wheelwright 1989). Unlike Garber, Gamman and Makinen argue that transvestism is distinct from cross-dressing in that it is linked to sexual pleasure, where the transvestite experiences sexual arousal when wearing the clothing of the opposite sex, a pleasure akin to sexual fetishism. Similarly, Woodhouse (1989) argues that there is a difference between the cross-dresser and the transvestite based on the latter's desire to 'pass off' as a woman; cross-dressers, by contrast, aim to draw attention to the artificiality of their appearance. The distinction between the cross-dresser and the transvestite is explored further in Chapter 6, as is the topic of sexual fetishism.

Masquerade, gender exaggeration and ambiguity

Cross-dressing reveals the arbitrariness or masquerade of gender: if femininity can be put on at will by men, and masculinity worn in the style of 'butch', or by 'drag kings', then gender is stripped of its naturalness and shown to be a set of culturally regulated styles. Gender is thus dislocated from the body and shown to be performed through style: femininity and masculinity are not the product of female or male bodies and there is no natural connection between female bodies and femininity or male bodies and masculinity. However, if this is the case, it is not just cross-dressers who perform gender and wear drag; we all do, since all dress has only an arbitrary relationship to 'natural' sex: *all* of us (cis) men and women performatively reproduce gender through their dress and bodily deportment.

Judith Butler's (1990, 1993) notion of performativity offers a radical critique of the sex/gender binary challenging the idea of natural sex upon which gender norms are built, calling into question the very notion of sex. She argues that heterosexuality is the 'regulatory framework' for organising bodies and desires into two sexes. Sex, like gender, is shown to be cultural with no essential properties. Indeed, the closer one examines biological sex, the harder it becomes to define. For every specified natural characteristic thought to define the categories of man/woman (chromosomes, hormones, reproductive organs) there are numerous naturally occurring anomalies and many people who display biological features of both male and female bodies. The male/female two-sex model construes to create (define, assert, enforce) two-sexed bodies rather than assign a third sex. The question asked of new parents, 'is it a boy or a girl?' is just one of the many ways in which bodies in most (but not all) societies reinforce and reproduce the two-sex model demanded by compulsory heterosexuality. The two-sex model is held in place in other declarations, discourses, and practices: sex as well as gender is performative, reproduced through endless iterations. In this way, Butler uses the idea of performativity to 'make trouble' by subverting commonly held ideas about sex/gender. It is also a political strategy: if the sexed body only gains its meaning through the performances of gender that are culturally regulated according to heterosexual ideology, they can be undone or challenged. Butler's work has been foundational in 'queer theory', which examines the way in which sexual desire has been historically and culturally constructed. For queer theorists, language marks out and defines sexuality, which has important implications for gender identity.

Butler's ideas about performativity can be traced back to earlier theorists, although she departs from them in important respects. The psychoanalyst Joan Rivière (1929) has been particularly influential in suggesting that gender is performed through dress and body style. Her famous essay 'Womanliness as Masquerade', written in 1929, argues that women working in jobs considered 'masculine' or women with 'masculine ambition' had to hide behind a façade of 'femininity' so as to avoid retribution by men: 'womanliness therefore could be assumed and worn as a mask, both to hide the possession of masculinity and to avert the repercussions expected if she was found to possess it' (1986: 39). These women, often successful, professional women, therefore adopted in exaggerated form, the signifiers of 'femininity' and might behave in a flirtatious manner with men they encountered. This exaggerated performance allayed some of their anxieties about their femininity and their desire for masculinity. However, crucially, she suggests that there was no simple distinction between 'real womanliness' and a 'masquerade of femininity': 'the reader may now ask how I define womanliness or where I draw the line between genuine woman and the "masquerade". My suggestion is not however, that there is any such difference; whether radical or superficial, they are the same thing' (Rivière 1986: 39).

The woman who acts in exaggerated feminine fashion is also sometimes referred to as a 'homeovestite': a 'manly' woman who covers her tracks with a quintessentially feminine performance. The women who might fall into this category include Pamela Anderson, Dolly Parton or even Barbara Cartland, who exaggerate, almost parody, femininity. The difference between Butler's and Rivière's ideas is that whereas Butler challenges the very category of sex, Rivière remains at the level of gender in her analysis, leaving intact the binary male/female. However, despite these differences, Rivière and Butler both illustrate the way in which body styles and styles of dress work to construct gender that is cultural rather than natural.

Transgender politics

Trans politics owes much to the ideas developed by Butler and others, as it sets out to challenge the very idea of natural sex, which underpins the sex/gender distinction. In doing so, transgender politics challenges the very category of woman central to feminist debate and political action. If sexed bodies are not natural but cultural – if there is no sex only gender – then there is no natural basis or reality to the biological woman. Since feminists of the second wave have historically claimed women are oppressed *because of biology* (women's role in reproduction controlled by men and restricting their roles in society), the dismantling of sex makes much 'gender trouble' for feminism and feminist politics as well, according to Butler. Indeed, contemporary transgender politics has brought to the fore tensions between second-wave feminists and the trans community over what the ontological (being) claims to be 'woman'. Sometimes referred to today as 'gender-critical' feminists argue the importance of retaining some sense of a natural, biological woman – gender identity based on sex – as opposed to those who argue that gender identity should be based on identification and do not see sex as a stable category with any innate qualities or ontological basis in nature. These debates have been vitriolic in recent years with the author J. K. Rowling at the centre of Twitter controversies over her assertions as to the idea and rights of biological women.

The complexity of transgender identity and politics can be examined through the ways trans identities are expressed through dress and bodily deportment. Not all trans identities are disruptive of dominant understandings of sex and gender. Indeed, some ways of understanding trans identity still place emphasis on the ontology – of *being* a particular body – that depend upon the idea of 'authenticity'. This is salient in the 'wrong body paradigm', which dominates much popular discussion of transgender people with respect to how they experience their bodies/identities. For example, Lovelock (2017: 676) argues that the dominant narrative, at least in the US and Britain, is the idea that 'transgender people possess an authentic gendered core, which is located within an initially mismatched corporeality'. Lovelock takes the example of Caitlin Jenner whose transformation from Bruce Jenner was revealed in a fashion spread in *Vanity Fair* and displayed through conventional feminine tropes, 'delicate "natural" make-up and perfectly coiffed hair' (2017: 675) as well as through breast implants and other surgeries. The 'wrong body paradigm' shapes the reading of Jenner's new body and identity as revealing a 'natural' truth that does not challenge sex. That is to say, the claim is simply that Jenner's body was wrongly sexed, while her newly aligned body conforms to conventional gendered norms of feminine embodiment. Indeed, Lovelock sees this paradigm as *consolidating* normative conventions of gender through the 'construction and maintenance of a beautiful feminine appearance' (2017: 676) necessary to be an 'authentic' (trans or cis) woman. As Lovelock (2017: 677), argues, while theoretical debate conceptualises trans as 'occupying a potentially resistant, disruptive or subversive position in relation to the essentialised categories of binary gender', the 'wrong body paradigm' highlights how representations of trans people can also do the opposite. Representations of Caitlin Jenner articulate the idea of an essential femininity that is expressed through the body and beauty work. Such feminine beauty work is not transgressive but conforming to the oppressive 'beauty myth' (Wolf 1994) that has strait-jacketed (cis) women for centuries.

In this way, trans is not automatically challenging to gender, it only has *potential* to unsettle gender norms and ideas. Trans is 'a battleground' according to Brice (2021: 303), with trans bodies conceptualised as either inherently 'subversive or regressive'. Clearly, celebrity transwomen, such as Caitlin Jenner, need to be distinguished from transgender activism, much of it challenging the dominant gender binary. The problem for Lovelock is that gender is seen as either innate (sex) or externally imposed (gender) so that '[A]ttempts to theorise gender identity through social construction, discursive performativity, or embodied phenomenology all make the error of reducing gender (or sex as its corollary) to an attribute of pre-given individuals' (2021: 303). Instead, Lovelock invites us to see gender not as the property of the pre-given individual but as 'a field of tensions and possibilities' (2021: 303). Individuals draw on these possibilities in their social encounters in the production of themselves as gendered, but '*gender remains a property of their relationship with the collective, rather than a property of the individual per se*' (Brice, 2021: 303 [emphasis added]).

Adopting this approach to bodies and gender means that we can look at the ways trans individuals encounter the distributed field of gender and see how they manifest 'certain dispositions, affinities, aptitudes, and capacities which make up style as much as the wearing of clothes and accessories' (Brice 2021: 303) without pointing to some pre-existing origin or natural state. Applying this alternative way of understanding (trans)gender, we can consider how Jenner's expressions of her new identity draw upon conventions of femininity. This conceptualisation avoids essentialising narratives about original or authentic identity because it emphasises gender identity as a *process*, shifting away from '*being* to *becoming*' (ibid: 303). This approach side-steps the problem of the origins of trans in the idea of an essential/biological pre-given reality to consider instead the ways in which trans lives are lived and expressed and come into being. If gender is not the attribute of individuals but a collective set of properties, we focus attention on the gender machinery itself.

One final thought relating queer politics and transactivism to fashion is to note how, in recent years, these debates have sought to challenge and change the narrative about gender within the fashion industry, so closely part of the machinery of gender norms and conventions with its many practices such as menswear, womenswear, male and female Collections, stereotypical representations of gender, etc. The industry is slowly waking up to these challenges. For example, many transgender models, such as Andrej Pejic, have gained prominence in recent years. Pejic has walked in both male and female runway shows, a testament to at least some blurring of the distinction between male and female clothing lines, male and female modelling distinctions, and practices of masculine and feminine styling. A new generation of fashion designers openly celebrate trans identity.

Figure 14. An example of trans-fashion, 'The Groom' from design house NARCISSISM.

For Santana Queirós, owner of House of NARCISSISM (narcissism on Instagram), the brand was 'conceived as an activistic, political act – and only secondly fashion-driven. The main goal was to create a sustainable platform to showcase the biggest range of trans individuals to customers' (interview with author). However, it is also true that such exceptions to the norm receive such attention precisely because they are rare.

Gender and fashion: fashion studies in the twenty-first century

The rise of fashion studies in recent years meant some changes in scholarly debates about gender and critique of fashion: where once feminists were antagonistic to fashion, certainly in the 'second-wave' movement, recent scholars are more likely to see it as resource for performance and play with identity, with some making direct challenge to the historical animosity of the women's movement towards fashion and beauty (Black 2004; Scott 2005). This is not to say that fashion is no longer criticised, just that it is not, de facto, always seen as a problem for feminists. In recent years, fashion has been centre stage in public and scholarly critique around the issue of industry images of the female body, either as 'unrealistic' or 'unhealthy', captured by the waves of media anxiety concerning 'size 0' models. While space does not allow me to go into much detail here on this, it is worth noting that some recent academic attention has moved the debate on from simple critique of images of fashion representations, vis-à-vis the skinny fashion model body, typical of some second-wave feminist critique (Shaw 1995; Morris et al. 2006; Prabuet al. 2002) to analysis of a range of broader social questions as to the rise, significance and structure of modelling itself.

A growing scholarship on modelling as a distinct area of fashion studies literature that connects fashion modelling to broader questions and analysis of work, gender, race and so on (see Entwistle and Slater 2012 for a detailed discussion). As Basberg Neumann (2012: 138) argues, the post-linguistic turn has meant the 'analytic division between the model industry and its representations on the one hand, and the models themselves on the other' has opened up, with scholarly interest examining a range of issues concerning fashion, gender, work and consumption (Brown 2011, 2012; Entwistle 2002, 2004, 2009; Evans 2005, 2008; Mears 2008, 2011, 2012a, 2012b; Mears and Finlay 2005; Wissinger 2007a, 2007b, 2009 and 2015). Some of this is historical analysis of the development of modelling agencies and their role within wider consumer culture; for Brown and for Wissinger it is within the context of North America, while for Maynard (1999, 2012) it is the slightly later developments in modelling within the Australian context. Alongside this, there is a growing interest in understanding the nature of work inside this world, with Mears' (2011, 2012) and Basberg Neumann's (2012) ethnographic analysis based in part on their own experiences as a model, attending to the routine work practices, relationships and pressures of fashion modelling.

There remain important questions *vis-à-vis* the way in which fashion operates and disseminates ideas about gender and the body – a less than squeaky clean industry, which has, quite rightly, been subject to some media scrutiny in terms of how it treats often very young women (and men). But the questions go much deeper than this, to examining the nature of this gendered work, the gendered performances it sustains, the different forms of aesthetic labour, and so on. My own work (Entwistle 2002, 2004; see also, Entwistle and Mears 2012), for example, looked specifically at male models and the ways in which they perform their gendered identity in a female-dominated occupation that celebrates and rewards women for looking attractive but places less value, untypically, on men. As I have argued, then, however 'plastic' gender may be, heteronormative gender performativity retains its grip on every day and routine practice, even while non-traditional work pushes at the boundaries of gender norms.

Conclusion

While many in Western societies are questioning the gender binary 'male/ female', at least in terms of dress (as well as many other aspects of social life) conventions still reproduce the distinction. Almost all clothing still carries a baggage of associations with either 'masculinity' or 'femininity' and attempts to blur these associations (fashions for men in skirts, for example) are only ever tokenistic or subversive with respect to the dominant conventions. Women's fashions are more fluid than men's fashions but even here, any trend towards suits, angular shapes or coarser fabrics are described as 'masculine' or sometimes 'androgynous', both of which point to the importance of gender as a way of making sense of fashion. Garments are still gendered too: the skirt, is the most heavily gender-coded garment in the West, worn almost exclusively by women. Understanding dress as situated practice means seeing how particular situations demand gendered different codes and norms. Gender is therefore a fluctuating phenomenon, differently denoted according to the specific social contexts. I have suggested here that gender intersects with class, while other factors and settings, such as peer group and occupation, etc., which all make different distinctions of gender accordingly. Gendered dress is sometimes explicitly enforced in the dress codes of certain occupations, or can be more subtly enforced by social convention, as in the case of certain professional occupations where a skirt is 'preferred'.

In sum, we might want to believe that gender is a less salient feature today. However, if we think back to elite, aristocratic fashions of earlier centuries that did not mark gender differentiation as strongly in terms of silhouette, we could argue that gender is more noticeable in dress than it used to be. So, while fashions are blurring today, the boundaries of gender are still tangibly in place as gender remains a significant component of our experience of our bodies. Even as transgender debates and activism set out to challenge the gender binary, dominant representations and dominant structures within fashion and beyond, distinctions between male/female, masculinity/femininity in fashion continue to play on gender, even while it periodically deconstructs it.

6
Identity: Fashion, Adornment and Sexuality

If adornment is close to the body, it would seem to go without saying that it is close to sexuality. Modern sexuality is rooted in our (sexed) body, making the things we use to decorate our bodies, potentially at least, sexually charged. Moreover, since our bodies are the location of sexual feelings, it is no surprise to find the properties of adornments, the feel of cloth or the smell of leather, linked to bodily pleasures and eroticised, even fetishised. Steele (1985: 9) goes as far as to argue that 'because clothing is intimately associated with the physical body, at the deepest level all clothing is erotic', as is the 'quest for beauty' which is an inherent feature of fashion. However, it would be misleading to assume that bodily adornments such as clothes, jewellery, tattoos simply reflect a pre-sexed and pre-sexual body; in fact, they do much more than this, they embellish the body, infuse it with sexuality. The materials commonly used simultaneously cover and reveal the body, adding sexual meanings to the body that would otherwise not be there. It is often said that nakedness is uninteresting, not 'sexy', while clothing adds a mystery to the body that makes it more provocative. The imagination is an important component in sexuality and clothing which keeps parts of the body hidden can stimulate fantasy and increase sexual desire: indeed, striptease depends upon the mystery of clothes and the imagination of the viewer which are negated once all is revealed.

Clothing is linked to eroticism if we take eroticism to be an 'aspect of inner experience as contrasted with animal sexuality' (Bataille 1986: 29); in other words, if we take it to refer to feelings and passions of the imagination. Animals may have sex but they do not eroticise; only humans with their subjective and imaginative qualities do so. According to Bataille (1986: 29), the decisive factor in the human erotic experience is 'an intangible aspect [...] not an objective quality' of the chosen loved object. If eroticism is imaginative and subjective, this may explain why the erotic objects of others are not always appealing to someone on the 'outside' of the experience (it is not just beauty that is in the eye of the beholder). This is true of all erotic experience: we might find our desires increased by certain items of clothing and we might find our own experience of sex enhanced using clothes. This may explain why nudist camps have little 'erotic' appeal to most: indeed, nudism is not associated with the sexual body but some notion of the 'natural' body. That clothes 'add' sexuality to the body is further evidenced by the fact that nudists will often wear some form of adornment for evening social events as a prelude to a sexual encounter. So, as Steele argues, 'by concealing the body, clothes excite sexual curiosity and create in the viewer the desire to remove them' (1985: 42). Clothes and other bodily adornments are part of the vocabulary with which humans invent themselves, come to understand others and enter meaningful relationships with them. It would therefore seem inevitable that they are incorporated into the vocabulary of desire and into the imaginative, erotic encounters one has with others. Fetishism provides a particularly extreme case where the object of choice, be it a person, article of clothing, piece of fabric or shoe, is transformed in the imagination of the fetishist who endows the object with special powers. However, fetishism exists on a continuum of sexual behaviour; for most people, whether fetishists or not, clothing and adornment play an important feature in erotic life because of their ability to stimulate the imagination.

In this respect, it is not surprising to find fashion obsessed with sex. Fashion, says Steele, is 'a symbolic system linked to the expression of sexuality – both sexual behaviour (including erotic attraction) and gender identity' (1996: 4). Fashion frequently plunders 'underground' sexual subcultures (which as a result are no longer entirely 'underground') and the iconography of sadomasochism and fetishism now reaches the catwalk and the high street. In this respect, Steele argues that 'to understand contemporary fashion, it is crucial to explore fetishism' (1996: 5). Fashion has also drawn inspiration from gay and lesbian subcultures in its exploration of gender and sexual identity. In addition, the paradox of the sexually ambiguous transvestite has reached the attention of the mainstream media and produced a growing awareness of the sexual ambiguity of clothes.

In this chapter, I explore these associations between fashion, adornment, and sexuality. I use the term 'adornment' deliberately since it is equally applicable to cosmetics, jewellery such as earrings, ankle chains, naval and nipple rings, tattoos and other bodily embellishments and the role they play in the expression of sexuality. Adornments such as these, while coming in and out of fashion, have in some cases a close relationship to sexual behaviour and practices, and can be linked to an erotic act, a sexual predilection, or a sexual identity (homosexuality, transvestism or sadomasochism for example). In this chapter I suggest some of the ways in which clothing and adornment come to play a part in articulating sexual desires, sexual orientation and, indeed, sexual identity. However, as noted in the previous chapter, sexuality is a complex word, which is closely interlinked with sex and gender. It is therefore necessary to define this difficult and ambiguous term before examining the ways in which adornment can be linked to the behaviour and practices, ideas and representations of sexuality.

Sexuality, Bodies and Dress

Sexuality is a modern construct. The word did not emerge until the mid to late nineteenth century and took some time to gather all its contemporary meanings. Bristow (1997), referring to the Oxford English Dictionary, summarises some of the earliest uses of the word and notes how it developed alongside a growing Victorian preoccupation from the 1860s with classifying sexual types, such as homosexuals and bisexuals, within the context of normative heterosexuality. This Victorian obsession gave birth to sexology as a body of knowledge that seeks to understand sexuality and that started its project by producing typographies of sexual desires considered pathological, such as sadomasochism and nymphomania, as well as homosexuality and bisexuality. The word sexuality is closely related to sex, although that too is a difficult word to define since it can refer to an act (as in 'to have sex'), or to a set of anatomical characteristics (as in 'male' or 'female'). However, ironically, while linked to the sex and the reproductive capacities of men and women, sexuality, as a modern construct, is the product of the increasing separation of coitus from reproduction. Sexuality today is more than the sum of sex. It is closely linked to eroticism – to ideas, fantasies, desires, quite independent of the actual sex act or any imperative to reproduce. Thus, as Horrocks (1997: 1) notes, sexuality embraces a wide range of human existence which makes it 'not a simple or uniform phenomenon'.

The modern fascination with sexuality also owes much to psychoanalysis: we live in an age still dominated by the theories of Sigmund Freud, who proposed sex as the core of our identity, the key to a life of happiness and fulfilment. For Freud, babies are born with 'drives' focused on their bodily needs and pleasures. As well as finding pleasure in the satisfaction of basic bodily needs, babies exhibit the drive to be looked at and the drive to look. The libido for looking holds the key to understanding the development of our gendered identities, as well as providing an explanation for the potency of dress in terms of sexual desire. For Freud, boys and girls start out with a desire to look at the body and see the 'hidden' organs. It is this libido for looking that eventually catapults the boy through the Oedipal and castration complexes, since it is with looking that one comes to the recognition of sexual difference. Thereafter these drives, the voyeurism and exhibition, acquire a gender: boys develop a desire for looking and girls a desire to be looked at. For Freud, this split comes with the acknowledgement of castration when the boy, metaphorically, if not literally, stares up the skirt of the woman, and recognises her 'lack'. The shock of this realisation can be traumatic for boys, who may later come to develop different strategies to cope with this: the adult male may attempt to reduce the potential threat and fear of castration by repressing or compensating for the fact of castration. This might take the form of punishment of woman for her 'lack' and the trauma it produces, or by adding embellishments to the body of the woman. In the first instance, the shock is relieved through obsessive looking, or voyeurism, which fixates on, and interrogates, the body of the woman, often resulting in some kind of humiliation or punishment. In the second instance, it results in an obsessive fixation with a particular female body part, such as the feet, or object associated with it, such as shoes, which serve as a penis substitute. Often the fetish object is chosen because of its proximity, temporally or spatially, to one's first sexual memory: shoe fetishism, for example, is sometimes explained by reference to its close association to the experience (real or imagined) of being on the ground looking up a woman's skirt.

Foucault's first volume on the history of sexuality (1979) examines the Freudian legacy and the way in which sex became a topic of considerable debate during the Victorian era. He argues that sexuality was 'put into discourse' through endless prohibitions with the effect of producing sexuality as an important aspect of one's identity. Given its historical contingency, Foucault is critical of the common-sense idea that sexuality is a natural force, transcending time and place. On the contrary, he asserts that sexuality is not a force (which can either be repressed or liberated, as Freudian psychoanalysis and some Marxist philosophers have argued); instead, it has no 'essence', no innate or 'natural' qualities, but is the product of systems of power/ knowledge (such as psychoanalysis), which have produced it as important in the process of naming and classifying it. Sexuality, then, is the product of our cultural attitudes towards sex, which produce practices of sex as well as categories of sexual types.

It must be noted that sexual identity is closely linked to gender identity: the characteristics of gender are often rooted in commonly held notions of the sexuality of men and women. As discussed in Chapter 5, these attitudes to gender and sexuality – men's supposed 'assertive' or even 'aggressive' natures and women's supposed 'gentle' and 'passive' natures – stem from what Butler (1990) calls 'compulsory heterosexuality'. Ideas about gender are the product of ideas about (hetero-)sexuality to such an extent that the two are often conflated. Ideas about 'femininity' are closely linked to ideas about feminine sexuality, and this can be demonstrated by examining the way in which the two are conflated in debates about women's dress. This chapter examines the example of 'power-dressing' which, as a discourse on the dress of the 'professional' woman, illustrates particularly well the conflation of gender and sexuality. The female body, as this example demonstrates, is a body that is not only marked out as 'feminine' but saturated with 'sexual' meanings too.

The very complex network of associations between sexuality and sexual identity are woven into a whole variety of practices of adornment. Body adornment can be linked to sexual acts, give sexual pleasure, send out sexual signals, mark out sexualised identities. In this way, women's supposed interest in clothes and their desire to look 'sexy' is often naturalised, assumed by some sociologists and psychologists (as discussed in the previous chapter) to be a 'natural' inclination stemming from their desire to attract a suitable partner. Furthermore, men's desire to look at women, their pleasure in the 'props' and accessories of female dress, such as underwear, jewellery and the like, have become so naturalised that voyeurism or the 'male gaze' have become taken for granted as an aspect of male sexual psychology. The supposed 'natural' exhibitionism of women and voyeurism of men have of course been challenged by feminists and indeed, even Freud, who argues that these two distinctive 'drives' – the drive to be looked at and the drive to look – are present in both sexes at an early age; only later are they assigned a gender. When the sexual pleasures or identities run counter to 'normal' or 'natural' heterosexuality, then the look or style is often deemed 'deviant' or even 'pathological', as in the case of some opinions on clothing fetishisms. Once defined, deviance, especially sexual deviance, often enhances rather than undermines the appeal of something and this may explain, in part, why mainstream fashion frequently plunders 'underground' sexualities such as sadomasochism, fetishism or gay and lesbian identities. Such looks and styles allow the fashion-conscious to 'play' at the boundaries of so-called 'normal' sexuality.

Adornment and Sexual Attraction

Western culture invests much sexual meaning in the female body and as such women are often acutely aware of the potential power of clothes, jewellery and make-up as sexual tropes that can enhance one's sexual appeal. This has nothing to do with any 'natural' feminine identity but is the result of cultural associations that tend to see women closer to sex and sexuality than men. However, while the link between clothing and eroticism may seem obvious, it should not be confused with explanations of clothing/adornment based on some crude idea of 'sex appeal', such as Laver's theory of the 'shifting erogenous zone'. As discussed in the previous chapter, Laver's writings on fashion tend to draw on stereotypical ideas of femininity's close relationship to fashion. His idea of the 'shifting erogenous zone' illustrates the way in which women are constantly linked to the idea of seduction through appearance. Fashions for women, Laver (1969) argued, display a concern with seduction (he called it the 'Seduction Principle'). However, as argued in Chapter 2, such mono-causal explanations of fashion are too crude to explain the complexity of women's fashions and, indeed, ignore the sometimes overt sexual nature of male clothing at particular periods in history. The motivations behind dress cannot be reduced to a single explanation: at different times we dress for different reasons and on some occasions, women may dress for status and men to attract admirers. As Wilson (2007) argues, sex appeal is linked to standards of beauty that are enormously variable. Similarly, Steele's argument (1996) is critical of such a 'sex appeal' theory, which she sees as adopting crude ideas about female sexuality based on old-fashioned sex psychology.

The erotic charge of clothes may also stem from their ability to symbolise the sex organs. Freud interprets dress in terms of sex symbolism, arguing, for example, that fur symbolises pubic hair; ties and hats the penis; shoes, girdles or veils, the vagina. Adopting a psychoanalytic framework, Flügel (1930) argues that not only could certain items of dress symbolise the sex organs, but so could the entire clothing system, which attempts to reconcile the contra-dictory desire for modesty and exhibitionism. The appeal of clothes, according to Flügel, comes from the fact that they can simultaneously reveal and conceal the body, enhancing the imagination and stimulating desire. Given that the focus of fashion is the body, it is no surprise to find fashion almost obsessed with sex and sexuality. However, whereas clothing in any culture, Western or non-Western, traditional or modern, may be linked to private and public erotic ideals, the modern fashion system differs in the way that it commodifies the body and sexuality. In other words, the fashion obsession with the sexuality of the body is articulated through particular commodities that are constructed as sexual. Fashion imagery in magazines and in print advertisements play at the boundaries of contemporary mainstream ideas about sexuality.

Power-dressing, Femininity and Sexuality

As argued above, sex and sexuality are closely linked to ideas about gender. This can be illustrated by examining the way in which the female body is produced through the discourse on power-dressing as both a 'feminine' and a 'sexual' body. Power-dressing emerged in the late 1970s in the United States as an explicitly feminine discourse on how to present yourself at work. It addressed the so-called 'career' or 'professional' woman and produced a way of dressing that sought to mark out or gender the female body by rendering it distinctly 'feminine'. The recurring theme of power-dressing is concerned to manage one's sexuality so as to acquire authority, respect and power at work. The result is a uniform for work that treads a thin line between 'masculine' dress (i.e. the 'suit') and 'feminine' decoration aimed at 'softening' the tailored lines of the suit. Power dressing is closely related to the notion of 'dress for success', which had been heralded in the mid-1970s as crucial to the career success of men (Molloy 1980). As I have previously examined (Entwistle 1997), it became prominent in the early 1980s against the historical backdrop of the women's movement and the increasing visibility of women in previously male-dominated professions. The power-dressing uniform quickly became something of a cliché in the 1980s: tailored skirt suit in navy blue with smart blouse and something 'feminine' around the neck, such as a scarf or ruff. The style was embodied by Mrs Thatcher and many other 'professional' women in the public eye (even Princess Diana became associated with the style on some of her engagements). While power-dressing articulated many of the same concerns as 'dress for success', in particular, the common-sense idea that how you look determines your success at work, it is different from its male counterpart in that it considered a woman's sexuality to be a major obstacle to her career development. Why did concerns emerge at this time about the dress of professional and businesswomen, and why was it considered important for career women to pay particular attention to the potential sexual messages of their dress? Why was this issue unique to women? The answers to these questions lie in the cultural associations in Western thought of the female body with sexuality, which make female dress more sexually charged than male dress. This style of dressing, linked as it is to a whole discourse on the female body at work, demonstrates the degree to which women's bodies are sexualised bodies, and also the way in which gender is conflated with sexuality.

The professional and business workplace has historically been the domain of men and the way in which work is organised has traditionally followed patterns defined by men. Furthermore, the reproductive capacities of the female body led it to become associated with nature, reproduction and sexuality, which are especially problematic for working women, since sexuality is deemed inappropriate at work (Gatens 1991; Hearn et al. 1993; McNay 1992; Ortner 1974; Sheppard 1989, 1993). The public realm of work is concerned with the maximisation of profit and productivity and these are seen as achievable only through rational control over libidinal drives (Bataille 1986; Burrell and Hearn 1993; Hearn et al. 1993). The ability to do one's job in almost all occupations (except those in the sex industry) require that sexuality be left at home. Women's cultural association with sexuality is therefore potentially undermining for their role, status and authority at work. Feminists such as Hearn et al. (1993), MacKinnon (1979), Pringle (1988, 1993) and Sheppard (1993) have noted that sexuality is often used to undermine women at work. However, it should be noted here that while sexuality can undoubtedly be used against women, it can of course, be harnessed by women to further their own interests: not only does the prostitute dress to accentuate her body and attract clients, but a saleswoman might decide to dress in a short skirt in order to increase her chances of making more sales with men. In both instances, sexual power might translate into economic power, although how liberating or empowering this is, is open to question.

Power-dressing, however, does not attempt to harness sexuality in this way; it is directed at those women in occupations where sexuality is deemed inappropriate. Power-dressing manuals such as Molloy's Women: Dress for Success (1980) outline a set of rules that promise the career woman some control over her body and self-presentation in the face of male-defined notions of female sexuality and the potential objectifying male gaze in the workplace. According to Molloy, the professional or businesswoman needs 'authority' if she is to achieve success in her career. He considers two things as undermining of authority: looking too much like a 'secretary' and therefore not obviously 'professional'; and looking too 'sexy'. The clothing recommended by Molloy diminishes the potential sexuality of the female body. He advises women not to wear waistcoats for business because they draw 'attention' to the bust and his advice extends to the sort of jacket women should wear: it 'should be cut fully enough to cover the contours of the bust. It should not be pinched in at the waist to exaggerate the bust' (1980: 50). The jacket is the primary signifier of 'professional' and is set in sharp contrast to the sweater, which, as well as being associated with secretaries, is also a garment good for attracting men: 'a cashmere sweater on a woman with even moderate build is one of the greatest seduction garments in existence' (1980: 77). The popularity of the 'Sweater Girls' of the 1950s (stars like Lana Turner) testifies to this association. However, while the body of the career woman must not be deemed too sexual, this requirement does not mean that women ought to dress like men: on the contrary, women must maintain their 'femininity' at the same time as resisting the potential problem of eroticisation and objectification. However, Molloy not only warns career women not to look too sexual, he also advises against being too 'feminine' at work: wearing 'feminine' patterns such as floral print, or 'feminine' colours such as salmon pink are undermining to a woman's 'authority'. He suggests that scarves are good 'attention seeking devices' at work as they draw attention to the face and away from the (problematic) breasts. However, while avoiding looking too 'feminine', the aspiring career woman must also avoid being too 'masculine'. This is one reason he offers as to why trousers are generally to be avoided in the board room and the office. He says that although it can be acceptable in female-dominated companies, 'you are taking a chance if you have to deal with men' because apparently men do not like doing business with women in trousers (1980: 73). A woman in a skirt is therefore unmistakably 'feminine' and this, according to Molloy, makes her less threatening to men at work.

In this way, power-dressing attempts the impossible, negotiating a veritable tightrope for professional women, balancing the need to diminish sexuality with the need to maintain femininity in a man's world of work. The dress advocated as the most appropriate for the female professional worker is a compromise between the demand to contain the potential eroticism of the female body and the demand to look like a woman at the same time. The female business suit results in the female body divided in two: her torso is covered by a fitted jacket, which de-emphasises her breasts, but her femininity is signalled by the wearing of a skirt. By wearing a skirt to the office, the business or professional woman signals her commitment to 'femininity', even though she might be operating in very male-dominated arenas of work. This need for femininity within a man's world is put more plainly by an image consultant I interviewed as part of my research into the dress of professional women (Entwistle 1997b, 2000). She firmly advocates skirted suits for business encounters: 'men', she says, 'like to see a woman's legs'. Thus, while sexuality may be off-limits, the skirt, which potentially connotes 'femininity' is not just acceptable, but preferable. However, one might ask whether it is possible to maintain a distinction between the sexuality of the female body and conventions of femininity. Might it be the case that skirts on women are preferred not because they are 'feminine', but because the skirt draws attention to a sexualised area of the female body? Indeed, given the cultural associations of 'feminine' with 'sexual', it could be argued that the two cannot be pulled apart and the dress of women is the outcome of a conflation of the two. The contradictions of power-dressing illustrate the way in which the distinction between sexuality and gender often collapses, particularly where a woman is concerned. It demonstrates how 'woman' is made up, in part, from her associations with sexuality; the two are inextricably linked. The rules or conventions of dressing the female body for work demonstrate how it is still routinely associated with sexuality and how women, as objects of the male gaze, need to 'manage' their bodies to avoid associations with sexuality.

While the term power-dressing has gone out of vogue, the main tenets of this style of dressing have not. Career-minded, professional women still must manage their dress more carefully than their male colleagues and have not abandoned the skirted suit (Entwistle 1997a, 1997b, 2000). Professional and businesswomen continue to express concerns about how to present their bodies at work so as not to be read as 'sexual'. This concern with the body gives further evidence of the way in which women have had to become conscious of their bodies and responsible not just for their own sexuality, but for the sexuality of men who might be 'misled' into reading sexuality into their dress. One woman I interviewed suggested that women have to monitor their own dress for the benefit of men who might find it difficult to 'read' women and their bodies. She argues that

> dressing for work is about not throwing out any kind of sexual signal and I think the workplace is not the right place for that, you know ... but I think in the workplace, particularly with all these cases of sexual harassment, women have to be sensible and sensitive to men and their response to the response they might produce ... it is about not sending out the wrong signals be they sexual ... most men would be appreciative of women who don't dress provocatively. (Entwistle 1997a: 246–7)

This woman's statement implies that sexual harassment is something that women can have some control over if they dress appropriately and don't throw out a 'sexual signal'. However, given the instability of dress and the potential for any garment to be interpreted as sexual, no style of dressing can ever eliminate the problem of sexual harassment. Indeed, such an attitude is highly problematic, especially when, as in many rape cases, it is invoked to imply that rape is something women invite through their dress (Lees 1999). What this attitude illustrates is the way in which women's bodies are a potential liability at work because of their associations with sexuality. It is hardly surprising to find that the discourse on power-dressing attempts to diminish these associations but at the same time reproduces them in another form.

Fetishism and Adornment

Perhaps the most obvious illustration of the connection between adornment and sexuality is fetishism, where objects themselves become a focus of sexual excitement. While fetishism carries some stigma of 'perversion', it has enjoyed an interesting relationship to fashion since the 1960s or so, when fashion designers began to plunder underground sexual subcultures. At this time the fetish look reached the mainstream through television characters such as Emma Peel in The Avengers. The 'kinky' look combined leather, PVC, corsets, stockings and high heels. As Polhemus (1994) notes, many of these garments were created by the designer John Sutcliffe, who ran a small company called Atomage, which made clothes for underground fetish enthusiasts. This world was brought into the public arena and made more readily available by Malcolm McLaren and Vivienne Westwood's shop SEX where overtly 'kinky' clothes were bought by punks in the 1970s.

The term 'fetishism' has three meanings within three different intellectual traditions. It was originally used within anthropology to describe a sacred object, such as a talisman or totem, which was thought to be endowed with special or magical properties by a particular community. It was later taken up by Marx to describe the way in which commodities under capitalism come to have a life of their own, especially when the 'object world is endowed with intrinsic powers, properties, values and meanings' (Slater 1997: 112). Thus, 'commodity fetishism' refers to the way in which commodities come to acquire magic, often in the shape of 'sex appeal'. The third set of meanings, from psychology, sexology and psychoanalysis, is applied to the way in which some objects become associated with sexual feelings to such an extent that the individual needs that object in order to become sexually aroused and/or reach orgasm. As Steele (1996) notes, Alfred Binet and Richard von Krafft-Ebing were the first to use the word in the modern psychological sense. Krafft-Ebing defined fetishism as 'The Association of Lust with the Idea of Certain Portions of the Female Person, or with Certain Articles of Female Attire' (Steele 1996: 11). Krafft-Ebing also coined the terms 'sadism' (after the Marquis de Sade) and 'masochism' (after Leopold von Sacher-Masoch who wrote the classic erotic tale, Venus in Furs). In his analysis of fashion and fetishism, Kunzle defines fetishism as 'the individual displacement of private erotic feelings onto a non-genital part of the body, or onto a particular article of clothing by association with a part of the body, or onto an article of clothing in conjunction with its effect on the body' (1982: 1).

A fetish can therefore be a part of the body (legs, breasts or feet, for example) or an article of clothing associated with a particular part of the body (shoes, suspenders or bra); it can also be the combination of the item of clothing with its effect on the body (such as the feeling of constriction when wearing a corset or rubber suit). Any object that adorns the body can lend itself to fetishism – corsets, bras, high heels, as well as materials such as rubber, leather or PVC, whose properties of smell or constriction or shininess make them popular with fetishists. These materials outline the contours of the body and make the body smooth and shiny. Some fetishists enjoy dressing up in their chosen fabric so that their entire bodies are encased and constricted. Sexual pleasure comes from both the feeling of constriction and the sight of one's body as a complete, hermetically sealed object (in symbolic terms, a phallic object).

Fetishisms can of course become fashionable. Sometimes fetishes become so wide as to define the fashion of a particular people or period: as Kunzle notes, 'when fashion (group cultural expression) and fetishism (individual sexual expression) are perfectly harmonised, we may speak of a "cultural" or "national" fetish' (1982: 1); he gives the example of foot binding in China. Steele (1996) notes that Western fashions periodically borrow from fetishism: couture designers such as Vivienne Westwood, Versace and Thierry Mugler, as well as high-street stores have all at different times adopted some of the style of fetishism. However, while there is some convergence between fashion and fetishism, we need also to draw a distinction between them. Fashions may 'play' with the idea of fetishism but this playfulness is some distance from the actual experience of fetishism as it is commonly defined within academic literature. While Freud believed that a certain degree of fetishism is present in 'normal' love, most people are not fetishists in the 'pure' sense of the word as defined by psychologists. Freud argued that we may focus on a part of the body (the legs, buttocks, breasts) as part of our sexual desire in the 'other' but that the situation only becomes pathological when the longing for the fetish passes beyond the point of being merely a necessary condition attached to the sexual object and actually take the place of the normal aim, and further when the fetish becomes detached from a particular individual and becomes the sole sexual object (Gamman and Makinen 1994: 37). Gamman and Makinen agree with Freud's insistence on 'some degree' of fetishism being present in all of us, but disagree with him on his distinction between 'normal' and 'pathological'. Likewise, Steele warns of taking the term 'pathological' at face value. What Freud, Gamman and Makinen do agree on is the importance of distinguishing between different stages of levels of fetishism and for this they refer to the work of Paul Gebhard as particularly useful, since he is one of few researchers who looks at fetishism in terms of 'stages' or levels. For Gebhard, level one is when there is a preference for a certain type of sex partner, stimulus or activity, which is not really fetishism at all but akin to Freud's idea of 'normal' love. Level two is when there is a strong preference for certain kinds of partners and/or activities. Level three is when specific stimuli are necessary for sexual activity and when such objects are needed to experience sexual gratification and/or orgasm. Level four is when specific stimuli take the place of the sex partner and is fetishism of the most extreme kind. This is useful when drawing a distinction between fetishism as a sexual predilection and fetishism as fashion style. Fetishism 'proper' involves much more than simply adopting a fetishistic look; it is much more about sexual feelings produced when wearing particular garments. Thus, for Freud, as for most psychoanalysts, fetishism is only 'pathological' when an object becomes detached from the body of the beloved. Gamman and Makinen cite Freud's essay 'Fetishism' (1963), which moves from describing fetishes to giving them a psychoanalytic reading, arguing that they stand in for the 'lost' phallus of the mother. Freud is thus led to the theory that fetishists are more likely to be male, since men are more likely to seek a substitute for the penis and might fetishise the female body in order to allay castration anxieties. This association of men with fetishism is accepted by most psychologists working in the area of sexuality. Stoller (1985), for example, suggests that fetishism is a predominantly male phenomenon, although he describes a small number of women fetishists (such as a woman he encountered who was excited to the point of orgasm when wearing men's clothes). Gamman and Makinen (1994) have challenged this orthodoxy, suggesting that women can be fetishists and frequently do fetishise objects in their adoration of and/or fixation on pop stars, food and clothes. They refer to Freud's argument that 'half of humanity must be classed among the clothes fetishists. All women, that is, are clothes fetishists ... it is a question again of the repression of the same drive, this time however in the passive form of allowing one to be seen, which is expressed by the clothes, and on account of which clothes are raised to a fetish' (Freud in Gamman and Makinen 1994: 41).

Here Freud is not arguing that women are active fetishists, but that their idealisation of clothes is linked to the repression of their desire to be looked at. Gamman and Makinen assert that women's attachment to objects can and does involve active fetishism but their argument depends upon explaining fetishism not in terms of compensation for castration anxiety (as in classic psychoanalytic theory), which would imply that only men can be fetishists. They refer to an alternative view on the origins of fetishism, namely that it can be explained by reference to early memories about separation from the mother, an experience which is as traumatic for girls as for boys. Separation from the mother is sometimes allayed when the child fixes on certain objects associated with her, such as stockings and shoes, which can serve as substitutes in her absence. If this theory of fetishism is adopted, it would seem that women certainly fetishise and Gamman and Makinen offer plenty of examples to support this.

In recent years, images of women in fetishistic clothing have proliferated. A few famous women, such as the English designer Vivienne Westwood and the singer Madonna, have popularised the fetishistic look for women in their exploration of sex and sexuality. The style played an important role within punk subculture; female punks in the 1970s, in their garish make-up, suspenders and stockings, leather and chains, drew inspiration from subversive style to openly flout the conventions of femininity. Madonna's book *Sex* (1992) explores taboo areas of female sexuality such as sadomasochism, bisexuality and lesbianism and her image around the same time drew inspiration from such sexual subcultures. As Steele (1996) notes, fetishism periodically comes in and out of fashion and images of women in fetishistic clothing have become more commonplace since the 1960s. She argues that capitalism has played a part in the rise of fetishistic fashions 'both because fashion itself developed concurrently with the rise of capitalism and because the fashion industry has recently stolen a great many items from the fetishistic wardrobe' (1996: 55; see also Lunning 2013). Capitalism has the ability to incorporate much that is radical and controversial and does so as part of its search for new markets and continued consumption. In this way, it has brought previously underground sexual subcultures into the mainstream, albeit stripping the style of some of its original meaning. Since capitalism frequently uses sex to sell goods (as noted above, this is related to commodity fetishism), it is not surprising that goods that come ready made with sexual meanings are plundered.

However, while it is more acceptable today for women to explore sexuality openly and while fetishistic clothing is more openly available, there are still few accounts of women as practising fetishists. There may be exceptions to this: women's enjoyment of underwear may, for example, provide us with real female fetishists. The controversy surrounding the wearing of the corset in the late nineteenth century draws attention to the practice of tight-lacing, said by Kunzle (1982) to be practised among a small group of fetishists who, he claims, were sexually and socially assertive women. The corset controversy is an interesting one to examine because of the questions it raises as to the relationship between clothing, eroticism and sexuality.

The corset controversy

The corset is a garment that has strong associations with sexuality and eroticism in both past and present culture: once tied to the Victorian standard of beauty, it now has links with sadomasochism in pornographic iconography and enjoyed some popularity as a fashion item in the late 1980s (Steele 1996). More than any other piece of feminine attire, it has excited considerable controversy: seen as an instrument of physical oppression and sexual objectification by Roberts (1977) and Veblen (1953) and by Kunzle (1982) and others as a garment asserting sexual power, it is now acknowledged as a stimulant to sexual pleasure for its 'enthusiasts'. There are, therefore, numerous readings of the corset, which Kunzle (1982) and Steele (1985, 1996) are keen to point out. Both recognise the ambivalence of the corset and indeed, all clothing, which expresses two opposing desires: garments cover the body and also enhance and display it. Thus, Kunzle notes that 'the socio-sexual symbolism of tight-lacing and its ritual components reveal its essentially ambivalent purpose to enforce the sexual taboo by objectively oppressing the body, and simultaneously to break that taboo by subjectively enhancing the body' (1982: 2–3).

However, while both Steele and Kunzle agree on the erotic nature of the corset and argue that the established reading of the 'passive' Victorian woman oppressed by her stays needs revising, when it comes to interpreting the evidence on tight-lacing, there is some disagreement. For Kunzle, 'the history of tight-lacing is part of the history of the struggle for sexual expression, male and female' (1982: 2). He goes on to analyse Victorian women (and some men) who were tight-lacing fetishists and did so because they enjoyed the feeling of constriction produced by the corset to the extent that they might become sexually aroused by it. This practice he sees as sexually expressive, even liberatory, especially for women, for whom it represented an alternative to the asexual femininity on offer within dominant Victorian culture. The enemies of sexual expression for Kunzle were those dress reformers who condemned the corset on moral or health grounds, insisting on an ideology of femininity tied to domesticity. He goes on to argue that 'women used their sexuality, and sexualised forms of dress, as women always have, to rise out of a socio-sexual subject position. And they got morally scape-goated for their pains' (1982: 2).

His argument relies on evidence taken from magazines such as the *Englishwoman's Domestic Magazine (EDM)* which, between 1867 and 1874, published a series of articles and letters on tight-lacing and became the focus of a debate among tight-lacing fetishists and their detractors. He also draws heavily on personal accounts from diaries and interviews. Such sources suggested that tight-lacers could lace down to waists as tiny as 16, 15, 14 and even 13 inches and proclaimed the erotic as well as health benefits of such a practice. In addition, tight-lacers frequently spoke of the erotic pleasures of high heels, which, together with the tightly laced corset could, says Kunzle, induce pleasurable kinetic sensations of an erotic kind. In addition, the corset itself could play an elaborate role in sexual foreplay:

> the state of being tightly corseted is a form of erotic tension and constitutes ipso facto a demand or erotic release, which may be deliberately controlled, prolonged and postponed. To the male the corset represents an intricate erotic obstacle, the deft removal of which permitted the development of all kinds of erotic foreplay, and betokened amorous expertise. To the woman, unlacing meant (promise of) sexual release. (Kunzle 1982: 31)

By his own definition of fetishism as the displacement of erotic feelings onto a non-genital part of the body, an article of clothing associated with a particular part of the body, or an article of clothing in conjunction with its effect on the body, tight-lacing fetishism for Kunzle is not the same as corset

THE "SPÉCIALITÉ CORSET" (Regd. No. 10438).
DICKINS & JONES,

Figure 15. Advertisement for corsets, illustrating the restricted waist, considered beautiful in
the late nineteenth century. More than any other single item of clothing, the corset has been
singled out for widespread criticism. The Advertising Archives

fetishism. Corset fetishism focuses on the object itself, which is associated
with certain powers or properties of the loved one, as in the case of the
lover who unlaces his beloved. The tight-lace fetishist may not be interested
in the corset *per se*, but in the sensations produced by the tightly laced
corset and the erotic tension produced when wearing it, as in the case of
the woman for whom sexual release comes from being unlaced by her lover,
or in the male lover who takes pleasure in the tight effect the corset has
on the body of the beloved. There is, therefore, something sadomasochistic
about tight-lacing and many of the letters to the *EDM* are sadomasochistic
in their celebration of the tension, constriction and pain induced by tight-
lacing. Some have a common narrative structure in recounting memories
of being forced to wear a tight corset by a strict parent or teacher at a
boarding school. As Steele (1996) notes, the letters to the *EDM* focus on
three things: extreme body modification as a result of wearing a corset day

and night; a sadomasochistic pleasure in domination and humiliation; and cross-dressing – some of the correspondents were male cross-dressers who enjoyed wearing corsets.

Steele (1985, 1996) takes issue with Kunzle's claims for tightlacing fetishists as sexually and socially liberated individuals, as well as with the evidence on which he bases his argument. However, she first insists on the need to distinguish between ordinary fashionable corsetry as practised by most nineteenth-century women, and the minority fetishistic practice of tight-lacing: most corset wearing stayed within the realms of ordinary fashion, with only a minority of corset producers reporting greater demands for smaller and smaller corsets. Furthermore, the statistics that Kunzle draws on are inherently unreliable. Those quoted in letters to the *EDM* probably exaggerated the statistics for erotic effect; measuring corsets that still exist today is of little use, as there is no way of knowing how tightly these may have been laced. Concerned philanthropists in the nineteenth century gathered other statistics from lingerie shops, which were responsible for measuring women for their corsets. Some corsetiers claimed that the tighter the corset, the smaller it must have been laced. While it is not impossible to imagine some waists as small as 16 inches, Steele suggests that 'such waists are rare' and it is 'time to discard the myth of the 16-inch waist as a touch-stone for thinking about the nineteenth-century woman' (1996: 61). She also argues that while there were some habitual tight-lacers, tight-lacing has also to be seen as part of a spectrum of corset wearing. Habitual tight-lacers, or tight-lacing fetishists, she argues, were few and far between and we cannot therefore make generalisations from this small minority. It is impossible to know from the accounts in the *EDM* whether or not there were many female tight-lacing fetishists. While many of the letters to the *EDM* were signed with women's names, this does not mean they were actually written by women since, as Steele (1985) rightly points out, it is a common practice within pornographic literature to attribute sexual tales to a female character. This is not to say that there were no Victorian tight-lacers, as Kunzle claims, but the evidence he provides is inconclusive. While the corset gradually disappeared from women's fashions in the early twentieth century, it has retained its potency as an erotic garment and still represents one of the most significant fetish objects today. Steele examines corset wearing in the 1990s and quotes from interviews with a number of tight-lacers. One woman, Cathie J., began tight-lacing because of her husband's interest in corsets; she herself does not derive any sexual pleasure from it but does it 'to please [her] husband' (1996: 85). She is, however, careful to distance herself from any association with bondage. Another interviewed woman, Lauren, would seem to be a genuine fetishist, tight-lacing for herself and not a partner, and taking pleasure from how the corset feels on her body and the way it makes her body look. Among male tight-lacers, Fakir Musafar has achieved considerable fame for extreme body modifications and is a corset enthusiast. He argues that corsets are 'very erotic' in that they 'enhance sexual experiences ... all your internal organs and your sexual components are in different positions, with different tensions and so on' which, he says, makes sex while tightly laced with a tightly laced woman especially erotic (Musafar in Steele 1996: 81).

As Musafar's account testifies, the physical properties of clothing and the sensations they produce on the body can become the focus of erotic attention and fetishised. As Steele (1996) notes, fetishes tend to be broadly characterised into 'smellies' and 'feelies'. Rubber and leather are the focus of erotic attention in part because of their smell which for fetishists can be intensely erotic. They are also favoured for their tactile qualities of hardness and smoothness, which enable them to outline the contours of the body as well as constrain the body. Some fetishists like to dress up completely in their preferred fabric and this desire (as with tight-lacers) might mean their fetish is a constraint that borders on the sadomasochistic. However, as Steele notes, this focus on 'hard' fabrics is relatively recent and has come about partly as a result of modern technologies that enable the manufacture of rubber and PVC clothing. In the nineteenth and early twentieth century, 'soft' or 'feminine' fabrics, such as fur, silk, satin and velvet were the focus of erotic attention by fetishists. Leopold von Sacher-Masoch's *Venus in Furs* tells the tale of a dominatrix who always wore furs when she dominated and humiliated her lover. However, while Freud believed fur symbolised pubic hair and, while it has luxurious qualities, fur fetishism is in fact quite rare. In the nineteenth century, silk and satin fetishism was common among women as well as men. The psychoanalyst Wilheim Stekel (1930) described various fetishisms associated with women and found that in some cases doll fetishism was linked to an adult fetishism for certain fabrics. He summarises three cases of silk or satin fetishists, one of which was reported in the *Journal de médecine* in 1914 and describes a girl who, growing up in a silk weaver's family, found that caressing silk would send shivers of sexual pleasure through her. Her fetishism led her to steal silk from shops and she was arrested and convicted on a number of occasions; the connection between female fetishism for certain fabrics and kleptomania is also noted by Stekel (1930).

Transvestism

One arena of fetishism that would seem to be almost exclusively male is transvestism, which evidently very often starts from a fetish for women's silky underwear and later progresses to the desire to wear full female dress. The word 'transvestism' can refer simply 'to the act of cross-dressing, when one sex adopts the clothes of the other' (Ackroyd 1979: 10). However, contemporary definitions make it more specific – sexologists and psychologists see it as an act of cross-dressing accompanied by fetishistic obsessions, although this understanding of the term, indeed the term itself, has fallen out of usage in recent years. Ackroyd discussing male dressers draws an important distinction between the transvestite and the transsexual: the former is fetishistic in deriving pleasure from wearing clothes of the opposite sex while the latter moves out of this fetishistic stage to a more 'comprehensive form of feminine "passing" and desire to become the opposite sex' (1979: 14). However, this distinction is not apparent in all the literature: in his account of a 'transvestite', Stekel (1930) describes the case of a woman who exhibits a general distaste for her own sex and a strong desire to have the body of a man as well as dress like one; she experiences no fetishistic pleasure in wearing men's clothes and, for this reason, it would seem more accurate to describe her as a transsexual than as a transvestite. The distinction between transvestism and transsexualism is important, since it would seem that while men can fall into either category, there appear to be very few women who derive sexual pleasure from wearing the clothes of men, making transsexualism more common among women than transvestism. Furthermore, it would be a mistake to assume that the male transvestite shares the transsexual's aspiration to become feminine. As Ackroyd (1979) notes, he may leave clues, unconscious or not, to his masculine identity even when dressed as a woman. Some transvestites feel the need to 'pass' as a woman in public but many are satisfied simply dressing as a woman at home.

While cross-dressing can be found in history among both sexes (as discussed in the previous chapter), the reasons why women cross-dress tend to be social, economic and political rather than fetishistic; there are few accounts of women who cross-dress for sexual pleasure. When cross-dressing is associated with lesbianism, the experience of wearing men's clothes is not likely to be sexual *per se*, but, as argued below, it is worn to signal one's sexual identity as a lesbian, or out of a desire to flout conventions of feminine appearance and articulate a masculine identification. According to Ackroyd (1979), the reason why women do not derive sexual pleasure from men's clothes is because men's clothes are just not erotic. This explanation seems a little simplistic and does not take account of the way in which men's clothes have been eroticised. Historically men's clothing has been erotic, as the codpiece testifies, and in recent years men's underwear has become a centre of erotic attention.

The transvestite is also almost always heterosexual. His fetishistic interest in clothing is sometimes explained by reference to his desire, envy or admiration of women which lead him to dress like one. Some transvestites are open about the fetishistic pleasures of dressing as a woman. However, Ackroyd (1979) notes that other transvestites are less comfortable with this aspect of their dress and choose to play it down. The phenomenon of transvestism has been much discussed within psychological literature and many different theories put forward to explain it. In his analysis, Stoller (1968) explains transvestism by reference to Freud's idea of castration: a man dressed as a woman re-enacts the original childish belief in the phallic woman and subconsciously attempts to resolve or allay fears of castration.

Underwear and eroticism

Underwear is another obvious aspect of dress to be linked with sexuality, although it serves a good many other functions as well. Underwear as we know it today was not worn before the nineteenth century. As Willet and Cunningham note, 'underclothes have had – and still have – an important "psychological" interest' (1992: 11) and suggest that to consider this dimension we need to look at the meanings of underclothes within their own epoch. This is useful to bear in mind since the development of underwear in the modern sense 'was an important historical stage in the evolving eroticism of dress' (Steele 1996: 116). The first undergarments worn in the medieval period were simple shifts, which functioned to protect one's outer clothes from the dirt produced by the body and also to protect the body from contact with stiff, uncomfortable fabrics. In this respect, 'its function was purely utilitarian' rather than erotic (Willet and Cunningham, 1992: 21). From the fifteenth century, corsets were worn by the members of the elite and, although at first glance the small waist of the Elizabethan woman might seem to be linked to sexual attraction, the style was more about social status than eroticism.

As Foucault (1979) demonstrates, during the nineteenth century sexuality became the focus of intense interest within a whole range of discourses, a fact that belies the common-sense view of the Victorian era as one of sexual repression. However, while sometimes over-exaggerated, the Victorians did display a 'prudish' attitude towards the body and sexuality, which found expression in the layers of clothing worn. Whereas the fashionable woman at the beginning of the nineteenth century had worn little in the way of underwear beneath her diaphanous chemise, by the end of the century the female body was concealed behind a complex combination of camisole, corset, stockings and petticoat. However, once the body became hidden behind more and more layers of stiff clothes, erotic attention transferred 'to its coverings, which became a matter of furtive preoccupation' and once associated with the hidden parts of the body, underwear began to gather its erotic connotations and become the focus of sexual interest (Willet and Cunningham 1992: 11). This is evidenced by examining attitudes to women in underpants. In the early to mid-Victorian period, the taboo on women in bifurcated garments extended to underpants or pantaloons which, although worn by men, were considered indecent on women, who did not wear them until late in the nineteenth century; modesty called for some coverage when wearing a crinoline cage (which could easily be blown above one's head). However, while, as Steele notes, 'some men complained that the opportunity to glimpse women's genitals had decreased as women adopted underpants, a new voyeurism directed toward the underpants themselves was born' (1996: 120).

The late Victorian and early Edwardian period of the *belle époque* is sometimes singled out as the era when underwear for women became even more elaborate and sexually codified. By the late nineteenth century, the frou-frou rustle of five petticoats had become erotically charged, as had the lacy pantaloons then worn by women. Indeed, the erotic appeal of pantaloons and petticoats was the basis for the popular can-can, in which the kicking legs of the dancers revealed yards of lace (Steele 1996). During this period the eroticisation of the secret, hidden layers of the body reached new heights; in addition, new forms of layered erotic device, ranging from nipple piercing to cosmetics, were introduced to enhance the sexuality of the body. Sennett notes how

> the laceration of the breasts, the use of rustling undergarments and some forms of make-up, meant that sensual appeal came through preparations which were hidden by clothing. No one sees those rings unless they see the woman undressed, the petticoats can be heard up close but not seen. (1977: 189)

While the 'fashion' for nipple piercing (as for genital piercing) remained underground, gradually towards the end of the century, cosmetics and perfume began to be marketed for women, although the 'respectable' woman had to keep it discreet so as not to be mistaken for a prostitute.

When one considers its proximity to the body, it is not surprising that underwear is the focus of intense erotic interest. It is the last staging-post before the naked body is revealed, an 'intermediate position' between the clothed and naked body, which serves to invest a greater erotic charge to the process of undressing (Steele 1996: 116). Underwear therefore plays a crucial role in many different experiences of sexuality. It is important in sexual foreplay and can become the focus of male obsession as a result: it also lends itself to fetishism as the clothing worn closest to the body of the loved one and thus the clothing that intimately evokes the cherished body parts.

As with fetishism, underwear as outerwear has become fashionable in recent years and has associations with fetishism, since underwear is one aspect of dress that is commonly singled out and fetishised. Modern underwear has become pared down but the erotic appeal of certain items of underclothing has not diminished and erotic and pornographic material will often draw on the more elaborate aspects of female underwear for its effect. Stockings, suspenders, garters, bras and knickers still play their part in sexual arousal, although there is a considerable difference between women (and their lovers) who take pleasure in gossamer bras, knickers or suspenders and stockings, and fetishists for whom a focus on underwear is obsessive and divorced from the body of the loved one. Some extreme cases of fetishism involve such obsessive interest in underwear that women have had items stolen (Steele 1996). Stockings and suspenders feature heavily in erotic and pornographic literature and have acquired a set of associations that make them almost always erotically charged, even though the vast majority of Western women habitually wear pantyhose or tights (this might in part explain some of the appeal of stockings in today's pornography). The eroticism of the stocking comes also from what is revealed and concealed. As Steele (1996) notes, the suspender belt around the waist frames the genital area, while the edge of the stocking draws the eye to the flesh of the upper thighs. The contrast between gossamer fabric and flesh is made more tantalising when there is a degree of difference in terms of colour: she suggests that black stockings are the most alluring on a white woman, while white or red on a black woman has the same effect of marking the boundary of cloth and skin. These contrasts are sometimes played out in bras: black bras have greater tonal contrast on white skin, red or white on black skin. Now an accepted part of the female wardrobe, the bra is a modern invention. Breasts, which had been shaped by the whalebone corset, only relatively recently got their own item of clothing, 'somewhere around 1908 more by accident than design' (Hawthorne 1992: 24). As Hawthorne notes, many contemporary fashion designers held claim to having 'invented' it, including the fashion designer Paul Poiret. The film director Howard Hughes, also an industrialist who made a significant contri-bution to aeronautical engineering, designed Jane Russell's famous bra in *The Outlaws* (1943) and is sometimes considered to be the inventor of the bra as we know it today. As with all clothing, the bra works on the body to transform it: depending on the shape of the cup and the use of bones, the bra can dramati-cally alter the shape of the breasts, which are in turn shaped by fashions of the time. The bra reached its pinnacle (both literally and metaphorically) in the late 1940s and 1950s when, in the wake of Russell's uplifted appearance, conical shaped bras helped to promote the 'sweater girl' look of Hollywood actresses such as Lana Turner. During the 1960s an alternative, flat-chested look became popular; rather than thrust the breasts forward, bras could be purchased that squashed them flat.

What of men's underwear? Willet and Cunningham argue that 'man has never used provocative underclothing; its plain prose has been in singular contrast to the poetical allurements worn by woman' (1992: 16). This statement is not entirely true, since male underwear has been a feature of homosexual interest for much of the twentieth century; white vests, for example, are particularly eroticised in gay iconography. Furthermore, while men's underclothes have not carried the same erotic charge as women's within mainstream heterosexual culture, a relatively recent growth in erotic interest in men's underwear has paralleled the growth in images of men as sexual objects. A new 'narcissistic' man whose body became the object of an erotic gaze emerged in the 1980s. The most famous example was Calvin Klein's campaign of advertisements in 1982, showing tanned, muscular men in tight white underpants and boxer shorts (the largest of these billboards went up in New York's Times Square). While the erotic appeal of white cotton underpants for men still lingers, the market has opened up considerably and it is possible to buy male briefs in a whole variety of fabrics, rubber, leather and PVC. This would, on the face of it, seem to suggest that a more overt interest in male bodies and male undergarments is now permitted (Cole 2014). Some of this interest is erotic, as Cole (2014: 7) argues: '[M]en's underwear can [...] be seen to reflect and enhance sexuality and sensuousness, especially when considered alongside the idea that concealments plays a part in the eroticism of clothing, calling attention to what is beneath the clothes.'

Adornment and Sexual Identity

Bodies can be adorned not only with cloth, but cosmetics, jewellery, tattoos, scars and perfume, and these adornments can similarly become the focus of erotic attention. Tattooing, scarification and piercing are some of the oldest forms of body adornment and were originally closely tied to religious rituals and rites of passage in many different cultures. Within the West, such body modifications as nose rings, navel rings and tattoos are enjoying a vogue within fashion and have lost their associations with sacred rituals, though piercing and tattoos have a longer history (Rush 2005; Sweetman 1999a, 1999b). Sennett (1977) notes how in the 1890s there was a 'passing fashion' for piercing women's nipples. The practice was, and to some extent still is, isolated to gay, sadomasochistic and fetish subcultures, although it has gained some mainstream acceptance of late. Genital piercing remains a more marginal practice, although here again, there is now more discussion of it in the mainstream media than ever before. Part of the appeal of such piercing for its advocates comes from the pain of piercing itself which, to sadomaso-chists, is experienced as sexually pleasurable. However, once piercings have healed, advocates claim they can exaggerate sexual pleasure, intensifying sexual arousal and orgasm, as well as facilitating a range of sadomasochistic bondage games. Such 'extreme' fetishistic practices are linked to sexual subcultures, such as the Pervs, where, as Polhemus argues, 'there is a serious commitment to exploring a new sexuality – one that seeks to replace the casual, "Your place or mine" promiscuity of the 1960s "sexual revolution" with an approach that is more relationship-based, and more ritualistic (even spiritual)' (1994: 105).

Polhemus argues that in recent years, the Pervs have served to redefine and extend 'the meaning of sex itself' (1994: 105). In a world still coming to terms with the effects of AIDS, such exploration of sexuality through adornment has gained increasing visibility and acceptance. On the London club scene, there has been a growing interest in fetishistic practices: the magazine *Skin Two* and special club nights 'Submission' and the 'Torture Garden' have grown considerably over the 1990s, attracting a great deal of attention through the mainstream media. This popularity, says Polhemus, should not surprise us, 'Aids, gender-related issues and a growing awareness of the deficiencies of the last "sexual revolution" in the 1960s all point to the need for a new approach to erotic and sexual experience' (1994: 105).

Gay and Lesbian Dress and Sexuality

Fashion has been a place through which sex, gender and sexual identities are articulated. Historically, sexuality is carefully managed in the public sphere, and for marginal groups, such as gay men or lesbian women, visibility of one's marginality or non-normative identity was often through secret codes of dress. Dress articulated these marginal sexualities and otherwise 'secret' desires. Gay men have long used clothing and other forms of bodily adornments to signal to other gay men. 'Gays and lesbians have indeed learned to speak about their sexuality by not naming it directly, but through their clothing, style, and behavioral signifiers' (Vänskä 2014: 451). Cole's (2000) history of gay men's dress in the twentieth century explores these codes, from the underground subcultures when homosexuality was illegal to the influence of gay men's dress on contemporary fashion. The iconography of gay masculinity is littered with sexual codes: ultra-masculine styles based around leather and the overt stylisation of masculinity through certain uniforms are the two most obvious examples.

This theme of dress and the articulation of sexual identity is explored in relation to lesbian identities (Lewis and Rolley 1997; Rolley 1992). Rolley (1992: 33) notes how 'familial ties' in general are commonly made visible through dress and uniforms that 'serve both to distinguish wearers from the rest of society and to bind them together into a unified body'. In this respect, 'the lesbian couple who dressed alike emphasised both their special closeness and their difference from the rest of society' (1992: 33). In some cases, this relationship was articulated through similarity, dressing to appear like sisters or twins, but, says Rolley, this serves more to suppress rather than express the physical nature of the relationship. However, when, as in the relationship between Vita Sackville-West and Violet Trefusis, one of the women chooses to dress in a 'masculine' way, 'it served the dual purpose of both sexualising the women's relationship with each other and excluding any male intruder' (1992: 34). Thus, for the lesbian couple, clothes enable the articulation of the 'masculine lesbian body' and its desires. Masculine clothes also play a role in articulating difference within the lesbian relationship, which replicates the difference found in heterosexual relationships. Dress thus plays a crucial part in articulating sexual identities that would otherwise be invisible. This is the reason why dress and adornment have been so important to gay and lesbian communities. Commonly recognised styles of 'butch' and 'femme' within the lesbian community play on codes that make visible one's sexual orientations: 'how else was a woman recognisable as a lesbian except through her body, her clothes, and the dialogue between the two?' (1992: 38).

Explorations of lesbian identity through fashion and dress have examined the various representations of lesbians, from butch/femme to the media-friendly 'lipstick lesbian' phenomenon of the 1990s. Reddy-Best and Jones (2020: 160) consider the many mainstream cultural representations or 'multiple assemblages' of lesbian styles to argue that structure 'ways of seeing' lesbians through 'the lens of fashionability'. In many contemporary representations (such as *Vogue*, *Women's Wear Daily*, as well as in TV shows like *The L Word*) much of the butch/femme dichotomy has been watered down. While lesbian identity is now widely acknowledged in the media, they argue that it is still largely white and middle-class.

This scholarship on gay and lesbian fashion challenges the dominant story of fashion. In her essay that accompanies the Fashion Institute of Technology's 2013 *A Queer History of Fashion: From the Closet to the Catwalk* exhibition, Steele (2013: 8) examines the role that the LGBTQ+ community (gay, lesbian, bisexual and trans people) have played within the history of fashion as designers, stylists, photographers, models, make-up artists, hairdressers and so on, and their influence on style and fashion trends as a result. She notes, we might ask, '[W]ho cares whether a designer or other fashion professional is gay?' However, in answer she argues that sexuality permeates much of everyday life and to ignore the role of LGBTQ+ in fashion is to reproduce the systematic silencing of their voice and experience. Important also is recognising how gay style generally, on the street and in clubs and bars, in music and popular culture, has also been highly influential on fashion and dress trends. Gay men have had a closer popular association with fashion than lesbians and indeed, '[Un]til the last decade or three "lesbian style" might have been laughed out of court as an obvious oxymoron' (Wilson 2013: 167). Today, there is a flourishing of queer style, with openly queer creatives consciously challenging gender and sexual norms such as Santana Queirós, owner of House of NARCISSISM'.

In recent years, the idea of 'queer' has moved away from discussions of discreet, alternative sexual identities and subcultures, to looking at ways to challenge mainstream norms and practices. Brown (2019) offers three ways of understanding 'queer': first, the oldest meaning of the word refers to the idea of something odd or strange and something of this meaning is retained in more recent understandings. Second, queer refers to the insistence of an intersectional understanding, which shifts the focus away from white histories and experience to bring out alternative, oppositional positions, such as race and sexuality, oppositional to dominant norms. The third meaning of queer, emerging in the 1990s but still dominant today, refers to non-normative identities and challenges the very idea of fixed identities such as 'gay' and 'straight'. The idea of 'queering' fashion, which Brown does in her history of modelling in the US in the twentieth century, is to bring all three understandings to make strange and critique of modelling conventions.

Of course, this theoretical focus and new historical approach is paralleled by the increasing importance and awareness of LGBTQ+ rights and identities, which has both borrowed from queer theory discussed in Chapter 5. LGBTQ+ activism challenges all essentialist thinking both about sexuality and sex (as noted above). Citing the influence of Teresa de Lauretis in 1991 in the rise of queer theory, Vänskä (2014: 448) argues '[I]n its theoretical form, as queer theory, [...] queer became a method that has been successfully used to criticise identity-based gay and lesbian studies and to challenge heterosexist assumptions.' Once again, fashion has been enormously important in these political and theoretical debates about sex, sexuality and identity, as well as opening up spaces for everyday sartorial practices that challenge these dominant meanings. For Vänskä (2014: 448) it meant a flourishing of work at the intersection of queer theory and fashion studies. She notes 'For someone coming to fashion from critical gender studies, all theories about gender and sexuality have started to make sense in a new way – how important a role everyday sartorial practices have played in fashioning theories about gender and sexuality.'

A further point of research interest in recent years is the apparent 'pornifi-cation' of culture. Concerns have been raised, mainly in mainstream media, as to the ways sex permeates fashion trends and style, with increasing emphasis on looking 'sexy' and being sexual, examined through debates on the 'sexual subjectificaion' of culture (Gill 2003) It would appear to be the case that the iconography of porn has slipped down from the top shelf and now shares space in many mainstream locations. The mainstreaming of porn has its roots in many developments and space does not allow me to trace them all here. As Lynch (2012) shows in her extensive analysis of 'porn chic', there are multiple sites for this. She describes in her fieldwork how young families and grand-parents now feel comfortable eating at Hooters outlets in the USA and there are other indications too: the *Playboy* bunny logo has entirely broken free of its soft-porn roots and is now on t-shirts worn by teenagers. Indeed, *Playboy* has been given high-fashion kudos by models like Kate Moss, who appeared in *Playboy* magazine to 'celebrate' turning forty in 2014. In popular music, similar extensions of porn iconography are evident: from Rihanna's explicit videos to Miley Cyrus 'twerking' at the MTV awards. This sexualisation of the body has been widely criticised and regarded as proliferating sexual goods marketed at pre-pubescent girls: for example, here in the UK retailers have been taken to task for selling G-strings to girls and the store popular with young people, American Apparel, once a popular brand in the USA and UK, which has since closed down, was known for its quite risqué sexual advertising imagery, aimed at teenagers and young people. While this pornification would appear to be an empirical reality, it is worth sounding a note of caution when discussing its influence and 'harm'. Such concern has a familiar ring to it, part of the recurring moral panic that our children are becoming sexualised by popular culture that dates back at least to the post-war era and the first youth subcul-tures. And, indeed, as discussion on 'modesty' and dress above indicates, there may be equally powerful alternatives pulling in the other direction, at least for some young women. These are interesting issues that need further exami-nation in future research.

Conclusion

This chapter has examined the idea that fashion and dress are infused with sexual meanings. As Steele (1985) argues, because of its close association to the body, all clothing is in some way related to eroticism or at least has the potential to be erotically charged. It is therefore not just the spectacular and the extreme examples where we find the connections between the body, adornment and eroticism, but the ordinary and everyday aspects of dress, which are likely to be related to ideals of beauty at various times. Since dress and adornment often exhibit a strong concern with aesthetics, it is in some way connected with eroticism. Furthermore, as argued above, the more 'mundane' practice of dressing for work, particularly power-dressing, illustrates the extent to which the body and dress, especially for women, is infused with sexual meaning.

Clothing and adornment are also linked to expressions of sexuality and sexual identity. As discussed at the beginning of this chapter, clothes can 'add' sexual meanings to the body that would otherwise be less apparent. According to the context and the individual, dress and adornment can play an important part in the expression of one's sexuality and the articulation of desire, forming part of the complex ritual of sexual seduction. Individuals can deploy dress strategically for sexual ends and this is no more obvious than the dress of a sex worker, whose dress and demeanour are heavily sexually coded. As discussed above, particular styles of dress and fabric are linked to erotic pleasure and particular styles of dress have articulate sexual identities and orientations.

In examining the links between adornment and sexuality, this discussion has focused both on sexuality in many forms and settings, from ordinary ways professional women dress to more 'spectacular' expressions of sexuality through subcultural practices (fetishism and transvestism). It has also considered the challenges posed by queer theory and LGBTQ+ communities, as well as noting the influence of the latter within fashion. These themes concerning fashion, bodies, identities, and meanings, originally examined in the first edition, have obviously retained a central place within fashion studies scholarship. What the wealth of literature published since demonstrates is how much more diverse, complex, and rich our understandings and analysis of fashion and sexuality have become.

7

The Fashion Industry

In this final chapter I want to consider the materiality of fashion as an industry involved in the manufacture of desirable objects destined for our bodies. We have already considered the materiality of bodies and the role dress and fashion plays in shaping the identities of bodies throughout this book – indeed it is where we started it. But to fully account for fashion we need to consider the materiality of fashionable objects themselves: the designed and manufactured goods. Fashionable goods circulate across a wide range of social spaces that constitute the fashion industry and for a full analysis of fashion we need to consider all these spaces and the processes through which fashionable goods arrive on our bodies.

It is impossible to discuss the industry without considering the many criticisms levelled at it today – environmental, animal, and human well-being. These problems have their origins in the history of the industry and modernity. As Wilson argues, fashion is a 'child of modernity': it is central to modernity (European and elsewhere) with its associations with modernising 'progress' and the eternal movement of the 'new'. From the first industrial revolution, with its technological developments, to today's speeded-up experience of modern life, with the pace of change (materials, technologies, aesthetics) is a critical factor constituting modern-day fashion systems. Fashion origins lie in global trade routes and connections and capitalist colonialisation. In this respect, it has been at the centre of much critique for its role as an exploitative industry. From Karl Marx's (1990 [1867]) observations of 'sweated' labour in the nineteenth century, to today's labour and climate-change activists, fashion has always been an industry with significant problems. Criticism today is levelled at 'fast fashion' for fuelling unsustainable appetites for new, cheap clothes that have a large carbon footprint: from the exploitation of natural resources (like water) and environmental damage caused by toxic chemicals in their production, to the damaging impact of transportation (usually from East/South to West/North), to the inevitable wastage of these materials, which often end in landfill after only a few wears.

This newly revised chapter examines these criticisms, bringing up to date some of the contemporary positions *vis-à-vis* the fashion industry in which fast fashion has developed unsustainable patterns of production and consumption. First, the discussion summarises the history of the fashion industry within the European context and introduces some of the technologies and processes characterising fashion production. There are many problems within the industry that have continued today with fast fashion. Fine and Leopold's (1993; see also Fine et al. 2018) idea of 'system of provision' is utilised to consider fashion as an integrated industry with relations of production and consumption.

Second, the chapter focuses on fashion consumption and culture, especially markets and shopping. Addressing the consumption means considering fashion as a culture industry and aesthetic economy producing aesthetic value around fashionable goods. Therefore, consideration of the work of numerous agents in the production, distribution and consumption of fashion is required. Much theoretical work in this area focuses on important 'cultural intermediaries', who produce meaning and value around fashionable clothing. The rise of online fashion communication and the central importance of bloggers and other 'influencers' and their work of 'prosumption' is considered as a key development to producing aesthetic value in fashion in the twenty-first century.

The latter section of the chapter discusses contemporary debates about sustainability and the environment. Here, the influential framework of actor-network-theory or ANT is utilised to consider fashion *assemblages* of nature-culture and provides a useful way of thinking about fashion in the context of ethical and sustainability debates concerning human labour and urgency of the climate emergency. The concept of assemblage radically extends earlier accounts of fashion that acknowledge the many agencies involved in constructing fashion.

Historical Development of the Fashion Industry

The fashion industry is of major significance to the industrial and economic development of many countries. In Britain, the development of the textile industry set in motion the Industrial Revolution and this expansion of capitalism depended upon the exploitation of natural and human resources with devastating effects that continue today. In the twentieth century, 'Fordist' forms of capitalism meant businesses owned and controlled their own production – i.e. the factories – as indeed Henry Ford the twentieth-century car manufacturer did. However, fashion failed to mass produce like the car industry and instead preferred the more 'agile' subcontracting chains that are now touted as part of neo-liberal capitalism. This subcontracting system involves the plundering of natural resources abroad and the outsourcing of work to populations in the Global South and East in search of the cheapest labour globally, resulting in poor labour conditions under which these (mostly) women and children work. Fashion production has long fed off the labour of the most vulnerable workers, women and children. Indeed, in his account of capitalism and class divisions under industrialisation, Karl Marx (1990 [1867]) points to the ways in which human labour is exploited to produce commodities for profit in the textile industry in particular. His collaborator, Engels, 'whose father owned a textile mill in Manchester had already documented the poverty and misery that arose from the production of all kinds of commodities in England's industrial cities in the 1840s' (Sullivan, 2016: 36). Any analysis of fashion production needs to consider how class, gender and race become interconnected in this exploitation, as fast fashion in the twentieth and twenty-first centuries is largely produced by women of colour, located in countries in the South, like Bangladesh, or in immigrant communities in the USA, UK and elsewhere.

Thus, a great disparity opens between fashion as freedom of expression, playful and fun (for consumers) and fashion as an oppressive system (for producers): the body of the wearer contrasts strongly with the body of the worker who is almost invariably unable to afford the clothes she makes. Connecting production and consumption is not only intellectually necessary for a fuller analysis, but also politically essential. As Fine and Leopold (1993) argue, production and consumption are connected into 'systems of provision'. Thus, for production to be translated into consumption, income must be generated, habits formed, and products marketed; production is tied closely to consumption, but consumption practices alone do not determine entirely the relations of production. According to Fine and Leopold (1993: 72), 'these chains in the link between production and consumption confirm the problems of defining a single model, either for dependence or consumption upon production'. There are distinct imperatives organising the production and consumption of different sets of commodities – food, shelter, clothing, which leads Fine and Leopold to argue for 'systems of provision approach', which focuses attention on the way in which patterns of production and consumption intersect in any given commodity market. Braham (1997: 133) argues something similar when he says that

> it is much more compelling to try to consider fashion in terms of both its cultural and its economic aspects than to deal with one aspect or the other, though it has to be recognised that this approach does not fit well within established disciplinary boundaries.

The importance of marrying production and consumption in accounts of fashion is one that is emphasised in much of the recent scholarship on fashion reviewed in this chapter.

An Imperfect Industry

Fashion plays a central role in the development of economies and is very often the way in which economies modernise from rural to industrial, as was the case in Britain, the first nation to industrialise. This industrialisation was prefaced on colonialisation through which raw materials were sourced and imported. In the case of the British Industrial Revolution, it was cotton production that was a significant motor for industrialisation. Imported cotton, from India especially, became fashionable from the eighteenth century as a versatile fabric for household linens and later, as a dress fabric (Wilson 2007). The British cotton industry grew exponentially in the nineteenth century and Britain became a vast consumer of the natural resources of their colonies in the Indian subcontinent, thereby destroying the indigenous market. Chacchi (1984) argues that British rule led to the destruction of traditional handicrafts and handloom production in India, turning one of the oldest textile countries in the world into an importer of textile goods from Britain.

The same industry that squandered resources abroad depended upon the extensive exploitation of labour at home. Images of the dangerous and noisy mills and overcrowded, unhygienic sweatshops have come to stand as one of the defining features of production during the Industrial Revolution in Britain in the nineteenth century. As Howard (1997: 151) argues:

> the apparel industry has long been plagued by a noxious creature known as the sweatshop. The word conjures up images of sweltering tenements and dark lofts, of women and children toiling into the night for wages that will barely keep them alive ... It is the peculiar nature of this industry that such conditions can be found today more or less as they existed a hundred years ago.

Howard (1997: 152) goes on to quote the economist John R. Commons, who in 1901 offered the following definition:

> the term 'sweating' or 'sweating system,' originally denoted a system of subcontract wherein the work is let out to contractors to be done in small shops or homes ... the system to be contrasted with the sweating system is the 'factory system,' wherein the manufacturer employs his own workmen, under the management of his own foreman or superintendent, in his own building.

The reason for the development of this subcontracting chain lies in the 'peculiar nature' of fashion, according to Howard. More than most cultural products, clothing, especially for women, is very unpredictable: seasonal changes and movement of fashion mean that the production of clothes for women is particularly risky (as discussed in more detail below). No trader wants to be left with garments they cannot shift and so 'the industry has historically dealt with this unpredictability by pushing risk down through the production chain: from retailer to manufacturer to contractor and subcontractor and ultimately into the worker's home' (Howard 1997: 15).

The result of this 'dog eat dog' approach to subcontracting is poor pay and conditions for those at the very end of the chain, the women who sew the fabric and put the garments together. The existence of sweated labour today shows how incomplete the process of industrialisation has been within the textile and garment industries. If, as was thought in the nineteenth century and the early twentieth, technology is progress, one would expect that new inventions for the spinning of yarn and the cutting or sewing of cloth would have brought improvements for workers. At the very least, such technology might speed up the process of making garments. However, compared with other industries, such as cars, clothing manufacture is much less mechanised and technological developments have not eliminated the basic unit of production, the woman at a sewing machine. Thus, new technologies for making clothes developed over the nineteenth century did not elevate these conditions, since technology alone does not produce cultural change. Marx's prediction that the use of the sewing-machine would, with other progress forces, do away with 'the murderous, meaningless caprices of fashion' has not come about (Fine and Leopold 1993: 100). The sewing-machine has remained the primary piece of technology in clothing production even today and this dynamic makes clothing production at odds with other forms of mass production, for example the car industry. By contrast, fashion never fully reached mass production. Instead of large-scale machinery gradually replacing individual workers, the individual worker at an individual machine remains the staple of clothing production, even as the relationship was made increasingly more automatic. While the sewing-machine stimulated factory production and speeded up the time it took to make clothes, 'it also served to reinforce rather than undermine the craft basis of production' (1993: 102). As Fine and Leopold note, by 1882 there were sixty-eight different stitches in use by tailors with greater skill. The sewing-machine may have been designed as a labour-saving device but it also served to heighten what was expected in a dress, so that dressmakers were under pressure to produce more elaborate clothing. However, there was a parallel movement towards the reduction of skill: sewing tasks were broken down as technologies such as the buttonholing machine developed. Thus, say Fine and Leopold, while these inventions speeded up the pace of tailoring tasks, they did not increase the number of garments that could be made up simultaneously. An early exception to this was the introduction in the 1870s of a steam-powered cutting machine, which could cut up to twenty-four layers of cloth at a time.

Fashion and inequalities

The history of industrialisation within the clothing and textile industry is a history inextricably linked to colonial exploitation abroad, as well as the exploitation of labour at home. To unpack the fashion industry, according to Phizacklea (1990) is to unpack the interconnections between class, gender, race and ethnicity, connections that have deep historical roots. These patterns have their origins in pre-industrial times: in their analysis of gender relations in the textile and garment industry, Lown and Chenut (1984: 25) argue that

> built into the process of industrial and technological change were many notions concerning the appropriate gender behaviour of women workers, and many fears about the implications of any changes in the familiar patterns of gender roles.

They examine the structure of textile production prevalent in pre-industrial Britain under the cottage system (also known as the 'putting out' system), according to which wool production was organised by the husband/father in the home: merchants distributed wool to a male in the household responsible for supervising the spinning, which was done by women and children. Weaving was a job largely performed by men and acquired a higher status than spinning. Although some women were weavers, by the eighteenth century they had been gradually eased out by male weavers who, increasingly insecure about their position, established guilds to exclude women and children. With the coming of mechanised means to produce fabric (silk looms were the first to be mechanised, followed in 1718 by the first water-powered mill in Derby and later by steam-driven machines), production was moved out of the home and into the factories.

Under the factory system existing gender roles were reproduced – women and children were employed to operate power looms and men supervised. This division of labour was also a division of pay and status, since men were rewarded with higher wages than women, who were usually paid on a piece rate (i.e. by the amount of spun yarn produced). Industrialisation therefore reproduced unequal gender relations characteristic of pre-industrial times as well as the gendered division between 'skilled' and 'unskilled': tasks associated with men were awarded the higher status of 'skilled' than tasks associated with women. While there is nothing 'natural' about these divisions, ideas about the 'natural' capacities of men and women were employed to legitimate this arrangement. As Elson (1984) argues, myths abound about women in the textile and clothing industry: for example, women are not technically minded; they have 'nimble fingers'; they don't need to earn as much as men since they are dependent upon men. Elson also argues that such myths are still perpetuated in the developing world by governments who sell these ideas about their female workforce in order to attract multinational companies to produce in their countries. She then explores how these myths are underpinned by assumptions about male and female skills. Female skills are seen to 'just happen'; they are 'natural' and therefore without any real art or technique since, as Phizacklea (1990) argues, the acquisition of skill is located in the domestic arena and largely 'hidden' from public view and therefore from recognition. Thus, say Chapkis and Enloe (1984), rather than being 'cheap', women's labour is cheapened by cultural attitudes that fail to recognise it or give it adequate status and reward.

Thus, new technologies are adapted to fit culture rather than bring about change, as some people expect or hope. Existing myths about gender form part of the calculation of companies about what machinery to use and what labour to target. According to Lown and Chenut (1984), in the nineteenth century the textile company Courtaulds deliberately designed machinery that could be operated by young female hands and sought out female labour in areas where poverty levels were high. They decided on Halstead in Essex because it was a depressed farming area that had suffered greatly not only as a result of indus- trialization but through the movement of the wool trade to Lancashire. This provided Courtaulds with a ready-made pool of exploitable labour.

Lown and Chenut also examine the similarities and differences between textile production in France, the United States and India. For example, in the United States in the nineteenth century young women from rural communities formed the bulk of textile workers. Relocated from the countryside to factory towns, these girls and young women were expected to send home the vast proportion of their wages. Later in the century immigrant labour from eastern Europe was exploited. As Howard notes, 'between 1880 and 1900, more than 3 million European immigrants poured into our cities, Jews fleeing the pogroms of Russia, Italians and Slavs and other workers ... desperate for work at almost any wage' (1997: 152). As a major gateway to the 'New World', New York was fed by this steady stream of immigrants and soon developed as a major centre for garment manufacture. Today this pattern continues with poor immigrant women from South America making up the vast proportion of workers in the garment industry in the United States – each new wave of immigration providing a new group of vulnerable workers whose labour can be exploited.

Gender, Class and Ethnic Relations in the Fashion Industry

As noted earlier, inequality in the textile and clothing industry does not just run along inequalities of class: gender, race and ethnicity have also been well-documented by historians of fashion. As Chapkis and Enloe (1984) and Phizacklea (1990) argue, ethic women are targeted for recruitment into textile industries. Indeed, racism and ethnocentrism operate globally as Western companies legitimise their move to countries in the southern hemisphere by arguing that Asian women are naturally willing to work for longer, naturally more inclined to do repetitive work. As Chapkis and Enloe argue, 'Third world women – so the racist/sexist explanation goes – are "naturally willing" to work for less and "naturally tolerant" of harsher working conditions' (1984: 3). The link between ethnicity and sexism is complex: according to Enloe (1984), when ethnic groups are organised into a hierarchy, women tend to be pushed into less desirable jobs. This is confirmed by Phizacklea (1990) who examines the inter-connections between class, gender, race and ethnicity in the textile and clothing industries across Europe. She describes how the system of subcontracting takes different forms in different countries: in Germany, for example, retailers tend to subcontract to producers in Asian countries whereas in Britain it is generally entrepreneurs at home who co-ordinate the production of short-run clothes. These British firms are predominantly run by ethnic minority men at the end of the 'dog eat dog' subcontracting chain. The chain can mean up to 200 per cent mark-up on British goods and paltry sums for the subcontractors and female workers. Predominance of ethnic minority men in this industry is an important factor. As traditional jobs decline, many of these men have little option but to pursue an entrepreneurial route but, says Phizacklea (1990), if ethnic men have low status, women are positioned even lower. In fact, she encountered no female entrepreneur in preparing her study. Working conditions are sometimes carried out in conditions not unlike the 'sweated' conditions of the nineteenth century – in small and cramped rooms around the East End of London, for example. However, an even 'cheaper' form of production now readily used in Britain and other developed countries is home-working, where the labour is performed in the home and the home-worker pays the fixed costs of fuel, lighting and so on. The status of these women is not helped by their social position *vis-à-vis* immigration legislation in many countries where immigrant women enter as the 'chattel' of their male partner/breadwinner and therefore acquire secondary status in the labour market (Phizacklea 1990). Moreover, fear of racial attack makes home-working safer for such women. In this respect, their status and conditions of existence are tied to other power relations, not least widespread and pervasive racism that is frequently institutionalised. As waves of immigrants are excluded from mainstream job opportunities, they become concentrated in those sectors with poor pay and conditions, largely 'hidden' from view and therefore vulnerable to exploitation.

This naked exploitation of poor working-class women and ethnic minorities has not been met passively: the history of the textile and garment industries is littered with stories of resistance. As Ross notes, 'because these industries have seen some of the worst labor excesses, they have also been associated with historic victories for labor and hold a prominent symbolic spot on the landscape of labor iconography' (1997: 11). For example, Lown and Chenut (1984) note how in 1860 women at Courtaulds went on strike when the company tried to reduce piece rate. Although they were forced back to work after lockout, they were more successful in the following decade when employers, fearful of losing female workers to domestic service, had to improve pay and conditions. Female garment workers were at the fore of industrial action in the United States at the turn of the century when a series of strikes among garment workers left their mark on labour relations. The focus of industrial action was the eradication of the sweatshop, which did drop out of view temporarily, although, as Ross notes, it never really disappeared. Perhaps the most famous piece of industrial action in the garment industry is the Triangle Shirtwaist Company walkout of 1909, which sparked widespread strike action among 20,000 shirtwaist makers across the country. This was followed in 1910 by 60,000 cloak makers going on strike. This led to the 'Protocol of Peace', which 'required employers to recognise the union and a union shop, set up a grievance procedure and a Joint Board of Sanitary Control to police health conditions in the shops' (Howard 1997: 153). The optimism of this Protocol was quickly dispelled when 146 workers died six months later in the Triangle Shirtwaist factory. The Protocol led many manufacturers to close down their shops and contract their work out, thereby passing on the liability to monitor working conditions to the subcontractor. As Howard notes, this situation only served to push the sweatshop further to the margins, putting an artificial distance between the manufacturer and the subcontractor which under-mined the ability to maintain legal standards in the shops. However, in 1926 a commission was set up in New York to examine the conditions of work in the garment industry, intended to ensure that the manufacturer (or 'jobber') could not escape liability but must share 'joint liability' with the contractor. This did result in a steady rise in pay and conditions, so that by the mid-1960s 'more than half of the 1.2 million workers in the apparel industry were organised and real wages had been rising for decades' (1997: 155).

While it is often thought that such naked exploitation has since been eradi-cated, the 'basic dynamic has not changed in a hundred years' (Howard 1997: 151). Today, garment workers are still subject to the vagaries of volatile market forces, which is highly recession sensitive. They are disposable labour, brought in cheaply when there is work and laid off when the market slows down. What has changed to some extent is the location of sweatshops in today's global economy. It is also the case that new relations of exploitation have been built on race and ethnic difference as well as gender. Sweated labour can now be found in developing countries such as those of the Asian subcontinent; they can also be found among the immigrant populations of developed countries in the West. As Ross (1997) notes, the high hopes of the New Deal in the 1960s have been increasingly undermined by political and economic changes since the 1970s as recession, neo-liberalism, and laissez-faire economics, under the banner of 'free trade', have put increasing pressure on producers in the garment industry to search for ever cheaper labour. Today in the garment industry one finds the most vulnerable and exploited workers, whose pay and conditions are the first to go in this global battle. In addition, home-working has returned as a mode of production that keeps costs down and profits up for big corporations. More shocking is the discovery of indentured labour on

US soil – in 1995 the contractors El Monte were found to have imported Thai women to work in its Californian factory, where they had little freedom and were little more than wage slaves (Su 1997). These relations of exploitation need situating within the context of the clothing industry in general, and women's clothing production. However, attention also needs to be paid to recent challenges by garment workers in the Global South, where protests at pay and working conditions do occur, as in the case of protests in Darka, Bangladesh in 2018 for a raise in the minimum wage. In their analysis of the global production networks in China, Pun et al. (2020) note that despite severe pressures and global competition, garment workers in China do have some power to shape these networks. As they argue (2020: 751), '[L]argely neglected in previous studies is the fact that China's garment workers, though seldom engaged in large-scale strikes (Chan 2015), can exert some control over labour processes in the different layers of the garment sector.' Their empirical study of garment workers in the Shanghai area notes 'the changing patterns of control and workers' resistance, and workers' individual and collective strategies' (Pun et al. 2020: 746). Many Indian garment workers also came out in protest following the collapse of the Rana Plaza factory demanding changes to their pay and conditions.

Figure 16. Indian garment workers protest on the one-year anniversary of the Rana Plaza factory collapse. Source: Flickr/Solidarity Center

These critiques of fashion in the early literature on the industry focused almost entirely on the impact on workers – on labour conditions and exploitation of human resources. It is only more recently that the focus of attention has shifted to also include a look at the impact of the fashion industry on the environment, which is discussed in the final section of this chapter when examining debates about sustainability and ethics.

Fashion Consumption and Culture

If, as Fine and Leopold (1992: 101) argue, fashion is a 'hybrid', then studies need to attend to the material relations of production and consumption, and to the discursive relations in terms of how it speaks of identity, gender and sexuality. Over the last few decades, numerous fashion scholars have drawn attention to fashion as an important industry, which combines many agencies and processes located across production, distribution and consumption. Early sociological analysis of the industry from Blumer (1969) and Braham (2007) have been influential in describing the multiple agencies that work to produce fashion. While their analysis is still relevant, more recent scholarship has been concerned to evidence empirically the work of these multiple agents located in different sectors of the economy and within cultural organisations. The main aim of these sociological studies (such as the systems of provision approach discussed above and in the main Introduction) is to show need for integrated analysis to consider the overlapping and interconnected agents of production, consumption and the many mediating agencies in between – the various 'middlemen' [sic], to whom Leopold (1992) refers as fashion buyers and agents. Together, these agents' work links production to consumption. More recent work in fashion scholarship has focused particular attention on various mediating agencies such as journalism/magazines, fashion bloggers and Instagram 'influencers', who are, to use French sociologist Pierre Bourdieu's (1984) influential concept, 'cultural intermediaries' or CIs. These CIs are important for mediating between production and consumption and their important work involves defining and valorising fashion to generate its value as 'new', 'trendy', etc.

As Fine and Leopold (1993) argue, the history of fashion is a history of systems for making, distributing and consuming clothes. Made to measure clothing (bespoke tailoring and *haute couture*) co-exist today, especially in France, alongside mass-produced clothing, which is fragmented into different market segments. Clothing provision is also organised into segmented markets – those for children, men, and women – as well as markets of different sizes, with each of these developing different strategies for managing production. Each sector in fashion production has its own dynamics, linking a wide range of agents in the process. According to Fine and Leopold, if one can generalise about the directions taken by the clothing industry in the last 200 years, one can say that it has transformed from consumption of essential items of dress designed to last, to the purchase of multiple garments, bought cheaply and replaced frequently. In this way, fast fashion has begun to mimic the food industry, where goods are marketed as perishable.

Indeed, in terms of understanding contemporary fast fashion, it is important to consider the significance of timing, so critical in women's fashion. Since fashion is about constant change, it is characteristically concerned with timing changes in trends, ensuring the turnaround from design to manufacture and distribution is carefully coordinated. As Fine and Leopold (1993) note, in the 1920s the women's clothing industry was still operating under primitive levels of development compared with other consumer industries like cars and, indeed, in contrast to men's fashions where production has long been geared towards 'staples' such as suits, jackets, overcoats and the like. Fine and Leopold argue that rapidly changing styles over the twentieth (and one can argue even faster in the twenty-first century) has come to serve as a compensation for the failure to achieve mass production within women's clothing. In other words, as previously considered in earlier chapters, the story of fashion is the story of women's clothing and its rapid changing aesthetic but not because of some essential feminine psychological impulse or 'shifting erogenous zone' arguments put forward by early theories (Laver or Flügel, as discussed in Chapter 5). Instead, Fine and Leopold offer a more sociological explanation: they suggest the evolution of the fashion system represented an attempt to accommodate the failure to achieve mass production fully (Fine and Leopold 1993: 95). Leopold (1992) further undermines the arguments that link fashion to the essential frivolity or vanity of women, shifting attention away from the psychology of the consumer to the dynamics of the industry. Fashion as transient, fast-changing style has become the motor of women's clothing and this is the main reason for the injustices of the fashion system, especially today's fast fashion. Fast turnover of style puts pressure on manufacturers to work quickly and at low cost to reduce the risk of over-production for clothing which, once ready, is no longer 'in' fashion. Producers are more likely to rely on subcontracting, which can seek out the most 'flexible' workforce, i.e. the one that can be picked up and laid off at will, with no demand for sickness benefits, maternity leave and the like. In the United States and Britain, successive neoliberal governments over the years have driven down wage costs and produced a ready-made pool of such labour at home willing to work for paltry sums.

Demographic factors have also played an important part in the development of mass production in men's clothing: in particular, the movement of populations to the West served to stimulate clothing production for men whose requirements were not for fashionable but for practical clothing. Throughout the eighteenth century, Europe exerted an influence over fashions in the United States with merchants importing clothes from London and Paris. However, the growth in settlers in the Midwest swelled the population of rural dwellers.

As railways and waterways pushed westwards, this expanding population of male workers needed rugged and protective clothing, their demands spurring technical change in clothing production to increase availability of garments. As a result, tools and materials were adapted from engineering work to clothing production (for example, the use of rivets instead of the hand-sewn seam). Fine and Leopold (1993) argue that the link between new patterns of work and new clothes is shown in the cowboy, who, working in dusty conditions, required strong and protective clothing: a hat to protect his eyes, a bandana to shield his mouth and so on. Sailors and slaves also required clothing that was hard wearing and tough and these large groups of male workers acted as a stimulus for mass-produced clothes. The spur to industrialisation and mass production came from the fact that these early markets were large and uniform while the newly built railroads and waterways also helped to open up new distribution channels for domestic clothing production of menswear. The Civil War also aided this process by encouraging the development of the first standardised sizing in men's clothing to aid the production of uniforms. This was a significant development, since standard sizing is crucial for the advancement of ready-made clothing.

Women's clothing was hardly affected by such developments. Indeed, female work did not demand particular dress and women's culturally acquired skills for sewing also meant that many clothes were produced at home. Indeed, the sewing-machine not only stimulated factory production but also facilitated home dressmaking, spurring the development of commercial patterns made by companies such as Buttericks. Women's factory-made clothes did not begin to appear until the beginning of the twentieth century, corresponding to the increasing participation of women in the labour market, among other factors. Yet even by the close of the First World War the industrial development of women's clothing continued to lag behind men's, 'displaying characteristics increasingly at odds with those conducive to the spread of mass production' (Fine and Leopold 1993: 101).

Changing Patterns of Fashion Retail

Understanding fashion as a system of production, an economic and cultural practice, means tying production regimes to consumption together as many scholars have done in recent years. Fashion consumption has taken many different forms – early fashion consumption through bespoke tailors and home sewing has, gradually, been replaced by other ways to consume, notably the rise of the department store in the nineteenth century, followed by the shopping mall, with various forms of second-hand retail paralleling these developments. The shop or market is a location of economic exchange and a clearly cultural place too. In other words, shops and markets are spaces of economic activity (buying and selling) rooted in a whole series of other everyday practices and activities: indeed, one can consume without purchasing anything, as the term 'window shopping' suggests, the items consumed are not material goods but the spectacle of the shop itself. There are now many studies of spaces of consumption, ranging from the market, the department store and, more recently, the shopping centre and out-of-town warehouse 'designer villages' (e.g. Shields 1992; Slater 1993, 1997). The spatial organisation of these sites is said to be implicated in the constitution of 'modern' and 'postmodern' identities. These spaces are not only prime sites for the consumption of goods and images but play a crucial role in the articulation of desire, identity and subjectivity in modern, and some would say, postmodern culture. As Foucault (1977) demonstrates in his work on the prison, space is never inert or simply 'there' but active in the constitution of social relations. The layout of a building and the spatial arrangement of streets impact upon the movement of bodies, directing the individual and organising the flow of the crowd. In recent years, attention has been focused on aspects of shopping such as shop design and display that direct the gaze of the modern-day *flâneur*. Slater suggests that these spaces of consumption carry an 'enormous ideological load in the modern period and again today: the image of a thriving civil society' (1993: 188–9).

Markets, shops and department stores

Shops occupy an important place within the economic and cultural life of the town and the city. Braudel argues that 'without a market, a town is inconceivable' (Slater 1993: 191). The market (open-air or closed) is the earliest form of shopping space and is a crucial location for the sale of second-hand clothing. Until the early twentieth century when ready-to-wear fashion became available to most of the population, working-class people wore second-hand clothes purchased at markets in addition to clothes made at home. Clothing was a considerable expense but the second-hand market 'at least enabled such clothes to be recycled, to outlive their role as fashion goods' (Fine and Leopold 1993: 131). Today, while old-style second-hand markets still exist, they do so alongside department stores, shopping centres and, more recently, out-of-town warehouses and 'designer villages', which stock end-of-line fashions. The pursuit of second-hand clothing became popular once more in the 1960s and 1970s among the young, especially hippies, who rejected consumerist lifestyle as wasteful and ecologically damaging. As McRobbie (1994b) notes, there are various interpretations of this style. She cites Hall (1977), for example, who argues that the hippy style indicates an 'identification with the poor' as well as a rejection of middle-class style. However, second-hand style sets itself apart from middle-class values and the greyness of real poverty, a fact which leads some people (the novelist Angela Carter is acknowledged by McRobbie in this respect) to question whether rummaging through jumble sales makes light of those who search in need and not through choice. Much of the student and young professional's second-hand look is fashion driven, not about poverty dressing. McRobbie notes that 'second-hand style continually emphasises its distance from second-hand clothing' (1994b: 140) and involves the highly selective exercise of taste by the second-hand shopper. Whatever the reasons and whatever the interpretations made of second-hand clothing, the second-hand look has continued to be a popular one with many young people. McRobbie (1994) argues that most youth subcultures have relied on second-hand clothes for their style and that this style has influenced mainstream fashion and retail to the extent that shops aimed at young people often borrow from the tactics of the market traders when displaying their clothes. As McRobbie (1994) suggests, there are numerous cross-fertilisations between the two kinds of shopping. Today markets function more like mainstream stores than old-fashioned markets, accepting credit as payment and not simply cash and fixing prices, while mainstream fashion stores copy the look and cache of the street markets: for example, Anthropologie and Urban Outfitters closely resemble market stalls and bazaars. In this way, the division between street style and second-hand shopping and mainstream shops is thus blurred.

Markets are places of social meeting and interaction, of 'heterogeneous activities', which attract crowds and naturally lend themselves to spectacle (Slater 1993). Earlier, shopping arcades brought together a range of activities when they first appeared in the late eighteenth and early nineteenth centuries. (Slater 1993: 192), referring to Walter Benjamin's work on arcades, notes how they bring together 'within a single image the idea that a market is, culturally, a gathering place for crowds, offering diverse points of focus for diverse and contingent interests. Arcades are covered passageways, usually arched and with shops and cafés on one or both sides; in the eighteenth century they occasionally included brothels and other places of urban pleasure. The Palais Royal, built in Paris in 1780, 'contained one such arcade, considered emblematic in showing the roots of modern consumerism in the urban, spectacle-focused crowd' (1993: 193). According to Slater, the arcade brought together three forms of crowd-gathering: 'the pre-modern market, the leisure gatherings of "society", and the city itself' (1993: 193). Arcades thus constituted a space for consumption, part old, part new, which served to promote modern forms of retail and consumption. Unlike the older market, where tradespeople sold their wares directly to the public, they separated production from consumption. Thus, modern shops stimulated the rise of 'middlemen', such as the shop or stall holder who mediated between producers and consumers. In gathering several merchants, the arcade continued the tradition of the pre-modern market but depersonalised the relations between seller and shopper, for example by relying on fixed prices rather than haggling. The arcade was also a space where the fashionable of 'society' met to promenade. This served to stimulate 'the growth of specific consumer infrastructures, for example the modern shop and the commercialisation of leisure' (1993: 194). A diverse range of social types such as financiers, *flâneurs*, dandies and prostitutes, each pursuing their own interests within the same space, could choose to attend concert halls or vaudeville, meeting rooms or clubs. Such a range of activities was later incorporated into big department stores, which at one time housed reading rooms, rest rooms, restaurants and later, hair and beauty salons. As such, arcades were like cities in miniature, simulations of a city within the city itself, not unlike in the modern shopping centre. In recent years, shopping centres have sprung up on the outskirts of cities across the developed world; representative examples include, in Britain, the Arndale Centre in Manchester and, in the US, the Copley Center in Boston. Langman (1992) and Shields (1992) argue that the shopping centre has replaced the Gothic cathedral of feudal times and the factory of the industrial age to become the building/space par excellence of contemporary society. However, while seeming a new and 'postmodern' space, as we can see from Slater's discussion (1993), the shopping centre incorporates many aspects of modern as well as pre-modern consumption.

Shops have always enjoyed a special place in the city as spaces of pleasure, desire and fantasy. As Porter notes, 'the eighteenth century brought the emergence of high-class shops, in the City, in Piccadilly and Mayfair' (1990: 199). These shops opened up new pleasures and opportunities for 'respectable' women previously denied the freedom to wander through the city, although their movements were still more restricted than that of their male counterparts (Nava 1992). Shopping could be a pleasurable activity for men too: as the poet Robert Southey wrote in a letter, 'if I were to pass the remainder of my life in London ... I think the shops would continue to amuse me. Something extraordinary or beautiful is forever to be seen in them' (Porter 1990: 145–6). Shops were places to marvel at and enjoy: in the 'upmarket' shops of London, goods would be displayed seductively in the window. Shelley noted how 'cunningly' women's fabric was displayed:

> whether they are silks, chintzes or muslins, they hang down in folds behind the fine high windows so that the effect of this or that material, as it would be in the ordinary folds of a woman's dress, can be studied ... Behind great glass windows absolutely everything one can think of is neatly, attractively displayed, and in such abundance of choice as almost to make one greedy. (Porter 1990: 144)

Drapery shops led the way in terms of shop-front design but it was the department store, such as the Bon Marché in Paris or Whiteley's in Bayswater, London, which was the 'great Victorian innovation' (Porter 1990: 201). Up until the 1830s, shops had tended to be highly specialist but some shopkeepers, particularly drapers such as William Whiteley, saw the potential of expanding their product range and clientele (the prices in many such stores were beyond the reach of most people). By including more goods in one space, and by clearly pricing them, the expanding drapery shops of the mid-nineteenth century could afford cheaper prices and enable shoppers to see at a glance the cost of items without the embarrassment of having to ask the price of something. These drapery shops constituted proto-department stores built along the lines of indoor markets that were developed in the 1830s in such cities as Newcastle, where the Grainger market (completed in 1835) housed butchers, greengrocers and fancy goods stalls and 'acted as a magnet to this city redevelopment' (Lancaster 1995: 8). By taking 'the fear out of shopping' through clear pricing, these new stores grew alongside the new lower middle-class household (Porter 1990).

According to Lancaster, 'the origins of the British department store are firmly rooted in the twin processes of industrialisation and urbanisation' (1995: 7), although he acknowledges that such shops have roots that go back further than this. The first department stores in Britain sprang up in the north, for example in Manchester and Newcastle. Whiteley's, founded in 1864, was the first such store to open in London, initially as a drapers but expanding rapidly to provide jewellery, furs and other fancy goods. Soon after, large stores such as Dickins and Jones moved to Regent Street and expanded to become a department store in the 1890s, while the Army and Navy stores began business in 1871

The novelty of these proto-department stores and the later big department stores was their provision of a wide range of goods and services, including restaurants and rest rooms. They were also places in which to sit around and dream, and this was nowhere more apparent than in Aristide Boucicaut's Bon Marché in Paris, founded in 1852. In style, the Bon Marché borrowed from the international exhibitions: the Great Exhibition in Crystal Palace, London (1851), and later the Exposition Universelle in Paris (1855) and the world fairs of Chicago (1893) and St Louis (1904). Not only were prices clearly displayed as they had been at the Paris exhibition, but the shop's whole environment was created to be a spectacle, encouraging leisurely browsing.

One did not necessarily have to consume anything except the spectacle itself, although one was encouraged to imagine ownership of the goods displayed. The store was built on a grand scale, facilitating a new kind of freedom: 'anyone could enter, browse in departments, wander from floor to floor, without spending a centime. The earliest proto-department stores had been too small and formal to offer such anonymity' (Lancaster 1995: 18). By reducing fears about shopping and stimulating desires, the department store became a showcase for an expanding market of goods and commodities to a larger number of people than ever before. Department stores were respectable places for 'respectable' middle-class women to visit and socialise in public in the nineteenth century (Nava 1996)

Innovative shop design, window dressing and interior displays facilitated the spectacle of the drapery shop and the department store. While the eighteenth century had 'designed the seductive shop-front' what was lacking until the nineteenth century, says Porter, was good lighting. Giant shops like Swan

Figure 17. General view of the Bon Marché. Source: Wikimedia Commons

and Edgar's, which sprang up in the West End of London had great gas-lit windows that could serve as showcases for commodities (Porter 1990). Thus, new forms of lighting revolutionised modern architecture: as the architectural historian Reyner Baham put it, 'the sheer abundance of light ... effectively reversed all established visual habits by which buildings were seen' (Leach 1989: 104). Nowhere was the zest for display more apparent than in the big city department stores of the United States: 'unlike Europeans, who often articulated aesthetic desires in high art, Americans channeled their desires almost entirely ... into the creation of mass commercial forms' (Leach 1989: 100). The commercial designers in the US worked to generate 'theatrical effects' and 'enchantment', 'interpreting and dramatising commodities and commodity environments in ways that disguised and transformed them into what they were not' (Leach 1989: 100). Not only did these designers have new forms of lighting at their disposal, but they could also exploit new materials and techniques, for example, new ways of using glass to create etchings, glazes and frosting as well as new kinds of colour produced by aniline dyes, all with the aim of enticing and dazzling those who entered. Shop display became increasingly important in the late nineteenth century and it is 'appropriate that the first significant advocate of display was the greatest of all American fairy-tale writers, L. Frank Baum, creator of the 'Land of Oz' (Leach 1989: 107). Baum's philosophy, evident in his fairy-tales and his interest in merchandising, celebrated consumption, display and artificial spectacle. As well as writing, dabbling in photography and film and working in retail and marketing, he founded the first magazine devoted to display, Shop Window, and assembled the first National Association of Window Trimmers. According to Leach, for Baum 'display was fantasy, childhood, theater, technological play, and selling all rolled into one' (1989: 10). He saw the importance of display in attracting the attention of passers-by and in stimulating desire for consumption; in doing so, he 'raised the status of the shop window to first place among advertising strategies' (1989: 110). What is at stake in all this is the production of a world of fantasy premised on the consumption of goods and commodities. Between the late nineteenth century and the early twentieth, America became the 'Land of Desire', a place that stimulated the consumption of commodities. This was a world that emphasised individuality and individual satisfaction, an increasingly secular world of leisure and consumption that played on hedonism, the libido, dreams and longings. It is no surprise therefore to find that the 'metaphor of consumption as a "dreamworld" dominated nineteenth-century discussions of consumption' (Slater 1993: 196).

The emphasis on spectacle is still a feature of large shops and department stores, especially over Christmas, when goods are extravagantly displayed, often in dreamscapes and fantasy settings. Shop display has become an important component in retailing practice: the modern department store as well as many shops are well versed in strategies for attracting the gaze and directing the feet of consumers through space and time. In today's shop interiors 'polished wood, solid-metal finishing, large plate-glass windows, dressing mirrors, show cards, props, spotlighting and so on' call on shoppers to partake in a spectacle, thus organising 'ways of looking for consumers' (Nixon 1996: 61). In his analysis of the construction of masculinity in the 1980s, Nixon (1996) examines the ways in which retailing practices, such as shop design and interiors, orchestrated the selling of menswear in shops such as Next and Top Man. For Nixon, the design innovations taking place in menswear in the 1980s were shaped 'by their insertion within a set of practices of selling' (1996: 47). In other words, an important part of the selling of new styles for men was their location in particular sites of consumption that were consciously designed. Nixon's account of menswear, unlike other studies that examine fashion by abstracting it and treating it to textual or semiotic analysis, insists that the consumption of a particular fashion is not separate from retail practice; from such things as shop design and layout. These practices are important in the process of marking out particular styles and particular subjectivities associated with them, in this case, the 'new man'. In this respect, Nixon considers the way in which shop design and fashion retailing (along with magazines such as Arena) operated in conjunction with each other to produce forms of spectatorship for men in relation to the 'new man' of the 1980s.The same could be said of many contemporary big-name department stores and high-street shops, which carefully manufacture the environment of the shop to create the appropriate look. When Ralph Lauren introduced 'Polo' to Selfridges in the mid-1990s in London, the layout was carefully orchestrated by designers from the fashion house to ensure the appropriate image was created for the label.

It is apparent that fashion exists not simply as an abstract force or idea, but is put into practice through the actions of individual agents, producers, buyers, magazine editors, journalists, retailers and consumers within the various subsections of the fashion system/s. For it to become the dominant style/s, fashion has to be translated, made meaningful, a process that cuts across economic and cultural practices to the extent that it is impossible to separate the economic from the cultural since, as du Gay (1997) argues, these do not exist in isolation but mutually constitute each other. However, as Leopold (1992) and Fine and Leopold (1993) argue, this is not recognised in the literature, which tends to focus on either consumption or production, without examining the ways in which they intersect. What is left implicit but unspoken by du Gay and Fine and Leopold is that the body is the prime object of fashion. As argued throughout this book, fashion is an important site for discourses on the body and identity produced across various sites and practices, ranging from designers who design on the body, models who wear and help promote the fashions, to journalists and retailers who interpret the body styles through text and image. The seamstresses who sew the garments cannot be ignored since fashion is produced through the labour (and exploitation) of these individuals. Consumers cannot be left out of the picture since fashions become popular only once they are consumed and worn: in other words, through the active articulation and interpretation of fashion in everyday dress produced at the level of the individual body. Understanding fashion requires understanding the interconnections between these various bodies: the discursive, the textual and the lived body and between the actions of agents who are themselves embodied.

Fashion as Culture Industry: Fashion Industry from the Twentieth Century

These developments in the production and consumption of fashion have shaped the industry as we know it today, in the twenty-first century. Production within the twentieth century has not changed very radically from the nineteenth century: similar conditions for women's clothing continue, particularly production based around sewing machines and sweated labour, which has accelerated with fast fashion. These problems are addressed below when discussing sustainability. Consumption practices still involve the retailing of fashion through shops, although many department stores and shopping centres are struggling to compete with online retailing. Significant changes in the twenty-first century extended participation in fashion to more of the population. Although full mass production has not occurred in fashion, something like mass fashion did emerge in the twentieth century. Another major change has been a move away from centralised fashion trends, dictated by leading fashion houses. The rise of youth subcultures and popular high-street stores has shifted the directions of fashion flow and influence and this greater participation, coupled with the importance of street style gradually challenges the stubborn idea that fashion is the preserve of an elite.

From elite style to popular fashion

In the late nineteenth and twentieth centuries Paris was the key fashion city, with the work of early couturiers (such as Charles Worth and later Coco Chanel) dictating the dominant fashion trends of the day. Although *haute couture* was (and still is) a limited market for the very wealthy, these early couture houses disseminated trends via pret-a-porter collections that were influential across other segments of fashionable dress. Gilbert (2006: 22) notes how

> [I]n the early twentieth century there was a formal institutionalization of the distinction between couturiers and other fashion professionals with the establishment of La Chambre Syndicale de la Couture Parisienne in 1910. Organised fashion shows and seasonal collections also began in this period.

However, he argues, 'the post-war period from the 1960s onwards, was [...] characterised by a less concentrated and more differentiated ordering of fashion's major centres' (Gilbert 2006: 25) with cities like New York and later Shanghai reconfiguring 'the global geographies of the fashion system in the second half of the twentieth century' (2006: 25). Numerous developments helped shift the centre of power including the rise of mass fashion, much of it influenced by pop music and youth cultures as sources of fashion style since the 1960s. Trends are now said to 'bubble up' from high street to fashion catwalk (Polhemus 1994).

These developments have served to blur the division between high fashion and everyday fashion; the latter hardly lags behind 'high' fashion and in many cases dictates the trends that are only later picked up by couture. With new sources of fashion coming up from the street, the orderly dissemination of high fashion from couture collections each season is no longer viable. This leads Braham (1997: 145) to argue that we now have 'multiple fashions systems': fashion moves up, down and along from various starting-points and in several directions, rather than emanating from a single source or 'trickling down' from the elite to the majority. This decline in the role of the couture as the central fashion innovator has not meant that couture is irrelevant to contemporary fashion. Indeed, one of the striking features of fashion in recent years is the degree to which couture designs, along with their diffusion ranges and franchising of their name to lower price point commodities, such as perfume, have become part of the everyday currency of fashion. As Braham says, just because designers look to the street does not mean to say there is no reason to be interested in high fashion. First, this borrowing from the street may enhance the prestige of designers. Further, compelling evidence of the influence of designers also lies in the vast economic scope of these fashion houses, which are owned by multi-million-dollar conglomerates operating on a global scale. But these designer brands sit alongside popular high-street brands such as Zara and Hennes. As Braham (quoting Davis) acknowledges, the concerns of such multi-national financial backers serve to constrain designers by insisting that some of their designs should be popular and simple enough to be easily translated into mass-produced high-street designs. This economic imperative blurs the line between high fashion and everyday fashion and can be seen in the large number of franchising agreements between fashion houses and manufacturers (of sunglasses, underwear, perfume and cosmetics, etc.). For example, the High Fashion Industry Accord, signed in Italy in 1971, shows how important alliances between design houses, fabric and garment manufacturers and financial backers have become. Under this Accord, Italian couturiers receive subsidy if their new lines conform to guidelines agreed with major garment manufacturers who can easily reproduce their designs for mass markets. These examples provide evidence of the degree to which the couture designer is now much more part of the everyday world of commodity culture than the exclusive world of elite fashion.

Much scholarly research on consumption in the 1990s focused on highly differentiated 'taste markets' (Nixon 1996; Mort 1996) supported by 'niche marketing', which capitalises on new tastes. An apparently unending growth of symbolic material and images during the 1980s and 1990s – from advertising, marketing and retail design work – is said to weave meanings around commodities to the point where, according to Baudrillard (1983), the thing consumed is the image not the commodity. Such developments, including the increasing globalisation of production and consumption with the rise of multi-national brands such as Zara, have been characterised under the rubric 'post-Fordism', which refers to changing production and consumption regimes whereby production is tied ever closer to consumption through technologies of 'just-in-time' production. Major retailers, like Zara and Topshop, pioneered this approach, with sales data at the tills directly feeding into the design and production strategies to ensure that consumer sales and trends are matched to production runs. The fast turn-around of these data into fashionable dress (sometimes as short a cycle as six weeks or less) explains how the term 'fast fashion' has come to characterise much of our high-street fashion retailing. This has only accelerated with Instagram 'swipe-up' and click-to-buy features that provide almost instantaneous communication of trends from consumers to retailer/producer.

In Britain, the other factor that needs consideration in any discussion of fashion is the art school or college, which plays an influential role in the training of designers. Since the 1960s and the rise of celebrity youth designers such as Mary Quant and later, Vivienne Westwood, British fashion design has become world renowned for its imagination and innovation. This continued in the 1990s with the British 'invasion' of Parisian couture: John Galliano first at Givenchy and now at Christian Dior, Alexander McQueen at Givenchy, Stella McCartney at Chloé. According to Angela McRobbie, these designers are examples of a relatively new phenomenon, the designer as *auteur*, a phenomenon fuelled by fashion magazines, which play on the idea of the designer as genius. However, they represent the smallest minority of fashion designers, most of whom do not go on to achieve celebrity status but must carve out work for themselves in an increasingly crowded market. McRobbie (1998: 1) considers the way in which these designers constitute a 'new cultural worker'; in some ways 'prime examples' of 'Thatcher's children', who are 'enterprising' in their ability to sell their skills, either freelancing for corporate chains such as Next, or as independent designers selling direct to the public through market stalls. With the growth of subcultures, many young designers since the 1960s have found they can service these through small outlets and market stalls, resulting in a rise of 'subcultural entrepreneurialism': this 'self-generated, self-employment demonstrated the existence of a sprawling network of micro-economies initially inside the youth subcultures, and then extending far beyond them' (McRobbie 1998: 8) and latterly, feminised entrepreneurship networks, post austerity (McRobbie 2013, 2018).

Fashion: culture industry, circuits, and networks

Clearly, what this discussion points to is that fashion is as much about *culture* as it is about *economy*, if, indeed, any such clear distinction can be drawn between them, since economic activity is always culturally embedded, while culture can be and is frequently commodified, which retailing perfectly exemplifies (du Gay 1997). But many questions can be asked about the ways economic and cultural calculations are made. Who defines what is a fashion trend? Who selects what items – from a myriad of possibilities – to make available to consumers? These questions prompt us to consider the processes, practices and agents responsible for connecting producers/designers and consumer.

One way to think of fashion is as a *culture industry*: it is about material objects given a specific aesthetic value as the new thing/trend. Fashion is not alone in this respect: a premium is placed on 'new' trends and fashions in many markets (architecture, interior design, furniture, etc.). However, fashionable clothing tends to change more rapidly than buildings and this is especially true within the European fashion system, where very regular aesthetic swings are evidence in women's fashion in particular, as Leopold argues: each is its own system of provision, as discussed above.

A number of theoretical and methodological approaches from the 1980s onwards attempt to capture the multifarious aspects that make up fashion. One of the earliest is the 'circuits of culture' (du Gay 1997) that examines how goods move from production to distribution and consumption, and how each moment in the exchange shapes the meanings of these goods in successive feedback loops. Their famous case study of the Sony Walkman can be applied to understanding a fashion trend because it considers many actors responsible for bringing goods to market. Indeed, many agents are responsible alongside designers' work in shaping fashion value: fashion buyers, journalists, bloggers and Instagrammers, pop stars and celebrities and a host of more invisible intermediaries. The question of who defines what is 'fashion', needs to be answered by connecting these actors. Such attention to the whole circuit also points away from overarching theories of fashion (argued in Chapters 2 and 3 as being reductive) to consider the day-to-day workings of the fashion industry, which coordinate to produce goods that have aesthetic value at a given time. Hence, the value of a sociological lens to fashion means considering fashion as the product of a complex set of interactions between various agents set in temporal and spatial relations to one another – between design houses, fabric and clothing manufacturers and retailers and the fashion-buying public.

In the last few decades, numerous sociological accounts have attempted to examine some of the interactions and practices within the fashion industry. Although he does not draw on empirical work, Blumer (1969) is an early sociologist examining fashion as coordinated activities across different key agents in the industry. His idea of 'collective selection' points to the way fashion circulates inside the industry. He argues that designers' designs showcase many ideas, only some of which are picked up by journalists and buyers, who then disseminate looks for consumption. There are similarities in the choices that they make, which Blumer puts down to the fact that they share similar tastes and preferences and are all immersed in the same world of fashion, trained to spot trends. However, consumers also are key to things becoming popular: a style becomes fashion not when the elite wear it, but when it corresponds to 'the incipient taste of fashion-consuming public' (Braham 1997: 139). Every agent wants to be seen to catch the mood of the time and, in doing so, taps into the same cultural trends (in pop music, film, art, etc.). Similarly, Braham (1997: 134) notes, what is distinctive about the fashion code is that it must pass through the filter of the fashion industry. Thus, the suggested code modifications displayed on the catwalks of Paris stand to be rejected, toned down or embraced not only by a host of publicists, critics, journalists and fashion leaders, but also by garment manufacturers and store buyers (1997: 134).

However, without empirical data, Blumer and Braham's work lacks evidence, suggestive of an approach to the study of fashion rather than substantially showing us *how* fashion is produced. Indeed, 'it is altogether more demanding to begin to delineate the precise contents of this communication or to trace its operation' (Braham 1997: 142). More recently, ethnographic fieldwork has focused on these operations: e.g. Aspers' (2006) study of fashion photographers, Entwistle's (2009) study of fashion buyers and model agents, Lynge-Jorlén's (2016, 2017, 2020) study of niche fashion magazines and stylists. Meanwhile, Volante's (2021) analysis, drawing on practice theory, considers how routine practices within fashion work to produce an 'inertia' to change that, in his view, reproduces the thin body as the fashionable ideal (as discussed in the final section below).

Some of this scholarly work draws on Bourdieu's concept of cultural inter-mediaries (CIs) who shape culture in general and fashion tastes in particular. As Maguire and Matthews (2012: 551) put it:

> [T]he term 'cultural intermediaries' has been good to think with: it has been a productive device for examining the producers of symbolic value in various industries, commodity chains and urban spaces, highlighting such issues as the blurring of work and leisure ... and material practices involved in the promotion of consumption.

They note two different tracks for this research, one that looks at CIs as new middle-class *mediators/workers*, the other focusing on *mediation/work*. Thus, McRobbie (1998: 4) notes, 'the expanded market for images has created the need for a new workforce of image makers and, once again, the cultural intermediaries step in to play this role', while more recent analysis within actor-network-theory (ANT) focuses on processes of mediation and the 'quali-fication' of goods, drawing more on the influential sociology of Michel Callon (1998a, 1998b; see also Callon et al. 2005)

These sociological studies of fashion answer Fine and Leopold's much earlier criticism of separation of scholarly research between studies of economic analysis of production on the one hand, and cultural analysis of consumption on the other. Indeed, this more recent scholarly research on CIs is a hybrid of economy and culture: CIs are new economic workers, whose role within production is vital to the economy, as well also key cultural taste-formers whose work of mediation is calculating both economic and cultural value. In the following section, I expand further on both approaches – Bourdieu's sociology of fields and Callon's economic sociology/sociology of markets and how they have been applied to fashion. I conclude that noting these theorists and approaches are not incompatible and combining them enables a fuller picture of how fashion markets/fields are 'made up'.

The field of fashion

Bourdieu's (1984, 1993a, 1993b, 1993c) field analysis has been enormously influential in analysing fields of cultural production, such as fashion. His concepts are useful in understanding the circulation of value (cultural, symbolic) inside markets, with *capital* and *habitus* as particularly significant. Capital can take numerous forms – economic, cultural, social – and is unevenly distributed *across* and *within* fields: fields are hierarchically organised (art valued over fashion, for example), and within them some 'players' hold more capital and thus more status/power than others. All fields deploy specific forms of capital: 'fashion capital' inside fashion (Rocamora 2009; Entwistle and Rocamora 2006). As Bourdieu (1993b) puts it in his analysis of *haute couture* fashion in France, there are 'established players' with high capital, like Balmain, who seek to hold on to their long-established power, and 'newcomers', like Courrèges, who seek to challenge established fashion houses and make their mark. Newcomers challenge old positions but ultimately not the field's existence itself. While power and influence may appear to come from 'charisma' unique to players, as Bourdieu (1993b) argues, in answer to the question 'who can replace Chanel?', even the most charismatic actor can ultimately be replaced. Karl Lagerfeld wielded considerable charismatic power after Coco Chanel.

Within the field, capital is routinely mobilised and transferred. Bourdieu uses both religion and magic as analogies to describe the process whereby the capital of significant players confers value to things in the field: e.g. an editor, stylist, photographer or blogger is like a 'cleric' inside the church with the power to 'consecrate' things by their very selection. Bourdieu's own analysis of French designers suggests the power of key clerics gives objects meaning and status, much in the same way as the religious object, communion wine, is 'turned into blood' in a process known as 'transubstantiation'; or as 'magic' in that the transfer has an alchemic power to change the meaning of the object, be it a model or designer label (Bourdieu 1993c). A more modern example: when influential British style magazine of the 1990s *The Face* chose rising 'cult' photographer Corinne Day, who chose the young, unknown model Kate Moss for the 'Summer of Love' cover in 1990, a transfer of capital occurred within the field (or along the network, to use Callon's analogy discussed below) and led to the consecration of Day and Moss in the process. This transfer of cultural/ fashion capital constructs symbolic value across the field, or network, which can, ultimately, convert into economic value if, like Moss, you end up as 'the face of' a design house and a 'supermodel' (see Entwistle 2002, 2009 for further discussion). This process sees significance/value attributed to things – an 'It' handbag, or particular 'hot' designer – through the work of those cultural intermediaries whose high cultural/fashion capital creates value: 'Cultural intermediaries impact upon notions of what, and thereby who, is legitimate, desirable and worthy, and thus by definition what and who is not' (Maguire and Matthews 2012: 552).

Bourdieu's field theory is seductively appealing, for its conceptual language readily applies to many fields of cultural production. However, some of his ideas about fashion need updating and evidencing. Indeed, as Rocamora's (2002) critique of his work argues persuasively, his analysis of (French) fashion, focusing on *haute couture*, did not take account of many post-war developments in popular fashion and street style. Secondly, Bourdieu's account of fashion is largely theoretical (he did not carry out empirical work on fashion). Despite these issues, his work still has application. Entwistle and Rocamora's (2009) critical reassessment of his work demonstrates how the field can be empirically observable as a space of action. Their examination of the fashion week collections applies field theory to the very real spaces of the fashion show and exhibition, where the legitimated positions within the field are mapped out in physical space. For example, the power of field players is mapped into the seating plan around the catwalk/runway, which itself is set into the space to create a field of visibility of these positions, since it carves the audience in two and sheds light on the people who are awarded a front row seat. In this light are made visible the important editors (such as US *Vogue's* Anna Wintour), and key celebrities and other fashion dignitaries. Moreover, field position is also performed – embodied – through the visible *'habitus'* (clothes, taste and deportment) of fashion, as well as the rituals of the 'air kiss'.

Markets as Networks

Empirical questions remain as to how do some things get defined as 'fashionable' today? What are the day-to-day practices and processes that make up fashion? Rather than take for granted that we know who these cultural intermediaries are, and what they do, empirically grounded studies of fashion need to trace the emergence and circulation of fashion. We could, for example, ask how does this or that garment or style get selected, following it from design studio to shop-floor to consumer? How does this model come to be seen as 'hot'?

In recent years, an empirically informed sociology of markets has emerged, sometimes referred to as 'new' economic sociology and drawing on the work of French sociologist, Michel Callon (1998a, 1998b, 1999; Callon et al. 2005, 2007). Callon's actor-network theory (ANT) approach focuses on routine ways in which goods within a market are chosen, calculated and circulated. Although his work examines 'harder' markets in finance, science and technology, the emphasis on empirical observation of markets in action – seeing how actors *in situ* put markets together – is useful for analysing fashion markets.

Markets, for Callon, are particular 'assemblages' – configurations of actors often in specially designed spaces, which enable particular sorts of interactions. Significantly, the 'actor' in ANT can be a human or non-human: *anything that 'acts' can be an actor*. In my analysis of fashion buyers (Entwistle 2009) we can see that a fashion buyer acts to bring things to store for sale, but during their work they interact with non-human actors, such as financial instruments and devices, e.g. spreadsheets. A spreadsheet 'acts' because it provides information (sales of a certain line are down) that visualise weekly sales figures in 'virtual' form (Carrier and Miller 1998), prompting action by the buyer; for example, low sales figures may prompt a special offer or sale. Thus, once in place, non-human devices are actors prompting human actors to act.

Thus, markets are made up of heterogeneous actors, linked into 'networks' that support various calculations. Indeed, calculative action is a critical component of all markets: sellers have to calculate what to buy, in what quantity, for which consumer. Unlike in classical economics, calculation is not the privilege of isolated, sovereign individuals coming together to serve their own interests. This view of the essential calculating actor is a theoretical artifice of economics, according to Callon (and indeed, to Bourdieu as well). Instead, market calculations are 'formatted' within actor-networks so that calculations are aided/distributed across a range of practices and devices that facilitate numerous interactions. Callon (1998a) famously gives the example of the strawberry market analysed by Garcia-Parpet (2007), which brings buyers and sellers together into a particular sort of interaction that prompts forms of market calculation. Applying this approach, Sommerlund (2008) notes how fashion mediation occurs through spaces and devices and she examines three in particular: fashion fairs, showrooms and look-books. 'Following the actors' as ANT instructs us to do as sociologists means we examine how actors meet one another, what happens in the interaction and how it shapes 'qualities' seen in the product.

According to Callon et al. (2005) all markets entail *calculation of qualities*: in the case of fashionable dress, this might be 'fashionability' or 'trendiness'. In addition, these qualities are assessed in relation to price point: 'cheap' might be important or 'quality' depending if you're in the fast-fast or designer market. Callon et al.'s (2005) analysis shows how all goods pass through a series of 'tests' that literally enable these qualities to be assessed. I apply this in my analysis of model agents' work (Entwistle 2004, 2009). Model agents ('bookers') define and shape the model quality/qualities, which are by no means self-evident or straight-forward 'good looks' but often far more esoteric. Indeed, bookers seek an ineffable 'certain something' in a potential model and this quality involves many calculations of physicality (symmetry of face/height/age) and 'photogenic' ability. Potential models are therefore 'tested' with a Polaroid or digital image (indeed it is called a 'test' shot). Assuming they have potential, a model might then be sent on a 'test-shoot' with a photographer, or a 'go-see' with a client like a fashion editor. If these significant others (CIs in Bourdieu's analysis) see similar qualities to the model agent they are booked for a job and thus 'qualify' as a model. This testing process continues throughout the model career, as their qualities are continuously qualified/requalified and objectified into their portfolio or 'book'.

Although they don't use Callon, Godart and Mears (2009) and Mears (2011) also describe similar mechanisms and calculations in their analysis of fashion modelling. Models, as with recent thinking on brands (Lury 2004), are 'assemblages': they are made up from heterogeneous connections and relationships along a complex network, as Entwistle and Slater (2012) have argued. Testing takes place in fashion retail as well: buyers test the qualities of garments in numerous ways – looking, handling, examining, trying on when out on a 'buy'. They question whether this is 'on trend' and ask 'how many to buy?' 'in what sizes?' Such mundane questions of calculation routinely made by those inside fashion markets therefore explain how/why some things (goods) make it in the market *as fashion*. These calculations are neither straightforwardly 'aesthetic' nor 'economic', but simultaneously both.

Among the many field/network positions within fashion that generate and disseminate fashion are various agents of communication (magazine/ newspaper editors, photographers, stylists) who generate ideas about trends and circulate fashion images: as Moeran (2016: 35) notes, it is 'the use of language that transforms clothing into *fashion*'. Precisely how representations shape fashion has been the focus of much scholarly debate and there have been many different communication forms. Early analysis of print media, drawing on semiotics, focuses on fashion codes (written and visual) and their power to shape understandings of clothing and bodies, often looking at gender (Barthes 1984; Crane 2000; Williamson 1978). More recent cultural studies of fashion magazines have looked beyond the fashion text to see how meaning is generated between producers, texts and readers' (Edwards 1997; Jobling 1999; Moeran 2010, 2016). A small empirical literature focuses attention on the work of journalists and stylists inside fashion magazines (Lynge-Jorlén 2012; 2016, 2017; McRobbie 1998), while more recent studies have focused on digital media production (Rocamora 2017, see discussion below).

ANT is motivated by a concern with empirical observation: to observe the calculations by actors inside markets. This means questioning 'common sense', opening up routine practices that are ordinarily 'black boxed' – a term borrowed from Science Technology Studies or STS, closely aligned to ANT, which describes things so routinely take for granted they are little examined in everyday life. 'Black boxes' are the stuff of actors' worlds and, once opened up by sociologists, are shown to be dependent upon actors' knowledge and expertise. Like field, actor-networks are physically located, since all markets occupy social space (online or offline). Callon's (1998a, 1999, 2005) concern with the specificity of markets as spaces of interaction is therefore useful: high fashion is promoted at various international 'fashion-week' shows, which are important trade events that bring together particular actors virtually or face-to-face. They encourage particular interactions and generate value around designers, models, goods. As Halliday (2022: 1–2) argues '[T]he fashion show is both an artistic medium and a trade event' and important in managing field relations, as Entwistle and Rocamora (2006), above, argue.

Figure 18. Runway model watched by fashion insiders. Source: photo by author

This ANT approach can be combined with Bourdieu's field analysis. While they appear to be quite different, network and field are both spatial metaphors that designate a way of thinking about markets and the relationships and interactions that take place within. Moreover, both see that the power to act (in network or field) comes not from unique charisma of individuals: Bourdieu directs us to think about positions between actors, while Callon directs us to consider network relations. The main difference is that Bourdieu's actors are always human, with embodied properties of capital, *habitus* and taste guiding their actions, while Callon considers the agency of non-human as well as human actors and how they come together. Both approaches enable us to trace the ways in which calculations of value are made within fashion markets. For example, to understand the art market Herrero (2010) observes how art dealers buy art in auction houses, focusing on the *habitus* of dealers as well as devices such as the catalogue and the materiality of the artwork, and how these come together to create art value. My work (Entwistle 2009) similarly details capacities of human agency (*habitus*, taste, etc.,) and the agency of non-humans in creating aesthetic value in fashion markets.

Combining both theorists enables us to examine traditional human *inter-mediaries* (like model bookers or fashion buyers), as well as routine processes and *practices of mediation*, at which Fall (2002, 2004) urges us to look. Specifically,

Callon's work enrols consumers/consumption within his network analysis, unlike Bourdieu's sole focus on those within the field of production/industry. As noted above, spreadsheets are one device mediating consumer choices as sales figures create multiple 'feedback loops' (McFall 2002) that inform buyers' future sales projections. This allows consideration of what some scholars call 'prosumers' and 'prosumption' (Ritzer and Jurgenson 2010; Ritzer 2014), concepts that suggest, convincingly, that consumers are now fully enrolled in production processes and calculations. This focus on consumption as production along with the ANT idea of networks resolves the problem of one-sided accounts that privilege either 'production' or 'consumption', to enable analysis of complex interactions between them. In doing so, the artificial distinction between 'economy' and 'culture' is blurred: clearly consumption/culture are part and parcel of economic calculations. That said, more recent work on prosumption has challenged the assumed universality of consumer interactions with production and pointed to differences in how non-Western consumers engage with fashion production (Tse and Tsang 2021; see also Tse et al. 2020). Clearly, more nuanced, contextual research is needed to fully account for the ways Web 2.0 is changing the production-consumption regime than Ritzer's original, Western-focused analysis.

The focus can be widened further, as many of the mediations within a market are not even directly between 'production/producers' and 'consumption/ consumers' but between business to business producers inside the market, as with Cronin's (2004) work on 'multiple regimes of mediation' and also Reynolds' (2021) study of fashion agents. In recent years, an explosion of interest in online fashion communication extends mediation between production and consumption even wider. This significant development in social media and online retail since the last edition of this book therefore requires consideration.

Fashion in the Twenty-First Century

Recent analysis of fashion culture and communication has focused attention at the online, digital dissemination of fashion via blogs and Instagram. Sometimes referred to as 'new media', Rocamora (2017) queries the newness of these new media, asking 'how new are fashion blogs?' (2011: 92; see also Rocamora's (2011, 2013)) and notes the continuities between new and old media. She also offers new ways of conceptualising new media, distinguishing between fashion *mediation* and the *mediatisation* of fashion. Digital media has changed the landscape of fashion communication in significant ways, but there are also many continuities between new and old media representations. On the one hand, digital media continues to speed up modern life. As discussed in earlier chapters, modern societies are described as faster than traditional societies and what is striking about digital fashion representations is the high velocity at which this communication travels and the reach of such communications in terms of audience (see Rocamora 2012, 2013 for detailed discussion). Compared to the earliest forms of fashion communication – a physical fashion doll depicting court dress in the seventeenth and eighteenth centuries – would have taken considerable time to travel across Europe; even an early print or newspaper in the nineteenth or early twentieth centuries would have had a restricted audience. However, today's digital media enables instantaneous communication: fashion shows are broadcast live on the internet (Halliday 2022), and Instagram posts can be seen by thousands or even millions in the space of a few minutes. In this respect, fashion communication is now faster and more ubiquitous.

Fast communication through such 'comptuterised technologies' (Rocamora 2013: 66) speeds up response times between producers and consumers, with Instagram directly connecting to retail, through 'swipe up' and clickable links taking viewers directly to products. These real-time purchases provide instant dissemination of trends and real-time feedback for retailers. The affordances of digital platforms like Instagram negate the need for physical shops in some cases: all that is needed is an Instagram or webpage. This is historically significant: digital communication connects producers and consumers globally in instantaneous communication loops, which is quite unlike earlier communication technologies that disseminated fashion trends to an elite minority. However, more is at stake than simply faster *mediation* of fashion trends. While mediation 'refers to the media as conveyors of meaning' (Rocamora 2017: 507), digital communications enable *mediatisation* of fashion.

For Rocamora, mediatisation means 'the idea that the media have become increasingly central to the shaping and doing of institutions and agents, to their practices and experiences'. Thus, 'mediatisation refers to their *transformative* power' (Rocamora 2016: 507) to shape our encounters with fashion. She argues that new rhythms have been established with the internet, with immediacy and connection being the characteristics of this form of communication and notes that the style and tone of blogs is different: typos are tolerated that would not be allowed in print media, and there is a new informality and conversational style adopted in blog posts. Significantly, blogs present fashion in different ways to print through hypertext, which decentres the author and creates 'endless new reconfigurations' of media message. 'Hypertexts are networked texts' (Rocamora, 2013: 71). Blogs open up communication, as followers can respond and bloggers themselves, at least in the early days, and can challenge the old hierarchies of power such that 'fashion [...] is not centred on established designers and key cities'. On the other hand, however, not everything online is new: citing McLuhan (1967), Rocamara notes (2013: 100) 'a new medium always appropriates some of the characteristics of an older medium'. Moreover, what happens when new media appears, is that old media adapts and reconfigures itself in response. This process is referred to as *remediation*, 'whereby new and old media represent and refashion each other' (2013: 100).

Scholarly research on digital media has not only looked at the content of fashion online, but also analysed production, specifically the labour (and labourers) involved in producing it. There is a growing literature examining this group of workers and 24/7 nature of the work, emerging forms of identity/ self and online communities. Findlay (2015: 158) maps the rise of fashion bloggers from their original position 'as an alternative, creative means of identity play through fashion' to 'a genre imbricated with the commercial practices and values of the fashion industry'. She notes how the earliest blogs (around the mid-1990s) was mostly news oriented and written by men and maps the rising of the first fashion blog, *She She Me*, which she dates to 2001. These early blogs were mostly text-based, then later crystallised in the format we recognise today, namely documenting personal style – 'the practice of "what I wore"' (Findlay 2015: 166). The early blogs, which Findlay refers to as the 'first wave', such as *Bryanboy* and *Style Bubble*, involved wearing daily outfits and sending from bedrooms and were stylistically creative and playful with limited resources (thrift stores), for a DIY take on a high-fashion look. Importantly, their status was that of 'outsiders looking in, and not necessarily with the desire to be included'. Although Findlay doesn't reference Bourdieu, these bloggers could be seen in terms of being outside the field of fashion – 'bloggers were effectively writing from the side-lines' (2015: 169) and their amateur status contrasted sharply with the legitimised positions of fashion journalists and editors in traditional print media.

As bloggers received more recognition from the fashion industry (around 2008–2010) they professionalised, with paid work for sponsored content. According to Findlay, 2009 was a 'watershed' year when the early bloggers, invited to the front row of fashion shows, were joined by a 'second wave' of bloggers, whose sole purpose was paid content. Bourdieu's notion of field as a dynamic space of action might apply here: at one time bloggers were newcomers who challenged and shifted the boundaries of the field, while today they have become accepted as established 'players' (in his parlance) and firmly established within the field of fashion. Today's fashion blogs have been superseded by Instagram, with fashion bloggers now more likely to be posting only, or primarily, on Instagram and known as 'influencers'. Instagram fashion is diverse, with different Instagrammers positing on various aspects of fashion, sometimes focusing on high-end designers, as Laura Fantacci does (@laura.fantacci), or high street, with increasing numbers of posting on fashion thrift, such as Alexandra Stedman (@alex.stedman). Indeed, Instagram provides a platform for various campaigns, often established by organisations outside Instagram and organised by hashtags, such as #secondhandseptember that was started by UK Oxfam.

Other scholarly work has examined forms of fashion identity online. For Rocamora (2011: 411), citing Giddens (1991) blogging is an 'identity perfor-mance' through 'dress's performative quality', a visual diary that tells a 'story' about the self, like modern biographies/autobiographies. Today, Instagram also opens spaces of identity performance (Entwistle and Wissinger 2021). Today's Instagrammers (so-called influencers or digital content creators) share many continuities with bloggers. Citing Senft (2008), Abidin (2016a: 3) defines influencer as a kind of 'microcelebrity … who accumulates a following on blogs and social media'. Their mainstay are their outfits, many of which are ads, endorsements, or gifts, while high-profile Instagrammers (usually those with large follower numbers) attend major fashion events subsequently documented on the platform. With Instagram came the rise of the 'selfie', which is also analysed by Abidin (2016b), who argues that it is a way of marking one's presence at an event, possibly accumulating prestige as a result. The immediacy and informality of Instagram is enabled through its many changing affordances: from posts on the 'grid', to Instagram Live events, IGTV and reels, all enabling immediate engagement and fostering a sense of community.

Examining identity performance in social media, some scholars (Banet-Weiser 2012; Duffy 2017) consider the importance of 'authenticity' or 'realness' as the key appeal. However, what Duffy and Hund (2019) refer to as the "authenticity bind" highlights how this very quality of authenticity is at odds with the commercial pull of Instagram. One such community is examined in Entwistle and Wissinger's (2021) study of Instagram style mums, who articulate their mum identity and connect with other mums on the platform. Entwistle and Wissinger (2021) discuss the problems of authenticity in tension with commerce when looking at how Instagram style mums attempt to 'keep it real'. Mums attempt to remain stylish, curating an aspirational lifestyle – often paid for by brands – while also showing some of the real challenges of life as an 'ordinary' mum. One such style mum, Chloe Samwell-Smith (@chloelovestoshop) has grown a following on Instagram (106,000 at the time of writing in July 2022) and offers a mix of everyday fashion and snippets of her life as a mum of three (see Figure 19 below). Chloe has worked for many fashion and beauty brands (e.g. Free People and Amazon fashion), and also posts regular stories and reels about fashion and her life as a mum, which is both quite 'aspirational' (with a high-end aesthetic), as well as 'real' (many posts are about high-street fashion brands), with the challenges of parenting thrown into the mix. This balancing act is not always an easy one, however. One famous style mum, Clemmie (former moniker @motherofdaughters), highlights the problems of navigating authenticity and commodification: in 2019, after increasingly being criticised by her followers for becoming too commodified, she was accused of bullying and eventually had to delete her account.

Much scholarly attention has also been directed to the offline/behind-the-scenes labour of producing content on social media. Scholars interested in 'platformisation', which examines the invisible work on/behind these platforms, include Bishop (2018, 2020), Duffy (2017, 2019a, 2019b), Duffy and Wissinger (2017), Petre et al. (2019) and Scolere et al. (2018). This work examines the inherent inequalities of this social media, which tends to reward

Figure 19. Instagram style mum Chloe Samwell-Smith posts regularly about her fashion style. Photo courtesy of Chloe Samwell-Smith

male content creators over female and privileges normative ideals through algorithmic bias. Thus, however 'new' social media appears to be, it is more likely to be mirroring the biases and identities found in older media than to be transgressive or transformative. In other words, while platforms would appear to be more open and unmediated, the commercial imperatives of social media tend to reproduce inequalities, thereby undermining any potential openness of social media to be more democratic, as Entwistle and Wissinger (2022) suggest.

Fashion industry: twenty-first-century contemporary critiques

While fashion has long been criticised for its poor labour practices, as previously discussed, recent criticisms of the industry have increasingly focused attention on the urgent issue of climate change and the climate emergency (see, for example, Fletcher (2015) and Fletcher and Tham (2015)). Activism, through groups such as Extinction Rebellion in the UK, and growing academic scholarship, have focused attention on the impact of the fashion industry on the environment. This has not overtaken criticisms concerned with labour; indeed, environmental concerns are not directed solely at plant and animal life but at the multiple harms of the climate emergency to human life on the planet. Thus, problems associated with the contemporary fast-fashion model have focused attention on *both* poor labour practices and environmental damage and, indeed, there is often a clear link between these two problems, as when workers are exposed to environmental harm from working with particular chemicals, or living in areas impacted by the polluting effects of garment factories.

Fast fashion has extended and accelerated the problems already identified as part of fashion's industrial past. If fashion is a 'child of modernity', as Wilson so elegantly puts it, it has grown into an unruly and destructive teenager in the twenty-first century. The relentless search for novelty, at the core of its appeal throughout modernity, has been extended in fast fashion with cheap, disposable clothing widely available across the globe. Cheap clothes create and then appear to satisfy increasingly insatiable demands for novelty. When a bikini can be priced at just £1, it encourages over-purchase. However, cheap clothes are not durable clothes and hence they can be thrown away and quickly replaced. 'Between 2000 and 2014, clothing production doubled, with the average consumer buying 60 percent more pieces of garment compared to fifteen years ago. Yet, each clothing item is now kept half as long. The industry has truly entered the era of "fast fashion"'(UN Alliance aims to put fashion on path to sustainability – UNECE). Fast fashion has been significantly speeded up by data analytics; from just-in-time production to social media swipe-up features, trends can be tracked and responded to with very short lead times (as little as six weeks in some cases). This business model is the dominant one on the high streets of most cities, from Gap to Zara to H&M, as well as online with PrettyLittleThings and ASOS.

This distance between big fast fashion brands, with head offices located in the North and production in the South, removes the harmful impacts on both labour and the environment from sight/oversight, enabling brands to distance themselves from problems when they arise. Thus, brands like Zara and Gap have been accused of 'washing their hands' of poor labour pay and conditions, first documented from the 1990s (Klein 1990; Ross 1990) and resulting in such terrible disasters as the Rana Plaza garment factory collapsing in April 2013 with a loss of 1,127 garment workers (see Figure 20 below).

More recently, criticisms levelled at garment factories during the 2019 Covid pandemic, highlight poor labour practices still taking place on UK soil. As noted by Sullivan (2022: 495), Leicester was exposed as being at 'the epicentre of a twenty-first century "sweating" scandal in the mainstream media', with the online retailer Boohoo the focus of attention for endangering

Figure 20. The Rana Plaza factory collapse in 2013 graphically highlights the poor working conditions of factories located in countries in the Southern hemisphere. Source: Flickr/rijans

workers' lives in their Leicester factory during the Covid pandemic (see also activist campaign group, Labour Behind the Label report LBL-Boohoo-WEB.pdf (labourbehindthelabel.net)).

Long sub-contracting chains similarly prevent oversight of poor environmental practices that happen at a distance. Moreover, long chains also contribute to significant carbon emissions involved in the distribution of raw materials and finished goods globally. Such an appetite for cheap new clothes is unsustainable: carbon emissions from fashion alone are contributing to climate change, with the UN estimating that the production of clothing contributes to around ten per cent of greenhouse gas emissions, due to long supply chains and energy intensive production (UN Helps Fashion Industry Shift to Low Carbon – UNFCCC and UN Alliance aims to put fashion on path to sustainability – UNECE). Added to these problems, cheap clothes don't always wash well and end up in landfill. At all points in the lifecycle of a garment – from plant to factory to consumer to landfill – the carbon footprint increases. Further, the use of limited resources, like water, which is required in volume to grow crops like cotton, and the polluting effects of dyes at production and washing/detergent at consumption, it is apparent that the appetite for fast fashion is fast out-growing the Earth's finite resources and capacity for rebalancing/recovery.

These issues, now widely reported in mainstream media, have resulted in various attempts to make the industry more 'sustainable' and a growing academic literature and activism by organisations such as Fashion Revolution and Labour Behind the Label is attempting to address these problems. In response, the United Nations Alliance for Sustainable Fashion, an initiative of United Nations agencies and allied organisations, is seeking to make the fashion industry more sustainable, in line with the UN's Sustainable Development Goals. However, what does sustainable/more sustainable fashion look like and is it achievable? What would more ethical fashion production and consumption look like? What do these terms 'sustainability' and 'ethical fashion' really mean? Defining these terms and how they have been debated within the literature is the focus of this last section.

Sustainability

Calls for fashion to be sustainable/more sustainable have grown increasingly louder in recent years. However, what do they mean? Fletcher and Tham (2015: 3) draw a distinction between 'sustainability' and 'sustainable'. While these two are 'often employed as synonyms':

> *Sustainability* is a system property that is dependent upon the relationships between things that evolve through time and towards *the aspirational goal of thriving*; while *sustainable*, by contrast, describes the process of attempting to achieve this goal, often in instrumental, bounded, static ways. (2015: 3 [emphasis added])

However, for Ehrenfeld (2015: 57) the word is an 'empty word', and, at its emptiest, refers to 'the capacity of a system to object to produce something desired over an extended period' but unless or until that something is named, 'it has no practical significance'.

Indeed, the 'something' being sustained may be just a very small part of the overall process as Thomas (2007) highlights. One of the problems for her is that sustainability often results in single-issue responses by the industry, which instrumentally address one problem. For example, organic cotton is promoted by high-street brands as a more sustainable option. However, while organic production means avoiding harmful pesticides, this instrumental solution to a single problem clearly does not address the many other problems that might follow, such as the considerable carbon emissions that may arise from transportation of the cotton to be used in garment production and consumption. Within this rubric of focusing instrumentally on specific issues, Fletcher and Tham (2015: 3) identify three tendencies within debates around sustainable fashion – 'products, processes and services[practices]'. In terms of *product*, we can point to various innovations that have focused on new technologies of fibre production or, in the case of Ryan and Storey, constructing the 'disappearing dress' as part of their WONDERLAND: Plastics is Precious: The disappearing dresses – Ulster University. However, fashion design is far more than the specifics of any particular product design and Payne's (2021) excellent comprehensive analysis of fashion design embeds sustainability into every aspect of the design process. Arguing for a holistic approach – 'fashion systems thinking' – from design education through to products and how they reach us, would enable us to design a different fashion for the future.

Carrying on Fletcher and Tham's (2015) summary of approaches, we can identify a set of responses to sustainability that are concerned with *processes*, which also tend to be narrowly defined to single issue changes. For example, a narrow focus on process by fashion businesses is evident in 'corporate social responsibility' (CSR) which may result in some changes in how companies do their business, i.e. through recycling or other initiatives, but is also often piece-meal. Thus, for Ehrenfeld such small solutions are very limited. As he argues (2015: 58),'[P]inning hopes on technological (eco-efficiency) or techno-cratic (rules and regulations) fixes is a losing approach.' Fletcher and Tham (2015: 3) agree that often changes in some processes simply mean 'maintaining the status quo with key adaptations' to lessen environmental impacts. Fletcher and Tham go on to note that these adaptations, while worthy, 'fail to engage with fundamental underlying structures contributing to the unsustainability of fashion' (2015: 5).

Finally, Fletcher and Tham (2015) note the third response to sustainability is changing *services and practices*, especially by consumers in how they consume fashion. In recent years there has been a rise in alternative ways of consuming fashion, with peer-to-peer rental platforms on Instagram or rental business, clothes swapping, new crafting initiatives (Fletcher's 2015) and DIY 'hackactivism' (Von Busch 2010), which add to the already well-established practice of vintage and second-hand shopping. Some of these initiatives can be referred to as the 'circular economy' (Geissdoerfer et al. 2017) initiatives that recognise the lifecycle of the garment and aim to reduce and reuse all parts. Some recent developments can also be characterised by the notion of a 'sharing economy' (Hossain 2020). In their review article on the sharing economy, Schor and Vallas (2021: 370) note that it is a form of consumption that 'includes not only platforms for accessing accommodations' (as with Airbnb), and app-enabled 'rides' (such as Uber); it also includes forms of social networking that have a longer tradition, from 'food swap and donation apps; rental, gift, and loan sites for household items; clothing exchanges; repair cafes'. For Schor and Vallas, how the sharing economy is defined often hinges on the question of whether it is seen as an extension of capitalism (in terms of new ways to do business) or something more alternative and radical. It is possible, given the diversity, that it is not either/or. In terms of the fashion, clothes swaps where people meet to swap/share clothes, do not make any money for anyone, while clearly fashion rental companies are in the business of profit-making. Do any of these ways of consuming fashion promise a radical alternative to fast fashion? Only time will tell but at present such alternative initiatives are a minority practice and not significantly reshaping fashion consumption. Likewise, various slow fashion practices – second-hand shopping/thrift shopping, buying craft and luxury items made to last – are also not challenging the dominance of fashion and are only available to middle-class consumers. It is only when consumers in significant numbers stop purchasing most of their clothes from fast-fashion stores that such initiatives will have significant eco-impact.

Critical questions as to what sustainability means continue to be posed, however. For Ehrenfeld, the question is, 'What should we be striving to sustain?' If the answer is to sustain current capitalist growth or conventional GDP measurements, then the problem, he notes, is that this means merely 'reducing unsustainability' (Ehrenfeld 2015: 35). The UN Fashion Alliance offers an example of this problem:

> [T]hrough the Alliance, the UN commits to changing the path of fashion, *reducing its negative environmental and social impacts*; and turning fashion into a driver of the implementation of the Sustainable Development Goals.' [Emphasis added]

For Ehrenfeld and others (Fletcher and Tham 2015) this goal to 'reduce' is not enough to avert eco-disaster; what is needed instead is a 'new paradigm' that challenges Enlightenment (and capitalist) definitions of the good life. Thus, Ehrenfeld's (2015) calls for 'sustainability-as-flourishing' goes much further but for the most part, mainstream sustainability debates and action have often been about companies 'green-washing' their brand to allay consumer guilt. There are signs that some fashion companies are waking up to the problems of excessive consumption. As this book goes into production, Selfridges department store announced that it aims for half of all its transactions to be 'resale, repair, rental or refills by 2030' (see Butler 2022). However, whether or not this initiative is more sustainable, in terms of reducing overall consumption, depends how they define these transactions. If this initiative doesn't supplant existing consumption patterns, but instead adds to increase overall consumption, it is ineffective. When assessing the impact of such new approaches, the important indicator is whether it leads to cumulative reduction of overall consumption. Likewise, any activities such as resale and repair are only effective eco-efficiency measures if they generate economic value at a reduced environmental impact compared to new items. If these offers lead to additional purchases, then they have few benefits.[1]

Fashion ethics

A more thorough and radical approach to sustainability is proposed by Thomas, who argues the need for a 'holistic' response to the problems within

[1] With thanks to Kate Fletcher for her thoughts on this point in email correspondence.

the fashion industry. For this reason, she prefers the broader term of 'ethics'. Ethics can be defined as 'moral principles, rules of conduct' (Thomas 2017: 5), which form the basis for all actions with regard for human and non-human life. She suggests that this more holistic way of thinking goes above and beyond piecemeal single-issue actions characterising sustainability. It can be seen in recent debates about care, such as the Care Collective (2021) critique of neo-liberal 'carelessness' since the 1970s. They call for a new 'ethics of care' that values all forms of life – human, non-human, social and natural world. A concept of *fashion ethics*, if placed at the core of business practices or consumers' values towards fashion, would provide a more radical approach than small changes produced by sustainability.

I have argued elsewhere (Entwistle 2013), that an ANT approach provides the basis for understanding and linking up all agents (human and non-human) within the fashion network and, in doing so, avoids false binaries of nature/ culture, which dominate the literature on sustainability/ethics. For ANT, networks are nature/culture hybrids. Applied to fashion, we might approach the study of fashion goods as hybrids of natural materials, technologies and human bodies. For example, we can trace networks within the production of cotton/organic cotton from a plant/crop to various, social/cultural practices as cotton moves from plant into fabric production, and onto the work of marketing by brands and consumer choices. Seeing cotton within a network and tracing that network through its configurations provides a useful way of seeing how cotton is bound up with both natural and cultural worlds.

Ethics and diversity in fashion

Taking ethics (as opposed to sustainability) as the holistic term to inter-rogate the fashion industry provides us with a broad basis upon which to critique other practices within the fashion industry, namely the historic lack of diversity. This problem has been singled out for many years, especially by feminists and black scholars and activists, who point to the narrow, exclusive body aesthetics that excludes more bodies than it includes. For example, fashion representation has long championed a very skinny body, usually because it selects very young models. It has also been accused of celebrating white, European bodies, with few models of colour awarded high prestige beauty and fashion contracts, or featuring on the front covers of prestige fashion magazines, such as *Vogue*. There is now a significant body of literature that details the histories and practices of fashion modelling as a significant practice for the reproduction of idealised body aesthetics (Brown 2011, 2012, 2019; Entwistle 2009; Entwistle and Mears 2012; Entwistle and Wissinger 2012; Evans 2005, 2008; Haidarali 2012; Mears 2011, 2012a; Sadre-Orafai 2012; Soley-Beltran 2004; Volonte 2021; Wissinger 2015). These empirically based studies of model agencies, which point the finger at particular practices inside fashion modelling, account for the particular idealised body they are said to promote. Volonte (2021) looks at the narrow, thin aesthetic and argues there is an 'inertia' to change within industry practices, and also points to sizing technologies, all of which have reproduced the thin aesthetic, while positioning 'plus-size' models in opposition to this dominant norm (see also Peters 2017, 2019, for a history of plus-size modelling).

Further analysis inside agencies throws light on the work of the model agents. Mears (2008, 2011, 2012a), a former model herself, argues that agents hedge against risk and uncertainty by sticking to what they know, which is the familiar young, thin, white aesthetic. When black models are cast, they tend to be exoticised as 'ethnic' and chosen to feature in editorials that play on racial stereotypes. For example, Cheang's (2013) analysis of top *Vogue* photography in the twentieth century shows how some of the most famous fashion photographers have fallen back on colonial thinking when shooting *Vogue* covers and editorials. In this way, according to Wissinger (2012), race is both liability and an asset for black models, who must appeal to this appetite for exoticised looks when designers and editors call upon it. She argues that racist ideas are often obscured by this aesthetic language, which means 'Othering' black models' bodies.

Social media has, to some extent, challenged the dominance of the model agency because the relative openness and ability of consumers/users to showcase their own style has become a feature many brands have harnessed. A quick search with hashtags, such as #plussize or #plussizefashion, or #curvystyle and one can enter various communities of fashion, and it is the same with differently abled bodies, who now present alternative ideas and ideals of the fashionable body. Greater diversity appearing on social media platforms like Instagram have, perhaps, played a small part in challenging and changing these established fashion ideals, as Entwistle and Wissinger (2021) argue in their analysis of Instagram 'style mums', now actively pursued by brands as models and ambassadors. They note that style mums on Instagram are older and larger than the young, skinny fashion models who graced twentieth-century fashion magazines. Instagram has also been one place where we can see the rise of 'body positivity' activists and campaigns promoting greater body diversity. This newer, user-generated content is increasingly informing brands who now actively harness the labour of these prosumers as another way of reaching out to different and more diverse audiences. However, undoubtably, most Instagrammers are small players in the 'field' of fashion (or as small nodes in a 'network' of fashion), with limited power. Unless these Instagram users manage to acquire a large group of followers on Instagram, they will have limited influence, and they will only manage to acquire influence if they can ride the algorithms of social media. This is one reason that focus has shifted in recent years to platforms and the algorithms that give visibility to some, but not all users, as discussed above.

Therefore, critical questions remain as to whether we are seeing full diversity in fashion aesthetics and even on Instagram we might call upon both brands and the social media platforms to consider representation as an ethical responsibility. Brands do now want to be seen to address the narrow aesthetics and do increasingly use a broader range of bodies in their campaigns and in their use of social media influencers. However, much of these developments are also driven more by commercial imperatives than by ethics: social media brings companies closer to consumers in real time and, as a result, brands are waking up to the need to widen their appeal. Obligations to tackle diversity and be more inclusive in their designs (see Entwistle 2021 for fuller discussion) mean that ethical concerns also make good business sense. Social media platforms, in turn, must consider their ethical responsibilities *vis-à-vis* the algorithm. Although this is 'black-boxed' (users do not know the terms of the algorithm and therefore cannot delete it), critical questions remain as to whether the algorithm remains biased towards particular groups, reproducing existing inequalities (Bishop, 2018).

Conclusion

This chapter has shown that an understanding of the history of the fashion industry is important if one is to understand contemporary fashion industry developments and criticisms levelled at it. Critical attention has long focused on the industry for its poor practices regarding workers (pay and conditions) and latterly, its environmental impacts contributing to climate change and emergency. At the heart of the problem is the essential quality of fashion as the *new*, the continual process of rapid change at the heart of modernity that fashion expresses so well. If the world is to be saved from a climate disaster, then our appetite for novelty needs to be curtailed and our relationship to our wardrobes radically altered.

This chapter has done more than map out this history, however; it has also introduced readers to various approaches to the study of the fashion that try to capture the complex social, economic, and cultural connections that make up the entire industry. Earlier scholarly work had tended to focus either on production or consumption, as Fine and Leopold (1993) argue, but the more recent scholarly debates discussed here have attempted to map the industry in its entirety. More recently, approaches that study fashion as a culture industry have productively argued that we need to go beyond focusing on one or other part of the binaries economy/culture, production/consumption. As part of this broad literature, the influence of Bourdieu's work has been particularly significant, and his concepts of cultural intermediaries have focused on these mediating workers between production and consumption, the so-called taste-makers who help generate value (cultural/aesthetic) around objects. Recent work drawing on ANT also provides an analytical framework for analysing markets by considering the way actor-networks collectively produce fashion. As I have suggested, the work of Bourdieu and Callon is compatible in terms of the concepts and methodology employed, which consider how value is generated and calculated inside markets and how these are simultaneously cultural, aesthetic and economic. Theoretical concepts from Bourdieu, such as cultural capital, for example, emphasise that calculations are neither strictly 'economic' nor 'cultural/aesthetic' but hybridised practices, while Callon's empirical lens for observing market practices provides a way of tracing practices of calculation. In terms of how we study and critique the fashion industry's attempt to develop more ethical working practices, such theoretical tools will remain essential to our analysis.

Finally, the urgency of studying fashion was highlighted with discussion of the many criticisms of the industry in the twenty-first century around sustainability and ethics. Fashion's role in climate change is undeniable and fast fashion has rightly been criticised as unsustainable. However, fashion ethics denotes a broad base through which we can also criticise and challenge the ways in which fashion has historically lacked diversity. Increasing analysis and activism has focused on the narrowness of the fashionable ideal and how it is held in place inside the industry. Fashion has proved to be slow to change but increasing calls for greater diversity and inclusion are beginning to impact industry practices. What this chapter has hopefully shown is the value, intellectually, socially and politically, of careful and considered social researching within the fashion industry and the rich rewards of doing so.

Conclusion

Fashioned Bodies in the Twenty-First Century

Fashion and dress articulate the body in culture: fashion produces discourses on the body and materials to adorn it, while dress is the translation of fashion into everyday practice. This simple assertion made in the original 2000 edition of *The Fashioned Body* remains as true today as it ever did. In the twenty-first century we now have multiple sites to consider the role fashion plays in articulating bodies: along with the conventional print fashion magazine, we now have vast online spaces for fashion that promote and circulate fashion trends and fashionable bodies. Thus, fashion remains a powerful industry, disseminating the raw materials of dress and communicating ideas about style and aesthetics. In this way, fashion (as a system of dress) continues to set the parameters of everyday dress, while every day worn dress is the ultimate expression, or embodiment, of any fashion.

Fashion trends are more varied than they have ever been, as well as more democratic. Fashion, once the preserve of an elite – first in Courts and later to middle-classes in growing industrial cities – only really became popular in the early part of the twentieth century, retailed through department stores and shops. However, popular fashion as we understand it today only really takes off in the post-war era of mass consumption. Throughout the twentieth century trends were still largely generated (dictated) by a limited elite of designers through seasonal collections in the major fashion cities (New York, London, Milan, Paris), with high-street brands disseminating similar designs. Today's fashion trends are multifarious, however, and flow in many directions: from street styles and subcultures, as well as high-end designers, through online spaces like Instagram, and by celebrities and people with influence on social media. In this multi-stranded, complex world of style, no single skirt length or style predominates. In July 2022, mini-skirts can be worn one day, midi-dresses and maxi-skirts another, although certain looks are more likely to be worn by segmented consumer groups, with one group (teens) preferring some styles to another (mums of teens). It is not the case, therefore, that 'anything goes': membership of a particular subculture, one's religious affiliation, age, or class predisposition all act as important structuring influences upon a person's choice of clothes, orientating people to specific brands or stores (Vans if one is a skater, for example; UK retailer, Whistles, if one is a middle-aged female professional). However, for any successful fashion to *be* a fashion, it must still capture a 'mood' or emerging 'taste' of a particular group. In this way, fashion remains a social phenomenon, but one that works in tandem with other social influences. Fashion, as I argued throughout this book, is also deeply personal and intimate. As a social force, which we wear on the boundary of our body, we dress to fit into, and feel comfortable, in our skin *and* in our milieu.

More of us now participate in the dissemination of fashion trends as our bodies enter the circulation loops on social media. When we hashtag or tag a brand, comment on, or review, a garment we have purchased, or blog about a new brand, we participate directly in fashion's feedback loops, our labour of consumption simultaneously taken up by fashion production. Increasingly we are producers as well as consumers of fashion. Our bodies participate in very visible ways when we perform our fashionability online and share with followers. This does represent a shift in power away from the traditional cultural intermediaries, who were previously powerful gatekeepers to the industry (couture designers, fashion magazine editors or stylists, for example), and who controlled what bodies could be represented as fashionable. Now bodies of all shapes and sizes can be seen as fashionable bodies online, with Instagram the preeminent fashion space for all these performances of fashionablity. Platforms, to some extent, have replaced the traditional fashion industry gatekeepers in terms of controlling the visibility of users, as discussed by scholars interested in and critical of the power of these platforms.

I have raised questions in Chapter 7 as to how democratic social media platforms are when the algorithm is encoded to reproduce the same old inequalities found in other, earlier, media organisations. Recent developments online, with the rise of social media, enable faster circulation of fashion aesthetics. Trends are disseminated at instantaneous speed, beyond anything seen in earlier periods of history, or even in the twentieth century, and, so too, is the spread of images of bodies and body ideals. In providing a history of European/Western fashion in this book, however, I have shown how the idea of speed and fast turnaround of trends has been a fundamental characteristic of this fashion system since its inception, and what we see today is just a radical continuation. Similarly, the problems identified specifically with the system of provision known as fast fashion are problems that stretch back at least to the Industrial Revolution.

This book has only touched on emerging developments as we move into the second decade of the twenty-first century. However, what I hope to have provided with the new edition of this book – in its modified third form – is an overview, historical in scope, for ways in which fashion has been written and thought about. Locating fashion historically is important in terms of analysing what is happening today and what might happen next. History is as much about continuities as it is about disjuncture and ruptures. The fashion system we see today in Europe and beyond has emerged out of a long history of modernity. Recent challenges to this European/Western analysis have been discussed here and I remain excited to see where future work in this area will take us.

Finally, the book offers a set of theoretical tools, largely unchanged since the first edition, for future scholars to continue examining fashion. I have insisted that the body provides the missing link between the various, separate but inter-connected agents that make up the fashion system or network. Understanding the body in culture requires understanding both how the textual body (the body articulated in discourses produced by texts, such as the fashion magazine) relates to the experience of embodiment (the body articulated in everyday life through experiences and practices of dress). Understanding fashion and dress requires understanding the relationship between various bodies within the fashion industry, such as the producers and cultural mediators, and the actions and decisions taken by individuals on and with their bodies. In laying out the framework of situated bodily practice, and hopefully breathing fresh life into this approach in this edition, I hope to have suggested what such a study involves and therefore how a sociology of fashion and dress might continue to proceed into the twenty-first century.

References

Abidin, C. (2016a) 'Visibility Labor: Engaging with Influencers: Fashion brands and #OOTD advertorial campaigns on Instagram'. *Media International Australia* 161(1): 86–100.

Abidin, C. (2016b) '"Aren't These Just Young, Rich Women Doing Vain Things Online?": Influencer Selfies as Subversive Frivolity'. *Social Media + Society*, April–June 2016: 1–17.

Ackroyd, P. (1979) *Dressing Up*. London: Thames and Hudson.

Akou, H. M. (2001) *The Politics of Dress in Somali Culture*. Bloomington: Indiana University Press.

Aldersey-Williams, H. (2013) *ANATOMIES: A Cultural History of the Human Body*. London: W.W. Norton and Co.

Al Jazeera (2021) 'Law Against Islam': French Vote in Favour of Hijab Ban Condemned'. Religion News.

Allman, J. (ed.) (2004) *Fashioning Africa: Power and the Politics of Dress*. Bloomington: Indiana University Press.

Ang, I. (1985) *Watching 'Dallas': Soap Opera and the Melodramatic Imagination*. London: Methuen.

Appleford, K. (2013) 'Fashion and Class Evaluation', in S. Black, A. de la Haye, J. Entwistle, R. Regina, A. Rocamora and H. Thomas (eds), *The Handbook of Fashion Studies*. London: Bloomsbury.

Appleford, K. (2016) 'Being Seen in your Pyjamas: The Relationship Between Fashion, Class, Gender and Space'. *Gender, Place and Culture* 23: 162–80.

Armstrong, L. and McDowell, F. (2018) *Fashioning Professionals: Identity and Representation at Work in the Creative Industries*. London: Bloomsbury.

Ash, J. and Wilson, E. (eds) (1992) *Chic Thrills: A Fashion Reader*. London: Pandora Press.

Ash, J. and Wright, L. (eds) (1988) *Components of Dress Design, Manufacturing, and Image-Making in the Fashion Industry*. London: Routledge.

Aspers, P. (2006) *Markets in Fashion*. Hove: Psychology Press.

Aspers, P. and Godart, F. C. (2013) 'Sociology of Fashion – Order and Change'. *Annual Review of Sociology* 39: 171–92.

Bailey, R. (1992) 'Clothes Encounters of the Gynaecological Kind: Medical Mandates and Maternity Modes in the US 1859–1990', in R. Barnes and J. B. Eicher, *Dress and Gender: Making and Meaning in Cultural Context*. Oxford: Berg.

Bakhtin, M. (1984) *Rabelais and his World*. Indiana: Indiana University Press.

Banet-Weiser, S. (2012) *Authentic[TM]: the Politics of Ambivalence in a Brand Cultur.*, New York, New York University Press.

Barnard, M. (1996) *Fashion as Communication*. London: Routledge.

Barnes, R. and Eicher, J. B. (eds) (1992) *Dress and Gender: Making and Meaning*. Oxford: Berg.

Barry, B. (2015) 'Dapper Dudes: Young Men's Fashion Consumption and Expressions of Masculinity'. *Critical Studies in Men's Fashion* 2: 5–21.

Barry, B. (2019) 'Fabulous Masculinities: Refashioning the Fat and Disabled Male Body.' *Fashion Theory* 23: 275–307.

Barthes, R. (1985) *The Fashion System*. London: Cape.

Bartlett, D. (2010) *FashionEast: The Spectre that Haunted Socialism*. Massachusetts Institute of Technology.

Bartlett, D. (2015) 'In Russia, at Last and Forever: The First Seven Years of Russian *Vogue*'. *Fashion Theory* 10(1/2): 175–204.

Bartlett, D. (2022) 'The Politics of Transnational Fashion'. *Fashion Theory*, 26(4): 457–63.

Basberg Neumann, C. (2012) 'Managing Desire: The International Fashion Model', in P. McNeill and L. Wallenberg, *Nordic Fashion Studies*. Stockholm: Axl Books.

Bataille, G. (1986) *Erotism: Death and Sensuality*. San Francisco: City Lights Books.

Bathelt, H., Malmberg, A. et al. (2004) 'Clusters and Knowledge: Local Buzz, Global Pipelines and the Processes of Knowledge Creation'. *Progress in Human Geography* 28(1): 31–56.

Bathelt, H. (2007) 'Buzz-and-Pipeline: Toward a Knowledge-Based Multiplier Model of Clusters'. *Geography Compass* 1(6): 1282–98.

Bathelt, H. and Schuldt, N. (2008) 'Temporary Face-To-Face Contact and the Ecologies of Global and Virtual Buzz'. SPACES: online 6(2008–04): Toronto and Heidelberg: www.spaces-online.com.

Baudelaire, C. (1986) 'The Painter of Modern Life', in N. Cameron (trans.), *My Heart Laid Bare and Other Prose Writings*. London: Soho Book Company.

Baudrillard, J. (1981) *For a Critique of the Political Economy of the Sign*. St Louis, MO: Telos.

Baudrillard, J. (1983) *Simulations*. New York: Semiotext(e).

Bauman, Z. (1991) *Modernity and Ambivalence*. Cambridge: Polity.

Beck, U. (1992) *Risk Society: Towards a New Modernity*. London: Sage.

Beckert, J. and Aspers, P. (2011) *The Worth of Goods Valuation and Pricing in the Economy*. Oxford: Oxford University Press.

Beiner, T. M. (2007) 'Sexy Dressing Revisited: Does Target Dress Play a Part in Sexual Harassment Cases?' *Duke Journal of Gender Law & Policy* 14: 125.

Bell, Q. (1976) *On Human Finery*. London: Hogarth Press.

Belsey, A. and Belsey, C. (1990) 'Icons of Divinity: Portraits of Elizabeth I', in L. Gent and N. Llewellyn (eds), *Renaissance Bodies: The Human Figure in English Culture 1540–1660*. London: Reaktion.

Benjamin, W. (1989) *Charles Baudelaire: A Lyric Poet in the Era of High Capitalism*. London: Verso.

Benthall, J. (1976) *The Body Electric: Patterns of Western Industrial Culture*. London: Thames and Hudson.

Bentham, J. (1843) *The Works of Jeremy Bentham*, vol. 4, ed. J. Browring. Edinburgh, London: W. Tait, Simkin Marshall and Co.

Berger, J. (1972) *Ways of Seeing*. Harmondsworth: Penguin.

Berman, M. (1983) *All That is Solid Melts into Air: The Experience of Modernity*. London: Verso.

Berthelot, J. M. (1991) 'Sociological Discourse and the Body', in M. Featherstone, M. Hepworth and B. Turner (eds), *The Body: Social Process and Cultural Theory*. London: Sage.

Black, P. (2004) *The Beauty Industry: Gender, Culture and Pleasure*. London: Routledge.

Black, S., de la Haye, A. et al. (eds) (2013) *The Handbook of Fashion Studies*. London: Bloomsbury.

Blacking, J. (1977) *The Anthropology of the Body*. London: Academic Press.

Blumer, H. (1969) 'Fashion: From Class Differentiation to Collective Selection'. *International Quarterly* 10: 275–91.

Blumer, H. (1969) 'Fashion: From Class Differentiation to Collective Selection'. *Sociological Quarterly* 10: 275–91.

Bourdieu, P. (1984) *Distinction: A Social Critique of the Judgement of Taste*. Cambridge, MA: Harvard University Press.

Bourdieu, P. (1989) *Outline of a Theory of Practice*. Cambridge: Cambridge University Press.

Bourdieu, P. (1993a) *The Field of Cultural Production: Essays on Art and Literature*. Cambridge, Polity.

Bourdieu, P. (1993b) 'Haute Couture and Haute Culture'. *Sociology in Question*. London: Sage.

Bourdieu, P. (1993c) 'Who Creates the Creators?' *Sociology in Question*. London: Sage.

Bourdieu, P. (1994) 'Structures, Habitus and Practices', in P. Press (ed.), *The Polity Reader in Social Theory*. Cambridge: Polity.

Bowstead, J. M. (2018) *Menswear Revolution: The Transformation of Contemporary Men's Fashion*. London: Bloomsbury.

Bradley, C. (1955) *A History of World Costume*. London: Peter Owen.

Braham, P. (1997) 'Fashion: Unpacking a Cultural Production', in P. du Gay (ed.), *Production of Culture, Cultures of Production*. London: Sage.

Brake, M. (1980) *The Sociology of Youth Culture and Youth Subcultures: Sex, Drugs and Rock 'n' Roll?* London: Routledge and Kegan Paul.

Brake, M. (1985) *Comparative Youth Culture*. London: Routledge and Kegan Paul.

Braudel, F. (1981) *The Structures of Everyday Life: The Limits of the Possible*. London: Fontana.

Breines, W. (2006) *The Trouble Between Us: An Uneasy History of White and Black Women in the Feminist Movement*. Oxford: Oxford University Press.

Breward, C. (1994) *The Culture of Fashion*. Manchester: Manchester University Press.

Breward, C. (1999) *The Hidden Consumer*. Manchester: Manchester University Press.

Breward, C. (2003) *Fashion*. Oxford: Oxford University Press.

Breward, C. (2004) *Fashioning London: Clothing and the Modern Metropolis*. Oxford: Berg.

Breward, C. and Evans, C. (eds) (2004) *The London Look: Fashion from Street to Catwalk*. New Haven and London: Yale University Press.

Breward, C. and Evans, C. (eds) (2005) *Fashion and Modernity*. Oxford: Berg.

Breward, C. and Gilbert, D. (eds) (2006) *Fashion's World Cities*. Oxford: Berg.

Brewer, J. (1997) *The Pleasures of the Imagination: English Culture in the Eighteenth Century*. London: Harper Collins.

Brewer, J. and Porter, R. (eds) (1993) *Consumption and the World of Goods*. New York: Routledge.

Brice, S. (2021) 'Trans Subjectifications: Drawing an (Im)personal Politics of Gender, Fashion, and Style'. *GeoHumanities* 7: 301–27.

Brill, D. (2008) *Goth Culture: Gender, Sexuality and Style*. Oxford: Berg.

Bristow, J. (1997) *Sexuality*. London: Routledge.

Brooks, R. (1989) 'Sighs and Whispers: A Review of a Bloomingdale Mail Order Catalogue for the Lingerie Department', in A. McRobbie (ed.), *Zoot Suits and Second-hand Dresses: An Anthology of Fashion and Music*. London: Macmillan Education.

Brooks, R. (1992) 'Fashion Photography, the Double-Page Spread: Helmut Newton, Guy Bourdin and Deborah Turberville', in J. Ash and E. Wilson (eds), *Chic Thrills: A Fashion Reader*. London: Pandora Press.

Brown, E. H. (2011) 'Black Models and the Invention of the US "Negro Market"', 1945–1960, in D. Zwick and J. Cayla, *Inside Marketing: Practices, Ideologies and Devices*. Oxford: Oxford University Press.

Brown, E. H. (2012) 'From Artist's Model to the "Natural Girl": Containing Sexuality in

Early Twentieth-Century Modelling', in J. Entwistle and E. Wissinger, *Fashioning Models: Image, Industry,Text*. London: Bloomsbury.

Brown, E. H. (2019) *Work!: A Queer History of Modeling*. Durham: Duke University Press.

Bryson, A. (1990) 'The Rhetoric of Status: Gesture, Demeanour and the Image of the Gentleman in Sixteenth and Seventeenth-Century England', in L. Gent and N. Llewellyn (eds), *Renaissance Bodies: The Human Figure in English Culture 1540–1660*. London: Reaktion Books.

Buckley, C. and Fawcett, H. (2002) *Fashioning the Feminine: Representation and Women's Fashion from the Fin de Siècle to the Present*. London: Berg.

Bullock, K. (2002) *Rethinking Muslim Women and the Veil: Challenging Historical and Modern Stereotypes*. London: International Institute of Islamic Thought.

Burrell, G. and Hearn, J. (1993) 'The Sexuality of the Organization', in J. Hearn, D. L. Sheppard, P. Tancred-Sheriff and G. Burrell (eds), *The Sexuality of Organization*. London: Sage.

Butler, J. (1990) *Gender Trouble: Feminism and the Subversion of Identity*. London: Routledge.

Butler, J. (1993) *Bodies that Matter*. London: Routledge.

Butler, S. (2022) 'Selfridges Wants Half of Transactions to be Resale, Repair, Rental, Refills by 2030'. *Guardian*. 2 September, 2022.

Calefato, P. (2004) *The Clothed Body*. Oxford: Berg.

Calefato, P. (2010) 'Fashion as Cultural Translation: Knowledge, Constrictions and Transgressions on/of the Female Body'. *Social Semiotics* 20(4): 343–5.

Callaway, H. (1992) 'Dressing for Dinner in the Bush: Rituals of Self Definition and British Imperial Authority', in R. Barnes and J. B. Eicher (eds), *Dress and Gender: Making and Meaning*. Oxford: Berg.

Callon, M. (1998a) 'Introduction: The Embeddedness of Economic Markets in Economics', in M. Callon, *The Laws of the Market*. Oxford: Blackwell Publishers/*The Sociological Review*.

Callon, M. (1998b) *The Laws of the Market*. Oxford: Blackwell Publishers/*The Sociological Review*.

Callon, M. (1999) 'Actor–Network Theory – The Market Test', in J. Law and J. Hassard (eds), *Actor Network Theory and After*. Oxford: Blackwell.

Callon, M., Meadel, C. et al. (2005) 'The Economy of Qualities', in A. Barry and D. Slater, *The Technological Economy*. London: Routledge.

Callon, M., Millo, Y. and Muniesa, F. (2007) *Market Devices*. London: Blackwell.

Campbell, C. (1989) *The Romantic Ethic and the Spirit of Modern Consumerism*. Oxford: Blackwell.

Campbell, C. (1993) 'Understanding Traditional and Modern Patterns of Consumption in Eighteenth-Century England: A Character-Action Approach', in J. Brewer and R. Porter (eds), *Consumption and the World of Goods*. New York: Routledge.

Campbell, C. (1997) 'When the Meaning is not a Message: A Critique of the Consumption as Communication Thesis', in M. Nava, A. Blake, I. MacRury and B. Richards (eds), *Buy this Book: Studies in Advertising and Consumption*. London: Routledge.

Carrier, J. and Miller, D. (eds) (1998) *Virtualism: A New Political Economy*. Oxford: Berg.

Cash, T. F. (1985) 'The Impact of Grooming Style on the Evaluation of Women in Management', in M. R. Soloman (ed.), *The Psychology of Fashion*. New York: Lexington Books.

Cheang, S. (2013) Book Section, *To the Ends of the Earth: Fashion and Ethnicity in the Vogue Fashion Shoot*, in D. Bartlett, S. Cole and A. Rocamora (eds), *Fashion Media*. London: Berg.

Chapkis, W. and Enloe, C. (eds) (1984) *Of Common Cloth: Women in the Global Textile Industry*. Transnational Institute.

Chase, C. (2010) 'Foucault, Femininity, and the Modernization of Patriarchal Fever', in R. Weitz, *The Politics of Women's Bodies: Sexuality, Appearance, and Behavior*. New York: Oxford University Press.

Chhachhi, A. (1984) 'The Case of India', in W. Chapkis and C. Enloe (eds), *Of Common Cloth: Women in the Global Textile Industry*. Transnational Institute.

Clarke, J., Hall, S., Jefferson, T. and Roberts, B. (1992) 'Subcultures, Cultures and Class', in T. Bennett, G. Martin, C. Mercer and J. Woollacott (eds), *Culture, Ideology and Social Process: A Reader*. Milton Keynes: Open University Press.

Colderidge, N. (1989) *The Fashion Conspiracy: A Remarkable Journey through the Empires of Fashion*. London: Mandarin.

Cole, S. (2000) *Don We Now Our Gay Apparel*. Oxford: Berg.

Cole, S. (2014) 'Jaks in Saks: Sportsmen and Underwear Advertising'. *Critical Studies in Men's Fashions* 1(2): 161–76.

Collier, R. (1998) '"Nutty Professors", "Men in Suits" and "New Entrepreneurs": Corporeality, Subjectivity and Change in the Law School and Legal Practice'. *Social and Legal Studies* 7(1): 27–53.

Collins, P. H. (2020) 'Defining Black Feminist Thought', in C. R. McCann, S.-K. Kim and E. Ergun (eds), *Feminist Theory Reader Local and Global Perspectives*. London: Routledge.

Collins, P. H. and Bilge, S. (2016) *Intersectionality*. John Wiley & Sons.

Cordwell, J. and Schwarz, R. (eds) (1979) *The Fabrics of Culture: An Anthropology of Clothing and Adornment*. The Hague: Mouton.

Cosgrove, S. (1989) 'The Zoot Suit and Style Warfare', in A. McRobbie (ed.), *Zoot Suits and Second-Hand Dresses*. London: Macmillan.

Coyle, A. (1982) 'Sex, Skill in the Organisation of the Clothing Industry', in J. West (ed.), *Work, Women and the Labour Market*. London: Routledge.

Craik, J. (1993) *The Face of Fashion*. London: Routledge.

Craik, J. (2009) *Fashion: The Key Concepts*. Oxford: Berg.

Craik, J. (2020) The Political Culture of Non-Western Fashion Identities. *Fashion, Style and Popular Culture* 7: 9–27.

Crampton, J. W. and Elden, S. (2007) *Space, Knowledge and Power: Foucault and Geography*. Farnham: Ashgate Publishing.

Crane, D. (2000) *Fashion and its Social Agendas*. Chicago: Chicago University Press.

Crane, D. (2012) 'Introduction', in A. M. Gonzalez and L. Bovone, *Identities through Fashion: A Multi-Disciplinary Approach*. London: Berg.

Crenshaw, K. (1989) 'Demarginalizing the Intersection of Race and Sex: A Black Feminist Critique of Antidiscrimination Doctrine, Feminist Theory and Antiracist Politics'. *University of Chicago Legal Forum*, 8.

Cronin, A. (2004) 'Regimes of Mediation: Advertising Practitioners as Cultural Intermediaries?' *Consumption, Markets and Culture* 7(4): 349–69.

Crossley, N. (1995a) 'Body Techniques, Agency and Inter-Corporality: On Goffman's Relations in Public'. *Sociology* 129(1): 133–49.

Crossley, N. (1995b) 'Merleau-Ponty, the Elusive Body and Carnal Sociology'. *Body and Society* 1(1): 43–63.

Crossley, N. (1996) 'Body/Subject, Body/Power: Agency, Inscription and Control in Foucault and Merleau-Ponty'. *Body and Society* 2(2): 99–116.

Crossley, N. (2006) *Reflexive Embodiment in Contemporary Society*. Berkshire, Open University Press.

Csordas, T. J. (1993) 'Somatic Modes of Attention'. *Cultural Anthropology* 8(2): 135–56.

Csordas,T. J. (1996) 'Introduction: The Body as Representation and Being-in-the-World', in T. J. Csordas (ed.), *Embodiment and Experience: The Existential Ground of Culture and Self.* Cambridge: Cambridge University Press.

Cumming, V., Cunnington, C. W. et al. (2010) *The Dictionary of Fashion History.* Oxford: Berg.

Davidoff, L. and Hall, C. (1987) *Family Fortunes: Men and Women of the English Middle Classes.* London: Hutchinson.

Davis, F. (1992) *Fashion, Culture and Identity.* Chicago: Chicago University Press.

de Grazia, V. and Furlough, E. (eds) (1996) *The Sex of Things: Gender and Consumption in Historical Perspective.* London: University of California Press.

de la Haye, A. (1988) *Fashion Sourcebook.* London: Macdonald & Co.

Derrida, J. (1976) *Of Grammatology.* Baltimore: Johns Hopkins University Press.

Diamond, I. and Quinby, L. (eds) (1988) *Feminism and Foucault: Reflections on Resistance.* Boston: Northeastern University Press.

Diprose, R. and Reynolds, J. (2008) *Merleau-Ponty: Key Concepts.* London: Routledge.

Ditcher, E. (1985) 'Why We Dress the Way We Do', in M. R. Soloman (ed.), *The Psychology of Fashion.* New York: Lexington Books.

Douglas, M. (1973) *Natural Symbols.* Harmondsworth: Pelican Books.

Douglas, M. (1979a) 'Do Dogs Laugh?: A Cross-Cultural Approach to Body Symbolism', in M. Douglas (ed.), *Implicit Meanings: Essays in Anthropology.* London: Routledge.

Douglas, M. (l979b) *Implicit Meanings: Essays in Anthropology.* London: Routledge.

Douglas, M. (1984) *Purity and Danger: An Analysis of the Concept of Pollution and Taboo.* London: Routledge and Kegan Paul.

Du Bois, W .E. B. (2004 [1094]) *Souls of Black Folk.* Routledge: London.

Duffy, B. E. (2017) *(Not) Getting Paid to Do What You Love: Gender, Social Media, and Aspirational Work.* New Haven: Yale University Press.

Duffy, B. E. and Hund, E. (2019) 'Gendered Visibility on Social Media: Navigating Instagram's Authenticity Bind'. *International Journal of Communication* 13: 4983–5002.

Duffy, B. E. and Wissinger, E. (2017) 'Mythologies of Creative Work in the Social Media Age: Fun, Free, and "Just Being Me"'. *International Journal of Communications* 11: 4652–71.

Duffy, B. E. et al. (eds) (2019a) 'Platformization of Cultural Production'. [Special issue]. *Social Media + Society* 5(4).

Duffy, B. E. et al. (2019b) "Platform Practices in the Cultural Industries: Creativity, Labor, and Citizenship." *Social Media + Society,* 5(4): 1–8.

du Gay, P. (ed.) (1997) *Production of Culture, Cultures of Production.* London: Sage.

Eckersley and Duff (2020) 'Bodies of Fashion and the Fashioning of Subjectivity'. *Body and Society* 26(4): 35–61.

Eco, U. (1986) *Travels in Hyperreality* (trans. W. Weaver). London: Picador.

Edwards, T. (1997) *Men in the Mirror: Men's Fashions and Consumer Society.* London: Cassell.

Edwards, T. (2009) *Fashion in Focus – Concepts, Practices and Politics.* London: Routledge.

Eicher, J. B., Evenson, S. L, and Lutz, H. A. (eds) (2008) *The Visible Self: Global Perspectives on Dress, Culture, and Society.* New York: Fairchild Publishers.

Eicher, J. B. et al. (eds) (2010) *The Berg Encyclopedia of World Dress and Fashion.* Oxford: Berg.

Elias, N. (1978) *The History of Manners: The Civilizing Process,* vol. 1. New York: Pantheon.

Elson, D. (1984) 'Nimble Fingers and Other Fables', in W. Chapkis and C. Enloe (eds), *Of Common Cloth: Women in the Global Textile Industry.* Transnational Institute.

Elson, D. and Pearson, R. (1981) 'Nimble Fingers make Cheap Workers: An Analysis of Women' s Employment in Third World Export Manufacturing'. *Feminist Review* 7 (Spring).

Emberley, Julia V. (1998) *Venus and Furs: The Cultural Politics of Fur.* London: I. B. Tauris & Co.

English, B. (2007) *A Cultural History of Fashion in the 20th Century.* Oxford: Berg.

Enloe, C. (1984) 'Racism at Work', in W. Chapkis and C. Enloe (eds), *Of Common Cloth: Women in the Global Textile Industry.* Transnational Institute.

Entwistle, J. (1997a) 'Fashioning the Self: Women, Dress, Power and Situated Bodily Practice in the Workplace'. PhD thesis, London: Goldsmiths College.

Entwistle, J. (1997b) 'Power Dressing and the Fashioning of the Career Woman', in M. Nava, I. MacRury, A. Blake and B. Richards (eds), *Buy this Book: Studies in Advertising and Consumption.* London: Routledge.

Entwistle, J. (1998) 'Sex /Gender', in C. Jenks (ed.), *Core Dichotomies in Sociology.* London: Sage.

Entwistle, J. (2000) 'Fashioning the Career Woman: Power Dressing as a Strategy of Consumption', in M. Talbot and M. Andrews (eds), *All the World and her Husband: Women and Consumption in the Twentieth Century.* London: Cassell.

Entwistle, J. (2002) 'The Aesthetic Economy: The Production of Value in the Field of Fashion Modelling'. *Journal of Consumer Culture* 2(3): 317–40.

Entwistle, J. (2004) 'From Catwalk to Catalogue: Male Models, Masculinity and Identity', in H. Thomas and J. Ahmed, *Cultural Bodies: Ethnography and Theory.* Oxford: Blackwell.

Entwistle, J. (2009) *The Aesthetic Economy of Fashion: Markets and Value in Clothing and Modelling.* Oxford: Berg.

Entwistle, J. (2010) 'Global Flows, Local Encounters: Spatializing Tacit Aesthetic Knowledge in High Fashion'. *SPACES:online.com* 2(8).

Entwistle, J. (2013) 'Introduction: Fashion, Identity and Difference', in S. Black, A. de la Haye, J. Entwistle et al., *The Handbook of Fashion Studies.* London: Bloomsbury.

Entwistle, J. (2021) 'Towards an Ethics of Fashion. Challenges and Advances.' *International Journal of Basque Studies RIEV* 66: 1–2.

Entwistle, J. and Mears, A. (2012) 'Gender on Display: Performance and Performativity in Fashion Modelling'. *Current Sociology* 7: 320–35.

Entwistle, J. and Rocamora, A. (2006) 'The Field of Fashion Realised: The Case Study of London Fashion Week'. *Sociology* 40(4): 735–50.

Entwistle, J. and Slater, D. (2012) 'Models as Brands: Critical Thinking About Bodies and Images'. *Fashioning Models: Image, Industry, Text.* London: Bloomsbury.

Entwistle, J. and Wilson, E. (1998) 'The Body Clothed. 100 Years of Art and Fashion'. London: Hayward Gallery.

Entwistle, J. and Wilson, E. (eds) (2001) *Body Dressing.* Oxford: Berg.

Entwistle, J. and Wissinger, E. (2006) 'Keeping Up Appearances: Aesthetic Labour in the Fashion Modelling Industries of London and New York'. *Sociological Review* 54(4): 774–94.

Entwistle, J. and Wissinger, E. (eds) (2012) *Fashioning Models: Image, Industry, Text.* London: Bloomsbury.

Ericksen, M. K. and Joseph, S. M. (1985) 'Achievement Motivation and Clothing Preferences of White-Collar Working Women', in M. R. Soloman (ed.), *The Psychology of Fashion.* New York: Lexington Books.

Evans, C. (2003) *Fashion at the Edge: Spectacle, Modernity and Deathliness.* London: Yale University Press.

Evans, C. (2005) 'Multiple, Movement, Model, Mode: The Mannequin Parade 1900–1929', in C. Breward and C. Evans, *Fashion and Modernity.* Oxford: Berg.

Evans, C. (2008) 'Jean Patou's American Mannequins: Early Fashion Shows and Modernism'. *Modernism/Modernity* 15(2): 243–63.

Evans, C. and Thornton, M. (1989) *Women and Fashion: A New Look.* Quartet Books.

Ewen, S. (1976) *Captains of Consciousness: Advertising and the Social Roots of the Consumer Culture.* New York: McGraw-Hill.

Fanon, F. (1986 [1952]) *Black Skins: White Mask*. London: Pluto Press.

Featherstone, M. (1991a)'The Body in Consumer Society', in M. Featherstone, M. Hepworth and B. Turner (eds), *The Body: Social Process and Cultural Theory*. London: Sage.

Featherstone, M. (1991b) *Consumer Culture and Postmodernism*. London: Sage.

Featherstone, M., Hepworth, M. and Turner, B. (1991) *The Body: Social Process and Cultural Theory*. London: Sage.

Featherstone, M. and Turner, B. (1995) 'Introduction'. *Body and Society* 1(1).

Featherstone, M. (ed.) (2000) *Body Modifications*. London: Sage.

Feher, M., Naddaff, R. and Tazi, N. (1989) *Fragments for a History of the Human Body, Part One*. New York: Zone.

Fine, B. and Leopold, E. (1993) *The World of Consumption*. London: Routledge.

Fine, B., Bayliss, K. and Robertson, M. (2017) 'The Systems of Provision Approach to Understanding Consumption', in O. Kravets, P. Maclaran, S. Miles and A. Venkatesh (eds), *The SAGE Handbook of Consumer Culture*. London: Sage.

Finkelstein, J. (1991) *The Fashioned Self*. Cambridge: Polity.

Fletcher, K. (2015) 'In the Hands of the User: The Local Wisdom Project and the Search for an Alternative Fashion System'. *Journal of Design Strategies* 7.

Fletcher, K. and Tham, M. (2015) *The Routledge Handbook of Sustainability and Fashion*. London: Routledge.

Florida, R. (2004) *Cities and the Creative Class*. London: Routledge.

Flügel, J. C. (1930) *The Psychology of Clothes*. London: Hogarth Press.

Foucault, M. (1976) *The Birth of the Clinic*. London: Tavistock Publications.

Foucault, M. (1977) *Discipline and Punish*. Harmondsworth: Penguin.

Foucault, M. (1979) *The History of Sexuality*, vol. 1. Harmondsworth: Penguin.

Foucault, M. (1980) 'Body/Power', in C. Gordon (ed.), *Power/Knowledge: Selected Interviews and Other Writings 1972–77*. New York: Pantheon Books.

Foucault, M. (1985) *The History of Sexuality*, vol. 2: *The Uses of Pleasure*. New York: Vintage Books.

Foucault, M. (1986) *The History of Sexuality*, vol. 3: *The Care of the Self*. Harmondsworth: Penguin.

Foucault, M. (1988) 'Technologies of the Self', in L. Martin, H. Gutman and P. Hutton (eds), *Technologies of the Self: A Seminar with Michel Foucault*. Amherst: University of Massachusetts Press.

Frank, A. W. (1990) 'Bringing Bodies Back In'. *Theory, Culture and Society* 7(1).

Freeman, C. (1993) 'Designing Women: Corporate Discipline and Barbados's Off-Shore Pink Collar Sector'. *Cultural Anthropology* 8(2).

Freud, S. (1927/1963) 'Fetishism', in *Sexuality and the Psychology of Love*. New York: Collier Books.

Friedan, B. (1963) *The Feminine Mystique*. London: Penguin

Gaines, J. (1990) 'Introduction: Fabricating the Female Body', in J. Gaines and C. Herzog (eds), *Fabrications: Costume and the Female Body*. London: Routledge.

Gaines, J. and Herzog, C. (eds) (1990) *Fabrications: Costume and the Female Body*. London: Routledge.

Gamman, L. and Makinen, M. (1994) *Female Fetishism: A New Look*. London: Lawrence and Wishart.

Gamman, L. and Marshment, M. (1988) *The Female Gaze: Women as Viewers of Popular Culture*. London: Women's Press.

Garber, M. (1992) *Vested Interests: Cross Dressing and Cultural Anxiety*. Harmondsworth: Penguin.

Garcia-Parpet, M. F. (2007) 'The Social Construction of a Perfect Market: The Strawberry Auction at Fontaines-en-Sologne', in D. MacKenzie, F. Muniesa and L. Siu (eds), *Do Economists Make Markets?: On the Performativity of Economics*. Princeton, Princeton University Press.

Gatens, M. (1991) *Feminism and Philosophy: Perspectives on Difference and Equality*. Cambridge: Polity.

Geczy, A. (2013) *Fashion and Orientalism: Dress, Textiles and Culture from the 17th to the 21st Century*. London: Bloomsbury.

Geczy, A. (2016) *The Artificial Body in Fashion and Art: Marionettes, Models and Mannequins*. London: Bloomsbury.

Geczy, A. and Karaminis, V. (eds) (2013) *Queer Style*. London: Bloomsbury.

Gertler, M. S. (2003) 'Tacit Knowledge and the Economic Geography of Context, or The Undefinable Tacitness of Being (There)'. *Journal of Economic Geography* 3(1): 75–99.

Giddens, A. (1991) *Modernity and Self-Identity: Self and Society in the Late Modern Age*. Cambridge: Polity.

Gill, R. (2003) 'From Sexual Objectification to Sexual Subjectification: The Resexualisation of Women's Bodies in the Media'. *Feminist Media Studies* 3(1): 100–6.

Gilroy, P. (2000) *Against Race: Imagining Political Culture Beyond the Color Line*. Boston: Harvard University Press.

Godart, F. C. and Mears, A. (2009) 'How do Cultural Producers make Creative Decisions? Lessons from the Catwalk'. *Social Forces* 88(2): 671–92.

Goff, S. and Loughran, K. (eds) (2010) *Contemporary African Fashion*. Bloomington and Indianapolis: Indiana University Press.

Goffman, E. (1971) *The Presentation of Self in Everyday Life*. London: Penguin.

Goffman, E. (1972) *Relations in Public*. Harmondsworth: Pelican Books.

Goffman, E. (1976) *Gender Advertisements*. London: Macmillan.

Goffman, E. (1979) *Stigma: Notes on the Management of Spoiled Identity*. Harmondsworth: Penguin.

Gonzalez, A. M. and Bovone, L. (eds) (2012) *Identities through Fashion: A Multi-Disciplinary Approach*. London: Berg.

Gorsline, D. (1953/1991) *A History of Fashion: A Visual Survey of Costume from Ancient Times*. London: Fitzhouse Books.

Granata, F. (2017) *Experimental Fashion: Performance Art, Carnival and the Grotesque Body*. London: Bloomsbury.

Greenblatt, S. (1980) *Renaissance Self-Fashioning: From More to Shakespeare*. Chicago: University of Chicago Press.

Haidarali, L. (2012) '"Giving Colored Sisters a Superficial Equality": Re-Modelling African-American Womanhood in Early Postwar America', in J. Entwistle and E. Wissinger (eds). *Fashioning Models: Image, Text, and Industry*. London: Bloomsbury, pp. 56–80.

Hall, S. (1977) 'The Hippies: An American Movement'. Birmingham: CCCS Stenciled Papers.

Hall, S. (2017) *The Fateful Triangle: Race, Ethnicity, Nation*. Cambridge, MA: Harvard University Press.

Hall, S. (2021) *Selected Writings on Race and Difference*. Durham: Duke University Press.

Hall, S. and Jefferson, T. (eds) (1977) *Resistances through Rituals*. London: Hutchinson.

Halliday, R. (2022) *The Fashion Show Goes Live: Exclusive and Mediatized Performance*. London: Bloomsbury.

Halttunen, K. (1982) *Confidence Men and Painted Women: A Study of Middle-Class Culture in America, 1830–1870*. New Haven and London: Yale University Press.

Harding, S. G. (ed.) (2004) *The Feminist Standpoint Theory Reader: Intellectual and Political Controversies*. London: Routledge.

Haug, F. (1987) *Female Sexualization*. London: Verso.

Hauser, K. (2004) A Garment in the Dock; or, How the FBI Illuminated the Prehistory of a Pair of Denim Jeans. *Journal of Material Culture* 9: 293–313.

Havelock, H. (1928) *Studies in the Psychology of Sex*. Philadelphia: F. A. Davis & Co.

Hawson, A. (2005) *Embodying Gender*. London: Sage.

Hawthorne, R. (1992) *Bras: A Private View*. London: Souvenir Press.

Hearn, J., Sheppard, D. L., Tancred-Sheriff, P. and Burrell, G. (eds) (1993) *The Sexuality of the Organization*. London: Sage.

Hebdige, D. (1979) *Subculture: The Meaning of Style*. London: Methuen.

Herrero, M. (2010) Performing Calculation in the Art Market. *Journal of Cultural Economy* 3: 19–34.

Holland, S. (2004) *Alternative Femininities: Body, Age and Identity*. London: Bloomsbury.

Hollander, A. (1993) *Seeing Through Clothes*. Berkeley: University of California Press.

Hollander, A. (1994) *Sex and Suits: The Evolution of Modern Dress*. New York: Alfred A. Knopf.

Holliday, R. (2001) 'Fashioning the Queer Self', in J. Entwistle and E. Wilson (eds), *Body Dressing*. Oxford: Berg.

Hoodfar, H. (1991) 'Return to the Veil: Personal Strategy and Public Participation in Egypt', in N. Radcliffe and M. T. Sinclair (eds), *Working Women: International Perspectives on Labour and Gender Ideology*. London: Routledge.

hooks, b. (1981) *Ain't I A Woman?*, New York: South End Press.

hooks, b. (2000) *Feminism is for Everybody: Passionate Politics*. London: Pluto Press.

Horrocks, R. (1997) *An Introduction to the Study of Sexuality*. London: Macmillan.

Hotchkiss, V. R. (1996) *Clothes Make the Man: Female Cross Dressing in Medieval Europe*. London: Garland.

Hossain, M. (2020) 'Sharing Economy: A Comprehensive Literature Review'. *International Journal of Hospitality Management*.

Howard, A. (1997) 'Labor, History, and Sweatshops in the New Global Economy', in A. Ross (ed.), *No Sweat: Fashion, Free Trade and the Rights of Garment Workers*. London: Verso.

Hudson, D. (1974) *Munby: Man of Two Worlds*. London: Abacus.

Ivaska, A. (2011) *Cultured States: Youth, Gender and Modern Style in 1960s Dar Es Salaam*. Durham, NC: Duke University Press.

Jansen, M. A. and Craik, J. (2016) *Modern Fashion Traditions: Negotiating Tradition and Modernity through Fashion*. London: Bloomsbury.

Jenkins, R. (1992) *Pierre Bourdieu*. London: Routledge.

Jeong, D., Chun, E. and Ko, E. (2021) Culture and Art Policy Analysis in Fashion Capitals: New York, London. *Journal of Global Fashion Marketing* 12: 77–94.

Jobling, P. (1999) *Fashion Spreads: Word and Image in Fashion Photography since 1980*. Oxford: Berg.

Jobling, P. (2005) *Man Appeal: Advertising, Modernism and Menswear*. Oxford: Berg.

Jones, J. (1996) 'Coquettes and Grisettes: Women Buying and Selling in Ancien Régime Paris', in V. de Grazia and E. Furlough (eds), *The Sex of Things: Gender and Consumption in Historical Perspective*. London: University of California Press.

Jones, J. M. (2004) *Sexing la Mode: Gender, Fashion and Commercial Culture in Old Regime France*. London: Berg.

Kalof, L. and Bynum, W. (eds) (2010) *A Cultural History of the Human Body*, vols. 1–6. Oxford: Berg.

Karademir-Hazir, I. (2020) Narratives of 'Getting it Right': Class, Culture and Good Taste in Clothing. *International Journal of Fashion Studies* 7(2): 147–65.

Karaminis, V. (2013) 'Born this Way: Lesbian Style since the Eighties', in V. Steele (ed.), *A Queer History of Fashion: From the Closet to the Catwalk*. New York: Yale, in Association with the Fashion Institute of New York.

Kawamura, Y. (2004a) *Fashion-ology: An Introduction to Fashion Studies*. Oxford: Berg.

Kawamura, Y. (2004b) *The Japanese Revolution in Paris Fashion*. Oxford: Berg.

Kawamura, Y. (2012) *Fashioning Japanese Subcultures*. London: Berg.

Kohler, C. (1963) *A History of Costume*. New York: Dover Publications.

Küchler, S. and Miller, D. (eds) (2005) *Clothing as Material Culture*. Oxford: Berg.

Kuchta, D. (1996) 'The Making of the Self-Made Man: Class, Clothing, and English Masculinity', in V. de Grazia and E. Furlough (eds), *The Sex of Things: Gender and Consumption in Historical Perspective*. London: University of California Press.

Kuhn, A. (1988) 'The Body and Cinema: Some Problems for Feminism', in S. Sheridan (ed.), *Grafts: Feminist Cultural Criticism*. London: Verso.

Kunzle, D. (1982) *Fashion and Fetishism: A Social History of the Corset, Tight-Lacing and other Forms of Body-Sculpture in the West*. Totowa, NJ: Rowan and Littlefield.

Kutulas, J. (2012) 'Dedicated Followers of Fashion: Peacock Fashion and the Roots of the New American Man, 1960–70'. *The Sixties* 5(2): 167–84.

Lancaster, B. (1995) *The Department Store: A Social History*. London: Leicester University Press.

Langman, L. (1992) 'Neon Cages: Shopping for Subjectivity', in R. Shields (ed.), *Lifestyle Shopping: The Subject of Consumption*. London: Routledge.

Laquer, T. and Bourgois, L. (1992) *Corporal Politics*. Cambridge, MA: MIT List, Visual Arts Centre.

Laquer, T. and Gallagher, C. (1987) *The Making of the Modern Body: Sexuality, Society and the 19th Century*. Berkeley: University of California Press.

Laver, J. (1950) *Dress: How and Why Fashions in Men's and Women's Clothes have Changed during the Past Two Hundred Years*. London: John Murray.

Laver, J. (1968) *Dandies*. London: Weidenfeld and Nicolson.

Laver, J. (1969) *Modesty in Dress*. Boston: Houghton Mifflin Co.

Laver, J. (1969/1995) *A Concise History of Costume*. London: Thames and Hudson.

Law, J. (2002) 'Economics as Interface', in P. du Gay and M. Pryke, *Cultural Economy: Cultural Analysis and Commercial Life*. London: Sage.

Leach, W. (1989) 'Strategies of Display and the Production of Desire', in S. Bronner (ed.), *Consuming Visions: Accumulation and Display of Goods in America, 1880–1920*. Ontario: Penguin.

Lees, S. (1999) 'When in Rome'. *Guardian*, 16 February, 6–7.

Leopold, E. (1992) 'The Manufacture of the Fashion System', in J. Ash and E. Wilson (eds), *Chic Thrills*. London: Pandora.

Lewis, R. (1996) *Gendering Orientalism: Race, Femininity and Representation*. London: Routledge.

Lewis, R. (2013) 'Fashion Forward and Faith-tastic! Online Modest Fashion and the Development of Women as Religious Interpreters and Intermediaries', in R. Lewis (ed.) *Modest Fashion: Styling Bodies, Mediating Faith*. London: Bloomsbury.

Lewis, R. and Rolley, K. (1997) '(Ad)Dressing the Dyke: Lesbian Looks and Lesbian Looking', in M. Nava, A. Blake, I. MacRury, and B. Richards (eds), *Buy this Book: Studies in Advertising and Consumption*. London: Routledge.

Lipovetsky, G. (1994) *The Empire of Fashion*. Princeton: Princeton University Press.

Lovelock, M. (2017) Call me Caitlyn: Making and Making over the 'Authentic' Transgender Body in Anglo-American Popular Culture. *Journal of Gender Studies* 26: 675–87.

Lown, J. and Chenut, H. (1984) 'The Patriarchal Tread: a History of Exploitation', in

W. Chapkis and C. Enloe (eds), *Of Common Cloth: Women in the Global Textile Industry*. Transnational Institute.

Luck, K. (1992) 'Trouble in Eden, Trouble with Eve: Women, Trousers and Utopian Socialism in Nineteenth Century America', in J. Ash and E. Wilson (eds), *Chic Thrills*. London: Pandora.

Lunning, F. (2013) *Fetish Style*. London: Bloomsbury.

Lurie, A. (1981) *The Language of Clothes*. New York: Random House.

Lynch, A. (2012) *Porn Chic – Exploring the Contours of Raunch Eroticism*. London: Bloomsbury.

Lynge-Jorlén, A. (2012) 'Between Frivolity and Art: Contemporary Niche Fashion Magazines'. *Fashion Theory* 16(1): 7–28.

Lynge-Jorlén, A. (2016) 'Editorial Styling: Between Creative Solutions and Economic Restrictions'. *Journal of Design, Creative Process & the Fashion Industry* 8.

Lynge-Jorlén, A. (2017) *Niche Fashion Magazines: Changing the Shape of Fashion*. London: Bloomsbury.

Lynge-Jorlén, A. (2020) *Fashion Stylists: History, Meaning and Practice*. London: Bloomsbury.

McCracken, G. D. (1985) *The Trickle-Down Theory Rehabilitated*. New York: Lexington Books.

McDowell, C. (1992) *Dressed to Kill: Sex, Power and Clothes*. London: Hutchinson.

McFall, L. (2002) 'What about the Old Cultural Intermediaries? An Historical Review of Advertising Producers'. *Cultural Studies* 16(4): 501–15.

McFall, L. (2004) *Advertising: A Cultural Economy*. London: Sage.

McKendrick, N., Brewer, J. and Plumb, J. H. (1983) *The Birth of a Consumer Society: The Commercialization of the Eighteenth-Century*. London: Hutchinson.

Mackinney-Valentin, M. (2017) *Fashioning Identity: Status Ambivalence in Contemporary Fashion*. London: Bloomsbury.

MacKinnon, C. A. (1979) *Sexual Harassment of Working Women*. New Haven: Yale University Press.

McNay, L. (1992) *Foucault and Feminism: Power, Gender and the Self*. Cambridge: Polity.

McNay, L. (1999) 'Gender, Habitus and the Field: Pierre Bourdieu and the Limits of Reflexivity'. *Theory, Culture and Society* 16(1): 95–117.

McNeill, P. and Karaminis, V. (eds) (2009) *The Men's Fashion Reader*. Oxford: Berg.

McNeill, P. and Wallenberg, L. (eds) (2012) *Nordic Fashion Studies*. Stockholm, Axl Books.

McRobbie, A. (1981) 'Settling Accounts with Subculture', in T. Bennett, G. Martin, C. Mercer and J. Wollacott (eds), *Culture, Ideology and Social Process*. London: B. T. Batsford.

McRobbie, A. (ed.) (1989) *Zoot Suits and Second-hand Dresses: An Anthology of Fashion and Music*. London: Macmillan.

McRobbie, A. (1991) *Feminism and Youth Culture: From 'Jackie' to 'Just Seventeen'*. London: Macmillan.

McRobbie, A. (1994a) *Post-Modernism and Popular Culture*. London: Routledge.

McRobbie, A. (1994b) 'Second-hand Dresses and the Role of the Ragmarket', in A. McRobbie (ed.), *Post-Modernism and Popular Culture*. London: Routledge.

McRobbie, A. (1998) *British Fashion Design: Rag Trade or Image Industry?* London: Routledge.

McRobbie, A. (2013) 'Fashion Matters Berlin: City-Spaces, Women's Working Lives, New Social Enterprise?' *Cultural Studies* 27: 982–1010.

McRobbie, A. (2016) *Be Creative: Making a Living in the New Cultural Industries*. Cambridge: Polity.

Maguire, J. S. and Matthews, J. (2014) *The Cultural Intermediaries Reader*. London: Sage.

Maguire, J. S. and Matthews, J. (2021) 'Are We All Cultural Intermediaries Now? An Introduction to Cultural Intermediaries in Context'. *European Journal of Cultural Studies* 15(5): 551–62.

Mascia-Lees, F. E. (2011) *A Companion to the Anthropology of the Body and Embodiment*. Oxford: Wiley-Blackwell.

Mauss, M. (1973) 'Techniques of the Body'. *Economy and Society* 2(1): 70–89.

Maynard, M. (2012) 'Fashion Modelling in Australia', in J. Entwistle and E. Wissinger (eds), *Fashioning Models: Image, Industry, Text*. London: Bloomsbury.

Mead, M. (1935) *Sex and Temperament in Three Primitive Societies*. New York: William Morrow.

Mears, A. (2008) 'Discipline of the Catwalk: Gender, Power and Uncertainty in Fashion Modeling'. *Ethnography* 9(4): 429–56.

Mears, A. (2011) *Pricing Beauty: The Making of a Fashion Model*. Los Angeles University of California Press.

Mears, A. (2012a) 'Size Zero High-End Ethnic: Cultural Production and the Reproduction of Culture in Fashion Modeling'. *Poetics* 40(2): 133–49.

Mears, A. (2012b) 'Made in Japan: Fashion Modelling in Tokyo', in J. Entwistle and E. Wissenger (eds), *Fashioning Models: Image, Industry, Text*. London: Bloomsbury.

Mears, A. and Finlay, W. (2005) 'Not Just a Paper Doll: How Models Manage Bodily Capital and Why They Perform Emotional Labor'. *Journal of Contemporary Ethnography* 34: 317.

Merleau-Ponty, M. (1976) *The Primacy of Perception*. Evanston and Chicago: Northwestern University Press.

Merleau-Ponty, M. (1981) *The Phenomenology of Perception*. London: Routledge and Kegan Paul.

Miller, D. (1987) *Material Culture and Mass Consumption*. Oxford: Blackwell.

Miller, D. and Woodward, S. (eds) (2011) *Global Denim*. Oxford: Berg.

Mitchell, C. and Weber, S. (eds) (2004) *Not Just Any Dress: Narratives of Memory, Body and Identity*. New York: Peter Lang.

Modleski, T. (1982) *Loving with a Vengeance: Mass Produced Fantasies for Women*. Hamden, CT: Shoe String Press.

Moeran, B. (2010) 'The Portrayal of Beauty in Women's Fashion Magazines', *Fashion Theory* 14(4): 491–510.

Moeran, B. (2016) *The Magic of Fashion: Ritual, Commodity, Glamour*. New York: Routledge.

Molloy, J. T. (1980) *Women: Dress for Success*. New York: Peter H. Wyden.

Moore, H. L. (1994) *A Passion for Difference*. Cambridge: Polity.

Moors, A. (2013) 'Discover the Beauty of Modesty: Islamic Fashion Online', in R. Lewis (ed.), *Modest Fashion: Styling Bodies, Mediating Faith*. London: Bloomsbury.

Morris, A., Copper, T. and Cooper, P. (2006) 'The Changing Shape of Female Fashion Models'. *International Journal of Eating Disorders* 8(5): 593–6.

Mort, F. (1988) 'Boy's Own', in R. Chapman and J. Rutherford (eds), *Male Order: Unwrapping Masculinity*. London: Lawrence and Wishart.

Mort, F. (1996) *Cultures of Consumption: Masculinities and Social Space in Late Twentieth-Century Britain*. London: Routledge.

Mulvey, L. (1975) 'Visual Pleasure and Narrative Cinema'. *Screen* 16(3).

Muniesa, F., Doganova, L., Ortiz, H., Pina-Stranger, Á., Paterson, F., Bourgoin, A., Ehrenstein, V., Juven, P.-A., Pontille, D. and Sarac-Lesavre, B. (2017) *Capitalization: A Cultural Guide*. Paris: Presse des Mines.

Nava, M. (1992) *Changing Cultures: Feminism, Youth and Consumerism*. London: Sage.

Nava, M. (1996) 'Modernity's Disavowal: Women, the City and the Department Store', in *Modern Times: Reflections on a Century of Modernity*. London: Routledge.

Negus, K. (1997) 'The Production of Culture', in P. du Gay (ed.), *Production of Culture/Cultures of Production*. London: Sage.

Negus, K. (2002) 'The Work of Cultural Intermediaries and the Enduring Distance Between Production and Consumption'. *Cultural Studies* 16(4): 501–15.

Newton, S. M. (1974) *Health, Art and Reason: Dress Reformers of the 19th Century*. London: John Murray.

Niessen, S., Leshkowich, A. M. and Jones, C. (eds) (2003) *Afterword Re-Orienting Fashion Theory Re-Orienting Fashion: The Globalization of Asian Dress*. Oxford: Berg.

Nixon, S. (1992) 'Have you got the Look? Masculinities and Shopping Spectacle', in R. Shields (ed.), *Lifestyle Shopping: The Subject of Consumption*. London: Routledge.

Nixon, S. (1996) *Hard Looks: Masculinities, Spectatorship and Contemporary Consumption*. London: UCL Press.

Norris, L. (2010) *Recycling Indian Clothing: Global Contexts of Reuse and Value*. Chesham: Indiana University Press.

Oakley, A. (1976) *Sex, Gender and Society*. London: Temple Smith.

O'Connor, K. (2005) 'The Other Half: The Material Culture of New Fibres', in S. Küchler and D. Miller (eds), *Clothing as Material Culture*. Oxford: Berg.

Okley, J. (2007) 'Research Embodiment by Way of "Techniques of the Body"', in C. Shilling (ed.), *Embodying Sociology: Retrospective Progress, and Prospects*. Oxford: Blackwell.

Ortner, S. B. (1974) 'Is Female to Male as Nature is to Culture?', in M. Rosaldo and L. Lamphere (eds), *Women, Culture and Society*. Stanford: Stanford University Press.

Ortner, S. B. (1996) *Making Gender: The Politics and Erotics of Culture*. Boston: Beacon Press.

Paoletti, J. (2015) *Sex and Unisex: Fashion, Feminism, and the Sexual Revolution*. Bloomington: Indiana University Press.

Parkins, I. (2012) *Poiret, Dior and Schiaparelli: Fashion, Femininity and Modernity*. Oxford: Berg.

Parkins, W. (ed.) (2002) *Dress, Gender, Citizenship: Fashioning the Body Politic*. London: Berg.

Partington, A. (1992) 'Popular Fashion and Working-Class Affluence', in J. Ash and E. Wilson (eds), *Chic Thrills: A Fashion Reader*. London: Pandora.

Paulicelli, E. (2004) *Fashion under Fascism: Beyond the Black Shirt*. Oxford: Berg.

Paulicelli, E. and Clark, H. (eds) (2009) *The Fabric of Cultures: Fashion, Identity, and Globalization*. London: Routledge.

Peiss, K. (2011) *Hope in a Jar: The Making of America's Beauty Culture*. Philadelphia: University of Pennsylvania Press.

Peiss, K. (2014) *Zoot Suit: The Enigmatic Career of an Extreme Style*. London: Bloomsbury.

Pellandini-Simanyi, L. (2016) 'Everyday Consumption Norms as Discourses of the Good Life in Pre-Socialist and Socialist Hungary'. *Journal of Consumer Culture* 16: 699–717.

Perniola, M. (1990) 'Between Clothing and Nudity', in M. Feher (ed.), *Fragments of a History of the Human Body*. New York: MIT Press.

Peters, L. D. (2017) '"Fashion Plus": Pose and the Plus-Size Body in *Vogue*, 1986–1988'. *Fashion Theory* 21(2): 175–99.

Peters, L. D. (2019) 'Flattering the Figure, Fitting in: The Design Discourses of Stoutwear, 1915–1930'. *Fashion Theory: Special Issue on The Body: Fashion and Physique* 23(2): 167–94.

Philips, J. C. (2012) 'On the Use and Re-use of Jewellery Elements', in R. Laffineur and M.-L Nosch (eds) *Kosmos*. Kliemo: University of Copenhagen, Belgium.

Phizacklea, A. (1990) *Unpacking the Fashion Industry: Gender, Racism and Class in Production*. London: Routledge.

Polhemus, T. (1988) *Bodystyles*. Luton: Lennard.

Polhemus, T. (1994) *Streetstyle*. London: Thames and Hudson.

Polhemus, T. and Proctor, L. (1978) *Fashion and Anti-Fashion: An Anthology of Clothing and Adornment*. London: Cox and Wyman.

Porter, R. (1990) *English Society in the Eighteenth Century*. London: Penguin.

Prabu, D., Morrison, G., Johnson, M. A. and Ross, F. (2002) 'Body Image, Race and Fashion Models: Social Distance and Social Identification in Third Person Effects'. *Communication Research* 29(270): online.

Pratt, A. (2008) 'Locating the Cultural Economy', in H. Anheier and Y. R. Isar (eds), *The Cultural Economy*. London: Sage, pp. 42–51.

Pratt, A. (2009) 'The Challenge of Governance in the Creative and Cultural Industries, Governance der Kreativwirtschaft: Diagnosen und Handlungsoptionen'. Transcript verlag, pp. 271–88.

Pringle, R. (1988) *Secretaries Talk: Sexuality, Power and Work*. London: Verso.

Pringle, R. (1993) 'Bureaucracy, Rationality, Sexuality: The Case of Secretaries', in J. Hearn, D. L. Sheppard, P. Tancred-Sheriff and G. Burrell (eds), *The Sexuality of the Organization*. London: Sage.

Pun, N., Tse, T., Shin, V. and Fan, L. (2020) 'Conceptualising Socioeconomic Formations of Labour and Workers' Power in Global Production Networks'. *Sociology* 54: 745–62.

Radway, J. (1987) *Reading the Romance: Women, Patriarchy and Popular Literature*. London: Verso.

Ramazanoglu, C. (ed.) (1993) *Up against Foucault: Explorations of some Tensions between Foucault and Feminism*. London: Routledge.

Ramírez, C. S. (2009) *The Woman in the Zoot Suit: Gender, Nationalism, and the Cultural Politics of Memory*. Durham: Duke University Press.

Reddy-Best, K. L. and Jones, K. B. (2020) 'Is This What a Lesbian Looks Like? Lesbian Fashion and the Fashionable Lesbian in the United States Press, 1960s to 2010s'. *Journal of Lesbian Studies* 24: 159–71.

Reed, J. and Medvedev, K. 2018. 'The Beauty Divide: Black Millennial Women Seek Agency with Makeup Art Cosmetics (MAC)', in Lynch, A. and Medvedev, K. (eds) *Fashion, Agency, and Empowerment: Performing Agency, Following Script*. London: Bloomsbury.

Reilly, A., Miller-Spillman, K. A. et al. (eds) (2012) *The Meanings of Dress*. London: Bloomsbury.

Reynolds, J. M. (2021) 'Eating, Sleeping, Drinking Fashion: Subjectivity, Space, Time and Affect in the Work of Fashion Agents'. PhD thesis, London: King's College.

Ribeiro, A. (1983) *A Visual History of Costume: The Eighteenth Century*. London: B. T. Batsford.

Ribeiro, A. (1992) 'Utopian Dress', in J. Ash and E. Wilson (eds), *Chic Thrills: A Fashion Reader*. London: Pandora.

Richardson, J. and Kroeber, A. L. (1973) 'Three Centuries of Women's Dress: A Quantitative Analysis', in G. Willis and D. Midgley (eds), *Fashion Marketing*. London: Allen and Unwin.

Riello, G. and McNeil, P. (2010) *The Fashion History Reader: Global Perspectives*. Routledge: London.

Ritzer, G. (2014) 'Prosumption: Evolution or Eternal Return of the Same?' *Journal of Consumer Culture* 14(1): 3–24.

Ritzer, G. and Jurgenson, N. (2010)'Production, Consumption, Prosumption: The Nature of Capitalism in the Age of the Digital "PROSUMER"'. *Journal of Consumer Culture* 10: 13–36.

Rivière, J. (1929/1986) 'Womanliness as a Masquerade', in V. Burgin, J. Donald and C. Kaplan (eds), *Formations of Fantasy*. London: Methuen.

Roach, M. E. and Eicher, J. B. (eds) (1965) *Dress, Adornment and Social Order*. New York: John Wiley & Sons.

Roberts, H. (1977) 'The Exquisite Slave: The Role of Clothes in the Making of the Victorian Woman'. *Signs* 2(3): 554–69.

Rocamora, A. (2009) *Fashioning the City: Paris, Fashion and the Media*. London: I. B. Taurus.

Rocamora, A. (2012) 'Hypertextuality and Remediation in the Fashion Media'. *Journalism Practice* 6: 92–106.

Rocamora, A. (2013) 'New Fashion Times: Fashion and Digital Media', in S. Black, A. D. L. Haye, J. Entwistle, A. Rocamora, and H. Thomas (eds), *The Handbook of Fashion Studies*. London: Routledge.

Rolley, K. (1992) 'Love, Desire and the Pursuit of the Whole: Dress and the Lesbian Couple', in J. Ash and E. Wilson (eds), *Chic Thrills: A Fashion Reader*. London: Pandora.

Ross, A. (ed.) (1997) *No Sweat: Fashion, Free Trade and the Rights of Garment Workers*. London: Verso.

Ross, R. (2008) *Clothing: A Global History*. Cambridge: Polity.

Rouse, E. (1989) *Understanding Fashion*. London: BSP Professional Books.

Rovine, V. L. (2004) 'Fashionable Traditions: The Globalization of an African Textile', *Fashioning Africa: Power and the Politics of Dress*. Bloomington: Indiana University Press, pp. 189–211.

Rush, J. A. (2005) *Spiritual Tattoo: A Cultural History of Tattooing, Piercing, Scarification, Branding, and Implants*. Berkeley: Frog.

Sadre-Orafai, S. (2012) 'The Figure of the Model and Reality TV', in J. Entwistle and E. Wissinger (eds), *Fashioning Models: Image, Text, and Industry*. London: Bloomsbury.

Said, E. (1985) *Orientalism*. Harmondsworth: Penguin.

Sampson, E. (2016) *Worn: Footwear, Attachment and Affective Experience*. London: Bloomsbury.

Schulze, L. (1990) 'On the Muscle', in J. Gaines and C. Herzog (eds), *Fabrications: Costume and the Female Body*. London: Routledge.

Scolere, L., Pruchniewska, U. and Duffy, B. E. (2018) 'Constructing the Platform-Specific Self-Brand: The Labor of Social Media Promotion'. *Social Media + Society* 1(3): July–September 2018.

Scott, A. J. (1999) 'The Cultural Economy: Geography and the Creative Field'. *Media, Culture and Society* 21: 807–17.

Scott, L. M. (2005) *Fresh Lipstick – Redressing Fashion and Feminism*. London: Palgrave.

Sekora, J. (1977) *Luxury: the Concept in Western Thought, Eden to Smollet*. Baltimore: Johns Hopkins University Press.

Sennett, R. (1977) *The Fall of Public Man*. Cambridge: Cambridge University Press.

Sennett, R. (1994) *Flesh and Stone: The Body and the City in Western Civilization*. London: Faber and Faber.

Sharman, L. (2021) 'Primary School Boys and Girls Wear Skirts to Promote Gender Equality'. *Evening Standard*, 4 November.

Shaw, J. (1995) 'Effects of Fashion Magazines on Body Dissatisfaction and Eating Psychopathology in Adolescent and Adult Females'. *European Eating Disorders Review* 3(1): 15–23.

Sheppard, D. L. (1989) 'Organisations, Power and Sexuality: The Image and Self-Image of Women Managers', in J. Hearn (ed.), *The Sexuality of the Organization*. London: Sage.

Sheppard, D. L. (1993) 'Women Managers' Perceptions of Gender and Organizational Life', in A. Mills, J. and P. Tancred (eds), *Gendering Organizational Analysis*. London: Sage.

Shields, R. (ed.) (1992) *Lifestyle Shopping: The Subject of Consumption*. London: Routledge.

Shilling, C. (2007) 'Sociology and the Body: Classical Traditions and New Agendas', in C. Shilling, *Embodying Sociology: Retrospective Progress, and Prospects*. Oxford: Blackwell.

Shilling, C. (2012) *The Body and Social Theory*. London: Sage.

Shukla, P. (2005) 'The Study of Dress and Adornment as Social Positioning'. *Material Culture Review* 61.

Silverman, K. (1986) 'Fragments of a Fashionable Discourse', in T. Modleski (ed.), *Studies in Entertainment: Critical Approaches to Mass Culture*. Bloomington: Indiana University Press.

Simmel, G. (1904) 'Fashion'. *International Quarterly* 10: 130–55.

Simmel, G. (1950) *The Sociology of Georg Simmel*. London: CollierMacmillan. Simmel, G. (1971 [1904]) 'Fashion', in D. Levine (ed.), *On Individuality and Social Forms*. London: University of Chicago Press.

Sims, M. (2003) *Adam's Navel: A Natural and Cultural History of the Human Body*. London: Allen Lane.

Slater, D. R. (1993) 'Going Shopping: Markets, Crowds and Consumption', in C. Jenks (ed.), *Cultural Reproduction*. London: Routledge.

Slater, D. R. (1997) *Consumer Culture and Modernity*. Cambridge: Polity.

Smith, A. (1986 [1776]) *The Wealth of Nations*. London: Penguin.

Smith, D. E. (2004) 'Women's Perspective as Radical Critique of Sociology', in S. G. Harding (ed.), *The Feminist Standpoint Theory Reader: Intellectual and Political Controversies*. London: Routledge.

Soley Beltran, P. (2004) 'Modelling Femininity'. *European Journal of Women's Studies* 11(3): 309–26.

Soloman, M. R. (ed.) (1985) *The Psychology of Fashion*. New York: Lexington Books.

Sommerlund, J. (2008) 'Mediations in Fashion'. *Journal of Cultural Economy* 1(2): 165–80.

Spooner, C. (2004) *Fashioning Gothic Bodies*. Oxford: Berg.

St Martin, L. and Gavey, N. (1996) 'Women Body Building: Feminist Resistance and/or Femininity's Recuperation'. *Body and Society* 2(4): 45–57.

Steele, V. (1985) *Fashion and Eroticism: Ideals of Feminine Beauty from the Victorian Age to the Jazz Age*. Oxford: Oxford University Press.

Steele, V. (1996) *Fetish: Fashion, Sex and Power*. Oxford: Oxford University Press.

Steele, V. (1999 [1988]) *Paris Fashion: A Cultural History*. Oxford: Oxford University Press.

Steele, V. (2001) *The Corset: A Cultural History*. Yale: Yale University Press.

Steele, V. (ed.) (2010) *The Berg Companion to Fashion*. Oxford: Berg.

Steele, V. (ed.) (2013) *A Queer History of Fashion: From the Closet to the Catwalk*. New York: Yale, in Association with the Fashion Institute of New York.

Steele, V. and Kidwell, C. B. (eds) (1989) *Men and Women: Dressing the Part*. Washington: Smithsonian Institute Press.

Stekel, W. (1930) *Sexual Aberrations: The Phenomenon of Fetishism in Relations*. New York: Liveright Publishing Corporation.

Stevenson, C. (2022) 'Radical Pedagogies: Right Here, Right Now!' *Fashion Theory* 26: 465–73.

Stoller, R. J. (1968) *Sex and Gender: On the Development of Masculinity and Femininity*. London: Hogarth Press Institute of Psychoanalysis.

Stoller, R. (1985) *Observing the Erotic Imagination*. New Haven: Yale University Press.

Su, J. (1997) 'El Monte Thai Government Workers: Slave Sweatshops', in A. Ross (ed.), *No Sweat: Fashion, Free Trade and the Rights of Garment Workers*. London: Verso.

Suthrell, C. (2004) *Unzipping Gender: Sex, Cross-dressing and Culture*. Oxford: Berg.

Sweetman, P. (1999a) 'Only Skin Deep? Tattooing, Piercing and the Transgressive Body', in P. Sweetman and M. Aaron, *The Body's Perilous Pleasures: Dangerous Desires and Contemporary Culture*. Edinburgh: Edinburgh University Press.

Sweetman, P. (1999b) 'Marked Bodies, Oppositional Identities? Tattooing, Piercing and the Ambiguity of Resistance', in S. Roseneil and J. Seymour. *Practising Identities: Power and Resistance*. London: St Martin's Press.

Sweetman, P. (2000) 'Anchoring the (Postmodern) Self? Body Modifications, Fashion and Identity', in M. Featherstone (ed.), *Body Modifications*. London: Sage.

Sydie, R. A. (1987) *Natural Women, Cultured Men*. London: Methuen.

Synnott, A. (1993) *The Body Social: Symbolism, Self and Society*. London: Routledge.

Tarlo, E. (1996) *Clothing Matters: Dress and Identity in India*. London: Hurst.

Tarlo, E. (ed.) (2010) *Visibly Muslim: Fashion, Politics, Faith*. Oxford: Berg.

Tarlo, E. (2013) 'Meeting through Modesty: Jewish–Muslim Encounters on the Internet', in R. Lewis (ed.) *Modest Fashion: Styling Bodies, Mediating Faith*. London: Bloomsbury.

Tarlo, E. and Moors, A. (eds) (2013) *Islamic Fashion and Anti-Fashion: New Perspectives from Europe and North America*. London: Bloomsbury.

Tarrant, N. (1994) *The Development of Costume*. London: Routledge.

Taylor, L. and Wilson, E. (1989) *Through the Looking Glass*. London: BBC Books.

Thornton, S. (1995) *Club Cultures: Music, Media and Subcultural Capital*. Cambridge: Polity.

Tiggemann, M. and Lacey, C. (2009) 'Shopping for Clothes: Body Satisfaction, Appearance Investment, and Functions of Clothing Among Female Shoppers'. *Body Image* 6(4): 285.

Triggs, T. (1992) 'Framing Masculinity: Herb Ritts, Bruce Weber and the Body Perfect', in J. Ash and E. Wilson (eds), *Chic Thrills: A Fashion Reader*. London: Pandora.

Tse, T., Shin, V. and Tsang, L. T. (2020) 'From Shanzhai Chic to Gangnam Style: Seven Practices of Cultural–Economic Mediation in China and Korea'. *Journal of Cultural Economy* 13(5): 511–30.

Tse, T. and Tsang, L. T. (2021) 'Reconceptualising Prosumption Beyond the "Cultural Turn": Passive Fashion Prosumption in Korea and China'. *Journal of Consumer Culture* 21(4): 703–23.

Tseëlon, E. (1992a) 'Fashion and the Signification of Social Order'. *Semiotica*. 91(1/2): 1–14.

Tseëlon, E. (1992b) 'Is the Presented Self Sincere? Goffman, Impression Management and the Postmodern Self'. *Theory, Culture and Society* 9(2).

Tseëlon, E. (1997) *The Masque of Femininity*. London: Sage.

Tseëlon, E. (2012a) 'Introduction', in A. M. Gonzalez and L. Bovone, *Identities through Fashion: A Multi-Disciplinary Approach*. London: Berg.

Tseëlon, E. (2012b) 'How Successful Is Communication via Clothing? Thoughts and Evidence on an Unexamined Paradigm', in A. M. Gonzalez and L. Bovone, *Identities through Fashion: A Multi-Disciplinary Approach*. London: Berg.

Tulloch, C. (2019) 'Style Activism: The Everyday Activist Wardrobe of the Black Panther Party and Rock Against Racism Movement'. *Fashion and Politics*: 85–104.

Turner, B. (1985) *The Body and Society: Explorations in Social Theory*. Oxford: Blackwell.

Turner, B. (1991) 'Recent Developments in the Theory of the Body', in M. Featherstone, M. Hepworth and B. Turner (eds), *The Body: Social Process and Cultural Theory*. London: Sage.

Turner, T. (1996) 'Bodies and Anti-Bodies: Flesh and Fetish in Contemporary Social Theory', in T. Csordas (ed.), *Embodiment and Experience: The Existential Ground of Culture and Self*. Cambridge: Cambridge University Press.

Twigg, J. (2013) *Fashion and Age: Dress, the Body and Later Life*. London: Bloomsbury.

Ugolini, L. (2007) *Men and Menswear: Sartorial Consumption in Britain 1880–1939*. Aldershot, Ashgate.

Vänskä, A. (2014) From Gay to Queer – Or, Wasn't Fashion Always Already a Very Queer Thing? *Fashion Theory*, 18: 447–63.

Veblen, T. (1953 [1899]) *The Theory of the Leisure Class: An Economic Study of Institutions*. New York: Mentor.

Vickery, A. (1993) 'Women and the World of Goods: A Lancashire Consumer and her Possessions, 1751–81', in J. Brewer and R. Porter (eds), *Consumption and the World of Goods*. London: Routledge.

Volante, P. (2021) *Fat Fashion: The Thin Ideal and the Segregation of Plus-Size Bodies*. London: Bloomsbury.

Von Busch, O. (2010) 'Exploring Net Political Craft: From Collective to Connective', *Craft Research* 1: 113–24.

Walker, E. (1999) 'Catwalk Special'. *Marie Claire*, February: 107–15.

Wallace, D. (2017) 'Reading "Race" in Bourdieu? Examining Black Cultural Capital Among Black Caribbean Youth in South London'. *Sociology* 51: 907–23.

Wallenberg, L. and Kollnitz, A. (2018) *Fashion and Modernism*. London: Bloomsbury.

Weatherill, L. (1993) 'The Meaning of Consumer Behaviour in Late Seventeenth- and Early Eighteenth-Century England', in J. Brewer and R. Porter (eds), *Consumption and the World of Goods*. New York: Routledge, pp. 206–27.

Weatherill, L. (1996) *Consumer Behaviour and Material Culture in Britain 1660–1760*. London: Routledge.

Weiner, B. and Schnieder, J. (eds) (1991) *Cloth and the Human Experience*. London: Smithsonian Institute Press.

Weller, S. (2007) 'Fashion as Viscous Knowledge: Fashion's Role in Shaping Trans-National Garment Production'. *Journal of Economic Geography* 7: 39–66.

Welters, L. and Lillethun, A. (2018) *Fashion History: A Global View*. London: Bloomsbury.

Wenger, E. (1998) *Communities of Practice*. Cambridge, Cambridge University Press.

Wheelwright, J. (1989) *Amazons and Military Maids: Women who Dressed as Men in the Pursuit of Life*. Liberty and Happiness. London: Pandora.

Willet, C. and Cunningham, P. (1992) *The History of Underclothes*. New York: Dover Publications.

Williams, D. L. (2019) 'Kangol Kool: Stylised Hats and the Performance of Black Dandyism', in A. Lynch and K. Medvedev (eds), *Fashion, Agency, and Empowerment: Performing Agency, Following Script*. London: Bloomsbury.

Williamson, J. (1978) *Decoding Advertisements: Ideology and Meaning in Advertising*. London: Marion Boyars.

Willis, G. and Midgley, D. (eds) (1973) *Fashion Marketing: An Anthology of Viewpoints and Perspectives*. London: Allen and Unwin.

Willis, P. (1975) 'The Expressive Style of a Motor-Bike Culture', in J. Benthall and T. Polhemus (eds), *The Body as a Medium of Expression*. London: Allen Lane.

Willis, P. (1978) *Profane Culture*. London: Routledge and Kegan Paul.

Wilson, E. (1991) *The Sphinx in the City*. London: Virago.

Wilson, E. (1992) 'The Postmodern Body', in J. Ash and E. Wilson (eds), *Chic Thrills: A Fashion Reader*. London: Pandora.

Wilson, E. (2005) 'Fashion and Modernity', in C. Breward and C. Evans (eds), *Fashion and Modernity*. Oxford: Berg.

Wilson, E. (2007) *Adorned in Dreams: Fashion and Modernity*. London: I. B.Taurus.

Wilson, E. (2013) 'What Does a Lesbian Look Like?', in V. Steele (ed.), *A Queer History of Fashion: From the Closet to the Catwalk*. New York: Yale, in Association with the Fashion Institute of New York.

Winge, T. M. (2012) *Body Style*. Oxford: Berg.

Wissinger, E. (2007a) 'Modeling a Way of Life: Immaterial and Affective Labor in the Fashion Modeling Industry'. *Ephemera: Theory and Politics in Organization* 7(1): 250–69.

Wissinger, E. (2007b) 'Always on Display: Affective Production in the Fashion Modeling Industry', in P. Clough and J. Halley (eds), *The Affective Turn: Theorizing the Social*. North Carolina: Duke University Press.

Wissinger, E. (2009) 'Modelling Consumption: Fashion Modelling Work in Contemporary Society'. *Journal of Consumer Culture* 9(2): 275–98.

Wissinger, E. (2012) 'Managing the Semiotics of Skin Tone: Race and Aesthetic Labor in the Fashion Modeling Industry.' *Economic and Industrial Democracy* 33(1): 125–143.

Wissinger, E. (2015) *This Year's Model: Fashion, Media, and the Making of Glamour.* New York: New York University Press.

Wolf, N. (1991) *The Beauty Myth.* London: Vintage.

Woodhouse, A. (1989) *Fantastic Women: Sex, Gender and Transvestism.* London: Macmillan.

Woodward, S. (2005) 'Looking Good: Feeling Right – Aesthetic of the Self', in S. Küchler and D. Miller (eds), *Clothing as Material Culture.* Oxford: Berg.

Woodward, S. (2007) *Why Women Wear What They Wear.* Oxford: Berg.

Wright, L. (1992) 'Out-grown Clothes for Grown-up People: Constructing a Theory of Fashion', in J. Ash and E. Wilson (eds), *Chic Thrills: A Fashion Reader.* London: Pandora

Yarwood, D. (1992) *Fashion in the Western World 1500–1900.* London: B. T. Batsford .

Young, I. M. (1995) 'Women Recovering our Clothes', in S. Benstock and S. Ferriss (eds), *On Fashion.* New Brunswick: Rutgers University Press.

Zhang, W. (2021) 'Politicizing Fashion: Inconspicuous Consumption and Anti-Intellectualism during the Cultural Revolution in China'. *Journal of Consumer Culture* 21(4): 950–66.

Index